THE CANINE-CAMPUS
CONNECTION

NEW DIRECTIONS IN THE HUMAN-ANIMAL BOND

Series editors: Alan M. Beck and Marguerite E. O'Haire, Purdue University

A dynamic relationship has always existed between people and animals. Each influences the psychological and physiological state of the other. This series of scholarly publications, in collaboration with Purdue University's College of Veterinary Medicine, expands our knowledge of the interrelationships between people, animals, and their environment. Manuscripts are welcomed on all aspects of human-animal interaction and welfare, including therapy applications, public policy, and the application of humane ethics in managing our living resources.

Other titles in this series:

Pioneer Science and the Great Plagues: How Microbes, War, and Public Health Shaped Animal Health
Norman F. Cheville

Cats and Conservationists: The Debate Over Who Owns the Outdoors
Dara M. Wald and Anna L. Peterson

That Sheep May Safely Graze: Rebuilding Animal Health Care in War-Torn Afghanistan
David M. Sherman

Transforming Trauma: Resilience and Healing Through Our Connections With Animals
Philip Tedeschi and Molly Anne Jenkins (Eds.)

A Reason to Live: HIV and Animal Companions
Vicki Hutton

Animal-Assisted Interventions in Health Care Settings: A Best Practices Manual for Establishing New Programs
Sandra B. Barker, Rebecca A. Vokes, and Randolph T. Barker

Moose! The Reading Dog
Laura Bruneau and Beverly Timmons

Leaders of the Pack: Women and the Future of Veterinary Medicine
Julie Kumble and Donald F. Smith

Exploring the Gray Zone: Case Discussions of Ethical Dilemmas for the Veterinary Technician
Andrea DeSantis Kerr, Robert "Pete" Bill, Jamie Schoenbeck Walsh, and Christina V. Tran (Eds.)

Pet Politics: The Political and Legal Lives of Cats, Dogs, and Horses in Canada and the United States
Susan Hunter and Richard A. Brisbin, Jr.

Free Market Dogs: The Human-Canine Bond in Post-Communist Poland
Michał Piotr Pręgowski and Justyna Włodarczyk (Eds.)

THE CANINE-CAMPUS CONNECTION

ROLES FOR DOGS
IN THE LIVES OF COLLEGE STUDENTS

Edited by
Mary Renck Jalongo

PURDUE UNIVERSITY PRESS | WEST LAFAYETTE, INDIANA

Copyright 2021 by Purdue University. All rights reserved.
Printed in the United States of America.

Cataloging-in-Publication data is on file at the Library of Congress.
Hardback ISBN: 978-1-61249-651-1
Paperback ISBN: 978-1-61249-648-1
ePub ISBN: 978-1-61249-649-8
ePDF ISBN: 978-1-61249-650-4

Cover artwork: Courtesy of Charles George, Megan Higgins, Mary Renck Jalongo and Haley Romanko

CONTENTS

PART ONE: DOGS ON CAMPUS

INTRODUCTION: LETTING THE DOGS IN   1
Mary Renck Jalongo, Editor, Springer Nature, Indiana, PA

1 TRANSITIONING TO COLLEGE LIFE: RESEARCH
EVIDENCE OF DOGS' EFFECTS ON HUMANS   31
Mary-Ann Sontag Bowman, School of Social Work, University of Montana, Missoula, MT, and Mary Renck Jalongo, Editor, Springer Nature, Indiana, PA

2 BRINGING POSTSECONDARY STUDENTS TOGETHER
WITH DOGS: DOG WELFARE, HEALTH, SAFETY,
AND LIABILITY CONSIDERATIONS   57
Laura Bruneau, Adams State University, Department of Counselor Education, Alamosa, CO, and Amy Johnson, Oakland University, School of Nursing Center for Human Animal Interventions, Rochester, MI

PART TWO: TYPES OF DOGS

3 SERVICE DOGS: PERFORMING HELPFUL TASKS
FOR PEOPLE WITH DISABILITIES   99
Mary Renck Jalongo, Editor, Springer Nature, Indiana, PA

4 EMOTIONAL SUPPORT ANIMALS: THERAPEUTIC
COMPANIONS FOR STUDENTS WITH
DISABILITIES IN CAMPUS HOUSING   133
Janet Hoy-Gerlach, Social Work, The University of Toledo, Ohio, Enjie Hall, Director of Campus Accessibility and Student Disability Services, The University of Toledo, Toledo, OH, and Bradley J. Menard, Director of Housing Services, The University of Toledo, Toledo, OH

5 THERAPY DOGS AND FACILITY DOGS:
SUPPORTING WELL-BEING   157
*Mary Renck Jalongo, Editor, Springer Nature, Indiana, PA, and Lorraine J. Guth,
Department of Counseling, Indiana University of Pennsylvania, Indiana, PA*

6 SHELTER DOGS: SERVICE-LEARNING PROJECTS
WITH ANIMAL WELFARE ORGANIZATIONS   185
*Mary Renck Jalongo, Editor, Springer Nature, Indiana, PA, and Tunde Szecsi,
College of Education, Florida Gulf Coast University, Fort Myers, FL*

PART THREE: INVOLVING CANINES ACROSS THE DISCIPLINES

7 INCREASING STUDENT ENGAGEMENT: ROLES
FOR DOGS IN COLLEGE COURSES   223
*Mary Renck Jalongo, Editor, Springer Nature, Indiana, PA, and Lorraine J. Guth,
Department of Counseling, Indiana University of Pennsylvania, Indiana, PA*

8 MEETING PROFESSIONAL EXPECTATIONS:
PRACTICA, INTERNSHIPS, VOLUNTEERISM, AND
COLLABORATIVE RESEARCH WITH FACULTY   249
*Jean P. Kirnan, Psychology Department, The College of New Jersey, Ewing, NJ, and
Taylor Scott, Graduate College of Social Work, University of Houston, Houston, TX*

PART FOUR: FUTURE DIRECTIONS

9 EVALUATING OUTCOMES: EVENTS, PROJECTS,
AND PROGRAMS INVOLVING DOGS   275
*Mary Renck Jalongo, Editor, Springer Nature, Indiana, PA, and Theresa McDevitt,
Academic Librarian, Indiana University of Pennsylvania, Indiana, PA*

10 POSSIBLE FUTURES: MOVING TOWARD A
MORE DOG-FRIENDLY CAMPUS CULTURE   305
Mary Renck Jalongo, Editor, Springer Nature, Indiana, PA

AFTERWORD   341

INDEX   345

ABOUT THE EDITOR   365

PART ONE

Dogs on Campus

INTRODUCTION
Letting the Dogs In

MARY RENCK JALONGO, EDITOR, SPRINGER NATURE, INDIANA, PA

A counselor organized Grief Awareness Day, an event to recognize and respect the frequently overlooked forms of grief that affect high school students. Within a small group of participants, one student spoke about the death of his best friend, a pit bull mix he persuaded his parents to rescue from the local animal shelter. The dog and the teenager had "grown up together" and this young man was still grieving that loss. As he talked, the teenager held a tiny vial hanging from his necklace between his thumb and forefinger; it contained ashes from the dog's cremation. Several of his classmates said that they were familiar with and approved of commemorating deceased dogs in this way. With that, the student who had been sharing his story turned around and tugged at the neck of his T-shirt to reveal an elaborate tattoo on his shoulders. A tattoo artist had used a photo of his dog's face to create the image. Other students admired the ink and their conversation continued as they described pets they had loved and lost.

In a year or two, these students probably will be part of the postsecondary student population. How did this younger generation move so far away from what was commonplace in this rural area 50 years ago: "outside dogs" living in pens, chained to doghouses, or relegated to a barn or porch? Many of these animals had little interaction with humans beyond—if they were lucky—regular food and water. So, who let the dogs in? How did it happen that they were ushered inside, integrated into daily lives, and allowed to captivate human hearts, as they evidently had for this group of high schoolers?

The data suggest that dogs have become companion animals in unprecedented numbers in the United States and many other parts of the world. To illustrate,

At an event on campus, two residential undergraduates take a selfie to send home. The dog's handler is a history professor. Photo Credit: Megan Higgins

consider the following statistics collected by a global industry trends company (Mintel Press Office, 2015; 2016; 2018):

- 75% of families with children under the age of 18 are home to one or more pets
- 67% of Americans own a pet and dogs are the number one companion animal among 18- to 44-year-old people
- 52% of US men and 49% of US women keep one or more dogs
- dog ownership is even higher among older millennials who have tended to postpone having children—75% of 30- to 39-year-old people own one or more dogs
- 51% of those who purchase pet products in the United Kingdom say they would rather cut back spending money on themselves than on their pets
- there is a "humanization trend" toward dogs in the United States, with many people reporting that they view their dogs as family members, apply

some of the same nutritional concerns that they have as people (e.g., natural foods) to their dogs, and collectively invest billions of dollars to make their dogs more comfortable and help to extend the animals' lives.

In addition to higher rates of keeping dogs indoors and regarding them as kin, roles for dogs in supporting the physical, psychological, and social functioning of human beings have expanded considerably (Seksel, 2019). A key source of support has been the ongoing study of the human-animal bond and canine cognition—often in research groups or university-affiliated human-animal interaction centers (O'Haire & Beck, 2018; O'Haire, Bibbo, Hoffman, Mueller, & Buechner-Maxwell, 2018). Research has provided verification of many observations that dog enthusiasts have been making for quite some time (Beck, Barker, Gee, Griffin, & Johnson, 2018). Box I.1 highlights some of the research that provides evidence of dogs' surprising abilities.

BOX I.1 EVIDENCE OF DOGS' REMARKABLE ABILITIES

- During 15,000 years of living together and earning the title of "best friend," dogs have become keen observers of human body language (Morey, 2010; Serpell, 2017). They are better at correctly interpreting the meaning of human gestures than any other animal on the planet (Hare & Woods, 2013; Miklosi & Topal, 2013). To illustrate, many primates do not "get" pointing at something to focus attention while most dogs do (Téglás, Gergely, Kupán, Miklósi, & Topál, 2012).
- Dogs are attuned to human emotions (Albuquerque, Guo, Wilkinson, Savalli, Otta, & Mills, 2016). Even when a stranger pretends to cry, most dogs will try to comfort the person by moving closer, nuzzling them, or placing their heads in the person's lap (Custance & Mayer, 2012). Using functional magnetic resonance imaging (fMRI), neuroscientists have found an area of the dog's brain that processes the emotional tone of human language (Berns, 2013).
- Well socialized dogs who interact frequently with humans often recognize about 200 words that have significance for them (e.g., "treat," "outside," "play"). A particularly brainy border collie, Chaser, demonstrated in a laboratory setting that he could identify over 1,000 nouns (Pilley, 2013). He knew the names of hundreds of different stuffed toys and would go and retrieve them by name (e.g., "Go get hedgehog"; "Go get rabbit").

- Humans tend to rely on sight more than their other senses, while dogs are "nose brained." The area of a dog's brain devoted to smell is 40% larger than that of a human being. Dogs have 300 million scent receptors and humans have just 6 million (Tyson, 2011). As a result, dogs can identify smells in tiny amounts. For example, we might be able to smell sugar in a cup of coffee, but they could smell it dispersed in the equivalent of two Olympic-size swimming pools (Horowitz, 2010).
- Dogs have separate chambers in their noses: one for breathing and one dedicated to smelling. This physiological characteristic also contributes to their superior sense of smell. In addition, they can move each nostril separately to point their nose in the direction of the smell (Tyson, 2012).
- Dogs can sort out smells in ways that humans cannot. We smell stew; they smell beef, carrots, and onions (Horowitz, 2010). Specially trained scent-tracking dogs can pick up a person's scent and follow it hours or even days after the person was there.
- Dogs' night vision is far superior to a person's. They can see about 5 times better than us in the dark. Also, due to the placement of their eyes, their field of vision is 250 degrees while ours is 180 degrees. It is not true that dogs see in black and white only; they also see colors, but not as vividly or full spectrum as people (Bradshaw, 2011).
- Dogs can hear a sound that is 4 times farther away than what a human can hear. This helps to explain how a dog knows that a family member is arriving home well before another person realizes it. A dog has 18 muscles controlling each ear; humans have 6. Those extra muscles help a dog to orient its ears to the direction that a sound is coming from (Bradshaw, 2011).
- Dogs are capable of detecting the presence of several different types of cancer on the breath, on an area of the human body, or in samples of blood, urine, or tissue taken from a human being. Specially trained dogs can identify cancer in laboratory settings earlier, more accurately, and with smaller tissue samples than those necessary for existing medical tests. Teams of medical detection dogs are nearly 100% accurate (InSitu Foundation, 2019).
- Dogs can be trained to alert to very specific smells. Bear, a Labrador retriever found as a stray, was trained to detect computer storage devices using the smell of the glue that holds the components together. Bear has found at least 100 pieces of critical evidence that might have been overlooked and has worked 125 cases (Li, 2019). He was responsible for locating the USB of child pornography that was used to convict former Subway spokesperson,

- Jared Fogle, on child pornography charges (Kim, 2015). Bear and other dogs like him are of inestimable value to law enforcement.
- Dogs who detect firearms and explosives are part of many law enforcement and security services. Where explosives and accelerants are concerned, the dogs' primary value is not that they are continually finding explosive devices. Rather, they avoid the huge expense and disruption of evacuating an area when false reports of bombs are made. Colleges are partnering with law enforcement or preparing/hiring officers to handle working dogs as a way to improve campus and event security (Ashroff, 2019).
- Dogs can be trained to guide the blind to navigate their worlds; alert people who are deaf or hard of hearing to the presence of sounds, such as the doorbell; interrupt damaging behaviors, such as the night terrors of those with PTSD; block a person with severe allergies from ingesting a dangerous food, such as peanuts; retrieve objects for people with mobility issues, such as dropped keys; and alert/respond to medical conditions, such as dangerously low or high blood sugar or blood pressure levels (Jalongo, 2018).
- Dogs can be trained to assist a person with a disability in an emergency situation. Hearing assistance dogs alert a person who is deaf when a smoke alarm goes off. Seizure alert and/or response dogs lead or follow the person to a safe place and remain at his or her side. Dogs learn commands such as "bring medicine" for a person with angina pain or "get phone" so that a person can contact a family member. Dogs also can be trained to use a specially designed big button phone that automatically dials 911 or other emergency notification systems to summon help (Byrne, Zeagler, Freil, Rapoport, & Jackson, 2018).
- Many studies of the recipients of service dogs have found that these dogs not only help by performing useful tasks for persons with disabilities, but also by acting as a conversation starter (Guest, Collis, & McNicholas, 2006). Nondisabled people are far more likely to speak to a person accompanied by a dog (Bould, Bigby, Bennett, & Howell, 2018). People with disabilities are more likely to venture away from home with their service dogs to support them.
- Numerous studies have demonstrated that dogs can offer support to learners engaged in challenging intellectual tasks (Gee, Fine, & McCardle, 2017; Kirnan, Siminerio, & Wong, 2016; Lenihan, McCobb, Diurba, Linder, & Freeman, 2016; Levinson, Barker, Van Zandt, Vogt, & Jalongo, 2017).
- Incorporating dogs into treatment plans for people with emotional, social, and/or behavioral issues frequently is more effective than other interventions (Bachi & Parish-Plass, 2017).

Research also has led the way in taking the next logical step by asking, in effect, "With these canine 'superpowers' in place, how might dogs be trained to become our helpmates in previously unexplored ways?" Take, for example, the medical alert dog. As little as 15 years ago, if someone had suggested that a dog could be trained to help a person with diabetes, most people would have dismissed it as ridiculous. Even today, people remain skeptical; the father of a child with type 1 diabetes commented, "I've been seeing reports in the media that dogs can be trained to alert to high and low blood sugar. Is that really a thing?" Yes, dogs really can be trained to do this (Hardin, Anderson, & Cattet, 2015). Researchers studying 27 glycemia alert dogs concluded that the dogs' accuracy in detecting dangerous blood sugar levels was even higher than what had been found previously with smaller samples; four of the dogs had 100% accuracy. The researchers noted that (1) the dog's training, (2) the human-dog bond, and (3) the match between a dog and its placement influenced the success rate (Rooney, Guest, Swanson, & Morant, 2019). Improving outcomes of the human-animal bond (Mills & Hall, 2014) relies on a cross-disciplinary blend of theory, research, and practice—the very approach that we use throughout this edited book. Scholars in human-animal interaction (HAI) advance the field when they develop theoretical frameworks, conduct rigorous quantitative and qualitative research, and identify evidence-based practices. In fact, this is the structure for each of the ten chapters in the book.

Another long-standing assertion among dog enthusiasts is that dogs and humans can form a deep, reciprocal bond. Or, as stated in everyday parlance, "my dog loves me" or "my dog understands me." A prison inmate involved in a service dog program wondered about this in his dog trainer's journal. He said that he was sitting in his cell with his head in his hands, feeling down and thinking about the long sentence left to serve. The six-month-old puppy he had been raising since it was 8 weeks old was resting quietly, but it got up, walked over, touched him with his nose, and then looked into his eyes as if to say, "Are you OK, buddy?" Although some might say the puppy "just wanted attention," it seemed to the inmate that the dog sensed his mood. The HAI field has made progress, not by being dismissive of anecdotal accounts such as this, but by using observations and hunches to spark scientific inquiry. A good example is the work of neuroscientist Gregory Berns (2013). He surprised his team by suggesting that they use fMRI on a dog. There were two big challenges: first, the dog had to stay perfectly still, and second, the clattering noises of the machine could be very disturbing to a dog. He trained his rescued golden retriever to hold still and the team fashioned some doggy noise-canceling headphones so that the tests could be run. More dogs were trained and tested. Over time, this line of research that began by asking, "What is my dog thinking?" has begun to map the canine brain, discovering, among other things, the region that is activated when responding to the emotional tone of human language (Berns, 2017). Other leaders in the field have studied the canine brain using different strategies. It is now possible to say with considerable confidence that dogs can indeed be attuned to people and display repertoires of behavior that are indicative of a human-animal bond (Horowitz, 2014; Miklosi, 2016; Serpell, 2017). Little wonder, then, that growing numbers of people are not just cohabitating with dogs, but also, as with the dog-tattooed high school student that introduced this chapter, plumbing the depths of the human-canine bond.

Yet even among those who own dogs and claim to love them, there is a very wide range of knowledge, skill, attitudes, and values. When a diverse population of postsecondary students is the focus, as it is for this book, it demands even more nuanced understandings than the perspective on dogs frequently attributed to white, middle-class, American females (Queen, 2014). Whether dogs come to campus or the students go out into the community to be with dogs, effective interpersonal communication, reciprocal respect, and concern for animal welfare are foundational to success.

This rest of this introduction begins by describing disparate perceptions of the dog's place in human society. Next, it defines some key terminology that will be used throughout the book to delineate seven important roles for canines. The third section forms a rationale for writing this book by applying these roles to the lives of postsecondary students. An overview of the structure of the book is outlined in the fourth and final section, which concludes with a sampling of interesting ways that colleges throughout the nation are providing expanded opportunities for college students and canines to interact.

DIFFERENT WAYS OF BEING WITH DOGS

To begin this discussion of diversity in the way that dogs are regarded, it is helpful to have some background on therapy dogs. Therapy dogs are quite different from service dogs. A service dog is trained (usually by a professional dog trainer) to perform helpful tasks for one person who has a disability. Therapy dogs, on the other hand, have been referred to as "everyone's best friend" because they accompany their owner/handler on visits to other people in the community. The purpose of a therapy dog is to elevate positive mood, invite conversation, reduce stress, and motivate people to participate in planned events. The great majority of therapy dogs are, first and foremost, the family dogs of their owners/trainers/handlers. Together, the handler/dog team participates in various community service activities, such as visiting health care facilities, schools, and libraries. These dogs are selected for their good temperament, interest in meeting and greeting new people, and relatively calm demeanor (MacNamara & MacLean, 2017). They then are trained beyond basic obedience to become visiting dogs. For instance, they are tested around orthopedic equipment, other dogs, and people of different ages so that they can visit residents of nursing homes as well as young children with special needs. Therapy handler/dog teams often carry liability insurance and are affiliated with a therapy dog organization. These organizations require the dogs to have an annual physical, be current on vaccinations, get tested for internal parasites, be well-groomed, and be under the control of the handler at all times during visits. Unlike service dogs, therapy dogs do not have public access rights; in other words, they do not have guaranteed access to housing, transportation, or public buildings. Therapy dogs need to be invited in. If you see a group of dogs on campus, they probably are therapy dogs. Sometimes called "comfort dogs," they are the ones that participate in various events, projects, and programs.

Some or most of this information may be unfamiliar to many students, faculty, administrators, and staff. When people hear that dogs will be coming to campus, they may object to the concept of dogs in the workplace, despite growing evidence that the presence of canines tends to exert a positive impact on workers' engagement in tasks, commitment to the organization, and prosocial behavior (Colarelli, McDonald, Christensen, & Honts, 2017; Hall & Mills, 2019). Of course, there are challenges and drawbacks to letting the dogs in at hundreds of postsecondary institutions. Concerns such as health and safety, ethnic differences, cultural sensitivities, fears/phobias of dogs, disruptions to the workplace, or property damage are legitimate, but most can be addressed through well-thought-out policies and procedures (Hall, Wright, McCune, Zulch, & Mills, 2017). Nevertheless, there may be dramatic differences between the way that many or most students see dogs and the perspectives of others in the campus community.

> One state university has a busy calendar of opportunities for students to interact with therapy dogs, including evening gatherings two or three times a month where students can convene at the counseling center to "just chill" and

"hang out" with therapy dogs. In a large multipurpose room, six visiting therapy dogs are seated with their handlers on blankets and each handler/dog team has a few college students clustered around them on the floor. People are chatting about the dogs in attendance (e.g., "Is she a rescue?" "Is this your dog?"), sharing information about their dogs (e.g., "Here's a picture of my dog." "He is so spoiled!"), and discussing college life (e.g., "What's your major?" "Do you have a lot of assignments due?"). Three male students from India arrive. They politely state that they are there to observe, not to participate. One of them explains that, in Delhi, there are thousands of stray dogs that are a nuisance and sometimes carry rabies and attack—or even kill—people. While some people in their country keep dogs, most of these animals live outside to function as watchdogs, and they would never be allowed into a school or business. As the trio walk around to watch the goings on, they have questions: "What is the purpose of that handkerchief?" (in reference to the Alliance of Therapy Dogs bandanas the dogs are wearing). "How do you know the dogs won't bite?" or "What kind of dog is that one over there?" As each question is answered, they discuss among their group in Punjabi, perhaps not wanting to offend anyone with their less-than-enthusiastic response to the strange behavior that they are witnessing.

At a subsequent event held during exam week, the therapy dogs are at the library for a "de-stress fest." Two female students from the Middle East look on curiously from a distance. They explain to an onlooker that dogs are viewed by many Muslims as impure. Still, the women are intrigued by a pair of fluffy Pomeranians. Watching their peers pet the dogs emboldens them to give the dogs a furtive little touch and then jump back. The women pause to use the hand sanitizer pump on the wall as they leave, talking animatedly about what just happened. The next time the dogs are at the library the pair returns. They avoid the large breed dogs but dare to pose next to the Pomeranians they met before, and one asks another student to take a photo with her cell phone. Both instantly send the picture off to their families and await their reaction. They anticipate that others will disapprove or, at the very least, be mystified by the bonds of affection that Americans evidently have with their dogs.

As these international students illustrate, dogs in many parts of the world represent a threat. They may be competitors for scarce food resources, carriers of parasites and disease, or even viewed as vermin themselves because the stray dog population has spun out of control. Of course, negative interactions with dogs are not limited to other countries. Even when the dominant culture is generally tolerant of dogs, students' interactions with dogs can vary considerably. Students from the United States may have been bitten by a dog, frightened by aggressive dogs, or witnessed a dog fight at a suburban dog park. Students may have personal experience with dogs being used by the military or law enforcement to pursue, apprehend, search, or attack individuals or to control crowds. When negative associations with dogs are strong, it should not be surprising if students choose to avoid some or all dogs.

As Serpell and Duffy (2014) describe, "dogs have traditionally been valued for their ability to perform an extraordinary number of working and social roles, including that of security guards, hunting aides, beasts of burden, weapons of war, entertainers, fighters, shepherds, garbage disposers, and pets, to name a few" (p. 32). At times, even practices that are illegal in the dominant culture persist. For example, pitting dogs against one another in a fight ring appeals to those who think dogs are disposable, are fascinated by pain and death, seek to gamble on the violent outcome, or plan to profit by arranging fights or selling the offspring of the fiercest dogs. Even within homes, owned dogs are sometimes all-too-convenient targets and voiceless victims of human frustration, rage, neglect, abuse, violence, and cruelty. Further, rather than being treated as friend or family, some people see dogs as a commodity, as in the case of commercial and backyard breeding operations used to mass produce puppies for sale. Bringing dogs indoors to cohabitate with people is, for some college students, completely out of the question, and the concept of being an animal guardian—versus viewing them as property—is an entirely foreign idea.

Even students who have lived with dogs and accumulated quite a bit of experience may hold widely divergent views of canines. Such differences need to be understood rather than ignored or glossed over by personal enthusiasm for the human-canine bond. This is not to say that we need to agree with mistreatment of dogs or practices that jeopardize their welfare, nor do we have to concede that there is no place for dogs on a college campus. There is ample research evidence collected across various disciplines and reported across all ten chapters of this book to support the assertion that dogs can exert a positive effect on the lives of human beings. Dogs visiting hospital patients offer a good example.

Physicians overwhelmingly support thoughtfully planned and carefully monitored opportunities for patients to interact with dogs. Doctors also recommend dog ownership to patients with and without disabilities. A survey of 1,000 family physicians published by Human-Animal Bond Research Institute (McCullough, Ruehrdanz, & Jenkins, 2016) found that 97% believed that there are health benefits associated with petkeeping. High percentages of physicians reported that bonds with pets "moderately to significantly" improved patients' relationships with staff (76%), physical condition (88%), mental health condition (97%), and mood or outlook (98%). The rewards outweigh the risks and the risks are managed (Linder Siebens, Mueller, Gibbs, & Freeman, 2017), because the conviction that there are salutary effects of positive interactions between humans and canines has support in the literature.

Yet one persistent challenge in exploring the role of canines in society is confusion about terminology. As with many emerging fields of study, arriving at clear understandings of key concepts and a shared vocabulary is an ongoing part of the process. Furthermore, the human-canine bond is an exceptionally interdisciplinary field of study and no one can be expected to understand every facet; that is one reason for deciding to write an edited, rather than a single-authored, book. Even those who have both professional credentials and extensive practical experience within their discipline are continually learning new things, refining their understandings, and revisiting terminology as they strive to keep current in this burgeoning field. With the goal of clarity in mind, we now turn to seven major roles that dogs frequently play in the lives of postsecondary students.

SORTING OUT TERMINOLOGY: SEVEN ROLES FOR DOGS

Roles for dogs during and after the attack on the World Trade Center will be used here to clarify terminology. First is the role of *family dog*. As people began their day on September 11, 2001, they were expecting to return home after work, school, or the other activities they had planned. Perhaps their dog was crated, left to roam the house, fenced in outdoors, or under the supervision of a family member or friend. Some people may have hired others to help, such as dog walkers or a "doggy day care." There was no way to anticipate how completely unhinged those plans would become. Indeed, the fate of the family dog created another type of mental anguish for many, while others viewed the family dog as the least of their worries in extreme crisis conditions. Further, as the national calamity rippled out beyond New York City to Washington, DC, and Shanksville, PA, the lives of many family dogs were forever changed.

Service dogs are individually trained to perform specific tasks for people with disabilities. An example of a *service dog* was a yellow Labrador retriever named Roselle. She had completed extensive training to become a guide dog for Michael Hingson, who was blind. In 2011, the American Humane Association named Roselle "America's Hero Dog" (American Veterinary Medical Association, 2011). She earned the title for guiding Hingson down 1,463 stairs of Tower 1, all the while immersed in chaos, tension, smoke, dust, and noise. Not only her owner, but also many others credited Roselle's calm demeanor with saving their lives that day.

In the aftermath of the disaster, the *working dogs* handled by professionals in various fields or professional dog trainers were called in. Some of these dogs assisted law enforcement by searching for explosives and firearms or aided in investigations on the ground by tracking terrorist cells at other bombing sites. At Ground Zero, there were many search and rescue dogs, usually handled by individuals who worked with first responders and emergency medical services in various communities. The iconic image of Riley, a golden retriever, being transported across a 60-foot canyon of destruction in a large basket operated by ropes and pulleys riveted the attention of a nation (Arnold, 2019). Even those who had not the slightest interest in dogs had to marvel at this dog's bravery, training, and skill. Initially, search and rescue dog teams had been hoping to save the lives of victims, but sadly, that was not the job; it was more a matter of locating human remains with the help of cadaver dogs. As work at the disaster sites went on day after day, the workers—both human and dog—were discouraged and exhausted.

It was then that *therapy dogs* were brought in to lift the search teams' spirits. As mentioned previously, therapy dogs usually are trained and handled by their owners; their purpose is to bring comfort and calm during stressful times and elevate positive mood. The presence of the therapy dogs shifted the focus from the workers' physical misery, overwhelming sense of loss, and feelings of national vulnerability to interactions with happy, friendly canines. It also encouraged conversations about dogs "back home."

Based on the American Veterinary Medical Association's (2020) definitions, there are three types of interventions that involve therapy dogs and all of them were widely implemented in the aftermath of 9/11.

1. *animal-assisted activities* (AAA) are "meet and greet" informal types of interaction in which therapy dogs visit with their handlers. The volunteer handler/dog

teams that interacted with workers from Ground Zero to support their emotional well-being are an example of animal-assisted *activity*.

2. *animal-assisted education* (AAE) involves therapy dogs in supporting academic goals and learning objectives. For example, a childcare program located near the World Trade Center enrolled students whose parent or parents were employed there. At the end of what the administrator called "the worst day of my professional life," no one came to pick up four of the children in her care. She had no other choice but to take them home with her and later learned that these students had been orphaned by the tragic event. Children and staff needed to heal, so she secured permission and then contacted a group of volunteer therapy dog handlers. The teachers selected books matched to the interests and reading levels of each student and scheduled 15-minute appointments during which the child could practice reading aloud with a handler/dog team. This is animal-assisted *education* because the therapy dogs were there to support learning and were part of a professional educator's plan.

3. *animal-assisted therapy* (AAT) incorporates the therapy dog in a professional treatment plan for an individual or group. Treatment goals are set and monitored by a professional working within his or her area of expertise, and progress toward achieving those goals is evaluated. Many counselors, psychologists, and psychiatrists found that, for some patients, dogs were an "icebreaker" that could help to build rapport between therapist and client. This qualifies as animal-assisted *therapy* because licensed mental health professionals made therapy dogs an integral part of their plan and assessed the impact on their clients (Bachi & Parish-Plass, 2017).

An estimated 25,000 people sustained physical injuries on 9/11; some would require physical therapy and ongoing rehabilitation services supplied by various health care facilities. At least some of these organizations were home to *resident animals* or *facility dogs*. Resident dogs at the facility such as "courthouse dogs" are present in waiting areas, during forensic interviews, and accompany victims as they testify. Facility dogs usually are the family dogs of an employee, trained as a therapy dog or at the assistance dog level, who accompany that person to work on a regular basis to support the goals of the organization. What differentiates facility dogs from visiting therapy dogs is that they are more of a permanent fixture at the institution. The resident or facility dog could encourage people to comply with physical therapy, for example, by brushing the dog or playing fetch with it to strengthen a hand and wrist after surgery.

Yet another category of dog, an *emotional support animal* or ESA, was important to those directly affected by the events of 9/11. An ESA is a companion animal who helps to reduce impairment experienced by an individual with a disability through simply being present and engaging in everyday interactions with that person; the need for an ESA should be verified in writing by a health care professional. Unlike service dogs, ESAs are not trained to do specific tasks to assist people. A canine ESA is essentially a therapeutic companion who offers the same physical, social, emotional, and psychological benefits to people that a pet does, simply by being there and interacting; it is the positive impact of such benefits on the functioning of a person with a disability that results in ESAs having limited federal legal recognition as an accommodation. Currently, ESAs are permitted in housing as accommodations for people with disabilities; people with ESAs do not have public access with their ESAs in the way that people with service dogs do. At the time of this writing, access for individuals with ESAs to public transportation and air travel was contested; the US Department of Transportation has just issued new rules limiting animal-related air travel accommodation to service dogs only.

In the wake of everything that happened after the tragedy, animals became homeless. Their owners may have perished, health issues may have made it impossible for them to take care of a dog, or changes in living arrangements and geographic relocation might have forced them to give up their dogs. If no other rehoming options were available, these animals probably went to an animal shelter or rescue to be put up for adoption. They became *homeless dogs in the care of animal welfare organizations*.

Each of these types of dogs—(1) family dogs, (2) service dogs, (3) working dogs, (4) therapy dogs, (5) resident/facility dogs, (6) emotional support animals, and (7) homeless dogs in the care of animal welfare groups—are or can become part of the experience of postsecondary students. All will be discussed in the next section.

DOGS IN COLLEGE STUDENTS' LIVES

This book is intended as a "guide to the galaxy" of the major ways that postsecondary students and canines might interact for their mutual benefit. Box I.2 highlights the seven categories of canines defined previously and describes these roles as they pertain to college and university students.

College study sometimes limits contact with students' network of known dogs, leaving students "dog deprived." Photo Credit: Megan Higgins

BOX I.2 ROLES FOR DOGS IN COLLEGE STUDENTS' LIVES

1. Family Dogs

These canines are an important part of students' history with petkeeping. Relationships with family dogs often undergo major changes during adolescence (Piper & Uttley, 2019). Residential students on and off campus may have had to leave family dogs behind. Some may be separated from their family dogs for extended periods of time. Commuter students living at home may continue to see their family dogs almost daily yet have less time for them; nevertheless, family dogs may provide routine and stability (Graham, Milaney, Adams, & Rock, 2019). More postsecondary institutions are offering dog-friendly residence hall and apartment housing options to college students and to students with families.

2. Service Dogs

Service dogs are individually trained to perform tasks that assist a person with a professionally diagnosed physical and/or psychological disability. College students also can be involved in the training phase of a service dog's preparation by helping to socialize the dog or raising and helping to train a service dog. For students with a disability who need help to perform tasks, the support of a service dog can make it possible for them to attend college when they otherwise would not. If, for example, a student has multiple sclerosis and the attendant physical mobility issues that result in the need for a scooter, the dog can assist the student to navigate the college campus, open doors, retrieve dropped objects, fetch medicine, and encourage communication with others.

A prison superintendent welcomes a goldendoodle pup destined to become a service dog through a prison dog training program. Staff will bring the puppies to campus to aid in their socialization.
Photo Credit: Mary Renck Jalongo

3. Working Dogs of Professionals

Dogs handled by law enforcement and first responders may be affiliated with campus police services or with justice organizations in the larger community. Specially trained dogs can improve campus security by searching for dangerous or illegal substances, such as drugs or firearms. They can be brought in to search for an abducted or missing student, locate evidence if a crime is committed, or track a perpetrator. There are even dogs trained to locate missing pets and reunite them with their owners.

4. Therapy Dogs

Visiting "comfort dogs" can fulfill important roles. For example, therapy dogs were on site when *The Champions*, a documentary about the successful rehabilitation of dogs seized from Michael Vick's BadNewz dog fighting kennels was shown (Dennett, 2016). Their presence attracted attention, resulted in a good turnout, and encouraged discussions about breed bias. Animal-assisted education occurred when the handler of a military war dog was a guest speaker for students enrolled in the Reserve Officer Training Corps (ROTC). The instructor for the class had made the visit part of the syllabus, linked it to learning objectives for the course, and required the students to complete further investigation into military working dogs (MWDs). An example of animal-assisted therapy occurred when a university counselor included a therapy dog in sessions with a student seeking help with test anxiety and charted the student's progress.

5. Resident or Facility Dogs

Resident dogs are at a facility full time, have a role in the facility, and are cared for by staff, volunteers, and residents. A facility dog is the family dog of a faculty member or administrator that accompanies the staff member to work regularly and is part of her or his professional practice. For example, an academic librarian might obtain permission to bring a certified therapy dog with additional insurance coverage through Alliance of Therapy Dogs to work nearly every day. The dog's presence helps students see library staff as more approachable, encourages them to enroll in library orientation sessions, prompts them to make better use of available library resources, and increases enrollment in elective courses on information literacy.

6. Emotional Support Animals (ESAs)

These dogs are the individual companions of a student who has is currently under treatment for a professionally diagnosed mental health issue. A licensed mental health professional has verified that the dog helps the student cope with a specific mental health challenge. For example, an undergraduate on the autism spectrum disorder (ASD) might formally apply to bring his dog to reside in the residence hall to help him deal with powerful emotions. The dog's presence serves to moderate some of the social awkwardness often associated with ASD.

7. Dogs Under the Care of Animal Welfare Groups

These dogs have become homeless and are in a shelter or perhaps in a temporary foster home until they can be placed for adoption. If the dogs were neglected, traumatized, or abused, they often need veterinary services, such as vaccinations, spay/neuter, or treatment for illness and/or injuries. College students sometimes volunteer to help homeless animals by doing such things as assisting

> with a fundraiser or working on a team to design a dog park. They may complete a professional internship that supports the organization in conjunction with their major field of study; for example, a student in advertising might design a new logo for the organization, a student in information science might create a database of volunteers, a student studying criminal justice might complete an internship with the dog warden, and a team of art majors could plan and paint a mural on one of the shelter walls. Many times, college students contribute by simply socializing and exercising dogs.

OVERVIEW OF THE BOOK

When we first proposed *The Canine-Campus Connection: Roles for Dogs in the Lives of College Students*, our goal was to produce a synthesis of theory, research, and practice that, to the best of our knowledge, did not exist previously. To better accomplish that aim, each of the ten chapters has a theoretical base. For example, the foundation for the chapter on therapy dogs is wellness; for the chapter on service dogs, it is inclusion; and, for the chapter on shelter dogs, it is service-learning. In addition, every chapter has a literature review that includes the relevant research from across the disciplines, and all chapters include descriptions of exemplary programs in place at colleges and universities.

The book is organized into four sections. Part one examines the interactions between postsecondary students and canines by reviewing the literature on the human-canine bond. It establishes what must necessarily be the top priority when people and dogs are brought together: the health and safety of both. Part two highlights four major categories of dogs that students are likely to interact with on and off campus: service dogs, emotional support animals, therapy dogs, and homeless dogs. Part three emphasizes ways in which dogs can influence student learning during classes and across aspects of their professional development. Part four considers future directions. It takes the stance that enriching and enlarging interactions between college students and canines will require university personnel who plan to evaluate events, projects, and programs. It also will require colleges and universities to develop a more dog-friendly campus culture.

Part one consists of two chapters. In chapter 1, Mary-Ann Sontag Bowman from the School of Social Work at University of Montana collaborates with the book editor to review the research evidence on human-canine interactions.

The chapter also addresses the feelings of loss that many residential students experience when they leave beloved family dogs behind. In any type of planned college or university-affiliated activity that brings students and dogs into contact, the welfare of both is the top priority. Chapter 2 is coauthored by Laura Bruneau, from the Department of Counselor Education at Adams State University, and Amy Johnson, from Oakland University's School of Nursing and Center for Human Animal Interventions. Together they have produced a very thought-provoking examination of what constitutes behaviorally healthy human-canine interactions in the postsecondary context.

Part two contains four chapters on categories of dogs that frequently are part of contemporary college students' experiences: service dogs (chapter 3), emotional support dogs (chapter 4), therapy dogs (chapter 5), and homeless dogs (chapter 6). Chapter 3 by Mary Renck Jalongo, editor with Springer Nature, draws upon her background in education as well as her teaching of inmate dog trainers in prison programs to discuss service dogs for students with disabilities. Chapter 4 on ESAs is a collaboration among Janet Hoy-Gerlach, a sociologist at the University of Toledo, and her colleagues, Enji Hall (with student disability services) and Bradley J. Menard (with student housing). They provide authoritative advice and practical guidance on canine ESAs and policies/procedures. The role of therapy dogs in supporting human wellness is the focus of chapter 5, coauthored by Lorraine J. Guth (counseling) and Mary Renck Jalongo (emerita, curriculum, and instruction). In addition to their work at Indiana University of Pennsylvania, both are owners/handlers of certified and insured therapy dogs and are involved in therapy dog activities on campus. Opportunities for college students to work with homeless dogs and shelter or rescue organizations is the focus of chapter 6. It is coauthored by two educators: Tunde Szecsi from Florida Gulf Coast University and the book's editor. Both have worked extensively with projects that provide postsecondary students with service-learning through partnerships with animal welfare groups.

Part three includes two chapters that examine ways that dogs can support learning and professional development for students. Chapter 7, authored by Mary Renck Jalongo and Lorraine J. Guth, is grounded in contemporary theory of student engagement. It describes how visits from professionals who have incorporated dogs into their practice can motivate college students to learn. In chapter 8, two researchers from The College of New Jersey—Jean P. Kirnan and Taylor Scott—use their collaborative research project with students to illustrate how experiences with dogs can be a springboard for practica, internships, volunteerism, and collaborative research that develops the next generation of professionals.

The fourth and final section of the book is essentially an answer to the question, "How can we arrive at even better human-canine interaction, both for new and continuing initiatives?" Chapter 9 builds a strong argument for the role that systematic evaluation plays in events, projects, and programs. Coauthored by Theresa McDevitt, an academic librarian at Indiana University of Pennsylvania, and the book's editor, the chapter illustrates how logic models can be applied to the task of evaluating human-canine interaction projects on campus. The authors also draw upon six years of experience in offering opportunities for college students to interact with dogs on campus and disseminating their survey findings to college and university librarians. The tenth and final chapter, written by Mary Renck Jalongo, looks to the future of dogs on and off campus and ways to build a more dog-friendly culture. Its theoretical base is Quality of Life (QoL), and the book concludes with the argument that, for many postsecondary students, faculty, administrators, and staff members, the presence of dogs can exert a positive influence on the lives of human beings. That message is important enough to bear repeating, so this introduction concludes in the same way.

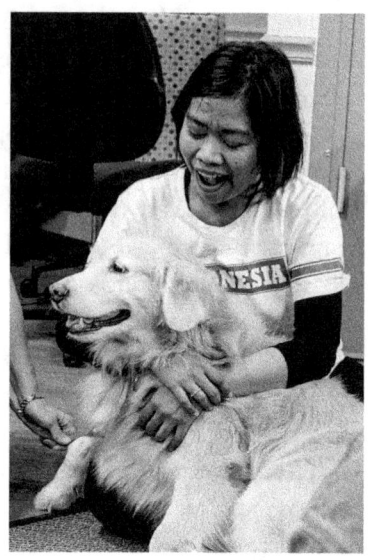

An international student interacts with a visiting therapy dog during one of the dog's frequent visits to the health and wellness center. Photo Credit: Megan Higgins

CANINES AND QUALITY OF CAMPUS LIFE

The assertion that dogs can improve quality of life on campus is more than a matter of individual enthusiasm for dogs, the convictions of a cadre of college/university personnel who like dogs, or even an insistence on majority rule. Support for connecting college students and canines comes from self-report data gathered from participants, through program evaluations, during assessment of outcomes, and as empirical research from various traditions (i.e., qualitative, quantitative, and mixed methods). A few of the ways that dogs can contribute to campus culture follow.

- *Dogs can improve safety.* Some students and staff may reject dogs completely yet benefit when dogs are used to increase security at campus gatherings (Ashroff, 2019). Partnering with law enforcement and working dogs from the community can assist in locating evidence, finding victims, and tracking perpetrators. Specially trained dogs can detect a wide range of threats to health and safety in minimally disruptive ways, for example, illegal substances, locating molds, insect pests (e.g., bedbugs or termites), or underground gas leaks.
- *Dogs can encourage physical activity.* Students who might otherwise remain sedentary can be motivated to exercise by an interest in dogs, and the dogs' appreciation for the activity helps to build a commitment to exercise (Yordy & Graff, 2019). When postsecondary institutions establish programs that engage students in fostering shelter dogs or training service dogs, they then create a need for dog exercise areas. St. Charles Community College (2019) in Missouri, for example, has an expansive, dog-friendly walking trail on their 228-acre campus that encourages students to get moving and keep fit.
- *Dogs can aid student recruitment.* Experts say that the best campus tours are interactive, tell a story, and help prospective students see the campus through the eyes of a successful student (Staff Writer in Schools, 2016). At one campus, parents and students had the choice of going on their campus tour with or without a dog. Those who elected the "with dog" option were guided by an undergraduate ambassador majoring in pre-veterinary studies. She had participated in a service dog training program on campus and her canine companion on the tour would soon "go off to college himself" to be placed/trained with a person who has a disability. This campus tour addressed all three recommendations on effective campus tours: it engaged the participants, the story was interesting, and it provided a student's perspective on the institution. Given that more postsecondary students are seeking institutions where their ESAs and service dogs are welcomed, bringing dogs into recruitment activities makes sense. For many postsecondary students, the institution they select will need to meet the spirit of the Americans with Disabilities Act and Fair Housing Act rather than just the letter of the law.
- *Dogs can help to counteract negative emotions.* Stress and anxiety among contemporary college students is a recognized threat to their well-being (Pendry & Vandagriff, 2019). Another emotional response that can have negative consequences for overall functioning is feeling disaffected or bored. When this emotion is intense, the prospect of attending class can seem onerous and skipping class soon leads to academic difficulties. When service dog puppies in training arrived on campus, they counteracted ennui. There is extensive evidence, based

on research conducted by the Royal Society for the Prevention of Cruelty to Animals (RSPCA) (2012) in the United Kingdom, that many people find the charm of puppies irresistible. Giving college students a chance to experience a young pup's boundless enthusiasm, passion for play, and over-the-top displays of affection can elicit a wide range of positive emotions. Dogs give us permission to let our guard down, show affection, and use baby talk. In many ways, it can be a form of emotional refueling.

- *Dogs can develop professional knowledge, skills, and dispositions.* A group of nursing majors decided to complete the training and participate in what one referred to as "the best thing, ever"—the opportunity to raise service dog puppies while living in a dog-friendly residence hall. "I've learned responsibility, patience, and how to work with others" a student wrote in his journal, "those are skills you can apply to any job." Participants in this program also developed more specific abilities related to the medical field, such as practicing daily care rituals, maintaining records on the puppies' health, and working with fellow health care professionals in veterinary medicine. For universities that partner with service dog providers, such as the partnership between Miami University in Oxford, Ohio, and 4 Paws for Ability, the dogs fostered by students also participate in commencement ceremonies (Kiefaber, 2013).

- *Dogs can support students in crisis.* During their student teaching experience, four preservice teachers were assigned to the same school building. They had completed many of their classes and practica together and treated each other as respected colleagues. It was a shock when one of them was on her way to school one morning, hit a patch of ice, lost control of her car, and was killed. After obtaining permission from all concerned, university counseling services arranged an afterschool onsite meeting for the remaining student teachers. A staff counselor, a doctoral candidate in psychology, and the Counseling Center's therapy/facility dog were there. The dog was familiar to the student teachers and, as they stroked his fur, they began to open up about how the loss affected them. There is considerable evidence that dogs do encourage college students to talk and disclose new information, even about difficult topics (see Caparelli, Miller, Wright, & London, 2019). Therapy dogs can play a key role in commemorations of historic tragedies as well, such as the 50-year anniversary of the Kent State University shootings (2020) during which unarmed student protestors were shot by the Ohio National Guard in 1970.

- *Dogs can support student retention.* The presence of dogs can support retention efforts by promoting positive social relationships (Wood et al., 2015). A military veteran with physical and psychological wounds who is in a wheelchair and waiting in the hallway for class to begin might otherwise feel as though he does not "fit in." However, with his service dog at his side, he finds himself engaged in animated conversation with his classmates. Service dogs not only perform helpful tasks, but also increase positive social interaction between their owner/handlers and nondisabled peers (Audrestch et al., 2015; Guest, Collis, & McNicholas, 2006; Wiggett-Barnard & Steel, 2008). This sense of belonging often strengthens students' resolve to persist and complete their academic course of study.

- *Dogs can increase student participation.* It can be extremely disappointing for college and university personnel to offer student support services or plan special events that few students access or attend. For example, when dogs were stationed inside a student health fair at our local university, the organizers reported that it was the best attendance the event had ever attracted. Student awareness of and access to special services is another issue. Research indicates that college students who have struggled with mental health issues in the past may want a fresh start, be reluctant to disclose their condition, and refuse professional help, even when it is provided free of charge (Cadigan, Lee, & Larimer, 2019). One strategy for destigmatizing the use of mental health services on campus is to plan events involving therapy dogs that all students can—and do—attend. An added benefit of such events is that students who need support later have already met counseling services staff, see them as more approachable, and know where to go and who to ask for help.
- *Dogs can expand horizons for students.* Five years of volunteering with college students at a no-kill shelter has been enlightening. Although one might expect that anyone who volunteers has extensive experience with dogs, many times this is not the case. Some of the volunteers apparently are filling a previously unmet need and say they were not allowed to have a dog due to parent work schedules, housing restrictions on animals, family members with phobias or allergies, and so forth. Others say that, although their family kept dogs, they did not agree with their parent(s) who insisted on a particular breed, did not embrace the idea of rescue, or kept dogs outdoors. In a few cases, students volunteer purely because a shelter appears to be the most interesting option among the service-learning sites. Students sometimes come from communities—both in the United States and in other countries—where their ideas about dog care conflict with those of the majority and where shelter/rescue services are unavailable or inadequate. They seek to gain an insider's perspective on how these organizations operate in the hopes that, someday, they might influence people at home to change. On rare occasions, students who confess to being afraid of dogs volunteer in the hopes that the experience will help them overcome their fears.

• *Dogs can be part of career preparation.* Some researchers are recommending that professionals in various fields could benefit from planned efforts to make human-animal relationships part of college curricula (Castillo, Silcox, & Fischer, 2019). Particularly in the social sciences and helping professions, graduates of various academic programs are apt to encounter dogs when they begin work. It would not be unusual for nursing students completing their clinical experience to see therapy dogs in a health care setting, for instance. Just knowing the laws governing service dogs and ESAs is important for professionals in culinary schools and hospitality management types of careers. Justice workers, for example, are likely to encounter dogs used by law enforcement, dog training programs in correctional facilities, and courthouse dogs that support victims during interviews or court testimony.

This is just a small sampling of a few ways that canines are now woven into the fabric of many, if not most, college students' lives. Increasingly, dogs have become part of the postsecondary school culture. Just typing in the search term "college students" and specifying roles for dogs (e.g., "service dogs," "shelter dogs," "emotional support animals") will yield thousands of articles, both in the professional literature and in the popular media, about each topic. Perhaps more than ever before, dogs are regarded not only as loyal companions, but also as helpmates, professional work partners, game changers, and even lifesavers.

REFERENCES

Albuquerque, N., Guo, K., Wilkinson, A., Savalli, C., Otta, E., & Mills, D. (2016). Dogs recognize dog and human emotions. *Biology Letters, 12*(1), 1–5. https://doi.org/10.1098/rsbl.2015.0883

American Veterinary Medical Association. (2011). Guide dog named American Hero. *JAVMA News.* https://www.avma.org/javma-news/2011-12-01/guide-dog-named-american-hero-dog

American Veterinary Medical Association. (2020). Animal-assisted interventions: Definitions. https://www.avma.org/policies/animal-assisted-interventions-definitions

Arnold, R. (2019, September 10). Remembering the hero dogs of 9/11. https://www.dogingtonpost.com/remembering-the-hero-dogs-of-911

Ashroff, Z. (2019, September 9). USC K-9 dogs detect firearms, explosives at campus events. *The Daily Gamecock*. https://www.dailygamecock.com/article/2019/09/uscpd-K9-unit

Audrestch, H. M., Whelan, C. T., Grice, D., Asher, L., England, G. C., Freeman, S. L. (2015). Recognizing the value of assistance dogs in society. *Disability Health Journal, 8*(4), 469–474. https://doi.org/10.1016/j.dhjo.2015.07.001

Bachi, K., & Parish-Plass, N. (2017). Animal-assisted psychotherapy: A unique relational therapy for children and adolescents. *Clinical Child Psychology and Psychiatry, 22*(1), 3–8.

Beck, A. M., Barker, S., Gee, N. R., Griffin, J. A., & Johnson, R. (2018). Background to human-animal interaction (HAI) research. *Human-Animal Bond Bulletin, 6*, 47–62.

Berns, G. (2013). *How dogs love us: A neuroscientist and his adopted dog decode the canine brain*. Boston: New Harvest/Houghton Mifflin Harcourt.

Berns, G. (2017). *What it's like to be a dog: And other adventures in animal neuroscience*. New York: Basic Books.

Bould, B., Bigby, C., Bennett, P. C., & Howell, T. J. (2018). "More people talk to you when you have a dog": Dogs as catalysts for social inclusion of people with intellectual disabilities. *Journal of Intellectual Disability Research, 62*(10), 833–841. https://www.ncbi.nlm.nih.gov/pubmed/30125042

Bradshaw, J. (2011). *Dog sense: How the new science of dog behavior can make you a better friend to your pet*. New York: Basic Books.

Byrne, C., Zeagler, C., Freil, L., Rapoport, A., & Jackson, M. M. (2018). Dogs using touchscreens in the home: A case study for assistance dogs operating emergency notification systems. ACI 2018 Conference Proceedings, Article 12. https://doi.org/10.1145/3295598.3295610

Cadigan, J. M., Lee, C. M., & Larimer, M. E. (2019). Young adult mental health: A prospective examination of service utilization, perceived unmet service needs, attitudes, and barriers to service use. *Prevention Science, 20*(3), 366–376.

Caparelli, A. L., Miller, Q. C., Wright, D. B., & London, K. (2019). Canine-assisted interviews bolster informativeness for negative autobiographical memories. *Psychological Reports, 123*(1), 159–178.

Castillo, Y. A., Silcox, D., & Fischer, L. (2019). Evaluating educational training impact on pre-service students' attitudes toward human-animal relationships. *Integrated Journal of Social Sciences, 6*(1), 6–11. http://www.pubs.iscience.in/journal/index.php/ijss/article/view/827

Colarelli, S. M., McDonald, A. M., Christensen, M. S., & Honts, C. (2017). A companion dog increases prosocial behavior in work groups. *Anthrozoös, 30*(1), 77–89. https://doi.org/10.1080/08927936.2017.1270595

Custance, D., & Mayer, J. (2012). Empathic-like responding by domestic dogs (*Canis familiaris*) to distress in humans: An exploratory study. *Animal Cognition, 15*(5), 851–859. https://doi.org/10.1007/s10071-012-0510-1

Dennett, D. (2016). *The champions.* New York: FilmRise. (DVD, 92 min).

Gee, N. R., Fine, A. H., & McCardle, P. (Eds.). (2017). *How animals help students learn: Research and practice for educators and mental health professionals.* New York: Routledge.

Graham, T. M., Milaney, K. J., Adams, C. L., & Rock, M J. (2019). Are millennials really picking pets over people? Taking a closer look at dog ownership in emerging adulthood. *Canadian Journal of Family and Youth, 11*(1), 202–227. https://doi.org/10.29173/cjfy29454

Guest, C. M., Collis, G. M., & McNicholas, J. (2006). Hearing dogs: A longitudinal study of social and psychological effects on deaf and hard-of-hearing recipients. *The Journal of Deaf Studies and Deaf Education, 11*(2), 252–261. https://doi.org/10.1093/deafed/enj028

Hall, S., Wright, H., McCune, S., Zulch, H., & Mills, D. (2017). Perceptions of dogs in the workplace: The pros and the cons. *Anthrozoös, 30*(2), 291–305. https://doi.org/10.1080/08927936.2017.1311053

Hall, S. S., & Mills, D. S. (2019). Taking dogs into the office: A novel strategy for promoting work engagement, commitment and quality of life. *Frontiers of Veterinary Science, 6,* 1–17. https://www.frontiersin.org/articles/10.3389/fvets.2019.00138/full

Hardin, D. S., Anderson, W., & Cattet, J. (2015). Dogs can be successfully trained to alert to hypoglycemia samples from patients with type 1 diabetes. *Diabetes Therapy, 6*(4), 509–517. https://doi.org/10.1007/s13300-015-0135-x

Hare, B., & Woods, V. (2013). *The genius of dogs: How dogs are smarter than you think.* New York: Plume.

Horowitz, A. (2010). *Inside of a dog: What dogs see, smell, and know.* New York: Scribner.

Horowitz, A. (Ed.). (2014). *Domestic dog cognition and behavior: The scientific study of Canis familiaris.* New York: Springer.

InSitu Foundation. (2019). Canine cancer detection. http://www.dogsdetectcancer.org

Jalongo, M. R. (Ed.). (2018). *Children, dogs and education: Caring for, learning alongside, and gaining support from canine companions.* New York: Springer Nature.

Kent State University. (2020, January). May 4th, 50th commemoration. https://www.kent.edu/may4kentstate50

Kiefaber, A. (2013, May 9). In-training service dogs to walk at graduation. *USA Today*. https://www.usatoday.com/story/news/nation/2013/05/09/service-dogs-walk-graduation/2148537

Kim, S. (2015, August 26). Meet the dog investigators say helped catch ex-subway spokesman Jared Fogle. https://abcnews.go.com/US/meet-dog-investigators-helped-catch-subway-spokesman-jared/story?id=33330258

Kirnan, J. P., Siminerio, S., & Wong, Z. (2016). The impact of a therapy dog reading program on children's reading skills and attitudes toward reading. *Early Childhood Education Journal, 44*(6), 637–651.

Lenihan, D., McCobb, E., Diurba, A., Linder, E., & Freeman, L. (2016). Measuring the effects of reading assistance dogs on reading ability and attitudes in elementary schoolchildren. *Journal of Research in Childhood Education, 30*(2), 252–259.

Levinson, Vogt, M., Barker, W. F., Jalongo, M.R., & Van Zandt, P. (2017). Effects of reading with adult tutor/therapy dog teams on elementary students' reading achievement and attitudes. *Society and Animals, 25*(1), 38–56.

Li, J. (2019, January 14). How Bear the electronic detection dog went from a life on the streets to sniffing out key evidence. https://www.insideedition.com/how-bear-electronic-detection-dog-went-life-streets-sniffing-out-key-evidence-49953

Linder, D. E., Siebens, H. C., Mueller, M. K., Gibbs, D. M., & Freeman, L. M. (2017). Animal-assisted interventions: A national survey of health and safety policies in hospitals, eldercare facilities, and therapy animal organizations. *American Journal of Infection Control, 45*(8), 883–887.

MacNamara, M., & MacLean, E. (2017). Selecting animals for education environments. In N. R. Gee, A. H. Fine, & P. McCardle (Eds.), *How animals help students learn: Research and practice for educators and mental health professionals* (pp. 182–196). New York: Routledge.

McCullough, A., Ruehrdanz, A., & Jenkins, M. (2016). HABRI Central Briefs: The use of dogs in hospital settings. https://habricentral.org/resources/54871/download/hc_brief_dogsinhospitals20160115Access.pdf

Miklosi, A. (2016). *Dog behavior, evolution, and cognition.* Oxford: Oxford University Press.

Miklosi, A., & Topal, J. (2013). What does it take to become "best friends"? Evolutionary changes in canine social competence. *Trends in Cognitive Sciences, 17*(6), 287–294.

Mills, D., & Hall, S. (2014). Animal-assisted interventions: Making better use of the human-animal bond. *Veterinary Record, 174*(11), 269–73. https://doi.org/10.1136/vr.g1929

Mintel Press Office (2015, June 22). One-quarter of US pet owners worry that pet food is making their pet obese. https://www.mintel.com/press-centre/food-and-drink/one-quarter-of-us-pet-owners-worry-pet-food-is-making-their-pet-obese

Mintel Press Office (2016, September 7). Dogs really are man's best friend: 71% of US males own a dog. Retrieved from: https://www.mintel.com/press-centre/household-press-centre/dogs-really-are-mans-best-friend-71-of-us-males-own-a-dog

Mintel Press Office. (2018, October 16). UK pet care buyers would rather cut back spending on themselves than on their pet. https://www.mintel.com/press-centre/retail-press-centre/uk-pet-care-buyers-would-rather-cut-back-spending-on-themselves-than-on-their-pet

Morey, D. F. (2010). *Dogs: Domestication and development of a social bond.* New York: Cambridge University Press.

O'Haire, M., & Beck, A. M. (2018). Human-animal interaction interdisciplinary centers and institutes: A decade of progress. *Human-Animal Bond Bulletin, 6,* 1–2. https://www.purdue.edu/vet//chab/ohaire/files/documents/HAI_2018_HAIB_OHaire.pdf

O'Haire, M., Bibbo, J., Hoffman, C. L., Mueller, M. K., Ng, Z., & Buechner-Maxwell, V. A. (2018). Overview of centers and institutes for human-animal interaction in the United States. https://www.purdue.edu/vet/chab/ohaire/files/documents/HAI_2018_HAIB_OHaire2.pdf

Pendry, P., & Vandagriff, J. L. (2019). Animal visitation program (AVP) reduces cortisol levels of university students: A randomized controlled trial. *AERA Open.* https://doi.org/10.1177/2332858419852592

Pilley, J. (2013). *Chaser: Unlocking the genius of a dog who knows 1000 words.* New York: Mariner Books.

Piper, L. J., & Uttley, C M. (2019). Adolescents and pets. In L. Kogan & C. Blazina (Eds.), *Clinician's guide to treating companion animal issues* (pp. 47–75). New York: Academic Press. https://doi.org/10.1016/B978-0-12-812962-3.00004-6

Queen, R. (2014). The overwhelming predominance of women in the world of dog rescue: The state of Michigan as a representative case study enhanced by relevant interview data from rescuers elsewhere. In A. Marovitz and K. Crosby (Eds.), *American dog rescue and the discourse of compassion* (pp. 64–79). Ann Arbor, MI: University of Michigan Press.

Rooney, N. J., Guest, C. M., Swanson, L. C. M., & Morant, S. V. (2019). How effective are trained dogs at alerting their owners to changes in blood glycaemic levels? Variations in performance of glycaemia alert dogs. *PLoS One, 14*(1), 1–16. https://journals.plos.org/plosone/article?id=10.1371/journal.pone.0210092

Royal Society for the Prevention of Cruelty to Animals (RSPCA). (2012). *Do puppies have secret powers: Understanding the irrational behavior of the puppy buying publics.* London, UK: Author.

Seksel, K. (2019, July 22). The "pet effect": The benefits of the human-animal connection. https://www.deltasociety.com.au/post/the-pet-effect-the-benefits-of-the-human-animal-connection

Serpell, J. (Ed.). (2017). *The domestic dog: Its evolution, behavior, and interactions with people* (2nd ed.). Cambridge: Cambridge University Press.

Serpell, J. A., & Duffy, D. L. (2014). Dog breeds and their behavior. In A. Horowitz (Ed.), *Domestic dog cognition and behavior: The scientific study of* Canis familiaris (pp. 31–58). New York: Springer.

Staff Writer in Schools. (2016, February 24). 3 engagement strategies for a more interactive campus tour. https://guidebook.com/mobile-guides/interactive-campus-tour

St. Charles Community College. (2019). Walking trails. https://www.stchas.edu/student-life/health-fitness/walking-trails

Téglás, E., Gergely, A., Kupán, K., Miklósi, A., & Topál, J. (2012). Dogs' gaze following is tuned to human communicative signals. *Current Biology, 22*(3), 209–212.

Tyson, T. (2012, October 4). Dogs' dazzling sense of smell. http://www.pbs.org/wgbh/nova/nature/dogs-sense-of-smell.html

Wiggett-Barnard, C., & Steel, H. (2008). The experience of owning a guide dog. *Disability Rehabilitation, 30*(1), 1014–1026. https://doi.org/10.1080/09638280701466517

Wood, L., Martin, K., Christian, H., Nathan, A., Lauritsen, C., . . . McCune, S. (2015). The pet factor-companion animals as a conduit for getting to know people, friendship formation and social support. *PLoS ONE.* https://doi.org/10.1371/journal.pone.0122085

Yordy, M., & Graff, E. (2019). Evaluation of dog walking programs to promote student nurse health. *Building Academic Communities Journal, 3*(1), 17–22. https://doi.org/10.18061/bhac.v3i1.6573

1

TRANSITIONING TO COLLEGE LIFE

Research Evidence of Dogs' Effects on Humans

MARY-ANN SONTAG BOWMAN, SCHOOL OF
SOCIAL WORK, UNIVERSITY OF MONTANA, MISSOULA, MT,
AND MARY RENCK JALONGO, EDITOR, SPRINGER NATURE, INDIANA, PA

INTRODUCTION

A small group of students began to gather in a circle around one of the visiting therapy dogs on campus. "Awww," one student said, "I miss my dogs so much! I haven't seen them for eight weeks now." "What kind of dogs do you have?" another student asks, and the phones come out so that they can share photographs of their family dogs. One young man says that, when he called home, his parents put him on speakerphone. Their dog—a Siberian husky—"went nuts" when she heard his voice. The conversations continue as some students remain while others decide to move to another group and dog. A student remarks, "I think that leaving my dog behind when I went off to college was one of the hardest things" and several other students nod agreement. One says, "I think it's hard because there's no way to explain why you aren't around or when you'll be back." During a quiet moment, a young woman who has the dog's head in her lap says, as her eyes fill with tears, "My dog was adopted from a shelter and has been with me since I was 6 years old. Last year, when my parents called to say that he was not doing well, I felt like dropping everything else and rushing home to see him, but I just couldn't—it was exam week. He passed before I could get there. It just kills me that I wasn't there for him at the end."

Walking dogs at the shelter was part of this international student's service-learning and physical fitness plan. Photo Credit: Mary Renck Jalongo

A student pursuing a graduate degree in counseling who was assisting with a therapy dog event on campus said, "A professional counselor who works in a grief support program for children came to speak with our class about ways that her therapy dog functions as her work partner. Her dog, a golden retriever, was there during the presentation. She shared a heartbreaking story about a young brother and sister. While they were away visiting a grandparent, their home caught fire and they lost both parents, a sibling with special needs, and their two dogs. The funeral home director contacted her because the remaining family members had requested that the therapy dogs be there for the children. The brother and sister arrived before the viewing carrying large stuffed toy dogs that a family friend had bought for them. The toys resembled their deceased dogs and the children had carefully printed each dog's name on its collar tag. When the children were greeted by the therapy dogs, they hugged them and talked about their dogs that died."

An elementary education major who was completing her student teaching described how she made her students' assignments more meaningful and valuable by connecting with the animal welfare group she had volunteered with over the past three years: "We partnered with the local humane society and my sixth graders wrote descriptive paragraphs about each animal using a checklist of its traits, a photo of the dog's kennel card, and brief observational notes provided by staff and volunteers. Then we posted on Petfinder. Students also used free software called PicMonkey to make posters for each animal using the photos supplied. Their posters appeared on the shelter's Facebook and Instagram pages. We checked the dogs' status frequently and the students were excited when each homeless animal got adopted." In her student teaching journal, she reflected on the fact that some of the students who were not normally that enthused about writing were highly motivated by this project.

As these comments from students suggest, dogs are very much a part of the lives of many college students. In addition to their family dogs, students can seek out interaction with dogs during on-campus events, encounter them in conjunction with coursework, and make them part of off-campus internships. This chapter begins by defining the human-animal bond and human-animal interactions. It argues that, although people obviously form bonds with other animals, dogs have maintained their status as best friends of humans. Canines also are the most diverse species; are pets in the majority of US households; dominate as therapy, service, and emotional support animals; and have acquired an impressive repertoire of responses to humans. Next, the chapter examines the rationale for sustaining college students' opportunities to interact with dogs. For residential students, being separated from their family dogs is a frequently overlooked and underestimated aspect of adjusting to college. Given that many traditional-age college students have had a family dog since early childhood, their beloved dogs may be close to (or reach) the end of their lifespans during the students' college careers. We use theories of attachment and loss to highlight the need of many college students to continue to have contact with a network of various types of dogs—their family dogs, therapy dogs visiting campus, service dogs, and dogs housed in shelters (Jalongo, 2015). The third section of chapter 1 examines research on the salutary effects of positive interactions between humans and canines; it also reports on exemplary postsecondary programs that strive to normalize the environment by keeping students in contact with canines. The chapter concludes with evidence-based recommendations to guide the initial implementation of projects/programs as well as to enhance the effectiveness of existing ones. We contend that keeping canines in students' lives is, for many students, an important way of supporting the transition to college life.

DEFINITION OF THE *HUMAN-ANIMAL BOND* AND *HUMAN-ANIMAL INTERACTION* (HAI)

As a visiting therapy dog and handler team made their way to a gathering for newly admitted freshmen held at the university library, three students who were engaged in animated conversation passed by on the opposite side of the street. One young man stopped short and called out, "OMG! Somebody brought a greyhound to campus?!" He dashed across the street, sank to his knees, and cradled the dog's face in his hands. Then he gently circled her long neck with his arms and buried his face in her fur. The dog was accustomed to giving and receiving hugs in this way, and reciprocated by resting her head on his shoulder and nuzzling his face. "My big ex-racer died over the summer. She was 12," the young man said. He rose to his feet and shared a photo. "Thank you for bringing her. Love this breed and can't wait to get another one. That's the first thing I'll do when I have a job and get my own place. You have no idea what this meant to me today." The two friends he had been chatting with joined them and, as they walked away together, he was telling them all about the great dog he had grown up with and answering questions about former track dogs.

This experience illustrates both the human-animal bond and human-animal interaction. The American Veterinary Medical Association (AVMA) (2018) describes the human-animal bond as a "mutually beneficial and dynamic relationship between people and animals that is influenced by behaviors essential to the health and well-being of both. This includes, among other things, emotional, psychological, and physical interactions of people, animals, and the environment" (unpaged). They further assert that the human-animal bond plays a role in individual and community health, has existed for thousands of years, and fulfills both human and animal needs. Human-animal interaction (HAI) is a more general term. It "encompasses any situation where there is interchange between human(s) and animal(s) at an individual or cultural level. These interactions are diverse and idiosyncratic, and may be fleeting or profound" (AMVA, 2018, unpaged).

Interactions between humans and animals are both historical and important; they include many species of animals, both domesticated and wild. The lives—and deaths—of animals have been, and remain, intertwined with humans in significant and diverse ways. Across the ages, connections between animals

A retired racing greyhound and registered therapy dog gets to be big dog on campus. Photo Credit: Megan Higgins

and humans might be best understood in terms of utility. Humans have tended to focus on the purpose(s) the animal serves, many times to the death or detriment of the animal, such as when animals are used as meat or milk, in clothing, for transportation, or as test subjects in research. Another role for animals is that of a work partner, such as dogs that help to hunt or herd. Even the companionship offered by valued domesticated animals is based on utility; few humans, after all, coexist with pets exclusively for the benefit of the animal.

Humans may indeed be grateful for the important roles animals play, but it is often in the way that a human is grateful for a comfortable couch. From a legal standpoint, animals are property, with all rights imbued in being someone's property. To illustrate, the service dogs of military veterans, as well as military working dogs, continue to be categorized as equipment. Nevertheless, some reject this notion of animals as property, understanding them instead as sentient beings with roles as companions and even elevating them to the status of family members. Millennials—the 28–43 age group in 2021—represent a portion of the undergraduate student population and dominate the group of students pursuing graduate degrees.

In 2016, 59% of them did not have children (Fleming, 2016); however, 71% of male and 62% of female millennials did own dogs (Bhattarai, 2016), many consider canines to be family, and refer to themselves "pet parents" rather than owners. Human-animal interactions are, therefore, complicated and nuanced, reflecting individual and community differences that may set up value conflicts and ethical conundrums, and can challenge those responsible for establishing community human-animal interactions policies, procedures, and programs.

Dogs have a long history of coexisting with humans. In fact, humans and dogs have interacted for at least 15,000 years (Savolainen, Zhang, Luo, Lundeberg, & Leitner, 2002). For example, depictions of what we now call sight hounds, traditional hunting dogs with speed and a keen eye such as salukis and Afghan hounds, have been found on pottery dating back to approximately 4000 BC in what is now Iran (Hole & Wyllie, 2007). Images of sight hounds also appear in the hieroglyphics of ancient Egypt (Ikram, 2013). Although the reasons for the initial interactions are unknown, humans have long had close associations with dogs. At some point, humans began manipulating the breeding of dogs, developing breeds for specific purposes. Doberman pinschers, for example, were developed by a German tax collector who wanted a dog that had an impressive appearance and would protect him on his rounds as he insisted on being paid. Dobermans are a mixture of Rottweiler, Weimaraner, and Manchester terrier, among others (Turner, 2017). Hundreds of dog breeds have been created, and each is intended to serve some human purpose. The American Kennel Club recognizes 197 dog breeds, The Kennel Club recognizes 211 dog breeds, and the Fédération Cynologique Internationale currently recognizes 344 breeds (Breeding Business, 2018). Dogs are one of the most diverse species on the planet (Kane, 2016). The range in size, facial features, body types, fur/hair coats, and temperaments is enormous.

Dogs support human endeavors in a variety of ways. To name just a few, they partner with hunters, provide protection, serve alongside military personnel, work with law enforcement, are members of ranching teams, and offer new freedoms and opportunities for individuals who are differently abled. That uniquely canine ability to function in so many different roles that benefit humans creates and supports mutual dependence and the formation of close bonds with their people. Modern life has shifted the function of dogs for so many because much of the traditional "work" of a dog is no longer necessary or desired. However, perhaps benefiting from thousands of years of mutual dependence, dogs are not being eliminated as their traditional utility decreases, but rather are having their roles in the lives of humans transformed. The role of dogs in providing companionship as well as emotional and social support to humans has expanded considerably in recent years, so much so that they have been described as "the social dog" (Kaminski & Marshall-Pescini, 2014). In the great majority of instances, what people describe as "the ideal dog" in large-scale surveys conducted in different countries is a dog that is obedient, friendly/affectionate, healthy/long-lived, and gentle with children (Diverio, Boccini, Menchetti, & Bennett, 2016; King, Marston, & Bennett, 2009).

Dogs are the most popular companion animal in the United States, with 38% of American households including at least one dog (American Veterinary

Medical Association, 2018). In addition to their value as companions, an interesting function of today's canines is contributing to local and national economies. The US pet industry is worth $75 billion (American Pet Products Association, 2019). Dogs generate jobs as well as both small and large businesses. Although perhaps fewer dogs are working in their more traditional capacities, they continue to partner with humans in a multiplicity of ways, demonstrating a uniquely canine adaptability to the needs and wants of humans.

A review of popular literature promotes dog ownership as a route to better human health. For example, an online article titled *The 10 Health Benefits of Dogs (and One Health Risk)* (Sturt, n.d.) identifies a variety of health benefits associated with dog ownership, from lower blood pressure to decreased rates of allergies in grandchildren. But the truth may be more nuanced. While it is true that dog ownership appears to have favorable health outcomes, it is not clear that those benefits are exclusively the result of owning a dog (Utz, 2014). For example, a frequently cited longitudinal study followed patients recovering from a myocardial infarction (MI) and found that, one year later, dog owners had a higher survival rate than those without dogs (Friedmann, Katcher, Lynch, & Thomas, 1980). However, it also has been argued that other variables, such as depression, lack of social support, and anxiety, may have been present at higher levels in the group without dogs. In fact, some of the original researchers on the team have pursued this line of inquiry further (Friedmann, Thomas, & Son, 2011). Interestingly, they found that, using a regression model that included depression, lack of pet ownership, and the interaction between the two, lack of pet ownership continued to be the only significant independent predictor of mortality (Friedmann et al., 2011). Still, it could be argued that those capable of keeping a pet were in some ways stronger and healthier than the comparison group or perhaps that these people had more supportive spouses/companions living with them that made it possible to care for a dog (Friedmann et al., 2011). This line of inquiry points out how difficult it is to conduct rigorous research that assesses the impact of the human-canine bond. In many ways, it is like attempting to conduct research on other abstract ideas, such as love or empathy. It taxes the creativity of even the most skilled and experienced researcher. Whether dogs are the causal factor in better health outcomes or healthier people with better human support networks are more likely to keep dogs, canines figure prominently in the lives of many individuals and families.

THEORIES OF ATTACHMENT AND LOSS

Dogs are physically present and available to humans. They tend to be acutely responsive, invite interaction, and express emotional connections. Quite simply, dogs make many humans feel good, and those positive feelings can generate a sense of connection, comfort, and safety critical for the successful formation of attachment. Bowlby (1958) defines an attachment bond as a close, emotional relationship between two individuals. The question then becomes whether this can apply to the human-canine bond. Ainsworth and Bell's (1970) classic studies of the bond between mothers and their young children identified attachment behaviors, including resisting separation, seeking proximity, and relying on the attachment figure as a "safe haven" or "secure base" (for a history, see Rosmalen, van der Veer, & van der Horst, 2015). Several studies have applied these criteria to observational research on the human-canine bond (Gácsi, Maros, Sernkvist, Faragó, & Miklósi, 2013; Horn, Huber, & Range, 2013; Palmer & Custance, 2008; Prato-Previde, Custance, Spiezio, & Sabatini, 2003; Topál, Miklósi, Csányi, & Dóka, 1998). Likewise, reviews of the literature have argued that the child-canine bond, for example, is a particular category of attachment behavior (Jalongo, 2015; Zilcha-Mano, Mikulincer, & Shaver, 2011).

Kurdek (2008) developed an instrument designed to assess four features of attachment: safe haven, secure base, proximity maintenance, and separation distress (p. 441). Reporting on a study of over 900 college students who completed his measure of attachment features, Kurdek (2008) found that "pet dogs are rated favorably on each feature of attachment but are especially likely to exhibit the attachment features of secure base and proximity maintenance" (p. 263). In a subsequent study of nearly 1,000 older adults, Kurdek (2009) concluded that some adults do establish attachment bonds with dogs; Beck and Madresh (2008) concurred.

Kobak (2009) disagreed. In a response to Kurdek (2009), Kobak (2009) noted the lack of agreement on what constitutes attachment in adults and suggested that allowing dogs to be considered attachment figures "requires establishing and validating criteria for what constitutes an attachment bond and when a relationship partner can be called an attachment figure" (p. 447). Apparently, since attachment theorists haven't yet sorted out how to define and assess attachment bonds much beyond infancy and very young childhood, Kobak (2009) seems to suggest it might be premature to add yet another potential adult attachment figure to the conversation. Instead, he queries whether the relationship or bond between human and dog might be better understood as a form of affectional bond. Of course, one could argue the lack of clear definition or rigorous methodology to assess adult attachment figures does not mean they are not occurring, including with dogs.

Kobak, however, did not have the last word on this conundrum. Rockett and Carr (2014) conducted an extensive literature review designed, in part, to explore animals as attachment figures. Their review led them to assert that "there are theoretical arguments and empirical evidence in support of the notion that attachment theory offers a valuable framework within which to structure the examination of human-animal relationship studies" (p. 427). Sometimes researchers spend quite a bit of time studying what humans are already doing—in this case, enjoying their companionship with dogs. To illustrate, a survey of 241 college students with pets asked them to evaluate their reasons for having a pet (Staats, Wallace, & Anderson, 2008). Among the dog owners, 39.9% of students said that having a dog lessened their feelings of loneliness. It would be difficult to argue that dogs could fulfill this function without some form of attachment present. In an interview about the study, Staats said:

> We might not think of college students as being lonely, but a lot of freshman and sophomores are in an early transition from living at home to living in dorms or off-campus. College is a stressful environment for them and sometimes they can feel isolated or overwhelmed with the change.... Many students said that their pets fulfill a significant role that is missing in their lives. The pets are not a substitute for human social interaction and support, but they do provide important interaction for these kids who might otherwise feel isolated from their current environment. (Ohio State University, 2008, unpaged)

There is another dimension of the human-animal bond that bears further examination. The formation of attachment with something defined under the law as property creates interesting challenges. Attachment theory helps us understand that attachment figures are important to individual well-being and that loss of an attachment figure is problematic (Sontag-Bowman, 2018). Most of us would understand, therefore, the value of supporting and maintaining attachment relationships when possible and especially during periods of emotional stress. And yet, we routinely send our young adults away to college, separating them from multiple attachment figures and/or affectional bond relationships.

The traditional college student typically is engaging in developmentally appropriate separation from primary adult caregivers, but that doesn't mean those relationship disruptions are easy. Further, the loss of friends and other human relationships is a significant burden on young adults who transition to college, and homesickness is a retention risk factor (Sun, Serra Hagedorn, & Zhang, 2016). Student support services focus on building supportive communities around students, providing potential replacements for lost human relationships. These are not, however, comparable replacement for the loss of a longtime canine companion.

The benefits derived from attachment to a dog are uniquely canine—they are not easily met in new human relationships. And while one dog is not another, just as humans are not interchangeable, there may well be benefit in inviting continuing connections with dogs in the same way universities and colleges offer opportunities for students to develop new human attachments.

RESEARCH AND INSTITUTIONAL INITIATIVES

There are a variety of ways that dogs can be involved in campus life—or not. Baylor University (n.d.) introduces their Pets on Campus policy with the statement: "Pets on campus can pose a significant risk to Baylor and its community" (unpaged). The policy goes on to exclude specific breeds of dogs, putting them in the same "prohibited animals" category as poisonous reptiles and constricting snakes. Interestingly, the Pets on Campus policy can be found on the same webpage as their statement on the institution's commitment to diversity and inclusion. Other campuses have a more welcoming tone in their pet policies, including some campuses that allow pets from home to visit college students.

Emotional support animals (see chapter 4) are, by law, allowed in college housing. Service dogs have broad access to campuses under the Americans with Disabilities Act. Some colleges and universities have service-learning courses or programs that incorporate volunteer activities with dogs, either on-site or at local agencies (see chapter 6). But the most significant way that dogs seem to be integrating college campuses is through programs designed to reduce student distress by giving students opportunities to interact with registered and insured therapy dog handler teams (see chapter 5).

Results from the American College Health Association (2018) survey describes a cohort of distressed college students. One-third of respondents reported that stress has impacted their academic performance, and 65% reported overwhelming anxiety in the previous 12 months. Twenty-two percent of the respondents had been treated for—or diagnosed with—anxiety in the previous 12 months. While it is difficult to know which of the many challenges associated with life as a college student are generating the distress described by students, it is important to understand anxiety as a frequent symptom of grief, which is normal and expected following any significant loss or change, including loss of a beloved dog (Planchon, Templer, Stokes, & Keller, 2002).

Further, a reduced capacity to handle stress is also an expected and normal response to loss and change. When one begins to add up the changes and associated losses experienced by first-year college students, in particular, the level of distress among freshmen has context and is understandable.

Colleges and universities use a variety of strategies, activities, and programs to ease the transition for new students and to support existing students. None of these is a "magic bullet," ensuring complete happiness and 100% retention, but rather each works in concert with others to reach diverse student bodies with varying social and emotional needs. The key to implementing effective strategies is truly understanding and appreciating the issues facing students.

One student shared on *Reddit*, "the worst part of being at college is not being around my dogs." Given the high number of students who can be expected to have left dogs behind when they come to college campuses, addressing the needs of students such of this one should be a priority. One way that this is being done at campuses in North America is through campus-based dog programs. These programs are varied and diverse, but all offer students a chance to interact with dogs and the results appear to be beneficial for those who elect to participate.

Castellano (2015) described the growth of canine-assisted interventions on campus as having gone from essentially nonexistent in 2005 to the norm by 2015 (para. 2). Dogs on Campus, a therapy dog program at Kent State University started in 2005, describes itself as the first in the country (n.d., para 2). While it is difficult to accurately establish the number of programs, multiple sources identify the number of animal-related campus programs at over 900 (see, for example, Herzog, 2017). Concurrent with the increases in these types of programs are expanded efforts to establish the value and efficacy of campus-based animal-assisted activities (AAAs) and animal-assisted therapy (AAT) programs. These research endeavors have primarily focused on aspects of student distress and, almost without exception, these efforts involve dogs.

Stewart, Dispenza, Parker, Chang, and Cunnien (2014) reported the results of an exploratory study that brought handler/dog teams to visit students at a college residential hall. The impact on the 55 participants was assessed with pre- and posttest measures of loneliness and anxiety. Students' self-report data indicated positive changes in the measures of loneliness and anxiety immediately following the AAT intervention, leading the authors to conclude, "the results of this study reveal that AAT outreach interventions may be an efficient and effective way for university and college counseling centers to meet the growing demands of their student populations in a way that students view as relevant" (p. 341). Further, the authors noted an additional benefit of the AAT outreach was involving students who may not have used the services of the institution's counseling center previously.

Daltry and Mehr (2015) also saw the value of AAT in both improving student welfare and expanding the reach of a campus counseling center. A drop-in program was developed using two certified therapy dog teams visiting the student union building approximately 15 times per academic year. The authors described the success of this program as follows: "Over time, dog therapy has become the counseling center's most popular and well-liked outreach activity. Students schedule and plan around the dates the dogs will be on campus, often coming early to the student union center to wait for their arrival, and not uncommonly shouting the dog's name when one enters the building. As many as 15 to 20 students will sit in a large circle, talking and socializing with one another as the dog makes his or her rounds with each one" (p. 75). Informal written feedback obtained from 54 students indicated that the program provided stress relief for students and created enhanced perceptions about—and awareness of—the campus counseling center.

Crossman, Kazdin, and Knudson (2015) studied the impact of a single, brief session with a dog on the self-reported distress of medical students and residents. Participants (n=67) were assigned to one of three study conditions: no-treatment control, a group in which participants looked at photos of the dog involved in the study, and a third group in which students interacted individually with the dog/handler team for 7–10 minutes. Using pre- and posttest measures to assess impact, the authors concluded "that interaction with a dog can reduce the subjective experience of distress, and that this effect is not limited to the effects of merely taking a break or engaging some other novel and distracting activity" (p. 656). Drop-in sessions seem to be the most common use of dogs on campuses, but they are not the only way that dog-assisted campus interventions

A faculty member posted this sign on the door during office hours. If a student would prefer not to have the dog there, they meet in another location. Photo Credit: Mary-Ann Bowman

with college students have been developed and studied. Binfet and Passmore (2016), for example, explored the impact of an eight-week AAT intervention on first-year college students, and specifically, how an AAT intervention impacted homesickness, life satisfaction, and connection to the campus community. All 44 participants had reported being homesick. They were assigned to either an eight-week AAT group or a wait-listed control group. The AAT intervention involved therapy dogs with handlers who had been trained to interact with college students on campus. At the end of the eight weeks, participants in the AAT experimental group reported reduced homesickness as well as increased life satisfaction and connection to campus. Over the same period, the control group (those who had been wait-listed) reported increased homesickness; furthermore, their self-reports of life satisfaction and connection to campus did not change.

Many of the studies that describe the impact of canine-assisted interventions use psychological measures that students complete before and after interactions with the dog(s) (more on this is in chapter 9). However, some researchers have added physiological measures in addition to the psychological measures of distress. Fiocco and Hunse (2017), for example, tracked electrodermal activity of participants and found the experimental group (dog-assisted) experienced less physiological reaction to a stressful event than did the control group (no dog). Muckle and Lasikiewicz (2017) used blood pressure as a stress measure in a study exploring the impact of an AAA on student stress at a Singapore university. The authors reported improvement in both psychological and physiologic measures of stress after a one-hour AAA session involving trained therapy dogs. Delgado, Toukonen, and Wheeler (2018) assessed both psychological and physiologic (salivary cortisol, blood pressure, heart rate) measures of stress in a group of 48 nursing students who interacted with a friendly dog for 15 minutes. The authors report that "improvement in mood and reductions in perceptions of stress were notably significant, and physiologic measures also showed significant positive changes" (p. 152). Jarolmen and Patel (2018) used blood pressure readings to assess interactions with dogs on student stress before and after exams; these authors also reported positive physiologic responses to AAA involving dogs.

It is sometimes suggested that robotic dogs might be a way to address the objections (i.e., phobias, allergies) and inconvenience of live dogs in the workplace. Those who are enthusiastic about dogs respond that it is "just not the same," pointing to the absence of a bond. However, there are numerous variables to consider. The first drawback of robotic dogs is the expense; if they are more sophisticated than a child's toy, the cost is prohibitive. An AIBO dog, for example, costs about $9,000 US dollars and, even if a robotic dog were donated to the university, arranging for and affording repairs might pose challenge. Given that visiting therapy dog teams are all volunteer, robotic dogs do not compare favorably from an investment standpoint. Furthermore, many people have a decided preference for real dogs over robotic dogs, despite increasingly sophisticated technology (Konok, Korcsok, Miklosi, & Gacsi, 2018). It is very telling that, when manufacturers make improvements to robotic dogs, the direction of the advances in technology consist of coming closer to attributes and behaviors of real dogs. Robotic dogs used with dementia patients, for example, had plush "fur," appeared to breathe, blinked their eyes, and oriented their heads toward sounds. These patient-robot interactions appeared to have some salutary effects (Sicurella & Fitzsimmons, 2016); however, the cognitive functioning of this group differs dramatically from that of college students. Limited repertoires of interactivity with humans can cause robotic dogs to fall short in other ways as well. Advanced robotic guide dogs may assist the blind in navigating their physical world, yet fail to provide the emotional and social support that 375 North

American guide dog owners attributed to their service dogs (Stern, 2017). Yet another reservation about robots is the capacity of an inanimate object to maintain attention after the initial novelty effect wanes. In one Danish study of the elderly in nursing homes, live dogs elevated mood, elicited more conversation, and sustained interaction over a longer period than robotic animals or stuffed toys (Thodberg et al., 2016). Perhaps even more important—given the increase in mental health issues of today's college students—is that other documented health benefits—such as the positive influence of live dogs on heart functioning—have not been associated with human/robotic dog interactions (Silva, Lima, Santos-Magalhaes, Fafiaes, & de Sousa, 2019).

RECOMMENDATIONS FOR PRACTICE

Although it might be tempting to attribute young adult college students' mental health issues to being privileged or coddled, and therefore to dismiss those issues, their lives have been made more complex by technology. Contemporary college students have to multitask in unprecedented ways and be exceptionally nimble as thinkers to navigate their rapidly changing worlds. Theirs is a "high-tech, low-touch" life that immerses them in social media, yet frequently results in interpersonal isolation. The new communication environment is instantaneous. Social media publicizes mistakes and "epic fails" and, at the same time, sets unrealistic expectations for stunning achievements with world-changing implications. A recent article in *The Guardian* (Shackle, 2019) reported that, at the same time that the United Kingdom set a national goal of at least 50% of students pursuing college degrees, there has been an upsurge in student anxiety, mental breakdowns, depression, dropping out, and suicides. The experts interviewed for the article attribute this to a variety of influences. Higher education has become increasingly high stakes. Students often find themselves worrying about failure, struggling financially, accumulating debt through loans, dealing with housing issues, navigating relationships, juggling studies with paid work, wondering about employment prospects, and taking on extra obligations to make themselves stand out from the rest. All of these concerns reported in 2019 surely have been exacerbated by the COVID-19 world health pandemic in 2020. Counseling and mental health services have not kept pace with the demand and, even when support is available, many students are reluctant to disclose a condition they have, preferring instead to get a "fresh start" rather than deal with prejudices. During recent years in Britain, many universities—including Cambridge, Brunel, London Metropolitan, and Warwick—have organized therapy pet programs. The great majority of these interventions involve bringing therapy dogs to campus during exam week. Researchers have continued to document the positive impacts of canine-assisted programs on the well-being of college students, but also are beginning to examine these programs with additional sophistication. For example, Ward-Griffin et al. (2017) introduced the question of whether the positive impact of a single, drop-in visit with a therapy dog and handler on college students was sustained over time (ten hours). Utilizing a prepost design with both an experimental and a control group, the authors found that college students who experienced a single visit with the therapy dog reported "reductions in stress and increases in happiness and energy levels immediately after the therapy dog sessions" (p. 471). These positive changes in student well-being were primarily short-term and not strongly sustained over time, according to the authors, leading them to suggest "it may be especially useful for such [therapy dog] sessions to take place during particularly stressful periods of the school year, such as exam periods, or even for therapy dogs to be present during stressors, such as while students complete assignments" (p. 472).

Fiocco and Hunse (2017) examined whether an interaction with a therapy dog can serve as a buffer against an immediate future stressor. College students were randomly placed into two groups and then completed two instruments to assess stress level and affect. The control group rested for ten minutes after completing the instruments while the treatment group interacted with a therapy dog for ten minutes. Both groups then completed a specific stressful activity (Paced Auditory Serial Addition Task). The authors report that the treatment group (ten minutes with a dog) experienced significantly less physiological reaction to the stressful event than did the control group (no dog), but they did not find a difference between the groups in terms of self-reported stress level and affect. This work suggests that therapy dogs might be useful as a form of stress "inoculation" in undergraduate students immediately prior to—not simply during—a stressful event.

McDonald, McDonald, and Roberts (2017) also explored the impact of dog exposure on college students immediately prior to a stressful event (an exam). However, this study used a friendly, well-mannered pet dog who was not certified or trained as a therapy dog. Forty-eight students were divided into two groups prior to taking an exam. The control group spent 15 minutes in one room engaging in whatever quiet activity they wanted, and the experimental group spent the 15 minutes engaging with the pet dog. Students in both groups had their blood pressure checked as a measure of stress response prior to their random assignment in a group, and at the end of the 15-minute period. Blood pressure differences were noted between the groups. The control group (no dog) had an increase in blood pressure while the dog-exposed group had a decrease in blood pressure at the end of the 15 minutes. McDonald et al. (2017) also demonstrated the value of dog exposure as a potential buffer against a future stressful event.

The question of handler impact on therapy dog sessions with college students was addressed by Grajfoner, Harte, Potter, McGuigan, and Williams (2017). The researchers looked at the impact of a brief (20-minute) dog visit on college students' well-being, mood, and level of anxiety. In their study, 132 college students were randomly assigned to one of three groups: standard visit with therapy dogs in which handlers interacted with the students, visit with therapy dog but minimal handler interaction, or visit with the handlers but no dogs. Students reported decreased anxiety and positive changes in mood and well-being immediately following their visits with the dogs. Further, the authors concluded that based on their findings, "it is the interaction with the therapy dog that affects these changes, with the handler providing a presence either neutral, or somewhat negative" (p. 7). In other words, this study suggests that it is the dogs—not the human contact—that contributes to positive changes from college students' interactions with trained therapy dog teams.

The question of "dose" (time needed for successful intervention) is one that is now receiving some attention. Binfet, Passmore, Cebry, Struik, and McKay (2018) found that students averaged 35 minutes when they were able to control the length of time spent in a canine-assisted intervention session. However, others have noted positive changes occur after shorter times (Crossman et al., 2015; Fiocco & Hunse, 2017; McDonald et al., 2017). Given the disparate measures of impact, confounding variables, and different programmatic goals, the question of how much time is optimal in campus canine-assisted remains unanswered.

The type and training of dogs involved in programs is another area of variability with implications for students, programs, campuses, and the dogs. Daltry and Mehr (2015) shared their belief that programs should "use certified therapy dogs rather than regular pets, given the training and certification therapy dogs have" (p. 77), and yet McDonald et al. (2017) and others have had similar success with a friendly pet dog. The robust program at University of British Columbia (Building Academic Retention through K9s or BARK), prepares dogs for the program and conducts holistic evaluation of teams. The recent book by Binfet and Kjellstrand Hartwig (2019) titled *Canine-Assisted Interventions: A Comprehensive Guide to Credentialing Therapy Dog Teams* should help to standardize training and expectations of dog-handler teams involved in campus-based dog programs. Even for handler/dog teams that may be registered and insured through a different therapy dog organization, the insights from this research are valuable.

What does seem clearly established is that campus canine-assisted programs are perceived by students to be beneficial. In the event there was any lingering doubt, Binfet et al. (2018) addressed this yet again with a large population of university students (n = 1,960), reporting that "spending time with therapy canines

This Bernese mountain dog pulled a cart on Arbor Day at the University of Montana, and helped to attract students and other community members to the tree planting event. Photo Credit: Kenneth Stolz

significantly reduces students' self-reports of stress" (p. 200). Further, students' perceived reduction in stress following interactions with dogs is supported by studies that have measured their improved physiological stress responses after a session with a dog. We may not completely understand the variables that are in operation here, or the optimal ways to deliver canine-assisted services, but dogs on campus appear beneficial to students, according to students. What is less well understood is the impact of dogs on other members of the campus community.

> I am a dog-loving professor at a university. I have multiple dogs that I train and show in a variety of dog sports. I have used my own certified therapy dogs in my work with children and adults. I have been involved as a guide dog puppy raiser. One of my dogs regularly comes to work with me. These realities give me a certain informed perspective about dogs on campus.
>
> Service dog vests are readily available online. The law—rightly—prohibits asking for verification of the authenticity of the service dog designation. I suspect these things help explain how an ill-mannered Saint Bernard on a prong collar got in a canine kerfuffle with a small terrier in one of my classes—both dogs were wearing service dog vests. Maybe they were just having a rough (ruff?) day?
>
> In another class, a student showed up with a medium-sized dog. After the class was over, I met with her to discuss the presence of the dog. She explained that he was her emotional support animal (ESA), that the Office for Disability Services told her that she could bring the dog to class if instructors agreed, and that all of her other instructors were allowing the dog in the classroom. Peer pressure! I called the Office for Disability Services. They were adamant that it is not their policy to permit ESAs in the classroom, and that they had not told the student she should ask her instructors about this. I met with the student again and let her know that she could not bring the dog to class unless he was a service animal, which she acknowledged he was not. Yes—the dog-loving professor was the one who denied access to a dog in the classroom.
>
> My experiences with dogs on campus and in the classroom have caused me to become both cautious and a bit cynical. It is hard for me to believe that the lunging, barking dogs with prong collars and vests I too often see on campus are trained service dogs.
>
> And I worry about all this—for those dogs who are clearly not prepared for life on a busy campus, for the real working service dogs and their humans who do not deserve to be considered with skepticism, for students and other

dogs who are at risk of an unfortunate encounter with an unmanaged dog, and for students who are compromising their personal integrity and honesty by passing their dogs off as something they are not.

The impact of dogs on a campus community is an important and additional area of consideration. Students are critical members of a campus community, and they appear to benefit from dog programs on campus. But a campus is a community that both includes students and exists around students. Unfortunately, there has been limited effort to understand how campus employees—faculty, staff, and administrators—experience campus programs involving dogs.

Foreman, Allison, Poland, Meade, and Wirth (2019) attempted to address this gap in the professional literature. The researchers designed and implemented a study to explore the perceptions of employees from three areas impacted by campus dog activities at one university. Specifically, the researchers were interested in staff and faculty perceptions of both benefits and risks of existing dog visitations in their work environments at one university. Data were collected via an online survey. Respondents (n=138) did not perceive dog-related activities in their workspace as especially risky, and in fact, barking was rated as the highest risk of dogs in the workplace. There was broad support for the dog activities, with 87% of the respondents agreeing "that if the proper protocols are in place, visitation dogs should be permitted in the workplace" (p. 46). However, support for the visitation dogs was not unanimous and Foreman et al. (2019) make the excellent point that "it is important to take into consideration the diversity of opinions of employees and ensure that there is a mechanism for them to express support or displeasure for the presence of dogs or other visitation animals in the workplace" (p. 48).

The physical presence of dogs on campus and/or programs that connect students to dogs in the community are not the only ways that members of a campus community can support students through canines. Office photos of dogs or other pets are signals of kindred spirits to students who are missing their family dogs, and they routinely generate stories and photo sharing that bring back for that student the canine who is so missed, if only for a short time. Classroom discussions and lectures that are about family, relationships, and similar topics can include attention to companion animals, thereby normalizing the feelings and experiences of students. There are many ways members of a campus community can acknowledge and respect the relationship between humans and dogs, and in doing so, students are supported.

CONCLUSION

There are likely few student support programs that would win the unanimous endorsement of every member of a campus community. The reality is that, just as not everyone thinks that football is an appropriate college activity, not all people agree that dogs should be permitted on campus. The goal of student support programs should not be to find the exact one thing that will work for all students, because that simply does not exist. Rather, the goal of successful student support services should be about understanding student needs and implementing a variety of interventions that promote student well-being and success; for a sizeable subgroup of college students, this points to activities involving dogs.

A significant number of college students experience a unique form of loss when they leave their dogs behind to attend college. While campuses work hard to help students both to maintain their connections to humans at home and develop new relationships, similar attention is not always given to the nonhuman relationships that have been left behind; this is both a mistake and an opportunity. Dogs on campus can make a difference not only for an individual student in that moment, but also for groups as they facilitate social interactions and promote future help-seeking behavior.

An undergraduate kept in contact with animals by volunteering at a no-kill shelter and later adopted a homeless animal. Photo Credit: Mary Renck Jalongo

Dogs are generous; they do not seem to begrudge humans for the ever-evolving ways we involve them in our lives. Some dogs are happy to lean into a stranger, and in doing so, a student is invited to see stress and anxiety for what it is: temporary. Dogs permit distressed students to experience that things can feel differently. Done well, dogs on campus can provide a needed uplift, foster and support connections to a campus community, and even facilitate a journey to needed counseling services. Perhaps that is their greatest gift—hope. In that way, special dogs can literally become lifesavers for some students.

REFERENCES

Ainsworth, M. D., & Bell, S. M. (1970). Attachment, exploration, and separation: Illustrated by the behavior of one-year-olds in a strange situation. *Child Development, 41(1)*, 49–67. https://doi.org/10.2307/1127388

American College Health Association. (2018). *American College Health Association-National College Health Assessment II: Reference group executive summary spring 2018.* Silver Spring, MD: Author.

American Pet Products Association. (2019). Pet industry market size & ownership statistics. https://www.americanpetproducts.org/press_industrytrends.asp

American Veterinary Medical Association. (2018). AVMA releases latest stats on pet ownership and veterinary care. https://www.avma.org/News/PressRoom/Pages/AVMA-releases-latest-stats-on-pet-ownership-and-veterinary-care.aspx

American Veterinary Medical Association. (2018). The human animal bond. https://www.avma.org/KB/Policies/Pages/The-Human-Animal-Bond.aspx

Baylor University. (n.d.). Pets on campus. https://www.baylor.edu/student_policies/index.php?id=87826

Beck, L., & Madresh, E. A. (2008). Romantic partners and four-legged friends: An extension of attachment theory to relationships with pets. *Anthrozoös, 21*(1), 43–56.

Bhattarai, A. (2016, September 13). Millennials are picking pets over people. *The Washington Post.* https://www.washingtonpost.com/news/business/wp/2016/09/13/millennials-are-picking-pets-over- people

Binfet, J., & Kjellstrand Hartwig, E. (2019). *Canine-assisted interventions: A comprehensive guide to credentialing therapy dog teams.* New York: Routledge.

Binfet, J., & Passmore, H. A. (2016). Hounds and homesickness: The effects of an animal-assisted therapeutic intervention for first-year university students. *Anthrozoös, 29*(3), 441–454.

Binfet, J., Passmore, H. A., Cebry, A., Struik, K., & McKay, C. (2018). Reducing university students' stress through a drop-in canine-therapy program. *Journal of Mental Health, 27*(3), 197–204.

Bowlby, J. (1958). The nature of the child's tie to his mother. *International Journal of Psychology, 39*(5), 350–373.

Breeding Business. (2018, June 18). How many dog breeds are there? https://breedingbusiness.com/how-many-dog-breeds-are-there

Castellano, J. (2015). Pet therapy is a nearly cost-free anxiety reducer on college campuses. https://www.forbes.com/sites/jillcastellano/2015/07/06/pet-therapy-is-a-nearly-cost-free-anxiety-reducer-on-college-campuses

Crossman, M. K., Kazdin, A., & Knudson, K. (2015). Brief unstructured interaction with a dog reduces distress. *Anthrozoös, 28*(4), 649–659.

Daltry, R. M., & Mehr, K. E. (2015). Therapy dogs on campus: Recommendations for counseling center outreach. *Journal of College Student Psychotherapy, 29*(1), 72–78.

Delgado, C., Toukonen, M., & Wheeler, C. (2018). Effect of canine play interventions as a stress reduction strategy in college students. *Nurse Educator, 43*(3), 149–153.

Diverio, S., Boccini, B., Menchetti, L., & Bennett, P. C. (2016). The Italian perception of the "ideal companion dog." *Journal of Veterinary Behavior, 12,* 27–35. https://doi.org/10.1016/j.jveb.2018.07.003

Dogs on Campus. (n.d.). About dogs on campus. https://dogsoncampus.org/about

Fiocco, A. J., & Hunse, A. M. (2017). The buffer effect of therapy dog exposure on stress reactivity in undergraduate students. *Journal of Environmental Research and Public Health, 14*(7), 707. https://doi.org/10.3390/ijerph14070707

Fleming, J. (2016, May 19). Gallup analysis: Millennials, marriage and family. *Social and Policy Issues.* https://news.gallup.com/poll/191462/gallup-analysis-millennials-marriage-family.aspx

Foreman, A., Allison, P., Poland, M., Meade, B. J., & Wirth, O. (2019). Employee attitudes about the impact of visitation dogs on a college campus. *Anthrozoös, 32*(1), 35–50.

Friedmann, E., Katcher, A. H., Lynch, J. J., & Thomas, S. A. (1980). Animal companions and one-year survival of patients after discharge from a coronary care unit. *Public Health Reports, 95*(4), 307–312.

Friedmann, E., Thomas, S. A., & Son, H. (2011). Pets, depression and long-term survival in community living patients following a myocardial infarction. *Anthrozoös, 24*(3), 273–285. https://doi.org/10.2752/175303711X13045914865426B8

Gácsi, M., Maros, K., Sernkvist, S., Faragó, T., & Miklósi, A. (2013). Human analogue safe haven effect of the owner: Behavioural and heart rate response to stressful social stimuli in dogs. *PLoS One, 8*(3), e58475.

Grajfoner, D., Harte, E., Potter, L., McGuigan, N., & Williams, J. (2017). The effect of dog-assisted intervention on student well-being, mood, and anxiety. *International Journal of Environmental Research and Public Health, 14*(5), 483–491. https://doi.org/10.3390/ijerph14050483

Herzog, H. (2017). Therapy dogs for homesick college students? https://www.psychologytoday.com/us/blog/animals-and-us/201708/therapy-dogs-homesick-college-students

Hole, F., & Wyllie, C. (2007). The oldest depictions of canines and a possible early breed of dog in Iran. *Paléorient, 33*(1), 175–185.

Horn, L., Huber, L., & Range, F. (2013). The importance of the secure base effect for domestic dogs—evidence from a manipulative problem-solving task. *PLoS One, 8*(5), e65296.

Ikram, S. (2013). Man's best friend for eternity: Dog and human burials in ancient Egypt. *Anthropozoologica, 48*(2), 299–307.

Jalongo, M. R. (2015). An attachment perspective on the child-dog bond: Interdisciplinary and international research findings. *Early Childhood Education Journal, 43*(5), 395–405.

Jarolmen, J., & Patel, G. (2018). The effects of animal-assisted activities on college students before and after a final exam. *Journal of Creativity in Mental Health, 13*(3), 264–274.

Kaminski, J., & Marshall-Pescini, S. (2014). *The social dog: Behavior and cognition.* Burlington, VT: Elsevier Science

Kane, S. (2016, February 24). Dogs are the most bizarre species on Earth, and these photos prove it. https://www.businessinsider.com/dog-breed-diversity-same-species-2016-2

King, T., Marston, L. C., & Bennett, P. C. (2009). Describing the ideal Australian companion dog. *Applied Animal Behaviour Science, 120*(1–2), 84–93.

Kobak, R. (2009). Defining and measuring attachment bonds: Comment on Kurdek (2009). *Journal of Family Psychology, 23*(4), 447–449.

Konok, V., Korcsok, B., Miklosi, A., & Gacsi, M. (2018). Should we love robots? The most liked qualities of companion dogs and how they can be implemented in social robots. *Computers in Human Behavior, 80,* 132–142. https://www.sciencedirect.com/science/article/pii/S0747563217306234

Kurdek, L. (2008). Pet dogs as attachment figures. *Journal of Social and Personal Relationships, 25*(2), 247–266.

Kurdek, L. (2009). Young adults' attachment to pet dogs: Findings from open-ended methods. *Anthrozoös, 22*(4), 359–369.

McDonald, S., McDonald, E., & Roberts, A. (2017). Effects of novel dog exposure on college students' stress prior to examination. *North American Journal of Psychology, 19*(2), 477–484.

Muckle, J., & Lasikiewicz, N. (2017). An exploration of the benefits of animal-assisted activities in undergraduate students in Singapore. *Asian Journal of Social Psychology, 20*(2), 75–84.

Ohio State University. (2008, December 28). College students find comfort in their pets during hard times. *ScienceDaily.* www.sciencedaily.com/releases/2008/12/081223091318.htm

Palmer, R., & Custance, D. (2008). A counterbalanced version of Ainsworth's Strange Situation Procedure reveals secure-base effects in dog-human relationships. *Applied Animal Behavior Science, 109*(2–4), 306–319.

Planchon, L. A., Templer, D. I., Stokes, S., & Keller, J. (2002). Death of a companion cat or dog and human bereavement: Psychosocial variables. *Society & Animals, 10*(1), 93–105.

Prato-Previde, E., Custance, D. M., Spiezio, C., & Sabatini, F. (2003). Is the dog-human relationship an attachment bond? An observational study using Ainsworth's strange situation. *Behaviour, 140*(2), 225–254. 10.1163/156853903321671514

Rockett, B., & Carr, S. (2014). Animals and attachment theory. *Society & Animals, 22*(4), 415–433.

Rosmalen, L., van der Veer, R., & van der Horst, F. (2015). Ainsworth's Strange Situation Procedure: The origin of an instrument. *Journal of the History of the Behavioral Sciences, 51*(3), 261–284. https://doi.org/10.1002/jhbs.21729

Savolainen, P., Zhang, Y., Luo, J., Lundeberg, J., & Leitner, T. (2002). Genetic evidence for an East Asian origin of domestic dogs. *Science 298*(5598), 1610–1613.

Shackle, S. (2019, September 27). "The way universities are run is making us ill": Inside the student mental health crisis. *The Guardian.* https://www.theguardian.com/society/2019/sep/27/anxiety-mental-breakdowns-depression-uk-students?utm_source=pocket-newtab

Sicurella, T., & Fitzsimmons, V. (2016). Robotic pet therapy in long-term care. *Nursing 46*(6), 55–57. https://doi.org/10.1097/01.NURSE.0000482265.32133.f6

Silva, K., Lima, M., Santos-Magalhaes, A., Fafiaes, C., & de Sousa, L. (2019). Living and robotic dogs as elicitors of social communication behavior and regulated emotional responding in individuals with autism and severe language delay: A preliminary comparative study. *Anthrozoös, 32*(1), 23–33. https://doi.org/10.1080/08927936.2019.1550278

Sontag-Bowman, M. (2018). Final gifts: Lessons children can learn from dogs about end-of-life, loss and grief. In M. R. Jalongo (Ed.)., *Children, dogs and education: Caring for, learning alongside, and gaining support from canine companions* (pp. 131–149). New York: Springer Nature.

Staats, S., Wallace, H., & Anderson, T. (2008). Reasons for companion animal guardianship (pet ownership) from two populations. *Society & Animals, 16*(3), 279–291. http://www.animalsandsociety.org/wp-content/uploads/2016/04/staats.pdf

Stern, T. (2017, October 17). Survey reveals the joys and obstacles for blind people and their guide dogs. https://www.guidedogs.com/blog/survey

Stewart, L. A., Dispenza, F., Parker, L., Chang, C., & Cunnien, T. (2014). A pilot study assessing the effectiveness of an animal-assisted outreach program. *Journal of Creativity in Mental Health, 9*(3), 332–345.

Sturt, K. (n.d.). The 10 health benefits of dogs (and one health risk). https://www.huffpost.com/entry/the-10-health-benefits-of-dogs-and-one-health-risk_n_57dad1b8e4b04a1497b2f5a0

Sun, J., Serra Hagedorn, L., & Zhang, Y. (2016). Homesickness at college: Its impact on academic performance and retention. *Journal of College Student Development, 57*(8), 943–957.

Thodberg, K., Sørensen, L. U., Videbech, P. B., Poulsen, P. H., Houbak, B., Damgaard, V., . . . Christensen, J. W. (2016). Behavioral responses of nursing home residents to visits from a person with a dog, a robot seal or a toy cat. *Anthrozoös, 29*(1), 107–121.

Topál, J., Miklósi, A., Csányi, V., & Dóka, A. (1998). Attachment behavior in dogs (*Canis familiaris*): A new application of Ainsworth's (1969) Strange Situation Test. *Journal of Comparative Psychology, 112*(3), 219–229.

Turner, J. F. (2017, July 20). The origin of the Doberman: History and fun facts. *Animal-wised*. https://www.animalwised.com/the-origin-of-the-doberman-history-and-fun-facts-80.html

Utz, R. (2014). Walking the dog: the effect of pet ownership on human health and health behaviors. *Social Indicators Research, 116*(2), 327–339.

Ward-Griffin, E., Klaiber, P., Collins, H., Owens, R., Coren, S., & Chen, F. (2018). Petting away pre-exam stress: The effect of therapy dog sessions on student well-being. *Stress and Health, 34*(3), 468–473.

Zilcha-Mano, S., Mikulincer, M., & Shaver, P. R. (2011). An attachment perspective on human-pet relationships: Conceptualization and assessment of pet attachment orientations. *Journal of Research in Personality, 45*(4), 345–357.

2
BRINGING POSTSECONDARY STUDENTS TOGETHER WITH DOGS

Dog Welfare, Health, Safety, and Liability Considerations

LAURA BRUNEAU, ADAMS STATE UNIVERSITY, DEPARTMENT OF COUNSELOR EDUCATION, ALAMOSA, CO, AND AMY JOHNSON, OAKLAND UNIVERSITY, SCHOOL OF NURSING CENTER FOR HUMAN ANIMAL INTERVENTIONS, ROCHESTER, MI

INTRODUCTION

Tom, a college freshman, had been struggling away from home. As it was still early in the first semester, he had not yet made many friends. Tom read about a "Paws to Relax" event at the university library and figured being around happy dogs would help him feel better. After he signed the consent form, he saw four dogs stationed around the room and went to the dog who had the least number of students sitting nearby. He sat down on the floor and shyly waited for a 50-pound Labrador to approach him. The dog, Dixie, walked over with her handler and sniffed his face and nuzzled him, making him smile. He scratched under her chin, and she pushed into him, putting her head over his shoulder, so it felt like a hug. Tom smiled again. The counselor who was also sitting at Dixie's station asked Tom questions about his experience at school. Tom began to talk about feeling lonely and being stressed. All the while, he stroked Dixie on her belly as she had rolled over for a belly rub. As other students moved in and out of the space, Dixie got up and greeted some of the new students. Tom respected Dixie's decision and continued to talk with the

Ryan brings Dutch, his 11-year-old Chihuahua mix, to visit students during exam week. Photo Credit: Mary Walsh

counselor for a short while afterward. He left with the counselor's card in hand, feeling a bit "lighter" and more connected to the university.

As this example illustrates, bringing dogs to college students or, conversely, students to dogs, can be beneficial if conducted correctly. Welfare considerations for both human beings and canines need to take precedence and guide decision making. It is vital to establish practices and policies that reflect the best research evidence available, as well as the recommendations of leading professional organizations. It is equally important to involve all stakeholders and consider liability issues. The chapter begins by defining behaviorally healthy human-canine interactions. It then discusses Wilson's (1984) biophilia hypothesis, the assertion that human beings have a natural tendency to seek contact with other living species. Without deliberate efforts to bring college students and nonhuman animals together in positive ways, campus life can fail miserably in recognizing this fundamental need. Animals of any type are a relatively rare sight at many colleges and universities unless they offer a veterinary program or are wild animals, such as squirrels or birds, whose habitats include some of the green spaces on campus. College towns are full of stories about students attempting to reestablish ties with animals in violation of their rental agreements and landlord's wishes, so much so that animal shelters in college towns often have a policy prohibiting adoptions by college students. Unless or until students understand the basic principles of humane education, animals usually are the losers in students' misguided attempts to affiliate with other living things. This chapter is about simultaneously considering the well-being of humans and dogs, which applies whether the dogs are owned by students or their families, briefly visiting the campus (e.g., therapy dogs), or spending most or all of the time on campus (e.g., facility dogs who accompany their handlers to work on a daily basis or service dogs of residential students). The third section of the chapter will examine research findings on animal welfare. The fourth and final part of the chapter will make recommendations to guide decision making at postsecondary institutions.

DEFINITIONS OF *BEHAVIORALLY HEALTHY HUMAN-CANINE INTERACTIONS*

Behaviorally healthy human-canine relationships are based on mutually beneficial, reciprocal interactions. When a human bonds with a dog, it produces a sense of safety and camaraderie that has the potential to augment the health, well-being, and standard of living for both (Jalongo & Ross, 2018). According to Fox and Gee (2016), a behaviorally healthy relationship is compatible with the idea of responsible companionship, in which pets are seen more as kin or family, rather than possessions or animals.

The Five Freedoms first established by the United Kingdom's Farm Animal Welfare Council (Brambell, 1965) have been serving as an anchor for conceptualizing and evaluating animal welfare by helping us to understand what a dog might need from a human, at the very *minimum*. The Five Freedoms are:

1. Freedom from hunger or thirst by ready access to fresh water and a diet to maintain full health and vigor.
2. Freedom from discomfort by providing an appropriate environment, including shelter and a comfortable resting area.
3. Freedom from pain, injury, or disease by prevention or rapid diagnosis and treatment.
4. Freedom to express (most) normal behavior by providing sufficient space, proper facilities, and company of the animal's own kind.

5. Freedom from fear and distress by ensuring conditions and treatment that avoid mental suffering.

However, we assert the Five Freedoms are insufficient, as they were intended to address abuse and neglect (Serpell, 2019). The Five Freedoms document sets the most basic standard of welfare and emphasizes the removal of something negative (e.g., pain), rather than the addition of something positive (e.g., pleasure) (Johnson & Bruneau, 2019). Several authors (Boissy et al., 2007; Ohl & van der Staay, 2012; Yeates & Main, 2008) have argued that welfare should measure more than the lack of negative states and include the existence of positive states. For dogs, this notion is especially important as the animals over time have adapted to interact with their environments (Ohl & van der Staay, 2012). Data from a recent study (Bir, Croney, & Widmar, 2019) suggest that the general population believes the two most significant welfare needs of breeding dogs are the availability of food and water and veterinary care. While these are essential aspects of animal welfare, they are not enough.

Further, animal welfare needs to be understood in context, including social and cultural values, something that is paramount, given the recent popularization of animal-assisted interactions (AAIs). Decades ago, Iannuzzi and Rowan (1991) offered Tannenbaum's (1989) Characteristics of a True Bond as an extension to the Five Freedoms when considering the ethical implications of AAIs. These characteristics remain relevant and provide a useful framework for understanding behaviorally healthy human-canine interactions. A true human-animal bond:

1. Involves a continuous, ongoing relationship rather than one that is sporadic or accidental.
2. Produces not just a benefit, but a significant benefit to both, and that benefit must be a central aspect of the lives of each.
3. Involves a relationship that is, in some sense, voluntary.
4. Operates in a bidirectional fashion.
5. Entitles each being in the bond to respect and benefit in their own right, rather than simply a means to an end.

Additionally, Mellor (2016) described animals as needing a "good life," not merely a "life worth living." In the case of a good life, the owner ameliorates negative experiences *and* fosters more positive ones. These attitudes and behaviors can be instilled early on as children learn how to take care of a dog, including but not limited to food, water, exercise, rest, safety, grooming, and affection (Jalongo & Ross, 2018). Also, when dogs are adequately trained and given affection, they learn prosocial behaviors, strengthening the overall bond between children and animals (Jalongo & Ross, 2018). Indeed, love for animals is most likely learned early on as children are taught to treasure, trash, or terrorize a dog (Raupp, 1999); if dogs are treasured, there is a significant investment into enhancing their well-being. However, if children see dogs treated as objects, or even abused, they may engage in unethical and immoral treatment of dogs later in life (Jalongo & Ross, 2018). In a perfect world, these prosocial values would extend to other dogs and animals, promoting a duty of care toward animals.

COLLEGE STUDENTS AND DOGS

College students demonstrate a strong bond with their companion animals, and as such, the role of pets in everyday life for college students is becoming increasingly popular (Adams, Sharkin, & Bottinelli, 2017). Eckerd College, for example, has been allowing dogs on campus since 1973. A small college with a current enrollment of 1,800 students, there are over 200 animals, including dogs, cats, hamsters, and lizards (Beach, 2019). At Eckerd, students can even bring pets from home to help with adjustment to college life. The open-pet policy has been described as a way to infuse warmth on the campus, and can help to build connections and community (Beach, 2019). In a survey of 246 college freshman, 93% considered the pets they left at home as essential components in their lives, and 96% of respondents expressed interest in a therapy animal program on campus (Adamle, Riley, & Carlson, 2009). Indeed, a trend in higher education is to expand programming to include therapy animals.

Due to the increasing mental health needs of students, including feelings of hopelessness, suicidal thoughts, depression, and anxiety (Binfet, 2017; Binfet, Passmore, Cebry, Struik, & McKay, 2018), university counseling centers need to connect with a larger group of students (Kronholz, Freeman, & Mackintosh, 2015). Mental health providers on campus frequently find that students are reluctant to disclose their mental health issues and seek support. Thus, outreach is critical: "mental health providers to be seen as active, accessible campus citizens" (Bonfligio, 2016, p. 99). Higher education certainly must take a more comprehensive position in educating students about mental health and wellness (Adams et al., 2017).

Programs involving dogs typically are low-cost and may help to decrease the stigma of mental health issues while increasing help-seeking behaviors (Daltry & Mehr, 2015; Kronholz et al., 2015). College students often underutilize campus resources and may attempt to manage stress on their own (Binfet et al., 2018).

For example, at Florida State University, students were more likely to attend a "Stress Buster Day" involving dogs and to approach counseling staff in an informal setting (Kronholz et al., 2015). Students also were likely to stay longer at such events and build rapport with counseling staff. Through social media, students shared their interactions with the therapy dogs, leading to good publicity for future gatherings. Finally, the staff noticed that handlers also experienced a human connection through the work (Kronholz et al., 2015).

Currently, programs range from small events such as stress relief during exam periods to larger research projects that assess the impact of AAI on college students (Binfet & Struik, 2018). In 2015, Crossman and Kazdin estimated that there were 900 animal-visitation programs on US college campuses, and that number surely has increased in recent years. More recently, Haggerty and Mueller (2017) reported that 62% of universities in the United States have programs that exclusively include visiting therapy dogs. Many times these programs are intended to reduce stress, which is a significant issue for college students (Binfet, 2017). The combination of life transitions, academic expectations, new social relationships, and financial pressures all contribute to such feelings (Adamle et al., 2009). Giving students a sense of belonging (Huss, 2012) and forging stronger connections with the institution is another purpose for visiting therapy dog events (Binfet & Passmore, 2016).

THEORY OF BIOPHILIA

The biophilia hypothesis first surfaced approximately 30 years ago, resulting from the independent work of E. O. Wilson and Stephen R. Kellert, from Harvard University and the US Fish and Wildlife Service, respectively. Wanting to discover the core of human relationships with the natural world, Wilson (1984) hypothesized that all humans make connections with other life forms, in addition to the natural world: "people have an innate tendency to focus on life and lifelike processes" (p. 1). Survival is an influence on this connection such that, by being attuned to nature, humans can more accurately assess threats to their own safety (Jalongo, 2015). When a dog's bark has the characteristics of "sounding the alarm," for example, this alerts the family to a potential threat.

Currently, domesticating and keeping dogs is prevalent around the world (Beck, 2013). In considering the traits of present-day dogs, they are disposed to protect people, property, and territory (Jalongo, 2015). As dogs have lived with humans, they have learned a lot from observing human behaviors. In particular, dogs can interpret and respond to humans' gaze, gestures, and body positions (Glenk, 2017). Dogs regularly make eye contact with humans; in particular, dogs attend to humans, following people that like them and staying away from people who do not (Smith, 1983). Yong and Ruffman (2014) found that dogs exhibited similar physiological responses as humans do after listening to a baby crying. Undoubtedly, as domesticated animals, dogs have become attuned to reading human behavior and emotions.

Assuredly, our connection to nature is fundamental to humans' survival, but the differences among biophilic values or expressions also are essential (Fine, 2014). For example, one might experience feelings of peace or serenity when safely seeing wildlife in their natural habitat, or when sitting by a babbling brook. Conversely, one might feel a sense of anxiety or apprehension encountering a poisonous snake—but both reactions are part of our biophilia (Fine, 2014). Enjoying time with our companion animals is also part of our biophilia. But the way we experience nature (e.g., love having pets, but dislike going to the beach) is going to vary from person to person; yet "our reliance on nature for our own well-being" (Fine, 2014, p. 45) is the same.

Specifically, nine biophilic approaches explain how people relate and interact with the natural world. These nine approaches (Kellert, 1997; Wilson, 1984) include: aesthetic (e.g., stopping at a scenic view); negativistic (e.g., perceiving danger); humanistic (e.g., viewing dog as family); naturalistic (e.g., swimming in a lake); symbolic (e.g., painting nature scenes); scientific (e.g., studying geology or biology); utilitarian (e.g., using natural resources such as hunting or fishing); dominionistic (e.g., hiking Mount Everest); and moralistic (e.g., doing volunteer work for an animal rights group). A person's unique pattern of biophilic expression is a combination of social learning, culture, and experience (Meltzer, Bobilya, & Faircloth, 2013; Shorb & Schnoeker-Shorb, 2010). Fine (2014) noted that no biophilic approach is inherently good or bad, but biophilia helps to understand how humans approach their relationships with the world and their survival as a species.

In particular, dogs serve fewer practical purposes and are treated more like family members; companion animals often meet social and emotional needs in humans (Wilkin, Fairlie, & Ezzedeen, 2016). These needs are seen quite clearly in the results of a study on the subjective experience of living with a companion dog (Maharaj, Kazanjian, & Haney, 2016). Twenty-seven dog owners participated in focus groups to describe how they perceive and relate to their family dogs, and how these experiences impact their sense of meaning in life. Results indicated that the human-canine relationship is infused with sacredness and spirituality that is influenced by the shortness of a dog's lifespan, the profoundness of the emotional bond, and a feeling of obligation to provide dogs with a meaningful life (Maharaj et al., 2016).

However, in looking at the word *biophilia*, which means "lover of life," it is clear that this term argues for a directional relationship. If biophilia is one-sided (e.g., humans like nature and living beings), this suggests that plants, nature, and animals are only here to suit humans' purposes. Therefore, the biophilia hypothesis should not be confused with the human-animal bond. Biophilia explains *humans'* need or desire to connect with nature, but it does not speak to the *animals'* need to interact with humans.

COLLEGE STUDENTS AND BIOPHILIA

Evidence exists that college students want to be around animals. Per a report in the *Chronicle of Higher Education* (Hoover, 2003), college students will go to great lengths to have a pet in college. For example, a facility manager at Michigan State University discovered enough "critters" in dorms over 15 years to fill a couple of pet stores, including snakes, gerbils, cats, rabbits, and lizards. However, many students are unable to keep a pet, often due to housing regulations and for financial reasons. Some animals find new homes, but many are left behind or simply released into the community to face an uncertain fate. Having pets provides a sense of identity for many students, increasing visitors and friendships for college students living in dorms. New college students often lose social support, including companion animals (Dell et al., 2015).

Further, a frequently cited study by Wells and Perrine (2001) investigated the presence of a companion animal in a professor's office on the students' perception of both the office and the professor. Two-hundred and fifty-seven students were randomly assigned to the three groups (picture of an office with a dog, cat, or no animal). When there was a dog in the image, students perceived the office to be more comfortable and professors to be amiable than when there was a cat or no animal in the office (Wells & Perrine, 2001). Results suggested that professors can influence their students' perceptions of them by having an animal on campus.

There is minimal opportunity for students to interact with other living species in college. Except for relatively rare sightings of wildlife on campuses, pets are not typically welcome; however, this is changing. First, elements of the various biophilic approaches may be seen on some campuses such as humanistic (e.g., viewing dog as family) or moralistic (e.g., doing volunteer work for animal rights group). Some colleges offer adventure programs (e.g., naturalistic) or student-led environmental advocacy groups (e.g., moralistic) and are increasing green spaces (e.g., aesthetic). Colleges, like other work settings and institutions, are starting to become more pet-friendly (e.g., humanistic; Wilkin et al., 2016).

For some animals, though, this might not be happening quickly enough. Dogs have been used in experimental research over the last two centuries, and while guidelines help to protect their welfare do exist (Foreman, Glenn, Meade, & Wirth, 2017), the experimentation often harms the dogs, which delivers the message that animals are to be used rather than to coexist. Further, four schools continue to use animals in medical student education, rather than human-based training methods, which are thought to provide a better teaching experience despite the extensive push-back from animal rights groups ("Ending Animal Use," 2015).

Moreover, live animal mascots may result in the exploitation of animals. Mascots are a symbol of a university and provide an identity for students, staff, faculty, and alumni. Nevertheless, they have come under scrutiny for many reasons, and in particular, universities must abandon the tradition when it comes to using live, sentient creatures as mascots (Baranko, 2011). Notably, Louisiana State University has a Bengal tiger named Mike, who is displayed on game days in front of huge crowds while being kept in a small cage. Cheerleaders will stand on top of the cage, and an LSU associate once admitted that Mike was "zapped repeatedly with a cattle prod to make him angry so that he will roar" (Baranko, 2011, p. 610). Likewise, Baylor University has used live bears since 1932, and has used over fifty bear cubs, which are replaced every two years. The bears live in a campus facility called "The Pit," and have demonstrated neurotic behavior typical of caged animals, such as crying (Baranko, 2011).

Although these are extreme examples, and many universities have switched to humans dressed in animal suits as their mascots (Baranko, 2011), there is still evidence of animal cruelty among college students. Animal cruelty has been reported on college campuses, with most of them involving Greek organizations and hazing rituals, such as burning a pig with heat lamps, beating a goose to death with a golf club, and throwing a puppy off a bridge (Hoover, 2003). There also is evidence of mistreatment. For example, animal shelters are inundated with animals who students cannot keep at the end of each semester. College students might make a rash decision to get a cute puppy, for example, only not to be able to care for the dog long-term due to employment, geographic relocation, and/or housing regulations. Not having a stable home and being returned to an animal shelter might lead to separation anxiety and other adverse health issues for the dog.

Another example stems from highly publicized programs at Yale Law School and Harvard University. Dogs Monty and Cooper, respectively, visit the libraries to provide stress relief. On a webpage, Yale described this program as "outside the box thinking, in an effort to provide creative non-traditional services to our patrons ... the provision of a therapy dog was considered an excellent extension to these services" (other "services" include lending bicycles, phone chargers, and iPads) (Aiken, 2012). As such, students were invited to "check out" Monty, a therapy dog, for up to 30 minutes as a way to increase student wellness (Williams, 2011). This program was popular; in fact, Monty was voted prom king and also invited to commencement (Chanen, 2011). Likewise, at Harvard University, Cooper is available a couple of days per week by reservation for 30 minutes with each student (Weinberg, 2014). Staff stated that Cooper enjoys a game of tug or giving kisses and described reserving Cooper as similar to checking out a book.

While these programs may appeal to some, we challenge the notion of a dog being an inanimate object that is borrowed. Treating living and feeling beings as objects ignores their rights (Epstein, 2002). Would dogs rather spend time with a stranger, or would they want to be at home in their own space? Dogs experience many of the same feelings as humans do, including love, joy, loneliness, and fear (Ng, 2019). For those readers who practice AAI, the example of art therapy comes to mind. Paints, brushes, and easels are tools to be used. These tools do not need a break, or food and water as a living, breathing therapy dog does. If we treat a dog like an inanimate object to serve a human agenda only, we send the misguided message to students that the dogs' agency and choice are immaterial.

Many programs on colleges and universities have begun as small outreach or ad hoc programs (Daltry & Mehr, 2015; Huss, 2012). For example, faculty members may bring their dogs to work on a designated day (Huss, 2012). The danger with these ad hoc programs is that there is little oversight, and adherence to best practices. Headlines and captions about programs tend to focus on how the students love these programs, not about whether the dogs enjoy them. More substantial, well-planned programs might also raise animal welfare issues. For example, Adams and colleagues (2017) described a "Puppies on the Quad" event to simultaneously help students relax during finals week and to support a rescue organization in adopting shelter cats and dogs. We have to ask though, who adopted these animals in the end? Are they college students who walked by and thought one was cute, oblivious to the fact that the dogs would need to be house-trained or without any commitment to long-term care? Huss (2012) expressed concern about college students' suitability for responsible pet care, particularly in college housing. This chapter now moves into addressing some of these broader questions about animal welfare.

RESEARCH ON ANIMAL WELFARE

As animals become more commonplace in college and university settings, so do the potential ethical, moral, and legal implications. Anecdotal reports from staff and personnel describe these programs as a "win-win" for both the students and the university. Animals indeed become symbols for the program or institution and may help with marketing (Foreman, Allison, Poland, Meade, & Wirth, 2019). However, programs need to be a "win-win-win," not just for the student and the university, but also for the animal. Indeed, Rooney and Bradshaw (2014) called attention to the notion of "what's good for us, is good for them" (p. 242), and caution against both anthropomorphism (assigning human qualities to animals) and anthropocentrism (assuming that the animal sees the world through human senses).

On one end of the spectrum, the animal rights movement calls into question the idea of animals being "used." This word, *use*, has particular significance in AAIs. Zamir (2006) contended that *using* animals to help people may be immoral, due to objectification, limiting their freedom, separating them from their kind, overworking them and increasing the likelihood of injury, and ultimately deciding how the animal should live. His commentary sets the stage for the quintessential question: *Does participating in human-animal interactions provide a suitable life for the animal?* If given a choice, would the dog stay involved in the human-canine interaction? Zamir (2006) admitted that, without a relationship with humans, a large number of dogs and horses would not exist, concluding with, "a world in which practices like AAT exist is an overall better world for these beings than one that does not include them, and this provides a broad, moral vindication of forms of AAT that rely on these beings" (p. 195).

According to the American Veterinary Medical Association (2019), the human-animal bond must be symbiotic; however, less attention to date has been given to the well-being of the animal (Ng, Albright, Fine, & Peralta, 2015; Vitztum & Urbanik, 2016). While stories about dogs on campus are cute and adorable, universities must prioritize animal welfare; to do otherwise risks exploitation of the dogs and sends unintended messages to students about consent. Therapy dogs are obedient and eager to please, yet "what can be perceived as a tolerant and quiet dog in the presence of an emotional human could actually be a dog suffering from learned helplessness" (Ng, 2019, p. 60). Stakeholders in AAI must guard against promoting human well-being at the expense of animal well-being.

The consensus in the research literature is that AAIs *do* raise concerns because there are no universally accepted standards about animal welfare. Looking back on the Five Freedoms, Ng (2019) provided an analysis of these in the context of AAIs. For example, handlers have been known to withhold water and food while visiting to prevent dogs from urinating or defecating while working. Freedom from discomfort might also be difficult due to the nature of unpredictable environments. Animal injuries might also occur and may be underreported. We know that stress is prevalent in AAIs, with some dogs being negatively impacted by distress in humans. And finally, the fifth freedom is a challenge:

> AAI is unlike any other animal activity in that it requires an animal to endure intimate, unsolicited affections from a human stranger for extended durations of time. Animals in these contrived circumstances must remain steady and cope with the interaction of unfamiliar people and strange settings without being able to choose whether to stay or leave, which prevents expression of normal behavior. (Ng, 2019, p. 62)

Thus, more research is needed, particularly on the cumulative effects of participation on the animal. Determining an animal's welfare is difficult because it frequently relies on the subjective evaluation of the observer (Ng et al., 2015) who may have a vested interest in the outcome. As Vitztum and Urbanik (2016) argued, factors used to determine an animal's suitability for participation in AAIs (e.g., physical health, training, etc.) typically has more to do with the welfare of humans than the animal—"like a three-legged stool, HAI is unable to stand alone on the perspective of the human" (p. 182).

The following welfare considerations apply to all dogs on college campuses, including companion animals, those considered emotional support dogs, therapy dogs, and service dogs. We recognize that service dogs are classified differently than the other types of dogs listed. By definition and protection from the Americans with Disabilities Act, service dogs aid the individual with a disability, and as such, rules and regulations related to service dogs do not necessarily apply to other classifications of dogs on campus. While service dog welfare also matters, this animal is not provided the same consideration of choice that other helping dogs have or should have. Dogs do not ask to be therapeutic partners, and gaining their consent and maintaining optimal welfare should be tantamount to avoid exploitation.

CANINE WELFARE

Because dogs have maintained their status as a best friend to humankind for centuries and are the animal most commonly integrated into AAIs, we have learned much about their welfare states. Historically, dogs have been bred mainly for hunting, herding, and guarding; thus, being touched, hugged, or approached by a stranger—or worse, a large crowd of people—can evoke distress (Glenk, 2017). While some dogs may tolerate these things, others may react negatively to such stimuli. Besides, dogs like to be touched in specific areas, such as the chest, chin, or base of the tail (Glenk, 2017); however, many people reach over the dogs to touch their heads, which is very intimidating. The physical environment also can be challenging, with strange sounds, smells, movement, or textures. Ng et al. (2014) found that unfamiliar settings can increase salivary cortisol levels. High temperatures and confined spaces are another source of stress for dogs (Marinelli, Normando, Siliprandi, Salvadoretti, & Mongillo, 2009).

A main purpose of bringing therapy dogs to college campuses is to soothe the anxiety of new students in a unique setting. This goal sometimes overshadows any consideration of the fact that dogs might experience the same feelings upon arrival to a campus setting. Some of the potential stressors outdoors and indoors might include:
- Current weather conditions
- Barometric pressure from changing weather patterns
- Sound of wind in the trees
- Flapping of flags or banners
- Squirrels and birds to chase

- Construction sounds
- Cars and other vehicles passing close by
- Smell of plants or animals
- Bikes passing close by
- Insecticide, fertilizer, and landscaping material smells
- Uncomfortable temperature on sidewalk
- Loud music
- Different surfaces to walk on
- Bee stings or other insects
- Personal belongings (e.g., purses, coats, hats, and sunglasses) can be scary
- Sliding glass doors
- Depth perception on stairs
- Variety of people
- People trying to touch the dog
- Wildlife or other dogs on campus
- Reflection in window
- Elevators
- Wheelchairs or crutches
- Buzzing sounds
- Alarms, elevator bells, and dings
- Smell of books, coffee, food, cologne, or perfume
- Cleaning product smells
- Groups of people indoors

New environments may be challenging for even the most docile and even-tempered dogs. In this line of work, we often hear people describe their animals as "perfect" or "real" therapy dogs. Good pets and "best friends" do not always make good candidates for AAIs (Glenk, 2017). Besides, people may misinterpret dog signals, which is a common reason for accidents, especially among children (Meints, Brelsford, Gee, & Fine, 2017). And, more importantly, having owned a dog or two does not necessarily make an owner an expert interpreter of canine communication (Meints et al., 2017). Dogs respond to stress in many ways, and typically follow the ladder of aggression model (Shephard, 2009) in which they move along a continuum of stress signals, with subtle signals such as yawning or lip licking to more severe and prominent signs such as freezing, growling, and biting (Campbell, 2016).

Dogs attempt to adapt to their environment through a variety of calming signals, particularly when experiencing stressful situations. Examples include lip licking, body shaking, yawning, tongue flicking, and licking self or objects (Glenk, 2017; McConnell & Fine, 2015). Fear and anxiety in dogs also are commonly expressed in attempts to retreat from the situation (Polgár, Blackwell, & Rooney, 2019). Forcing a dog to engage in human-centric social activities in which they do not have an opportunity to disengage may impact their well-being (Polgár et al., 2019). Sometimes, in their enthusiasm for community service, therapy dogs can be overscheduled by their handlers—another cause of stress. It is possible, though, that a dog can gain confidence over time with appropriate support and a good match with the recipient/environment.

However, each dog is unique and reacts to stress and new situations in various ways (Meints et al., 2017). One emerging topic is the use of leads in AAIs. Being on a leash may be required by therapy animal organizations as part of the liability insurance agreement or may be necessary for the safety of the dog. However, pulling dogs on a lead may result in increased levels of cortisol similar to the experience of hearing a sudden noise (Beerda, Schilder, van Hooff, de Vries, & Mol, 1998). In a more recent study, Glenk et al. (2013) found a significant difference in levels of salivary cortisol between dogs who were on or off lead during therapy sessions. Those dogs who were off lead had lower cortisol levels when working than those who were on lead during the session. However, some local laws, campus policies, and the insurance regulations of therapy dog groups may require all dogs to be on a leash at all times. Furthermore, some dogs may feel more comfortable being on a lead; thus, AAI handlers ideally should be able to decide what is best for their dog (Glenk et al., 2013). All in all, we need more information on the use of a lead during AAI and how to give dogs a choice in when to approach or avoid people during sessions.

As a veteran dog trainer once stated, "Dogs don't like surprises." Dogs tend to respond best to predictable behavior and a familiar environment (Ng et al., 2014). For example, dogs tend to prefer people who are steady and quiet (Jalongo, 2008). However, college campuses may not provide the ideal environment for AAI programming (Binfet & Struik, 2018). College students are often enthusiastic, have a lot of energy, and may squeal with delight at the sight of dogs on campus. Also, some college campuses have a remarkably diverse student body who may have extremely different views on how to interact with dogs. Space also is an issue on college campuses, and AAI events may be held in cramped spaces or public spaces that are considered high-volume areas (Binfet & Struik, 2018), which helps to attract more students. Unfortunately, more students in high-traffic areas may lead to more stress for the dogs.

It's no wonder best practices recommend that therapy dogs have several days of rest after an AAI session. In one instance, a program was halted when a therapy dog was diagnosed with Cushing's disease, which may have developed due to high, consistent stress (Glenk, 2017). However, what about programs that do not work with registered therapy dogs? Take, for example, a recent study that examined the impact of an untrained dog on stress levels in college students (McDonald, McDonald, & Roberts, 2017). The authors argued that there is a lack of trained therapy dogs at some colleges due to rural locations or a limited budget. If this type of program is being studied, this suggests these programs are occurring. And, if so, who is evaluating the temperament and the stress levels in these untrained, untested dogs? We now turn to other types of dogs that may be present on college campuses.

EMOTIONAL SUPPORT ANIMALS

For a full discussion about emotional support animals (ESAs) on college campuses, refer to chapter 4. However, a chapter on welfare must address the needs of these dogs. Powers (2013) noted that as our relationship with dogs has evolved, it makes sense that we question policies, regulations, and laws about human-animal companionship. There has been a spike in requests for ESAs on campuses for students struggling with symptoms of anxiety and depression. The National Institutes of Health estimated young adults 18 to 25 had the highest incidence of mental illness, with 22.1% affected (Bedrossian, 2018).

Central to this discussion are the questions about costs/benefits of keeping a pet on a college campus and documentation of a disability-related need assessed by a mental health professional. Younggren (2019) argued that while a person with depression might feel better when a pet is around, that does not mean there is a disability-related need for the animal. For example, psychotropic medication may be useful in treating depression, and as such, a person would need to take the medication daily as directed. But if a person can go to class or hang out with friends without their ESA, the ESA may be viewed as a companion animal rather than addressing a need. From an animal welfare perspective, one must consider whether an ESA can thrive in a college setting, given that there is no behavioral evaluation or suitability measure required for the dog (Taylor, 2016). For example, an elderly emotional support dog may find it difficult to move from the comforts and freedoms of a home to a residence hall that is small, noisy, and keeps him indoors or on leash nearly all of the time.

Specific university regulations help to mitigate the possibility of abuse or neglect of the animal. For example, an ESA request would be denied if the animal poses a direct threat to the health and safety of another person or would cause substantial damage to the property of others (Masinter, 2016). Further, ESAs must have vaccinations that are up to date, be reliably house-trained, free of internal and external parasites, and be small enough to live in the allotted space. Even more important are the dog care obligations of the ESA or service animal handler. There must not be any evidence of mistreatment or abuse and the animal cannot be left alone overnight, even under the care of a roommate (Masinter, 2016). Some other university-specific regulations also stipulate that an animal must be appropriately contained when the owner is not in the room, and the animal must always be under the control of the owner, such as on a leash, harness, or in a crate/carrier (*United States of America vs. Kent State University*, 2016; *United States of America vs. University of Nebraska at Kearney*, 2015). The decision to crate, for example, is a human-centric one, leaving the dog's welfare in question. For many dogs, being crated might be perceived as punishment, and lengthy periods of crating may constitute neglect or even abuse, especially if the animal is forced to "hold it" for many hours.

CANINES ON CAMPUS

Service dogs perform tasks for the benefit of a person with a disability, and as such, have full access to colleges and universities. Also, many workplaces are becoming more sensitive to the needs and wants of people with family pets (Wilkin et al., 2016). Adopting more pet-friendly policies may attract and retain employees, increase morale, and boost productivity (Foreman et al., 2017; Wilkin et al., 2016). Some work settings may allow employees to bring their pets to work every day, while others may participate in an annual "bring your dog to work day." Yet not all work settings are dog-friendly and may be stressful for the animal. Dogs must be able to play and engage in other typical behaviors (Foreman et al., 2017). Therefore, universities bear responsibility for ensuring animal welfare through policies and procedures, especially when multiple dogs are present (Foreman et al., 2017). Even service animals protected by the Americans with Disabilities Act of 2011 can be prohibited from facilities if the animal's presence is a threat to public safety. Service dog etiquette must also be implemented at the university level so that boundaries are maintained and respected (see chapter 3).

Foreman et al. (2019) surveyed 138 university employees about hazards and risks to resident visitation dogs, and the impact on well-being for students and employees. For the most part, employees believed the dogs presented minimal risk and had the potential to increase well-being for students. Of the issues noted by the respondents, allergies, religious and cultural beliefs, and phobias were of particular concern (Foreman et al., 2019). It's important to note the circumstances of the dogs that were included in this study; the dogs lived with faculty or staff members, but came to work each day to spend the day in various locations, including the counseling center waiting room, a freshman engineering tutoring center, and a student lounge (Foreman et al., 2019). Dogs typically sleep for more than half the day, so long work hours may be stressful to dogs.

Further, when many animals come to the same work environment, policies on how to address intra- and interspecies conflict must be implemented (Wilkin et al., 2016). Some dogs may be too anxious or aggressive to come to work each day, and clear guidelines for the person responsible for the dog are necessary. Health and safety guidelines also are essential, including "dog-proofing" the environment, designating dog-free zones, ensuring the health of dogs, establishing guidelines for safe interaction with animals, and maintaining hygienic practices (Wilkin et al., 2016). The decision to bring animals on college campuses needs to be carefully considered, thoughtfully implemented, and closely monitored. Fortunately, innovative programs and initiatives provide some best-practice guidelines.

INSTITUTIONAL INITIATIVES

As AAIs become more prevalent across disciplines, innovative programs are developing at many institutions. For example, at Southeastern Louisiana University, the Pet Project began as a collaboration between faculty and students in the Department of Communication Sciences and Disorders to support and enhance traditional clinic services (Davis, 2018). In this program, child clients read to a therapy dog named Oliver during their sessions at the Speech-Language-Hearing Clinic. Although Oliver's handler is an audiologist, she joins the sessions as a handler only so that she can ensure the situation is safe for Oliver, the children, and to help support the clinicians who are providing the services (Southeastern Louisiana University, n.d.).

The University of Central Florida has a program in which service dogs are being trained in university housing (O'Brien, 2016). This program mirrors innovative programming in many prison dog programs (Jalongo, 2019). While still a new program, STEP@UCF seeks to teach the general campus community about the impact of service dogs. After going through a rigorous selection process, students raise puppies for Canine Companions for Independence. The campus serves as a useful training ground due to the sights, smells, and distractions (Service Dog Training, 2019). Student trainers gain knowledge across disciplines, including but not limited to canine behavior, learning theory, record keeping, public relations, public speaking, and disability awareness, which can be useful skills after college (Service Dog Training, 2019).

QUALITY PROGRAM EXAMPLE

The University of New Brunswick and St. Thomas University offer excellent examples of how to manage therapy dog programs on a college campus while being mindful of health, liability, safety, and welfare issues. Dogs can be an enormous draw for university-sponsored events, attracting students who would not ordinarily participate. Many students experience feelings of loneliness and miss their families, including their pets. Bringing therapy dogs on campus allows students to interact in a safe environment while meeting other students, faculty, and in some cases, counselors and other student support providers. As social lubricants (Levinson, 1969), dogs often prompt communication with others when it might otherwise be uncomfortable. Indeed, opportunities to sit with, pet, or cuddle with a registered therapy dog may fill a void for some students.

The Student Health Centre (SHC) serves full-time students at the University of New Brunswick (UNB) and St. Thomas University (STU), which are both public universities in Canada. Combined, these schools enroll around 11,500 students. Events and visits from therapy dogs are open to students, faculty, and staff, and are well-publicized on the university websites.

Currently, dogs are the only species included in these programs. Although some therapy animal organizations do register a variety of species, the program leaders at SHC are trained in dog behavior and do not want to risk jeopardizing the welfare of other animals. Also, there are no local experts in the immediate vicinity who could assess the temperament, behavior, and welfare of different species.

Poster to advertise therapy dog event. Photo Credit: Patricia Eagan

The SHC hosts a variety of animal-assisted activities and animal-assisted education events where faculty and staff connect with students on many topics, including physical and mental health. For example, the PawstoDeStress program has unique visits from therapy dogs, in addition to other incentives such as hot chocolate, coloring areas, and calming jars. This program is designed to promote self-care during stressful periods, such as midterms and final exams, and provides a novel experience to engage students. This event also has benefits for the dog, such as spending time out of the house with their human

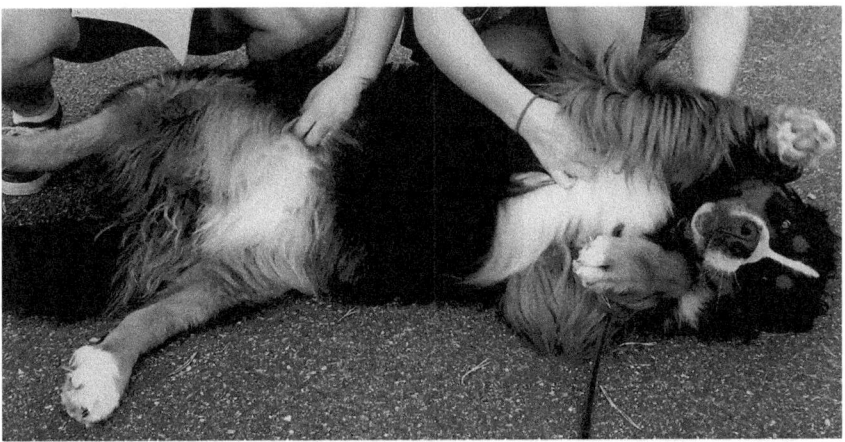

Rosi asks for a much-needed belly rub at PawstoDeStress. Photo Credit: Patricia Eagan

handlers. These "field trips" can provide mental and physical stimulation, in which the dog receives a lot of praise, treats, and belly rubs—all of which the dogs seem to enjoy.

In addition to the PawstoDeStress event, which is held twice a year at UNB and STU, other innovative programs include a Be My Valentine, in which a therapy dog distributes valentines across campus. Therapy dogs also are involved with meet-and-greet visits at student orientation and recruitment programs, as well as special ad hoc events, including Eating Disorder Awareness Week and Mental Health Week.

Without careful coordination of these events, the potential for injuries and negative experiences dramatically increases. For example, at the SHC, this lesson was learned early on when a group of second-year students planned an AAI event without being aware of specific protocols. These well-meaning students thought that gaining permission from the dean was all that was necessary. However, there were several incidents at these initial events. On one occasion, a woman and her pet dog walked in off the street because she was interested in therapy dogs. The student volunteers decided to set her up in a corner to interact with attendees without having any knowledge of the dog's temperament or medical history. At another event, there were too many dogs in the room, and no one was monitoring the dog areas, which led to some of the dogs interacting negatively. Many of the teams vowed never to return to the SHC. Luckily, no one was injured during these events, but it did result in specific protocols for future events.

Presently, the success of the AAI events at SHC is the result of relevant education and training, qualified personnel, careful planning, and specific protocols. Dog welfare considerations are critical to the success of the program. Using the model established by the SHC, as well as incorporating some of the research from above, recommendations for AAI events on college campuses, at a minimum, are as follows.

EDUCATION AND TRAINING.
Staff, volunteers, and dog handlers need to have education and training on the foundation of AAIs. Just being a dog owner does not mean that a person has the requisite knowledge and skills to assess canine behavior, train a dog, and mitigate the signs of stress in dogs. Education should be ongoing, but at minimum, an orientation should be held to cover such basics as interpreting dog body language, responding appropriately when dogs show signs of stress, and using gentle, positive methods of dog training. Of note, education needs to address the negative impact of using aversive training methods. The orientation also should contain safety planning, including but not limited to emergency preparedness, an evacuation plan, cleaning protocol, dog and human hygiene, and how to set up the room for optimal flow and welfare.

Another critical component is ensuring that the dogs have choices. The dogs, ideally, should choose with whom they want to interact, and if the dog is no longer interested in the interaction, this needs to be respected. As this can be difficult for new handlers and staff who are excited about their dogs being at the event, this should be practiced when possible. Objectively assessing one's dog for signs of stress is critical to this line of work. This knowledge is not only species- or breed-specific, but also occurs at the individual dog level. By prioritizing optimal dog well-being, the likelihood of an injury occurring or negative experience for all involved decreases drastically.

One way the SHC raises awareness of the dogs' welfare is by having posters or trading cards that include a photo of the dog, along with what the dog likes and dislikes. For example, the dog might not be able to have treats or be around more than one or two people at a time. Also, talking openly about consent ensures the dogs are actively seeking out contact with humans. A simple consent test can help to assess if the dog likes being touched. If the human stops the activity (e.g., scratching chest, rubbing belly), does the dog take action to make the activity start again? For example, a sign that a dog likes to be petted is that they freely move into the human's space, whereas a dog who ducks or moves away does not want to be petted at that moment.

When implementing an AAI program, the benefit to the animal must be clear. For therapy dogs who love social interaction with humans, these events also may serve as extra bonding time with their guardian. During the event, the dogs receive praise and a lot of attention, which most seem to love. The main job of the handler is to monitor the welfare of the dogs. Leading therapy dog organizations emphasize that handlers are obligated to be advocates for their dogs and remove them from situations that cause their dog to become stressed. At SHC, staff or volunteers provide a secondary welfare check. For example, there have been times when a dog is scheduled for a one-hour visit but seems to become tired after thirty minutes. During these instances, it is vital for staff to recognize the needs of the animal and provide a break or possibly end the visit early.

PERSONNEL.

The success of these programs relies on having a competent director to oversee all dog-related programming. Since 2008, the program director at the SHC is Patricia Eagan. As a human-animal intervention specialist with experience as a veterinary assistant and volunteer work as a therapy dog handler with over 1,500 client visits, Eagan was granted oversight of AAI programming at SHC. Having a collaborative working relationship with administration and other key groups on campus is also important. University leadership must be confident in the management of these programs and ensure that all policies and procedures are upheld.

Further, the approval process for AAI programming is critical and should be shared across campus. It is easy, and relatively common, for someone to bring a dog on campus and not be aware of the liability and legal issues associated with doing so. Thus, having a gatekeeper to oversee events is necessary. For example, at UNB, if students, faculty, or staff want an AAI event to take place, Eagan is available to review the request and assist in the planning and coordination of the event. Eagan and her team also debrief after every event to determine what worked, and what was concerning, for both the students and the dogs. To illustrate, after a handler remarked that having so many scents was challenging for the dogs, the group advertised events as "scent-reduced" so that participants would consider skipping the heavy perfumes.

One of Eagan's main priorities is evaluating the benefits for the dogs. Knowing the difference between dogs enjoying the work versus tolerating the work is the cornerstone to success. As Eagan described (P. Eagan, personal communication, May 30, 2019), "For dogs that enjoy a lot of tactile reinforcement, the PawstoDeStress events are a good match. Some dogs prefer to do tricks for praise, which is highly entertaining for the students, or some dogs like to greet and have brief interactions."

Further, knowing the volunteer therapy dog teams is essential. As Eagan elaborated, "When we know the teams well, we can advocate for the dogs before they are approved for specific events. We also encourage handlers to identify their dogs' top picks for positive reinforcement and share that with students as they approach to interact." Eagan also understands the importance of ongoing professional development. She continuously attends workshops, conferences, trainings, and reads the latest research on dog welfare to ensure SHC is always following best practices.

PLANNING AND PROTOCOLS.

Careful planning is vital for any AAI event. Event planning involves considering all foreseeable aspects. Gaining approval from all departments is an important, and sometimes complicated first step. For example, the dean of Student Services may have approved the event, but the building manager also needs to sign off. Thus, having a checklist and flowchart of the approval process from various departments and department heads is useful. Next, it is best practice to have many registered therapy dog teams at the ready. These events can become quite popular and crowded; at one institution, over 500 students and staff visited the library to interact with dogs during a two-hour event. Teams can elect to participate based on their strengths and interests, and each team is invited to participate for no more than an hour at a time. If a dog is uncomfortable one day or isn't feeling well, this does not mean that the team is excluded for future events, but will need to be reassessed regularly.

Other important aspects to planning include the flow of the event, the position of dogs so that they do not interact, considerations of sensory stimulation (e.g., bright lights, loud music, slippery floors), and easy access to exits and water bowls. For example, the SHC positions mats around the room strategically to keep the dogs away from each other, but also provides a substrate that is not slippery, which many dogs dislike. They also lower the room temperature and secure a location at the entrance where students can drop off their backpacks so as not to accidentally bump the dogs with them. Dogs are often wary of large silhouettes, which may include hats, winter jackets, and large bags. Space and floors also should be clean, which typically requires coordination with facility services.

Room set-up for students and handler/therapy dog teams before PawstoDeStress. Photo Credit: Patricia Eagan

On the day of the event, there needs to be a place for therapy dog teams to check in and to ensure they are wearing appropriate equipment per their therapy animal organization. Alliance of Therapy Dogs, for example, requires all dogs to be on a four-foot leash, and handlers are to wear sensible shoes with closed toes.

Volunteers can escort the team and be sure they are aware of exits in case of emergency. Volunteers who are well versed in dog body language and identification of stress in dogs should be stationed around the room to monitor the dogs, and act if necessary. The SHC sets up stations, so there are 20 feet of open space in between each station to avoid crowding the dogs.

Eagan and her team have evolved their policies and procedures over several years. These are fluid documents, subject to change as necessary. Policies and procedures are revisited, and agreed-upon changes are disseminated to the entire team.

RECOMMENDATIONS FOR PRACTICE

The concept of humane education is also impacting college programming. According to the "Professional Guidelines for Humane Educators" (Association of Professional Humane Educators, 2012), before including an animal in an activity, the professional must decide if the animal will benefit from participation as well as enhance the overall message. We need to be able to assess enjoyment and exhaustion in animals during an AAI, across different species and while considering the personality of the individual animal (Hedeger, Meisser, & Zinsstag, 2019), which is no easy task. Animal-assisted intervention must be mutually beneficial for it to be considered ethical, with the needs of the therapy animal taking precedence over the human (McCullough et al., 2018; Serpell, Coppinger, Fine, & Peralta, 2010). Although the research base is growing, there is considerable variation in studies on animal welfare and measures of cortisol, the hormone associated with stress in dogs and humans, are mixed (Glenk, 2017). In a recent study, however, McCullough et al. (2018) found a relationship between canine cortisol and canine behavior, suggesting that canine cortisol can be useful in researching dog welfare. In this study, 26 therapy dog-handler teams were studied, and results demonstrated that therapy dogs did not have increased physiological stress responses.

Future research should utilize multiple measures of dog welfare, not only behavioral observations (Ng et al., 2014), but also physiological measures such as tympanic temperature, heart rate, heart rate variability, salivary cortisol, and salivary oxytocin (Martin et al., 2019). For example, a recent study found that one 15-minute petting session between a calm person and a shelter dog led to dogs' decreased heart rate, increased heart rate variability, and changes in behavior associated with relaxation (McGowan, Bolte, Barnett, Perez-Camargo, & Martin, 2018). Howie (2019) advocated for respecting the individuality of the animal when choosing therapy animals. Not all animals are equally appropriate for a therapeutic setting or a particular activity. For example, if the goal of the intervention is to improve self-regulation, a dog that actively moves around, nudges the human, or gets the human to engage with them in some way is a better fit than a dog that stays quietly near humans, no matter what the human is doing (Howie, 2019). The Clothier Animal Response Assessment Tool, or CARAT (Clothier, 2007), may be a viable option for those who want to assess desired therapy animal characteristics. The CARAT looks at the following traits and how these traits interact with each other: sociability, patience, biddability, social tolerance, awareness, reactivity, arousal, resilience, energy, social use of space, exploratory, confidence, reliability, self-modulation, and impulse control.

Ng et al. (2014) endeavored to standardize AAI variables by studying college students as they interacted with a dog during an hour-long study break. When conducted in a controlled manner by the handler, this AAI did not increase salivary cortisol levels or stress signals in the dogs. The researchers believed that the influence of the dog handler helped to minimize stress responses in the dogs through facilitation of predictable interactions (Ng et al., 2014). Handlers must instruct participants how to interact with the dog safely and respectfully through posture, gestures, tone and voice, and eye contact. For example, the handler might show the recipient how the dog likes to be touched and where the dog does not.

Undeniably, the handler is a core element to any AAI. According to Binfet and Struik (2018), "recognizing that therapy dogs are but one-half of the dog therapy-handler team, it remains equally important to assess volunteer dog handlers for both how they govern the dog under their care and for their suitability for working with target clients" (p. 6). Handlers must understand the dog's baseline behavior at home so they can recognize signs of distress when they occur (Ng et al., 2014). When working with college students, handlers must be able to adapt to their needs as well (Binfet & Struik, 2018). Students may attend stressed, homesick, and sad; thus, handlers must be able to support students who are in various emotional states.

At the very least, handlers must be able to establish a rapport with the student, while simultaneously facilitating the canine-human interactions. Also, handlers must be sensitive to diversity issues based on gender, race, ethnicity, and other cultural influences (Binfet & Struik, 2018). Handlers must also advocate for their dog's physical health. A recent study (Boyle, Corrigan, Buechner-Maxwell, & Pierce, 2019) found that compliance with infection-control practices was inadequate among a small group of handlers. In essence, we need to learn more about the handlers in AAI; some studies have indicated that handlers have higher levels of cortisol on visitation days than on control days (Haubenhofer & Kirchengast, 2007; Schöberl, Wedl, Beetz, & Kotrschal, 2017), which may then impact the animal. Ng (2019) noted the potential for an overexcited handler to disregard the needs of the animal, possibly to meet his or her agenda. Thus, handlers should be calm and controlled, with the animals' interest at the forefront (Ng, 2019).

The structure of the AAI must also be considered. Binfet (2017) found that students felt less stressed for a short time, even after a brief intervention (e.g., 20 minutes) with a dog. Although the impact of the intervention was not sustained two weeks later, students described feeling a connection to their college community (Binfet, 2017). Further, Ward Griffin et al. (2017) found that a single, drop-in group therapy session with dogs immediately impacted student wellness, although these results diminished over time. The authors concluded that AAI sessions could take place during stressful periods during the school year (e.g., exam week), or for the dogs to be present during the stressor, such as when taking the exam (Ward et al., 2017).

As the field of AAIs continues to grow, so do policies, procedures, and guidelines. Two leading organizations in the area of AAIs have developed guidelines for practice. The Animal Assisted Intervention International (AAII) "Standards of Practice" (2018) were developed to assist individuals, organizations, institutions, and providers who implement AAI programming. The International Association of Human-Animal Interactions Organizations (IAHAIO) also has recently updated their white paper on "Guidelines for Wellness of Animals Involved in AAI" (2018). Together, these standards set the minimum required for AAI programming and are essential reads for any AAI provider. As Ng (2019) stated, "when we have done everything in our power to safeguard animal welfare, a positive AAI can be mutually beneficial for both the human and the animal" (p. 82). A condensed summary of these standards is provided in table 2.1; note, this listing is not exhaustive. In essence, dogs should welcome and enjoy human-animal interactions, and not just tolerate interactions with strangers (IAHAIO, 2018; PetPartners, 2019). Further, handlers must recognize that dogs are not *tools* to be used, but living, sentient beings (IAHAIO, 2018).

CONCLUSION: ONE WELFARE

All living things are interconnected; when the welfare of one species is severely compromised, it has a ripple effect across the health of other species. The recent COVID-19 global health crisis, as well as other pandemics, clearly indicate that this is the case: human beings cannot exist by disregarding other living animals and the environment. This type of thinking has led to "one health, one welfare" perspectives. Although the concept of One Health has long been recognized globally, the term is relatively new with the Centers for Disease Control that opened an office dedicated to these concerns in 2009 (CDC, 2016). Even more recently, the One Welfare framework (2019) extends One Health, by focusing on the interrelationships between animal welfare, human well-being, and the environment (Pinillos et al., 2016). As succinctly described by Jordan and Lem (2014), "Where there are poor states of human welfare there commonly exist poor states of animal welfare" (p. 1203). In essence, the One Welfare framework helps us to improve human problems while concurrently improving animal and addressing environmental issues. As Serpell (2019) notes, "all of us are better off when we seek to attain a balanced, sustainable, and mutually beneficial coexistence with other species," and symbiotic relationships between different species may be the norm, rather than an exception (para. 1).

For example, Jordan and Lem (2014) examined the impact of volunteering with a community veterinary outreach program that provides free care to vulnerable pet owners (e.g., people who are homeless). Twenty early career veterinary students described gaining knowledge, acceptance, and understanding of marginalized individuals, and the intersection of the well-being of animals and these owners. Students also gained increased awareness about poverty and homelessness, in addition to experiencing the power of the human-animal bond (Jordan & Lem, 2014). This program is an example of One Welfare, leading to enhanced empathy and compassion for all. By addressing the human-animal bond, these students began to recognize their work reaches beyond the health of animals, and promotes the mental and physical health of humans.

To date, most research on AAI is one-sided, mainly examining the benefits to humans and not the other way around (Serpell, 2019). Even though the field of human-animal interactions is developing best practices and guidelines for protecting the animals involved, these initiatives may be lacking, as "we cannot expect such relationships to be mutually beneficial when the needs and interests of the animals are viewed as subordinate to those of the humans" (Serpell, 2019, para. 2). In regard to AAIs, we must go beyond preserving the safety of therapy dogs, as important as that is, to ensure that the dogs enjoy these planned interactions. Doing so should also increase the benefit to the recipient (Serpell, 2019).

On a broader level, AAI programs should use these human-canine interactions as a chance to increase knowledge, respect, and care for the natural world (Serpell, 2019). Going back to the idea of treasuring, trashing, or terrorizing a pet (Raupp, 1999), developing empathy for animals who cohabitate with humans may lead to kindness and compassion for other animals. According to Paul and Serpell (1993), childhood pet keeping leads to support for animal protection as adults; as the number of companion animals has increased, so too has the percentage of adults who support animal protection organizations. Nurturing animals also means advocating for what is generally important to them.

The One Welfare framework works well when conceptualizing the needs of college students, as it is sensible to look at reciprocal benefits for humans and animals. When applying a One Welfare model to a college campus, there are many such opportunities. Examples include course-based field trips to observe the interactions between animals, humans, and the environment (Mor et al., 2018). Or a canine study-buddy or dog-walking program could be set up between student support or outdoor recreation services and local animal shelters. If the university allows, selected students also may be able to foster cats and dogs on campus, which could help to increase socialization and confidence building for both the student and the animal. In regard to AAIs, handlers and program leaders could incorporate a social responsibility aspect to the program. For example, students could learn about the roles of animals in various jobs and occupations (Jalongo & McDevitt, 2015).

Table 2.1 Best Practices for AAIs in College Settings

DOGS	HANDLER	RECIPIENTS	ENVIRONMENT
Be well socialized with an interest in interacting with humans and willing participation in AAIs	Receive training and possess knowledge of human-animal interactions, general animal behavior, and species-specific interactions; complete continuing education	Be willing and accepting of animal interactions and relate to animal in a gentle and nonthreatening manner	Allow the dog to maintain as much natural behavior as possible (e.g., sleeping, playing, going outside, etc.); appropriate room temperature, lighting, flooring textures, etc.
Be humanely trained (e.g., positive reinforcement and force-free approaches) and show a willingness to learn	Be able to detect signs of discomfort and stress before, during, and after the visit; respond to these signs quickly and appropriately, including terminating the session	Give the dog a choice to interact with them or not, and respect this decision	Form expert committee to oversee planning and supervision of the staff, handlers, and dog, including orientation, ongoing evaluation, and record keeping
Be registered with a reputable organization to ensure specific criteria are met for therapy dog, including role-play scenarios, interest in therapy dog work, and relationship with handler	Ensure the animal is healthy, rested, comfortable, and supported before, during, and after the sessions	Be informed and consent to interact with dog	Maintain a clean environment, including equipment; avoid overwhelming the dogs with certain smells; prohibit food or food preparation nearby
Be at least one year of age to have some maturity and attain a level of training that provides some predictability in behavior	Respect boundaries by not forcing animals to participate in ways in which comfort and safety are put at risk; use loose lead or no lead if the dog will be safe within a confined environment and it is permitted	Be healthy and not have diseases that can be spread from client to client via the animal; handwash before and after visiting	Always provide access to water as well as protection from the elements and potential toxins

Be adaptable to different types of people and equipment and, if stressed, be capable of returning to a normal or calm baseline within a couple of minutes	Do not overwork dogs and keep session length and frequency within the dog's threshold (e.g., 30–45 minutes and no more than two hours per day with rest days in between); assess every session before, during, and after	Visit with dog individually or in small groups, positioning self at the same level as the dog	Provide easy access to the outdoors for urination and defecation
Must not only be considered good pets by the owner, but also good candidates for AAI work	Provide measures to prevent zoonosis, including regular veterinary exams, vaccinations, careful monitoring, diet, and proper hygiene; know dog first aid	Interact appropriately with dogs (e.g., no rough play or teasing)	Provide ongoing risk assessment, and ensure provisions and protocols are in place to increase safety and reduce risk of injury
Be clean, well-groomed, and under a proper health care plan as determined by a veterinarian	Advocate for policies and procedures to ensure care is provided for animals; report any incidents	Learn the dog's stress signals and work on getting animals to trust them under direction of handler	Screen recipients when possible, and provide informed consent
Show minimal signs of anxiety and no aggression toward AAI participants; aggression must not be outside normal canine communication if working with other dogs	Maintain control of the dog at all times, and be the dog's best advocate; be open to what the animal is communicating	Be calm and predictable (e.g., being in a prolonged intense emotional state can be stressful and harmful to the dog)	Allow dogs to be comfortable (e.g., do not dress up animals in human clothes or costumes, or ask them to perform tricks or tasks if the dog exhibits signs of stress)
Be prepared for the environment, population, and work they are doing within college settings	Show empathy and sensitivity to participants and other professionals	Be open to learning about the dog, animal welfare, and what can be done to help animals	Provide ample breaks depending on activity and developmental level, and ensure a clear safety zone for the dog

Adapted from AAII (2018); IAHAIO (2018); and Ng (2019)

Colleges and universities would do well to integrate some key concepts from the Institute for Humane Education (IHE) (2019). For example, a "solutionary" is a person who not only identifies problems, but also someone who then develops just, humane, and sustainable solutions for people, animals, and the environment, sometimes referred to as MOGO, which stands for "most good." MOGO addresses the most fundamental question in humane education, namely, how can we do the most good and the least harm to other people, animals, and the environment in our everyday actions (IHE, 2019)? In essence, college students must be able to acquire knowledge, think deeply, make compassionate and responsible choices, and focus on solutions. All of these concepts pertain when the decision is made to bring college students and dogs together, and when we educate students about their duty of care for our natural world (IHE, 2019).

REFERENCES

Adamle, K. N., Riley, T. A., & Carlson, T. (2009). Evaluating college student interest in pet therapy. *Journal of American College Health, 57*(5), 545–548.

Adams, A. C., Sharkin, B. S., & Bottinelli, J. J. (2017). The role of pets in the lives of college students: Implications for college counselors. *Journal of College Student Psychotherapy, 31*(4), 306–324. https://doi.org/10.1080/87568225.2017.1299601

Aiken, J. (2012, September 19). Meet Monty. *Lillian Goldman-Law Library.* https://library.law.yale.edu/news/meet-monty

American Veterinary Medical Association. (2019). *Human-animal bond.* https://www.avma.org/KB/Resources/Reference/human-animal-bond/Pages/Human-Animal-Bond-AVMA.aspx

Animal Assisted Intervention International. (2018). *Standards of practice.* https://aai-int.org/aai/standards-of-practice

Association of Professional Humane Educators. (2012). *Professional guidelines for humane educators.* https://www.aphe.org/Resources/Documents/APHE%20Professional%20Guidelines%20r evised%202012%20March.pdf

Baranko, J. (2011). Hear me roar: Should universities use live animals as mascots? *Marquette Sports Law Review, 21*(2), 599–619.

Beach, L. A. (2019, May 19). More colleges are adopting pet friendly policies. *USA Today.* https://www.usatoday.com/story/life/2019/05/19/animal-house/3705183002

Beck, A. M. (2013). The human-dog relationship: A tale of two species. In C. N. L. Macpherson, F. X. Meslin & A. I. Wandeler (Eds.), *Dogs, zoonoses and public health* (2nd ed.). Boston: CAB International.

Bedrossian, L. (2018). Emotional support animals on campus: Know the facts, review your policies. *Disability Compliance for Higher Education, 24*(1), 6. https://doi.org/10.1002/dhe.30485

Beerda, B., Schilder, M. B. H., van Hoof, J., de Vries, H. W., & Mol, J. A. (1998). Behavioral and hormonal indicators of enduring environmental stress in dogs. *Applied Animal Behavior Sciences, 58*(3–4), 365–381. https://doi.org/10.1016/S0168-1591(97)00145-7

Binfet, J. (2017). The effects of group-administered canine therapy on university students' wellbeing: A randomized controlled trial. *Anthrozoös, 30*(3), 397–414. https://doi.org/10.1080/08927936.2017.1335097

Binfet, J., & Passmore, H. A. (2016). Hounds and homesickness: The effects of an animal-assisted therapeutic intervention for first-year university students. *Anthrozoös, 29*(3), 441–454. https://doi.org/10.1080/08927936.2016.1181364

Binfet, J., Passmore, H. A., Cebry, A., Struik, K., & McKay, C. (2018). Reducing university students' stress through a drop-in canine-therapy program. *Journal of Mental Health, 27*(3), 197–204. https://doi.org/10.1080/09638237.2017.1417551

Binfet, J., & Struik, K. (2018). Dogs on campus: Holistic assessment of therapy dogs and handlers for research and community initiatives. *Society and Animals, 26*(1), 1–21. https://doi.org/10.1163/15685306-12341495

Bir, C., Croney, C. C., & Widmar, N. J. O. (2019). US residents' perceptions of dog welfare needs and canine welfare information sources. *Journal of Applied Animal Welfare Science, 22*(1), 42–68, https://doi.org/10.1080/10888705.2018.1476862

Boissy, A., Manteuffel, G., Jensen, M. B., Moe, R. O., Spruijt, B., Keeling, L. J., . . . Aubert, A. (2007). Assessment of positive emotions in animals to improve their welfare. *Physiology & Behavior, 92*(3), 375–397.

Bonfiglio, R. A. (2016). Anticipating the future of mental health needs on campus. *New Directions for Student Services, 2016*(156), 97–104. https://doi.org/10.1002/ss.20195

Boyle, S. F., Corrigan, V. K., Buechner-Maxwell, V., & Pierce, B. J. (2019). Evaluation of risk of zoonotic pathogen transmission in a university-based animal assisted intervention (AAI) program. *Frontiers in Veterinary Science, 6*, 167. https://doi.org/10.3389/fveta.2019.00167

Brambell, F. W. R. (1965). *Report of the technical committee to enquire into the welfare of animals kept under intensive livestock husbandry systems.* Cmnd 2836, London: HMSO.

Campbell, E. J. (2016). Owners' abilities to recognise and comprehend signs of displays of aggression in their canine companions outwith the home environment. *Veterinary Nursing Journal, 31*(11), 329–333. https://doi.org/10.1080/17415349.2016.1224693

Centers for Disease Control. (2016). *One Health basics.* https://www.cdc.gov/onehealth/basics/history/index.html

Chanen, J. S. (2011). Going to the dogs: New addition to Yale's law library—therapy dog Monty. *ABA Journal, 97*(8), 14.

Clothier, S. (2007). *C.A.R.A.T. (Clothier Animal Response Assessment Tool): "Looking for the gem in every individual."* https://suzanneclothier.com/intro-to-carat

Crossman, M. K., & Kazdin, A. E. (2015). Animal visitation programs in colleges and universities: An efficient model for reducing student stress. In A. H. Fine (Ed.), *Handbook on animal-assisted therapy: Foundations and guidelines for animal-assisted interventions* (pp. 333–337). New York: Elsevier.

Daltry, R. M., & Mehr, K. E. (2015). Therapy dogs on campus: Recommendations for counseling center outreach. *Journal of College Student Psychotherapy, 29*(1), 72–78. https://doi.org/10.1080/87568225.2015.976100

Davis, R. (2018, May). A 4-legged approach to clinical education and research. *The ASHA Leader, 23*(5). 32–33.

Dell, C., Chalmers, D., Gillett, J., Rohr, B., Nickel, C., Campbell, L., . . . Brydges, M. (2015). PAWSing student stress: A pilot evaluation study of the St. John Ambulance Therapy Dog Program on three university campuses in Canada. *Canadian Journal of Counselling and Psychotherapy, 49*(4), 332–359.

Ending Animal Use in Medical Education. (2015, Spring). *Good Medicine, 24*(2), 9–13.

Epstein, R. A. (2002, December). Animals as objects, or subjects, of rights. *U Chicago Law & Economics, Olin Working Paper No. 171.* http://dx.doi.org/10.2139/ssrn.359240

Fine, A. H. (2014). *Our faithful companions: Exploring the essence of our kinship with animals.* Crawford, CO: Alpine Publications.

Foreman, A. M., Allison, P., Poland, M., Meade, B. J., & Wirth, O. (2019). Employee attitude about the impact of visitation dogs on a college campus. *Anthrozoös, 32*(1), 35–50. https://doi.org/10.1080/08927936.2019.1550280

Foreman, A. M., Glenn, M. K., Meade, B. J., & Wirth, O. (2017). Dogs in the workplace: A review of the benefits and potential challenges. *International Journal of Environmental Research and Public Health, 14*(5), 498–529. https://doi.org/10.3390/ijerph14050498

Fox, R., & Gee, N. R. (2016). Changing conceptions of care: Humanization of the companion animal–human relationship. *Society & Animals, 24*(2), 107–128. https://doi.org/10.1163/15685306-12341397

Glenk, L. (2017). Current perspectives on therapy dog welfare in animal-assisted interventions. *Animals, 7*(2), 7. https://doi.org/10.3390/ani7020007

Glenk, L. M., Kothgassner, O. D., Stetina, B. U., Palme, R., Kepplinger, B., & Baran, H. (2013). Therapy dogs' salivary cortisol levels vary during animal-assisted interventions. *Universities Federation for Animal Welfare, 22*(3), 369–378. https://doi.org/10.7120109627286.22.2.369

Haggerty, J. M., & Mueller, M. K. (2017). Animal-assisted stress reduction programs in higher education. *Innovative Higher Education, 42*(5–6), 379–389. https://doi.org/10.1007/s10755-017-9392-0

Haubenhofer, D. K., & Kirchengast, S. (2007). Dog handlers' and dogs' emotional and cortisol 6 secretion responses associated with animal-assisted therapy sessions. *Society and Animals, 15*(2), 127–150. https://doi.org/10.1163/156853007X187090

Hediger, K., Meisser, A., & Zinsstag, J. (2019). A One Health research framework for animal assisted interventions. *International Journal of Environmental Research and Public Health, 16*(4), 640. https://doi.org/10.3390/ijerph16040640

Hoover, E. (2003, September 12). Animal cruelty 101. *Chronicle of Higher Education.* https://www.chronicle.com/article/Animal-Cruelty-101/14206

Howie, A. (2019, April). *Respecting the individual animal while choosing therapy animals with the greatest potential for therapeutic benefit.* Paper presented at the International Association of Human-Animal Interactions Organizations Conference, Brewster, NY.

Huss, R. J. (2012). Canines on campus: Companion animals at postsecondary educational institutions. *Valparaiso University School of Law, 44*(2), 416–479.

Iannuzzi, D. A., & Rowan, A. N. (1991). Ethical issues in animal-assisted therapy programs. *Anthrozoös, 4*(3), 154–163. https://doi.org/10.2752/089279391787057116

Institute for Humane Education. (2019). *Who we are.* https://humaneeducation.org/who-we-are

International Association of Human Animal Interaction Organizations (IAHAIO). (2018). The IAHAIO definitions for animal assisted intervention and guidelines for wellness of animals involved in AAI. http://iahaio.org/wp/wp-content/uploads/2018/04/iahaio_wp_updated-2018-final.pdf

Jalongo, M. R. (2008). Beyond a pets theme: Teaching young children to interact safely with dogs. *Early Childhood Education Journal, 36*(1), 39–45. https://doi.org/10.1007/s10643-008

Jalongo, M. R. (2015). An attachment perspective on the child-dog bond: Interdisciplinary and international research findings. *Early Childhood Education Journal, 43*(5), 395–405. https://doi.org/10.1007/x10643-015-068-4

Jalongo, M. R. (Ed.). (2019). *Prison dog programs: Rehabilitation and renewal in correctional facilities*. New York: Springer.

Jalongo, M. R., & McDevitt, T. (2015). Therapy dogs in academic libraries: A way to foster student engagement and mitigate self-reported stress during finals. *Public Services Quarterly, 11*(4), 254–269. https://doi.org/10.1080/15228959.2015.1084904

Jalongo, M. R., & Ross, M. (2018). Building behaviorally healthy relationships between children and dogs. In M. R. Jalongo (Ed.), *Children, dogs and education: Caring for, learning alongside, and gaining support from canine companionship* (pp. 43–69). New York: Springer Nature.

Johnson, A., & Bruneau, L. (2019). Caring for and about dogs: Animal welfare considerations. In M. R. Jalongo (Ed.), *Prison dog programs: Rehabilitation and renewal in correctional facilities* (pp. 79–97). New York: Springer Nature.

Jordan, T., & Lem, M. (2014). One Health, One Welfare: Education in practice veterinary students' experiences with community veterinary outreach. *The Canadian Veterinary Journal, 55*(12), 1203–1206.

Kellert, S. R. (1997). *The value of life: Biological diversity and human society*. Washington, DC: Island Press.

Kronholz, J. F., Freeman, V. F., & Mackintosh, R. C. (2015). Animal-assisted therapy: Best practices for college counseling. *Ideas and research you can use: VISTAS 2015*. https://www.counseling.org/docs/default-source/vistas/article_7525cd23f16116603abcacff0000bee5e7.pdf?sfvrsn=bbdb432c_8

Levinson, B. (1969). *Pet-oriented child psychotherapy*. Springfield, IL: Charles C. Thomas, Bannerstone House.

Maharaj, N., Kazanjian, A., & Haney, C. J. (2016). The human–canine bond: A sacred relationship. *Journal of Spirituality in Mental Health, 18*(1), 76–89. https://doi.org/10.1080/19349637.2015.1047922

Marinelli, L., Normando, S., Siliprandi, C., Salvadoretti, M., & Mongillo, P. (2009). Dog assisted interventions in a specialized centre and potential concerns for animal welfare. *Veterinary Research Communications, 33*(1), 93–95. https://doi.org/10.1007/s11259-44 009-9256-x

Martin, F., McGowan, R., Anderson, R., Wang, L., Turpin, T. Smidt, J., ... Mohabbat, A. (2019). *Emotional welfare state of therapy dogs during animal assisted therapy in an outpatient setting*. Paper presented at the International Association of Human-Animal Interactions Organizations conference, Brewster, NY.

Masinter, M. R. (2016). Update policies for student requests for handling emotional support assistance animals in residence halls. *Student Affairs Today, 19*(9), 6. https://doi.org/10.1002/say

McConnell, P., & Fine, A. H. (2015). Understanding the other end of the leash: What therapists need to understand about their co-therapists. In A. H. Fine (Ed.), *Handbook on animal-assisted therapy: Foundations and guidelines for animal-assisted interventions* (4th ed., pp. 103–113). Waltham, MA: Academic Press.

McCullough, A., Jenkins, M., Ruehrdanz, A., Gilmer, M. J., Olson, J., Pawar, A., ... O'Haire, M. (2018). Physiological and behavioral effects of animal-assisted interventions for therapy dogs in pediatric oncology settings. *Applied Animal Behavior, 200*, 86–95. https://doi.org/10.1016/j.applanim.2017.11.014

McDonald, S., McDonald, E., & Roberts, A. (2017). Effects of novel dog exposure on college students' stress prior to examination. *North American Journal of Psychology, 19*(2), 477–484.

McGowan, R. T. S., Bolte, C., Barnett, H. R., Perez-Camargo, G., Martin, F. (2018). Can you spare 15 min? The measurable positive impact of a 15-min petting session on shelter dog well-being. *Applied Animal Behaviour Science, 203*, 42–54. https://doi.org/10.1016/j.applanim.2018.02.011

Meints, K., Brelsford, V., Gee, N. R., & Fine, A. H. (2017). Animals in education settings: Safety for all. In N. R. Gee, A. H. Fine, & P. McCardle (Eds.), *How animals help students learn* (pp. 34–48). New York: Routledge.

Mellor, D. (2016). Updating animal welfare thinking: Moving beyond the "Five Freedoms" towards "a Life Worth Living." *Animals, 6*(3), 21. https://doi.org/10.3390/ani603002

Meltzer, N. W., Bobilya, A. J., & Faircloth, B. (2013). *Effects of participation in a semester boarding school on students' biophilic expressions.* Paper presented at the International Society for Anthrozoology conference, Chicago, IL.

Mor, S. M., Norris, J. M., Bosward, K. L., Toribio, J. A. L., Ward, M. P., Gongora, J., ... Zaki, S. (2018). One health in our backyard: Design and evaluation of an experiential learning experience for veterinary medical students. *One Health, 5*, 57–64. https://doi.org/10.1016/j.onehlt.2018.05.001

Ng, Z. (2019). Advocacy and rethinking our relationships with animals: Ethical responsibilities and competencies in animal-assisted intervention. In P. Tedeschi & M. A. Jenkins (Eds.), *Transforming trauma: Resilience and healing through our connection with animals* (pp. 55–90). West Lafayette, IN: Purdue University Press.

Ng, Z., Albright, J., Fine, A. H., & Peralta, J. (2015). Our ethical and moral responsibility: Ensuring the welfare of therapy animals. In A. H. Fine (Ed.), *Handbook on animal-assisted therapy: Foundations and guidelines for animal-assisted interventions* (4th ed., pp. 357–376). Waltham, MA: Academic Press.

Ng, Z., Pierce, B. J., Otto, C. M., Buechner-Maxwell, V. A., Siracusa, C., & Werre, S. R. (2014). The effect of dog-human interaction on cortisol and behavior in registered animal-assisted activity dogs. *Applied Animal Behaviour Science, 159*, 69–81. https://doi.org/10.1016/j.applanim.2014.07.009

O'Brien, K. (2016). Puppy living on UCF campus to graduate soon. *Orlando Sentinel.* https://www.orlandosentinel.com/features/os-puppy-living-on-ucf-campus-to-graduate-soon-20160923-story.html

Ohl, F., & van der Staay, F. J. (2012). Animal welfare: At the interface between science and society. *The Veterinary Journal, 192*(1), 13–19. https://doi.org/10.1016/j.tvjl.2011.05.019

One Welfare. (2019). *About One Welfare.* https://www.onewelfareworld.org/about.html

Paul, E. S., & Serpell, J. (1993). Childhood pet keeping and humane attitudes in young adulthood. *Animal Welfare, 2*, 321–337.

PetPartners. (2019). *Criteria for prospective therapy animals.* https://petpartners.org/volunteer/become-a-handler/program-requirements

Pinillos, R. G., Appleby, M. C., Manteca, X., Scott-Park, F., Smith, C., & Velarde, A. (2016). One welfare–a platform for improving human and animal welfare. *Veterinary Record, 179*(16), 412–413.

Polgár, Z., Blackwell, E. J., & Rooney, N. J. (2019). Assessing the welfare of kennelled dogs: A review of animal-based measures. *Applied Animal Behaviour Science, 213*, 1–13. https://doi.org/10.1016/j.applanim.2019.02.013

Powers, K. R. (2013). Dogs in dorms: How the United States v. University of Nebraska at Kearney illustrates a coverage gap created by the intersection of fair housing and disability law. *Creighton Law Review, 47*, 363–388.

Raupp, C. D. (1999). Treasuring, trashing or terrorizing: Adult outcomes of childhood socialization about companion animals. *Society and Animals 7*(2), 141–159. https://doi.org/10.1163/156853099X00040.aw

Rooney, N., & Bradshaw, K. (2014). Canine welfare science: An antidote to sentiment and myth. In A. Horowitz (Ed.), *Domestic dog cognition and behavior* (pp. 241–274). Berlin: Springer-Verlag.

Schöberl, I., Wedl, M., Beetz, A., & Kotrschal, K. (2017). Psychobiological factors affecting cortisol variability in human-dog dyads. *PLoS ONE 12*(2), 1–18. https://doi.org/10.1071/journal.pone.017070

Serpell, J. (2019). One Welfare: Healthy environments for human and nonhuman animals. In *International Association of Human-Animal Interaction Organizations (Conference Handbook)*, IAHAIO, Brewster, NY, pp. 14–15.

Serpell, J. A., Coppinger, R., Fine, A. H., & Peralta, J. M. (2010). Welfare considerations in therapy and assistance animals. In A.H. Fine (Ed.), *Handbook on animal-assisted therapy: Theoretical foundations and guidelines for practice* (3rd ed., pp. 85–107). San Diego, CA: Elsevier.

Service-Dog Training and Education Program at University of Central Florida. (2019). *University of Central Florida.* https://knightconnect.campuslabs.com/engage/organization/stepucf

Shephard, K. (2009). The canine ladder of aggression. In D. Horwitz & D. S. Mills (Eds.), *BSAVA manual of canine and feline behavioural medicine* (2nd ed., pp. 13–16). Gloucestershire, UK: British Small Animal Veterinary Association.

Shorb, T. L., & Schnoeker-Shorb, Y. A. (2010). *The Kellert-Shrob Biophilic Values Indicator: A workbook.* Prescot, AZ: Native West Press.

Smith, S. L. (1983). Interactions between pet dogs and family members: An ethological study. In Katcher and A. Beck (Eds.), *New perspectives on our lives with companion animals* (pp. 29–36). Philadelphia, PA: University of Pennsylvania Press.

Southeastern Louisiana University. (n.d.). Communication sciences and disorders using animal assisted therapy. http://www.southeastern.edu/news_media/homepage/stories/csd.html

Tannenbaum, J. (1989). *Veterinary ethics.* Philadelphia, PA: Williams & Wilkins.

United States of America v. Kent State University Board of Trustees; Jill Church; Elizabeth Joseph; Brian Hellwig; Amy Quillin. 53 U.S. (2016).

United States of America v. University of Nebraska at Kearney and Board of Regents of the University of Nebraska. 288 U.S. (2015).

Taylor, J. S. (2016, July). Colleges see an uptick in requests for emotional support animals on campus. *ABA Journal, 7.* http://www.abajournal.com/magazine/article/colleges_see_an_uptick_in_requests_for_e motional_support_animals_on_campus

Vitztum, C., & Urbanik, J. (2016). Assessing the dog: Theoretical analysis of the companion animal's actions in the human-animal interactions. *Society and Animals, 24*(2), 172–185. https://doi.org/10.1163/15685306-12341399

Ward Griffin, E., Klaiber, P., Collins, H. K., Owens, R. L., Coren, S., & Chen, F. S. (2017). Petting away pre-exam stress: The effect of therapy dog sessions on student well-being. *Stress and Health, 34*(3), 468–473. https://doi.org/10.1002/smi.2804.

Weinberg, C. (2014, June 27). Loaner puppies: The latest elite college perk. *Bloomberg.* https://www.bloomberg.com/news/articles/2014-06-26/loaner-puppies-the-latest-elite-college-perk

Wells, M., & Perrine, R. (2001). Pets go to college: The influence of pets on students' perceptions of faculty and their offices. *Anthrozoös, 14*(3), 161–168. https://doi.org/10.2752/089279301786999472

Wilkin, C. L., Fairlie, P., & Ezzedeen, S. R. (2016). Who let the dogs in? A look at pet-friendly workplaces. *International Journal of Workplace Management, 9*(1), 96–109. https://doi.org/10.1108/IJWHM-04-2015-0021

Williams, T. (2011, March 21). *For law students with everything: Dog therapy for stress*. http://www.nytimes.com/2011/03/22/education/22dog.html?_r=0

Wilson, E. O. (1984). *Biophilia*. Cambridge, MA: Harvard University Press.

Yeates, J. W., & Main, D. C. (2008). Assessment of positive welfare: A review. *The Veterinary Journal, 175*(3), 293–300. https://doi.org/10.1016/j.tvjl.2007.05.009

Yong, M. H., & Ruffman, T. (2014). Emotional contagion: Dogs and humans show a similar physiological response to human infant crying. *Behavioural Processes, 108*, 155–165. https://doi.org/10.1016/j.beproc.2014.10.006

Younggren, J. N. (2019). *Role conflicts and emotional support animal certifications* [PowerPoint slides]. https://ce.nationalregister.org/wp-content/uploads/2019/04/Emotional-Support-Animal-National-Register-Slides.pdf

Zamir, T. (2006). The moral basis of animal-assisted therapy. *Society and Animals, 14*(2), 179–199. https://doi.org/10.1163/156853006776778770

PART TWO

Types of Dogs

PART TWO

3

SERVICE DOGS

Performing Helpful Tasks for People With Disabilities

MARY RENCK JALONGO, EDITOR, SPRINGER NATURE, INDIANA, PA

INTRODUCTION

In the Pennsylvania Department of Corrections, there are 24 prisons that offer the opportunity for carefully selected inmates to become dog trainers. Some of these programs work with animal welfare nonprofits while others work with service dog providers. Karley, a teenager who was the recipient of a service dog, wrote a thank you letter to her dogs' trainers that captures the many contributions of these animals:

> Independence is such a powerful word, one that is often taken for granted. Being a teenager, like other teenagers, I want as much independence as I can possibly get. But in April 2012 I was given a diagnosis that took my independence away from me, or so I thought. I suddenly went from running with my track team and playing basketball to having to use crutches and a wheelchair to get around.

Karley's life changed the day she got the call that she would be getting a service dog named Kaiser. Their story together had just begun. She wrote:

> With Kaiser by my side to support my walking and to help me conserve my energy, I began to slowly get back aspects of my independence that I thought were gone for good!
>
> I am now able to go out in public without needing anyone but Kaiser by my side. He picks up whatever I drop, opens the heavy doors that I can't, and

The college community helps to socialize a service dog in training during a campus visit. If he sat politely first, students could pet him. Photo Credit: Mary Renck Jalongo

helps me up the stairs I thought I would never be able to walk up again. . . . I can drive.

Kaiser is my best friend and he is the best thing that has ever happened to me. I can't imagine living my life without him. My service dog has brought me the ability to be completely independent. Kaiser is my gift that keeps on giving! (Karley & Kaiser, 2015, p. 18)

As this vignette illustrates, bringing a service dog into the life of a person with a disability can exert a powerful, positive influence on that person's willingness to meet new challenges, participate more fully in society, and achieve greater independence (McIver, Hall, & Mills, 2020). Service dogs of various types are seen at more postsecondary institutions than ever before. In the past, it was mainly guide dogs for the blind or visually impaired. Gradually, service dogs for people with mobility issues became more accepted. Today, service dogs that perform a wide array of tasks—for instance, emotional support for a military veteran with post-traumatic stress disorder (PTSD) or the diabetes alert dog of an incoming freshman—are a more common sight. In a few cases, college students have become involved as puppy raisers by collaborating with a service dog provider. As more and different types of service dogs become part of campus culture, modifications must be made to postsecondary institutions, not only to the policies that guide practice, but also to the physical environment. If a residential student arrives with a service dog, for example, it requires housing accommodations indoors and outside. The theoretical base for this chapter is inclusion—the concept that everyone needs to belong to a group, to be welcomed by others, and to have their unique contributions recognized and valued. College students with both visible disabilities (e.g., mobility issues) and invisible disabilities (e.g., traumatic brain injury) are at even greater risk of being excluded and experiencing social isolation. There is a growing body of research to suggest, however, that other people are much more likely to interact with individuals with disabilities of various types when they are accompanied by a service dog (Hart, Hart, & Bergin, 1987; McNicholas & Collis, 2000). Thus, service dogs not only perform helpful tasks for their human partners, but also tend to increase positive social interactions between their owners/handlers and other people. The second part of the chapter examines what postsecondary institutions have done to bring service dogs on campus in various capacities. Chapter 3 concludes with recommendations about policies and practices that integrate service dogs into the landscape of postsecondary institutions.

DEFINITION OF A *SERVICE DOG*

One of the things that makes dogs a companion of choice for so many people is that, taken as a group, canines are attuned to human emotions and accurately interpret human behavior better than any other species on the planet (Derr, 2011; Miklosi, 2016; 2018). For centuries, dogs have helped human beings by hunting, herding, guarding property, and accompanying soldiers during wartime.

In what appears to be one of the earliest recorded service dog type of activity, an engraving produced in the first century AD depicts a blind man being led by his dog (International Guide Dog Federation, 2019b). Informal pairings of blind people with dogs who helped them to navigate their environments have an exceptionally long history. Informal human/dog pairings such as this no doubt continued, but it was not until the 20th century that systematic training of dogs to support people with various types of disabilities occurred. Service dogs in the United States were first defined in legal terms through the Americans with Disabilities Act of 1990.

Interest in acquiring service dogs to assist people with various physical and psychological issues has increased dramatically in recent years. Perhaps the simplest way to define a service dog is to first show what it is not. Suppose that a college freshman wants to bring along the family's dog and obtain permission for the dog "to go everywhere" on campus. This request would be denied for several reasons. The main reason would be that the dog is neither specially selected and trained, nor is it performing essential tasks for an individual with a disability. Some of the differences between a typical pet dog and a service dog are:

- The dog is well-mannered and does not jeopardize the safety of others
- The dog is carefully selected and extensively trained
- The dog's human partner has a professionally diagnosed disability
- The dog provides an important service/function related to the disability
- The level and purpose of the dog's training is documented
- Some dogs may wear identifying gear (e.g., a vest)
- The dog and the student have been trained to work together

Stated concisely, a service dog is an animal that has been individually trained to assist an individual with a physical or mental disability (Vincent et al., 2015). The latest version of the Americans with Disabilities Act (ADA) Title III Regulations in the United States (2011) defines a service dog as:

> any dog that is individually trained to do work or perform tasks for the benefit of an individual with a disability, including a physical, sensory, psychiatric, intellectual, or other mental disability. . . . The work or tasks performed by a service animal must be directly related to the individual's disability. Examples of work or tasks include, but are not limited to, assisting individuals who are blind or have low vision with navigation or other tasks, alerting individuals who are deaf or hard of hearing to the presence of people or sounds, providing nonviolent protection or rescue work, pulling a wheelchair, assisting an

individual during a seizure, alerting individuals to the presence of allergens, retrieving items such as medicine or the telephone, providing physical support and stability to individuals with mobility disabilities, and helping persons with neurological and psychiatric disabilities by preventing or interrupting impulsive or destructive behaviors.

A good example of the progress made in public acceptance of service dogs comes from the US military. In the recent past, dogs trained to assist retired military personnel with physical mobility issues were gradually recognized as providing a unique form of support for those with physical, "visible" injuries and conditions. Respect for dogs that provide psychological support for "invisible" wounds has taken much longer. Impressed by the success stories and emerging research involving wounded warriors and their dogs, the Veterans Health Administration has changed its stance on service dogs for psychological conditions. Recently, the argument has been made that psychological trauma does affect mobility, because military personnel who have suffered this frequently are afraid to leave their homes. According to current policy (Veterans Health Administration, 2019), veterans with "chronic mobility issues associated with a mental health disorder" are eligible for a veterinary medical benefit if their dog was trained by an accredited service dog provider. This benefit for the service dogs of veterans includes veterinary office visits, an annual dental procedure, vaccinations, and equipment (e.g., a harness for a guide dog for the blind).

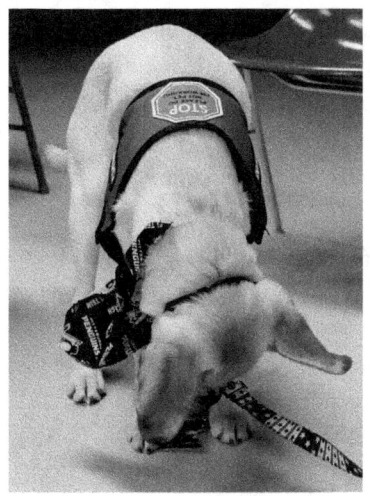

Picking up a dropped credit card is a task that a service dog can perform for a person with a disability. Photo Credit: Mary Renck Jalongo

A service dog is trained to perform helpful tasks directly related to the individual's professionally diagnosed disability. One route to official recognition for a service dog is to have the dog successfully complete the Public Access Certification Test. Service dogs are distinguished from pets and comfort animals because they are individually trained to work with a specific individual with a disability who cannot perform the task or accomplish the work independently.

Only service dogs have public access rights. Public access means the right to come into public buildings (e.g., schools, libraries), businesses that would otherwise not permit dogs (e.g., restaurants, offices), and transportation (e.g., bus, airplane). These rights are guaranteed by the Americans with Disabilities Act (ADA). Even service dogs in training are covered by the law if the trainer is engaged in the actual training process and activities of service dogs (Huss, 2012). Unfortunately, some unscrupulous people are falsely representing their untrained dogs as service dogs just so they can take the dog along with them. As table 3.1 suggests, there now are many different types of service dogs.

Service dogs frequently have extensive training, often being required to learn more than 60 different commands. Most service dog providers are nonprofit and rely on donations and grants to survive; therefore, they strive to be as cost-effective as possible. To increase chances of success, many prominent service dog providers have their own dog breeding programs. It is also possible to identify suitable shelter dogs with potential as service dogs (Batt, Batt, Baguley, & McGreevy, 2008); however, if there is no medical history (as with a stray dog), that may make it more difficult to predict if the dog will be physically sound (Weiss, 2002; Weiss & Greenberg, 1997). Of course, it depends on the type of service that the dog would be trained to do; the criteria for a dog to help a person who is legally blind, has PTSD, or someone who has become deaf would differ accordingly. To illustrate, those who train service dogs for people with mobility issues often assess a puppy's overall temperament (Volhard & Volhard, 2007) and have a special interest in puppies' tendency to pursue an object because service dogs of this type perform many retrieval tasks. The downside here is that puppies' behavior may not be all that consistent with their temperaments as adults (Robinson, Skiver Thompson, & Ha, 2016). In addition, the interrater reliabilities of these assessments can be relatively low (Riemer, Muller, Viranyi, Huber, & Range, 2014). Nevertheless, there are some behaviors in prospective service dogs that are reasonably reliable predictors of success (Harvey et al., 2016). In a very promising line of research, a team of neuroscientists (and dog trainers) first taught dogs to keep still during functional magnetic resonance imaging (fMRI) and designed sound-canceling earphones so that the loud noises made by the machine would not distress the dogs (Berns, 2013). After that, they began to study how dogs' brains reacted to rewards (Montague & Berns, 2002). More recently, they studied which service dog candidates were most responsive to hand signals given by different people (measured by activity in the caudate region of the brain), yet did not display excessive arousal (as measured by activity in the amygdala) (Berns,

Brooks, Spivak, & Levy, 2017). Longitudinal research will be necessary to determine which characteristics of dogs tested effectively predict their success as service dogs.

Another consideration in preparing service dogs is designing training methods that are based on scientific evidence (Bender & Strong, 2019). Neuroscientific study of dogs has led to many important insights about how they process information. For example, dogs appear to have regions of the brain that analyze the emotions in human voices (Andics, Gacsi, Farago, Kis, & Miklosi, 2014), and they are capable of studying human faces (Cuaya, Hernández-Pérez, & Concha, 2016). Findings such as these tend to support positive, reward-based approaches and the ethical standards of respected dog training groups (Certification Council for Professional Dog Trainers, 2017). There is little doubt that, although training a particular dog at a high level has many important general guiding principles, the individual characteristics of the dog need to be taken into consideration. It also takes a very skilled, perceptive, and compassionate trainer to avoid pushing the dog too hard, to decide when to nudge the dog forward in training, and to discontinue a training session out of consideration for the animal's welfare.

With the right combination of dog selection and appropriate training, dogs can perform many different tasks that enable college students to be more independent. Assistance Dogs International (2016) notes that service dogs work with individuals who need a medical alert or response; have difficulties with major life activities, including social skills, communication, attention, and learning; experience movement or mobility issues; and/or demonstrate anxiety or undesirable behaviors. Many people are familiar with dogs that guide visually impaired individuals or assist people with mobility issues by retrieving dropped items, opening doors, or turning light switches off and on (Crowe et al., 2014). Other physical tasks that service dogs frequently are taught to perform include serving as a brace when a person is getting up, sitting down, walking, or using stairs; assisting with transfer from bed to wheelchair or wheelchair to car; and transporting items, such as school supplies or books. Dogs can assist with self-help skills—for example, pulling off socks, bringing shoes, pulling up the blankets, or assisting balance and support when getting in and out of the bathroom. Service dogs frequently are trained to perform tasks that enable a person with a disability to be responsible for the dog's care, such as retrieving a leash, stepping into their service dog vest, and standing still to be brushed. Advances in technology have expanded the service dog's repertoire even further; for example, some dogs have been trained to operate a big button switch that summons emergency help (Byrne, Zeagler, Freil, Rapoport, & Jackson, 2018).

Historically, the progression of service dogs can be arranged as follows.

Table 3.1 Service Dogs' Roles in Supporting College Students

COLLEGE STUDENT'S CONDITION	DOG'S ROLE	DOG CHARACTERISTICS	ADVANTAGES
Physical mobility issues	Perform physical tasks (e.g., opening doors, retrieving dropped objects), provide balance and stability when walking, climbing stairs, or moving from bed to chair, etc.	Large, gentle, eager-to-please dogs with strength, stamina, and trainability (e.g., Labrador or golden retrievers)	Provide greater independence; build confidence about venturing outside; prevent falls; decrease dependence on others during everyday activities
Visually impaired or blind	Guide the person safely through various environments	Large dogs with the intelligence and training to disobey a command if the person is in danger. German shepherds and retrievers often are preferred	Enable the student to navigate unfamiliar places; avoid obstacles at ground level and at the head height of the person; increase independence and safety
Hearing impaired or deaf	Alert to specific sounds in the environment and lead person to the sound, if appropriate (e.g., when the person's name is called)	Small, frisky dogs to race back to get the person's attention are sometimes chosen; shelter dogs often are chosen for this role	Bring important sounds—telephone, smoke alarm, doorbell, siren, water left running—to the attention of the individual with hearing-impairment
Seizures (e.g., epilepsy, diabetic)	Seizure alert (anticipate oncoming seizures) and/or seizure response (assist after a seizure occurs). Remain at the person's side or summon help	Dogs exceptionally responsive to changes in a person's scent/behavior; seizure alerting often is—at least at first—spontaneous, so various breeds are used	Prevents falls and injuries, increases the human partner's confidence about going out in public

Trauma victim response	Alert to indicators of anxiety in the individual and provide a calming presence	Dogs of various breeds and mixed breeds attuned to a person's emotional state	Watch over the person; interrupt a behavior before it spins out of control (e.g., awaken the person during a night terror); provide a comforting presence and tactile stimulation (i.e., petting the dog); check home or other area for safety before entering; make a boundary/buffer between student and the source of anxiety
Severe allergies	Alert to the presence of the item that will cause anaphylactic shock in the student such as peanuts or milk products; block the person from contact with the substance	Dogs of various breeds	Recognize the allergen's presence when the person does not; retrieve medication (e.g., a pouch with an inhaler); go and get help or use a medical alert device
Autism spectrum disorder	Trained to provide emotional support to a person on the autism spectrum	Dogs of various breeds, often Labrador or golden retrievers	Offer a calming presence in stressful situations, particularly those involving social interaction

Sources: Burrows, Adams, & Spiers, 2008; Davis, Nattrass, O'Brien, Patronek, & MacCollin, 2015; Hardin, Anderson, & Cattet, 2015; Hart & Yamamoto, 2015; Jalongo, 2018; Rintala, Matamoros, & Seitz, 2008; Rooney, Morant, & Guest, 2013; Vincent et al., 2015

GUIDE DOGS FOR THE BLIND.
In 1927, Morris Frank was a 19-year-old from Nashville, Tennessee, who had lost his vision in two different accidents. His father read him an article in the *Saturday Evening Post* about the work of Dorothy Eustis, a professional trainer of German shepherd dogs prepared as working dogs for the military or law enforcement. While working with veterans, she had trained "seeing eye dogs" for wounded warriors who became blind. Frank wrote to her and they began a collaborative effort to open the first US seeing eye dog training facility in Morristown, New Jersey. In a brilliant public relations move, Frank announced to the media that he would be traveling to New York City and, although completely blind, he would be crossing a street down near the wharf that was notorious for being busy and dangerous by relying completely on his service dog. With an entourage of reporters and photographers in tow, Frank's service dog—a German shepherd he named Buddy—led him safely across and created a media sensation. Afterward, he sent a one-word telegram to Eustis: "SUCCESS!" Morris Frank devoted his life to educating others about the many ways that a guide dog could increase the independence of a person without sight. At first, there were many skeptics, but by 1956, every state in the United States had passed laws allowing blind people with guide dogs access to public spaces. The work of that Eustis and Frank started has continued to expand and thrive up to the present day. Referred to variously as "guide dogs," "leader dogs," and "seeing eye dogs," these canines continue to be the most widely recognized exception to rules governing the presence of dogs in public spaces. Formed in 1989, the International Guide Dog Federation (2019a) reported that 98 organizations across 32 different countries had joined the group that focuses on guide dogs for the blind by 2019. Yet preparing guide dogs for the blind is one of the most demanding forms of service dog training because the person's life may depend on the dog's behavior. The dog has to be exceptionally dependable and obedient, yet, at the same time, sufficiently confident to override a command and intelligently disobey if it would put the person in danger. A survey of administrators of guide dog programs found that approximately 300 out of every carefully selected 1,000 dogs failed to become successful leader dogs for the blind (Serpell & Hsu, 2001). This relatively low success rate and lengthy training process (often three years) mean that the demand for these dogs exceeds the supply, and that a legally blind person seeking a guide dog frequently is waitlisted for more than a year.

MOBILITY ASSISTANCE AND HEARING ASSISTANCE DOGS.
Commencing around the 1960s, formal training of service dogs capable of supporting individuals with conditions that limited their physical mobility (e.g., cerebral palsy, paralysis, traumatic injuries, balance issues) began to emerge. Dogs were trained to perform tasks that would mitigate mobility issues, such as retrieving dropped objects, turning the lights on/off, opening doors, helping to pull a wheelchair, and so forth. It would take another 30 years before the roles of these service dogs were defined and recognized by law through Dr. Bonita Bergin's research that formed the foundation for the Americans with Disabilities Act of 1990 (Platpets, 2015). Service dogs for people with visual impairments or severe mobility issues have the longest history and therefore enjoy more protection under the law (Ensminger, 2010; US Department of Justice, 2011).

During the 1960s, formal training programs for *hearing assistance dogs* for the deaf and hard of hearing were established. These dogs are trained to alert those with a hearing impairment (deaf or hard of hearing) to the presence of people or household and community sounds by making physical contact and, if appropriate, leading the handler to the source of the sound (IGDF, 2019b). Some ADI-accredited hearing assistance dog providers include America's VetDogs, Canine Companions for Independence, Dogs for Life, NEADS World Class Assistance Dogs, and International Hearing Dog, Inc. Recent research with individuals who have hearing assistance dogs indicates that these dogs do much more than "hear for" the person. Recipients of these dogs generally indicate that hearing assistance dogs help to reduce feelings of isolation, increase independence, increase positive interactions with the hearing community, build confidence in venturing out of the house, improve physical safety, promote empathy in the individual, elevate positive mood, encourage physical activity, provide physical contact/comfort, aid other family members who are responsible for the student's care, and bring positive recognition to the deaf community (Carlisle, 2015; Collins et al., 2006; Grandin, Fine, O'Haire, Carlisle, & Bowers, 2015; Guest, Collis, & McNicholas, 2006; Hart & Yamamoto, 2015; McNicholas & Collis, 2000; Sachs-Ericsson, Hansen, & Fitzgerald, 2002; Vincent et al., 2015; Wisdom, Saedi, & Green, 2009; Yap, Scheinberg, & Williams, 2017). For basic information on hearing dogs, see American Kennel Club Staff (2015).

SERVICE DOGS FOR DIAGNOSED PSYCHOLOGICAL CONDITIONS.
It was not until 1996 that service dogs for psychological conditions, such as post-traumatic stress disorder (PTSD) and autism spectrum disorder (ASD),

were trained and recognized. Matching a child with ASD to a service dog requires careful consideration of the particular characteristics of the child and the animal (Pawsitivity Service Dogs, 2019). The demand for dogs to assist children with ASD has risen exponentially in recent years (Berry, Borgi, Francia, Alleva, & Cirulli, 2013). As a result, students with ASD who attend college may have had one or more service dogs throughout their childhoods. A recent review of the research suggests that the major benefit of these dogs is social support (Hill, Ziviani, Driscoll, & Cawdell-Smith, 2019). Likewise, students who have experienced trauma—notably, military veterans—may arrive at college with a service dog. For example, a survivor of sexual violence might have night terrors and dogs can interrupt the nightmare as soon as they sense the person's agitation by waking them up. Dogs who support people with a history of trauma can be taught to enter the home first, operate a switch to turn on the lights, and search throughout the home. The difficulty with these "invisible wounds" is that uninformed and misinformed people are more likely to question whether the person has a disability or challenge the person's and dog's right of public access.

MEDICAL ALERT DOGS.
The most recent type of service dog prepared is the medical alert and/or response dog. These dogs anticipate and/or respond to seizures such as those experienced by people with epilepsy, dangerously low or high blood sugar levels (Hardin et al., 2015), severe allergies, and other medical conditions such as migraine headaches. About 30% of dogs react/respond spontaneously to medical conditions, such as an oncoming seizure, dangerously low or high blood sugar levels, migraine headaches, and so forth. It seems that changes in the chemistry of the human body are detected by the dog's superior sense of smell. Dogs who alert give the person time to prepare by retrieving medication, moving to a safer place, or retrieving the telephone so that the person can call for help. In other instances, the dog responds to the medical situation after the fact by summoning help and/or by laying down close to the person. Many people who have medical alert or response dogs would be reluctant to attempt to attend college classes without the reassurance that their service dog provides.

There is little question that dogs can provide an important service to people with special needs (Rodriguez, Bibbo, & O'Haire, 2019; Sachs-Ericsson et al., 2002). It is important to consider that people with disabilities may have multiple challenges and therefore require a dog that is trained for more than one purpose.

The rationale for creating a college student/service dog team is provided by the following benefits for service dogs' human partners that have been documented in the research:
- improving physical safety
- building empathy in the individual
- elevating positive mood
- encouraging physical activity
- reducing stress or anxiety
- supporting the person in complying with therapeutic treatment recommendations of professionals
- providing physical contact/comfort
- serving as a social catalyst and making connections with others
- aiding other family members who are responsible for the student's care
- increasing the person's sense of self-efficacy
- enabling the student to participate in more activities outside the home
- gaining positive recognition in the community (Carlisle, 2015; Collins et al., 2006; Grandin et al., 2015; Hart & Yamamoto, 2015; McNicholas & Collis, 2000, Vincent et al., 2015; Wisdom et al., 2009; Yap et al., 2017)

ISSUES WITH SERVICE DOGS

Approximately 48.9 million people—nearly 1 out of every 5—have a disability (United States Census, 2012). It is difficult to determine how many service dogs there are because few of them are registered; however, it is estimated that there are about 500,000 service dogs (United States Census, 2012). Postsecondary personnel may express the concern that hundreds of service dogs will suddenly appear on campus, yet, as these national statistics suggest, that is highly unlikely. There are many obstacles to acquiring a service dog as outlined in table 3.2.

Lori Breece is the director of the Service Dogs Program with United Disabilities Services Foundation in Lancaster, Pennsylvania, and has extensive experience training and placing service dogs. This group has over 50 years of experience and the program is accredited by Assistance Dogs International. She describes the challenges that service dog providers face as follows:

Table 3.2 Obstacles to Acquiring a Service Dog

OBSTACLE	EXPLANATION
High demand/low supply	Although the demand for service dogs has increased exponentially, the supply of service dogs has not kept pace (Assistance Dogs International, 2016). Most service dog providers are nonprofit groups that prepare fewer than nine dogs per year (Baughman et al., 2015). Waitlist times to acquire a service dog frequently are a year or more.
Moderate success rates	Training programs frequently are two years or more. Dogs can fail as service dogs for physical reasons (e.g., hip dysplasia), behavioral issues (e.g., becoming protective), or training problems (e.g., being too distractible).
Initial cash outlay	In the United States, the price tag on a fully trained service dog can range from $5,000 to as high as $50,000 (Konrad, 2009).
Training with person and dog	Highly respected service dog providers typically require that the person and dog complete training together. The investment of time and money—as well as the need to travel to the site—may be prohibitive for some people. Groups accredited by Assistance Dogs International also require the person/dog team to be reevaluated annually, which may be another impediment to acquiring a service dog.
Unrealistic expectations	Students may expect a fully trained service dog to be delivered to their doorstep and fail to recognize the time and effort required as well as the financial and emotional investments that are necessary. Although some people train their own assistance dogs, it is more common that the dog is trained by others. Just because a dog is trained by a handler, that does not mean that the college student with a disability can get the dog to work for him or her; it is critically important that the student and the dog learn how to work together, as a team. Thus, even after a service dog provider makes what appears to be an appropriate match for a student, it still might fail.

Currently, the Americans with Disabilities Act (2011) does not require a working dog to be certified or wear any identifying markings such as a cape or vest. Asking the person to identify his or her disability is not permitted. Only two questions are permitted when a person appears with a dog: (1) Is that your service dog? and (2) What tasks does the dog do for you?

Fake service dogs that are not trained are a big problem. A person can go online, register a dog, get a certificate/ID card, and purchase a vest for $99. Many people are doing this just so they can take their pets along, not because the dog is trained to assist in any way. Many times, these dogs go out in the public and give a bad reputation to real assistance dogs.

Our organization gets frequent calls from restaurants, airlines, and other public places that have dogs that are rude, display bad behaviors, urinate or defecate in their place of business, or even growl and snap at other customers/clients. A guest/customer can be asked to leave if the dog does any of these things and the handler can't control the animal. Of course, people must choose their wording carefully so that the dog, not the person, is being asked to leave, and the person can still come there to eat/shop/travel, etc. Not many places do this because people make such a fuss in a loud voice and threaten to call the police. The police could be called, but then, do they really know what the laws/rules/regulations are pertaining to assistance dogs?

Assistance Dogs International and service dog training agencies all over the country are working with local legislators to try and identify ways to manage these issues. Many are advocating a database accessed by reputable training agencies that would serve as a registry for dogs that have successfully completed their training programs. This could then be accessed by police and all agencies that are involved with the public. Nevertheless, this is a "soapbox issue" for service dog providers that is barely acknowledged and poorly understood by the public, much less fixed. My hope is that we can get enough people involved and work with our elected officials to make something happen that would protect people who genuinely need a service dog and are being penalized because others are misrepresenting untrained dogs as service animals.

Box 3.1 highlights the general behavior and training standards for all service animals as set forth by Assistance Dogs International. Although comparatively few service dog providers are accredited by ADI, these more rigorous standards may be the direction the country will take in the future as it strives to deal with the problem of fake service dogs.

Situations such as the following undermine the good work that people and dogs are doing to support people with disabilities:

A Labrador retriever trained as a service dog practices the sit/stay command.
Photo Credit: Mary Renck Jalongo

A customer enters a convenience store and notices a large German shepherd mix dog that is matted and muddy roaming around inside. The owner glares at the customer and says, "I can tell by the look on your face that you don't like dogs. This is my service dog. I know the law. I'm allowed to have her here." The customer replies, "Actually, I love dogs but if it is your service dog, it should be on a leash." The owner scoffs and says, "Oh, she's waaayyy past needing a leash." After calling the dog's name several times, the animal finally comes over to the owner, stands next to the cash register, and begins sniffing and slobbering on the candy bars on a display rack. With that, the customer responds, "What I really object to is that you are allowing your dog to lick the candy bar wrappers before people buy the candy."

This incident raises several issues about standards for service animals (see Box 3.1).

THEORY OF INCLUSION

Despite the challenges and obstacles to creating effective human-canine assistance dog teams, service dogs of various types are present at more postsecondary institutions than ever before. In the past, it was mainly guide dogs for the blind or visually impaired. Gradually, service dogs for people with mobility issues became more accepted. Today, "multipurpose" service dogs—for instance, providing emotional support for a military veteran with PTSD as well as assisting with mobility issues caused by physical injuries—are a more common sight. The theoretical base for this chapter is inclusion; the concept that it is important for people who are different in both obvious and more subtle ways to belong to the

BOX 3.1 BEHAVIOR AND TRAINING STANDARDS FOR ALL SERVICE ANIMALS

ASSISTANCE DOGS INTERNATIONAL

For over 75 years, Assistance Dogs International has worked successfully in public and won the public's acceptance by achieving high behavioral and training standards that set them apart from pets and other animals. To assure the comfort and safety of people with disabilities and the general public, high behavioral and training standards must apply equally to all service animals. ADI believes that all service animals intended for use in public, regardless of species, should be required to meet the same standards required of dogs specifically trained to assist people with disabilities. Any animal that can meet the existing standards for behavior, training, cleanliness, and public appropriateness should be allowed to work in public when accompanied by the person for whose disability it was specifically trained. These standards include:

Public Appropriateness
- Animal is clean and does not have a foul odor.
- Animal does not urinate or defecate in inappropriate locations.

Behavior
- Animal does not annoy any member of the general public.
- Animal's conduct does not disrupt the normal course of business.
- Animal works without unnecessary vocalization.
- Animal shows no aggression toward people or other animals.
- Animal does not solicit or steal food or other items from the general public.

Training
- Animal is specifically trained to perform more than one task to mitigate (lessen) the effects of its partner's disability, said disability being any condition as described by and covered under the ADA that substantially impairs one or more major life functions.
- Animal obeys the commands of its handler.
- Animal works calmly and quietly on a harness, leash, or other tether.

- Animal has been specifically trained to perform its duties in public and is accustomed to being out in public.
- Animal must be able to lie quietly beside the handler without blocking aisles, doorways, etc.
- Animal is trained to urinate or defecate on command.
- Animal stays within 24" of its handler at all times unless the nature of a trained task requires it to be working at a greater distance.

HOW TO DIFFERENTIATE A PET OR EMOTIONAL SUPPORT ANIMAL FROM A TRAINED SERVICE ANIMAL UNDER ADA

Many people say they derive emotional support from a pet's companionship, but ADI believes this relationship between an animal and an individual, standing alone, is not sufficient to cause an animal to be regarded as a service animal. If an individual with a mental, emotional, or physiological disability wants access rights with an animal as an accommodation, this animal must be trained as required by the definition of a service animal published in the CFR in October 1991 by the US Department of Justice.

The Americans with Disabilities Act (ADA) defines a service animal as a guide dog, signal dog, or any other animal that is individually trained to perform tasks or to do work for the benefit of a disabled person. The US Department of Justice illustrated what is meant by this training requirement, giving examples of tasks or work service animals are trained to perform, such as guiding the blind, alerting the deaf to specific sounds, and pulling a wheelchair or providing balance support to individuals with a mobility impairment.

"Individual training" is the process of deliberately teaching the animal using rewards and/or corrections to perform a task in response to a command or another stimulus, such as the onset of a seizure. A "task" is a certain desired behavior or set of behaviors the animal is trained to perform whenever needed to assist the animal's partner in a way that mitigates his or her disabling condition.

If an animal has not been specifically trained to perform identifiable tasks to assist a disabled individual, it does not qualify under ADA as a service animal.

group, to be welcomed by others, and to have their unique contributions recognized and valued. The burning questions of inclusion identified by Connor and Berman (2019) pertain to the college student/service dog pair, namely:
- Who belongs in school or university?
- How is belonging created or stifled?
- What does belonging look like?
- How can belonging address inequality?

Students may "look down" on fellow students for a variety of reasons—physical appearance, family socioeconomic status, sexual orientation, intellectual prowess, or even based on disregard for another student's major area of study. Without adult modeling and guidance, college students can become socially stratified and have few interactions with peers they view as "other." This stratification may be situational, such as when sophomores with the same major take required classes together, or it may be quite deliberate, such as when students in a Greek organization affiliate with a group they deem the most popular/beautiful or the most intelligent. College students with an identified disability are at even greater risk of being excluded and experiencing social isolation.

Postsecondary institutions are obligated to make accommodations for college students; however, students may elect not to disclose their special needs. In a review of research and report issued by the National Center for Learning Disabilities (2019), they identified several reasons why students might not divulge their disabilities:
- Wanting to establish an identity independent of disability status
- Shame or fear of being perceived as lazy or unintelligent or of getting an unfair advantage by requesting accommodations
- Fear of receiving no response or a negative response from faculty who may not know much about certain disabilities or about the laws that protect against discrimination
- Underestimating how important accommodations are to their academic success
- Not knowing what kinds of disability services are available in college or how to access them
- Having a high school transition plan that does not specify needed postsecondary accommodations and supports

When a student appears on campus with an assistance dog, it makes their disability status more apparent, yet can serve to create a different identity. A study by Sanders (2000) found that individuals who were visually impaired and had a guide dog acquired a new status as a competent dog handler; this perception by self and others existed independent of the person's physical challenges. A review of the research on psychiatric service dogs (PSDs) for military veterans with PTSD arrived at a similar conclusion: being part of a successful handler/dog team changed the way that the recipients of a trained service dog perceived themselves (Gilett & Weldrick, 2014).

Reactions of other people often serve to exclude individuals with disabilities, intensify social stigma, and lead to greater isolation. Even those who have no intention of responding negatively and want to be helpful frequently are uncertain about what to say or do. This often results in avoiding eye contact, maintaining greater personal distance, and keeping social interactions very brief (Eddy, Hart, & Boltz, 1988). Over the past thirty years, many studies have concluded that the presence of a service dog increases the likelihood that others will approach and interact with individuals with disabilities of various types (Hart et al., 1987; Hart, Zasloff, & Benfatto, 2012; McNicholas & Collis, 2000; Sachs-Ericsson et al., 2002; Shyne, Masciulli, Faustino, & O'Connell, 2012). Evidently, college students are no exception; they too are more apt to interact with a person with a disability if that person is accompanied by a dog (Coleman, Ingram, Bays, Joy-Gaba, & Boone, 2015).

RESEARCH AND INSTITUTIONAL INITIATIVES

Successfully navigating the law as well as the personal and practical issues surrounding service dogs' presence on campus is a challenge, yet some institutions have been responsive to and respectful of service dogs and their handlers.

In some parts of the world—mainly the United States, the United Kingdom, and European countries—service dogs have gained greater acceptance. The first consideration in making decisions about service dogs is to make the safety and welfare of all stakeholders a priority. Legally, dogs in general and service dogs tend to be categorized as property. Therefore, if a service dog causes damage or causes injury to someone, the legal owner would be liable (Huss & Fine, 2017).

In 2011, Weatherly listed the presence of service dogs in schools among the top three "hot" issues that educators were facing. Yet, as a team of researchers from the United Kingdom concludes, although service dogs are widely recognized by the public, acceptance of service dogs via government social policy lags behind (Audrestch et al., 2015). Service dogs have their "fair share of challenges, obstacles, and detractors" (Walthall, 2012, p. 151). Where service dogs are concerned, people with "hidden" disabilities often have the most difficult time gaining access to public buildings, restaurants, and public transportation. College students with a nonvisible disability and a service dog may have their right to enter a classroom, library, cafeteria, store, or shuttle bus challenged.

There are many considerations when making the accommodations mandated by law. These include:

1. Health and safety. A true service dog is reliably nonaggressive. However, when the dog's training is inadequate or when a dog is in pain, it might growl and snap at people or attack another dog on campus. If this occurs and is documented, then the handler can be required to remove the dog from campus because it jeopardizes the health and safety of others.
2. Diagnosis. According to ADA law, a service dog is individually trained to assist a person with a disability. Although school personnel cannot demand to know what a student's disability is, it does have to be professionally diagnosed (Ensminger, 2010).
3. Tasks performed. It is within the rights of personnel at the postsecondary institution to ask what tasks the dog has been trained to perform.
4. Identification. Although the ADA does not require service dogs to wear a harness and/or other items that clearly identify them as such, from a practical standpoint it may be easier for the student and dog to gain access—particularly in the surrounding community—with these items than without them. Assistance Dogs International-accredited organizations do require some form of identification that the dog is a service dog.
5. Animal welfare. When making accommodations, it is important to consider how the dog will be helped to adapt to campus life, particularly if the student is living in a residence hall on campus. An area where the dog can get exercise, go outside to eliminate, and a place designated for disposal of excrement is needed.
6. Reasonable accommodations. The institution has some rights to determine what constitutes a "reasonable accommodation." If, for example, classrooms have highly polished, slippery floors and a service dog has difficulty walking on them, does the student have the right to demand that the college install rubber mats or carpeting throughout? Expense may be an issue and, if this is not required by law for compliance with handicapped access rules, campus personnel may decline. There are other, less costly measures to address this, such as keeping nails and fur on the feet trimmed, paw

wax that reduces slippage, discs with a gritty outer surface that are affixed to the dog's paw pads with temporary adhesive, or booties that give traction on slippery surfaces.

The underlying concept of public access is that service animals require an exception to the "no pets allowed" policies in public areas so that people with disabilities can participate more fully in society. This meant, at first, guide dogs, but the laws expanded to include, among others, hearing dogs, dogs for the mobility impaired, seizure-alert and seizure-response dogs, and dogs providing psychological benefits to individuals with clinically diagnosed psychological conditions (Ensminger, 2010). One of the most helpful resources for educators in the United States is Michigan State University's Animal Legal and Historical Center website, particularly the Table of State Assistance Animal Laws (Wisch, 2019). It is updated frequently. Additional resources for educators on legal issues governing service dogs include Huss, 2016; Walthall, 2012; and Zirkel, 2011. These laws are undergoing rapid change and each state and municipality may have additional regulations, so it is important to consult current information.

RECOMMENDATIONS FOR PRACTICE

It isn't enough for postsecondary institutions to comply with the letter of ADA law; they also need to comply with its spirit. Students and staff need to be educated about service dogs because this is the key to successfully integrating these important animals into the campus community. Several studies that interviewed or surveyed people with disabilities found that the major obstacles to having a service dog were inappropriate responses to the dog by others or being denied access. In a cross-cultural study of college students from the United Kingdom and Japan, more positive attitudes toward service dogs were associated with more knowledge about them (Miura, Bradshaw, & Tanida, 2002). At the time the study was conducted, service dogs were not that common in Japan. Even though all the participants in the research were studying animal care at college, only 41% of Japanese students supported the use of assistance dogs, while 98% of the British students were in favor of service dogs.

Students are sometimes unsure about whether or how to interact with a service dog when they see one. They may have heard that people are not supposed to pet a service dog at work or read "do not pet" if the dog is wearing a vest that indicates this. The fact that *therapy* dogs *are* brought to campus specifically to interact

A seven-month-old goldendoodle being trained as a service dog rests quietly during a presentation in class. Photo Credit: Mary Renck Jalongo

with people tends to confound the issue in many people's minds, so it is helpful to educate the campus community about appropriate responses to service dogs.

Furthermore, some students and staff may feel sorry for service dogs, assuming that these animals are obligated to work hard and never get a chance to play, relax, or "just be a dog" when this is not the case. People may object to a dog's presence where food is served and sold or at a health clinic because they view dogs as a source of contamination/infection. Some individuals may have negative prior experiences with aggressive dogs used to protect property or packs of semi-feral and disease-ridden strays in their communities. The problem of stray dogs is not unique to other countries; there are still many places in the United States that have no humane organizations within a reasonable driving distance or overwhelmed shelters where dogs have just a few days to get adopted before they are slated for euthanasia. Furthermore, students and staff may come from a culture that does not have a tradition of pet keeping and values dogs for utilitarian purposes such as hunting or herding only. These differing perspectives of an appropriate role for dogs need to be taken into consideration when educating the campus community. Just as we have guidelines for civility that members of the campus community are expected to adhere to, there are also guidelines for educating students, faculty, administrators, staff, and visitors about interacting with service dogs and the people they assist (see Box 3.2).

ALTERNATIVE ASSIGNMENTS FOR DOGS TRAINED AS SERVICE ANIMALS

In German-speaking countries, teachers can bring their dogs to school if the dogs meet rigorous standards for training, are health checked, and the team is reevaluated annually. In the United States, some public schools have a facility dog that has extensive training or may even have passed the Public Access Certification Test. However, the dog is owned/handled by a staff member without a disability,

BOX 3.2 DOS AND DON'TS FOR BEHAVIOR AROUND A SERVICE DOG TEAM

1. **DO speak to the owner/handler rather than the dog**

The service dog and her handler are a team. If you want to talk to them, always speak to the person first rather than automatically approaching the dog. Remember, the animal is working, and her human's life could depend on her staying focused on her job.

2. **DON'T touch the dog without asking permission first**

Touching or petting a working dog is a distraction and may prevent him from tending to his human partner. The dog may be in the process of completing a command or direction given by his human, and you don't want to interfere.

Fortunately, most service dogs are trained to stay in work mode until they receive a release command from their handler. That's why many service dogs are able to ignore outside influences.

3. **DO keep your own dog a distance away from a working dog**

If you happen to have your dog with you when you encounter a service dog team, don't allow your pet to approach them without first talking with the handler to see if it's permissible.

Other animals are an obvious distraction to working dogs, and in a worst-case scenario, there could be an altercation between the two animals.

4. **DON'T offer food to a service dog**

According to Canine Companions for Independence, "Food is the ultimate distraction to the working dog and can jeopardize the working assistance dog team."

Not only are food and treats a potential distraction, but many service dogs are fed a specific diet and on a particular schedule.

5. **DO treat the owner/handler with sensitivity and respect**

Asking a service dog's handler personal questions about his or her disability is out of bounds. It's disrespectful and an intrusion of privacy.

Assume the service dog team can handle things themselves. If you sense they could use your help, ask first. And don't take it personally if your offer is rejected, as there's usually a good reason.

6. **DON'T assume a napping service dog is off duty**

All dogs nap, including working dogs. When her handler is sitting or standing for some length of time, it's perfectly natural and appropriate for a service dog to catch a few winks. She's still technically at work, however, so all dos and don'ts remain in effect.

7. **DO inform the handler if a service dog approaches you**

If a working dog approaches you, sniffs or nudges you, etc., politely let the handler know. Resist the urge to respond to the dog—the handler will correct the dog.

8. **DON'T assume service dogs never get to "just be dogs"**

Working dogs typically get plenty of rest, relaxation, and playtime. When they're home and out of their "work clothes," they're free to behave like any other dog. Since the jobs these wonderful animals do are often challenging and stressful, their handlers recognize they need plenty of downtime and exercise.

Source: "The Rules for Service Dogs: Don't Touch or Distract Them"
https://healthypets.mercola.com/sites/healthypets/archive/2016/01/23/behavior-around-service-dog-team.aspx

such as the principal. Rather than being individually trained to perform tasks that help the owner with a disability, the principal incorporates the dog into his/her professional practice. Thus, a child who is a reluctant reader might be given the opportunity to practice reading aloud with the handler/dog team to reduce stress, make reading more pleasurable, and motivate the child to practice. Likewise, a service dog can be owned/handled by a professional in authority at the postsecondary institution and function more as a facility dog. The dog would accompany a staff member to work on a regular basis and that staff member would also keep the dog as his/her family pet. The dog could be present at various events, such as homecoming, move-in day for freshmen, or available for drop-in visits from students. The way that this typically occurs is that a dog was prepared for the role of a service dog, but the service dog provider decided that the customary role was not a good match for the dog. If, for example, the service dog provider prepares dogs for people with mobility issues, dogs need to be physically sound to perform tasks such as opening doors or serving as a brace. Thus, a dog with previously undetected hip dysplasia would not be a good fit for those tasks, but might be a perfect fit for a person with mental health issues instead. Some dogs need lots of mental stimulation, physical activity, and thrive on varied human interaction. To give the dog a role to which he or she is best suited, working as a facility dog that is part of a lively organization is sometimes the decision. Although this tends to muddy the waters about whether or not the dog is covered by the ADA, there are many working dogs out there with extensive service dog training that have different roles than what was originally envisioned for them. When I speak with various community groups about service dog training, that is one common question: "What happens to the dogs that don't make it as service dogs?" The answer is that responsible service dog providers find a suitable placement and do right by the dog. Well-trained dogs with good temperaments are in great demand.

PARTNERSHIPS WITH SERVICE DOG PROVIDERS

Postsecondary institutions in some areas may find that there are no national therapy dog organization representatives nearby who are willing to travel a distance to participate in activities on campus. In cases such as this, it might be possible to find instead a service dog provider in the area and collaborate with that organization. In some instances, college students might live with service dogs in training in on-campus residential housing. In addition to or instead of this, service dogs could visit campus for events in much the same way that therapy dogs do. In the United Kingdom, the University of Sheffield's Counseling

After 16 months of training, this service dog is ready to be placed with a person who has mobility issues. They will learn to work as a team. Photo Credit: Mary Renck Jalongo

Services formed a partnership with Guide Dogs for the Blind that was mutually beneficial. The students were able to interact with calm, well-trained animals for informal group stress relief while the dogs had opportunities to be better socialized to a wide variety of people and experiences.

CONCLUSION

At each step in the evolution of service dogs, the ability of a dog to be trained and assist in various roles was questioned by skeptics who asked, in effect, "Can a dog *really* do that?" When strong bonds are formed between well-trained service dogs and their human partners, it can become a powerful partnership that is mutually beneficial. The person achieves greater independence and the dog is well cared for and treasured beyond estimation. Many college students with disabilities credit their service dogs with making it possible to pursue their higher education goals. The dog's role in helping them to surmount various obstacles is so essential that service dogs often participate in commencement ceremonies with their human partners. What is frequently overlooked is that service dog training is the equivalent of higher education for canines as well.

Although it is possible for a person with a disability to train his or her own service dog (depending somewhat on the severity of the disability), it is more often the case that service dogs are prepared by professional dog trainers. There is also some evidence that professionally trained service dogs are better equipped to fulfill their roles (Yamamoto & Hart, 2019). Although it may sound like an overstatement to the uninitiated, the best service dog trainers are equally committed to helping people with disabilities and to advocating for the dogs' well-being. Service dog trainers are animal guardians who provide compassionate care to service dogs; employ gentle, rewards-based training methods; respect each dog as a sentient being with unique strengths; and make thoughtful matches between people and service dogs. Rather than relying on past practical experience alone, they seek professional development and revise their practices based on scientific evidence. Reputable service dog providers also monitor the person/service dog dyad's progress and if, despite all efforts, the pairing is not working well, intervene to retrain human or dog or even make the difficult decision to find a more suitable placement for the dog. Pairing the right person with the right dog is no small accomplishment. When it works, it is exhilarating; when it fails, it is demoralizing. The cost of a failed placement is high, not only in terms of financial investment, but also in terms of disappointment for the person and disruption for the animal. Every effective service dog trainer is called upon to simultaneously advocate for people with disabilities as well as respect the dogs' needs.

Selecting service dogs for college students can pose additional challenges to this process. Traditional-age undergraduates are young adults who may be more physically active and socially interactive than many other clients. Rather than a relatively quiet single-family home, the student and service dog may live most of the year in a residence hall, and this might require exceptional resistance to distractions from the dog when it is working. Conversely, attending classes requires an extended period of sedentary behavior that may be uncharacteristic of a young dog. When college students complete practicum experiences or internships off campus, an extra effort of adaptation often is necessary as well.

Survey research conducted with people who have service dogs has identified the downside to having a service dog (Guest et al., 2006; Hogle, 2007; Rintala et al., 2008). First, the very fact that a person is accompanied by a service dog is a public proclamation of a disability, and the presence of the dog can attract unwanted attention. The uninformed or misinformed may seek to fulfill their own needs for canine companionship by treating service dogs as they would their family pets, and those in authority may challenge the person/service dog dyad's public access rights. Financial constraints are another hurdle, particularly if the dog becomes ill or is injured. The stressors for service dogs and their human partners as they navigate a busy college campus and diverse community can be intensified. Stated plainly, there are many moving parts to the task of completing courses and experiences across semesters and years. Ultimately, success depends not only on the individuals in the process, but also the interactions among key stakeholders in the process: the service dog trainer, the trained dog, the person with the disability, the campus community, and the surrounding community.

REFERENCES

American Kennel Club Staff. (2015, April 1). Canine companions perform important functions for hearing impaired people. https://www.akc.org/expert-advice/training/hearing-dogs

Americans with Disabilities Act Title III Regulations. (2011). Part 36 nondiscrimination on the basis of disability in public accommodations and commercial facilities. CFR

§ 35.104, § 35.136, § 36.104, § 36.302 amendments effective March 15, 2011. http://www.ada.gov/regs2010/titleIII_2010/titleIII_2010_regulations.htm

Andics, A., Gacsi, M., Farago, T., Kis, A., & Miklosi, A. (2014). Voice-sensitive regions in the dog and human brain are revealed by comparative fMRI. *Current Biology, 24*(5), 574–578.

Assistance Dogs International (ADI). (2016). http://www.assistancedogsinternational.org/members/programs-search

Audrestch, H. M., Whelan, C. T., Grice, D., Asher, L., England, G. C. W., & Freeman, S. L. (2015). Recognizing the value of assistance dogs in society. *Disability and Health Journal, 8*(4), 469–474.

Batt, L. S., Batt, M. S., Baguley, J. A., & McGreevy, P. D. (2008). Factors associated with success in guide dog training. *Journal of Veterinary Behavior: Clinical Applications and Research, 3*(4), 143–151. https://doi.org/10.1016/j.jveb.2008.04.003

Baughman, P., Foreman, A., Parenti, L., Scotti, J. R., Meade, B. J., Wilson, M.E., & Wirth, O. (2015). Project ROVER's survey of assistance dog providers. https://www.ncbi.nlm.nih.gov/pmc/articles/PMC4699314

Bender, A., & Strong, E. (2019). *Canine enrichment in the real world: Making it a part of your dog's daily life.* Wenatchee, WA: Dogwise Publications.

Berns, G. (2013). *How dogs love us: A neuroscientist and his adopted dog decode the canine brain.* Seattle, WA: Lake Union Publishing.

Berns, G. S., Brooks, A. M., Spivak, M., & Levy, K. (2017). Functional MRI in awake dogs predicts suitability for assistance work. *Scientific Reports, 7*(43704). https://www.nature.com/articles/srep43704

Berry, A., Borgi, M., Francia, N., Alleva, E., & Cirulli, F. (2013). Use of assistance and therapy dogs for children with autism spectrum disorders: A critical review of the current evidence. *The Journal of Alternative and Complementary Medicine, 19*(2), 73–80. https://doi.org/10.1089/acm.2011.0835

Burrows, K. E., Adams, C. L., & Spiers, J. (2008). Sentinels of safety: Service dogs ensure safety and enhance freedom and well-being for families with autistic children. *Qualitative Health Research, 18*(12), 1642–1649. https://doi.org/10.1177/1049732308327088

Byrne, C., Zeagler, C., Freil, L., Rapoport, A., & Jackson, M. M. (2018). Dogs using touchscreens in the home: A case study for assistance dogs operating emergency notification systems. ACI 2018 Conference Proceedings, Article 12. https://doi.org/10.1145/3295598.3295610

Carlisle, G. K. (2015). The social skills and attachment to dogs of children with autism spectrum disorder. *Journal of Autism and Developmental Disorders, 45*(5), 1137. http://dx.doi.org/10.1007/s10803-014-2267-7

Certification Council for Professional Dog Trainers. (2017). Code of ethics. http://www.ccpdt.org/wp-content/uploads/2014/07/Code-of-Ethics.pdf

Coleman, J. A., Ingram, K. M., Bays, A., Joy-Gaba, J. A., & Boone, E. L. (2015). Disability and assistance dog Implicit Association Test: A novel IAT. *Rehabilitation Psychology*, *60*(1), 17–26. http://dx.doi.org/10.1037/rep0000025

Collins, D., Fitzgerald, S., Sachs-Ericsson, N., Scherer, M., Cooper, R., & Boninger, M. (2006). Psychosocial well-being and community participation of service dog partners. *Disability and Rehabilitation: Assistive Technology*, *1*(1/2), 41–48.

Connor, D. J., & Berman, D. (2019). (Be)Longing: A family's desire for authentic inclusion, *International Journal of Inclusive Education*, *23*(9), 923–936. http://dx.doi.org/10.1080/13603116.2019.1602361

Crowe, E. K., Perea-Burns, S., Sedillo, J. S., Hendrix, I. C., Winkle, M., & Dietz, J. (2014). Effects of partnerships between people with mobility challenges and service dogs. *American Journal of Occupational Therapy*, *68*(2), 194–202.

Cuaya, L. V., Hernández-Pérez, R., & Concha, L. (2016). Our faces in the dog's brain: Functional imaging reveals temporal cortex activation during perception of human faces. *PLoS ONE*, *11*(e0149431). https://doi.org/10.1371/journal.pone.0149431

Davis, B. W., Nattrass, K., O'Brien, S., Patronek, G., & MacCollin, M. (2015). Assistance dog placement in the pediatric population: Benefits, risks, and recommendations for future applications. *Anthrozoös*, *17*(2), 130–145.

Derr, M. (2011). *How the dog became the dog: From wolves to our best friends.* New York: Harry Abrams.

Eddy, J. L., Hart, L. A., & Boltz, R. P. (1988). The effects of service dogs on social acknowledgments of people in wheelchairs. *Journal of Psychology*, *122*(1), 39–45. https://doi.org/10.1080/00223980.1988.10542941

Ensminger, J. J. (2010). *Service and therapy dogs in American society: Science, law and the evolution of canine caregivers.* Springfield, IL: Charles C. Thomas.

Gillett, J., & Weldrick, R. (2014). Effectiveness of psychiatric service dogs in the treatment of post-traumatic stress disorder among veterans. http://www.cf4aass.org/uploads/1/8/3/2/18329873/psd_and_veterans_living_with_ptsd_-_gillett_march_23_2014_2.pdf

Grandin, T., Fine, A. H., O'Haire, M., Carlisle, G., & Bowers, C. M. (2015). The roles of animals for individuals with autism spectrum disorder. In A. H. Fine (Ed.), *Handbook on animal-assisted therapy: Foundations and guidelines for animal-assisted interventions* (4th ed., pp. 225–236). Waltham, MA: Academic Press.

Guest, C. M., Collis, G. M., & McNicholas, J. (2006). Hearing dogs: A longitudinal study of social and psychological effects on deaf and hard-of-hearing recipients. *Journal of Deaf Studies and Deaf Education*, *11*(2), 252–261. https://doi.org/10.1093/deafed/enj028

Hardin, D. S., Anderson, W., & Cattet, J. (2015). Dogs can be successfully trained to alert to hypoglycemia samples from patients with Type 1 diabetes. *Diabetes Therapy, 6*(4), 509–517. https://doi.org/10.1007/s13300-015-0135-x

Hart, L. A., Hart, B. L., & Bergin, B. L. (1987). Socializing effects of service dogs for people with disabilities, *Anthrozoös, 1*(1), 41–44. https://doi.org/10.2752/089279388787058696

Hart, L. A., & Yamamoto, M. (2015). Recruiting psychosocial health effects of animals for families and communities: Transition to practice. In A. H. Fine (Ed.), *Handbook on animal-assisted therapy: Foundations and guidelines for animal-assisted interventions* (4th ed., pp. 53–72). Waltham, MA: Academic Press.

Hart, L. A., Zasloff, R. L., & Benfatto, A. M. (1996). The socializing role of hearing dogs. *Applied Animal Behaviour Science, 47*(1–2), 7–15. https://doi.org/10.1016/0168-1591(95)01006-8

Harvey, N. D., Craigon, P. J., Sommerville, R., McMillan, C., Green, M., England, G. C. W., & Asher, L. (2016). Test-retest reliability and predictive validity of a juvenile guide dog behavior test. *Journal of Veterinary Behavior, 11*, 65–76. https://doi.org/10.1016/j.jveb.2015.09.005

Hill, J., Ziviani, J., Driscoll, C., & Cawdell-Smith, J. (2019). Can canine-assisted interventions affect the social behaviours of children on the autism spectrum? A systematic review. *Review Journal of Autism and Developmental Disorders, 6*(1), 13–25.

Hogle, P. S. (2007). Survey finds high satisfaction with service dogs. *Animal Behavior Consulting: Theory and Practice*, Fall, 23–31. https://pamhogle.files.wordpress.com/2009/07/service-dog-satisfaction.pdf

Huss, R. (2012). Canines on campus: Companion animals at postsecondary educational institutions. *Missouri Law Review, 77*(2), 418–479. https://scholarship.law.missouri.edu/cgi/viewcontent.cgi?referer=https://www.google.com/&httpsredir=1&article=1288&context=mlr

Huss, R. J. (2016). Canines in the classroom revisited: Recent developments relating to students' utilization of service animals at primary and secondary educational institutions. *Albany Government Law Review*. http://www.albanygovernmentlawreview.org/Articles/Vol09-1/1.pdf

Huss, R. J., & Fine, A. H. (2017). Legal and policy issues for classrooms with animals. In N. R. Gee, A. H. Fine & P. McCardle (Eds.), *How animals help students learn: Research and practice for educators and mental health professionals* (pp. 27–40). New York: Routledge.

International Guide Dog Federation (IGDF). (2019a). About us. http://www.igdf.org.uk/about-us

International Guide Dog Federation (IGDF). (2019b). History of guide dogs. http://www.igdf.org.uk/about-us/facts-and-figures/history-of-guide-dogs

Jalongo, M. R. (Ed.). (2018). *Children, dogs and education: Caring for, learning alongside, and gaining support from canine companions.* New York: Springer Nature.

Karley & Kaiser. (2015). SCI Greene. *All Paws on Deck, 2*(2), 18.

Konrad, W. (2009, August 21). An aide for the disabled, a companion, and nice and furry. *The New York Times.* http://www.nytimes.com/2009/08/22/health/22patient.html

McIver, S., Hall, S., & Mills, D. S. (2020). The impact of owning a guide dog on owners' quality of life: A longitudinal study. *Anthrozoös, 33*(1), 103–117. https://doi.org/10.1080/08927936.2020.1694315

McNicholas, J., & Collis, G. M. (2000). Dogs as catalysts for social interactions: Robustness of the effect. *British Journal of Psychology, 91*(1), 61–70.

Miklosi, A. (2016). *Dog behaviour, evolution and cognition.* New York: Oxford University Press.

Miklosi, A. (2018). *The dog: A natural history.* Princeton, NJ: Princeton University Press.

Miura, A., Bradshaw, J. W. S., & Tanida, H. (2002). Attitudes towards assistance dogs in Japan and the UK: A comparison of college students studying animal care. *Anthrozoös, 15*(3), 227–242. https://doi.org/10.2752/089279302786992496

Montague, P. R., & Berns, G. S. (2002). Neural economics and the biological substrates of valuation. *Neuron, 36*(2), 265–284. https://doi.org/10.1016/S0896-6273(02)00974-1

National Center for Learning Disabilities. (2019). The state of LD: Transitioning to life after high school. https://www.ncld.org/transitioning-to-life-after-high-school

Pawsitivity Service Dogs. (2019). Autism. https://www.pawsitivityservicedogs.com/autism

Platpets. (2015, December 6). Tribute to Dr. Bonnie Begin: A master dog trainer and revolutionary. http://platpets.com/bonnie-bergin-a-master-dog-trainer-and-revolutionary

Riemer, S., Muller, C., Viranyi, Z., Huber, L., & Range, F. (2014). The predictive value of early behavioural assessments in pet dogs—a longitudinal study from neonates to adults. *PLoS ONE, 9*(7), 1–13.

Rintala, D. H., Matamoros, R., & Seitz, L. L. (2008). Effects of assistance dogs on persons with mobility or hearing impairments: A pilot study. *Journal of Rehabilitation Research Development, 45*(4), 489–503.

Robinson, L. M., Skiver Thompson, R., & Ha, J. C. (2016). Puppy temperament assessments predict breed and American Kennel Club group but not adult temperament. *Journal of Applied Animal Welfare Science, 19*(2), 101–114.

Rodriguez, K. E., Bibbo, J., & O'Haire, M. E. (2019). The effects of service dogs on psychosocial health and wellbeing for individuals with physical disabilities or chronic conditions. *Disability Rehabilitation, 42*(10), 1350–1358. https://doi.org/10.1080/09638288.2018.1524520

Rooney, N. J., Morant, S., & Guest, C. (2013). Investigation into the value of trained glycaemia alert dogs to clients with type 1 diabetes. *PLoS One, 8*(8). https://doi.org/10.1371/journal.pone.0069921

Sachs-Ericsson N., Hansen N. K., & Fitzgerald S. (2002). Benefits of assistance dogs: A review. *Rehabilitation Psychology, 47*(3), 251–277.

Sanders, C. R. (2000). The impact of guide dogs on the identity of people with visual impairments. *Anthrozoös, 13*(3), 131–139. https://doi.org/10.2752/089279300786999815

Serpell, J. A., & Hsu, Y. (2001). Development and validation of a novel method for evaluating behaviour and temperament in guide dogs. *Applied Animal Behavior Science, 72*(4), 347–364.

Shyne A., Masciulli L., Faustino J., & O'Connell C. (2012). Do service dogs encourage more social interactions between individuals with physical disabilities and non-disabled individuals than pet dogs? *Journal of Applied Companion Animal Behaviour, 5*, 16–24.

United States Census. (2012). Number of service dogs in the U.S. https://www.census.gov/newsroom/releases/archives/miscellaneous/cb12-134.htmlor

US Department of Justice. (2011). ADA 2010 revised requirements—service animals. http://www.ada.gov/service_animals_2010.pdf

Veterans Health Administration. (2019). Service dog frequently asked questions. https://www.prosthetics.va.gov/factsheet/PSAS-FactSheet-ServiceDogs.pdf

Vincent, C., Gagnon, D. H., Routhier, F., Dumont, F., Poissant, L., Corriveau, H., & Tousignant, M. (2015). Service dogs for people with spinal cord injury: Outcomes regarding functional mobility and important occupations. *Studies in Health Technology and Informatics, 217*, 847–851.

Volhard, J., & Volhard, W. (2007). Volhard puppy aptitude test. www.volhard.com/pages/pat.php

Walthall, J. T. (2012). Dog days in American public schools: Observations and suggestions regarding the laws, challenges, and amazing benefits of allowing service animals to accompany children with special needs to schools. *Campbell Law Review, 35*(1), 148–172. http://scholarship.law.campbell.edu/cgi/viewcontent.cgi?article=1565&context=clr

Weatherly, J. J. (2011, November). The top three "hot" issues educators face today in special education: RT/child-find, service animals and disability harassment. Paper presented at the Annual State Superintendent's Conference on Special Education, Florence, Wisconsin.

Weiss, E. (2002). Selecting shelter dogs for service dog training. *Journal of Applied Animal Welfare Science, 5*(1), 43–62. https://doi.org/10.1207/S15327604JAWS0501_4

Weiss, E., & Greenberg, G. (1997). Service dog selection tests: Effectiveness for dogs from animal shelters. *Applied Animal Behaviour Science, 53*(4), 297–308. https://doi.org/10.1016/S0168-1591(96)01176-8

Wisch, R. F. (2019). Table of state assistance animal laws. https://www.animallaw.info/topic/table-state-assistance-animal-laws

Wisdom, J. P., Saedi, G. A., & Green, C. A. (2009). Another breed of "service" animals: STARS study findings about pet ownership and recovery from serious mental illness. *American Journal of Orthopsychiatry, 79*(3), 430–436. https://doi.org/10.1037/a0016812

Yamamoto, M., & Hart, L. A. (2019). Professionally- and self-trained service dogs: Benefits and challenges for partners with disabilities. *Frontiers of Veterinary Science, 6*, 179. https://doi.org/10.3389/fvets.2019.00179

Yap, E., Scheinberg, A., & Williams, K. (2017). Attitudes to and beliefs about animal-assisted therapy for children with disabilities. *Complementary Therapies in Clinical Practice, 26*, 47–52.

Zirkel, P. A. (2011). Service animals in public schools. *Education Law Association, 46*(1), 4–9.

4

EMOTIONAL SUPPORT ANIMALS

Therapeutic Companions for Students With Disabilities in Campus Housing

JANET HOY-GERLACH, SOCIAL WORK, THE UNIVERSITY OF TOLEDO, OHIO, ENJIE HALL, DIRECTOR OF CAMPUS ACCESSIBILITY AND STUDENT DISABILITY SERVICES, THE UNIVERSITY OF TOLEDO, TOLEDO, OH, AND BRADLEY J. MENARD, DIRECTOR OF HOUSING SERVICES, THE UNIVERSITY OF TOLEDO, TOLEDO, OH

INTRODUCTION

Increasing numbers of students are requesting permission to bring their emotional support animals (ESAs)—often, dogs—to live with them on college campuses. There has been confusion about how to implement this as well as lawsuits arising when ESA requests are denied. More broadly, there is confusion about what an emotional support animal is; who is eligible for an ESA; how to obtain one; and the legal protections associated with having an ESA. This chapter begins with a vignette describing a student at a university, "Rocky," who desires to bring his dog, "Fitz," to live with him on campus as an emotional support dog to help alleviate his anxiety symptoms and panic attacks. Other typical issues for which college students may seek an ESA include but are not limited to depression, autism spectrum disorder, post-traumatic stress disorder, and chronic mental health symptoms due to a physical disability. Next, the chapter defines key terminology and concepts related to ESAs, including a definition of what an ESA is; how to obtain an ESA; and the legal policies that do and do not pertain to individuals with ESAs. The third section of the chapter will present a research base and conceptual foundation for understanding the benefits of ESAs for individuals living with chronic mental illness, specifically,

A reciprocal bond is the foundation for an emotional support animal. Photo Credit: Haley Romanko

the "stress-mediation" framework. This framework explains how the benefits (physical, psychological, emotional, and social) of interaction with an ESA can work together to help ameliorate symptoms, distress, and impairment related to living with chronic mental health symptoms and disability. The final section will conclude with a detailed description of the processes and practices used by the disability services office and campus housing to successfully integrate Fitz as an emotional support dog in a residence hall setting.

> Rocky, a college freshman, had always struggled with anxiety and occasional panic attacks when meeting new people or having conversations with groups of people he did not know well, or even when thinking about being in such social situations. During his first semester, Rocky enjoyed his coursework, but found living on campus in a residence hall surrounded by many people to be overwhelming. He had panic attacks nearly daily, dreaded being in his residence hall, and his grades began dropping. Rocky went to a local counseling center for help. In talking with his therapist, he realized that one thing that helped him feel much less anxious about anticipating social situations when he had lived at home was the presence of his mixed-breed dog, Fitz. Rocky's

family had adopted Fitz when Rocky was 15; Rocky said, "Fitz has always been my dog, we're tight, he somehow knows when I'm getting panicky, and stays close and somehow helps me feel better." Fitz, while friendly and generally well-behaved, did not have any special training to help Rocky; however, Fitz was very bonded to Rocky and attuned to him. Rocky continued to struggle with anxiety and panic attacks during the spring semester, was close to failing several classes, and was formally diagnosed with social anxiety disorder. He started to seriously contemplate dropping out of school. To help manage Rocky's social anxiety symptoms, Rocky's therapist suggested that Rocky bring Fitz to campus as an emotional support animal (ESA) who could live in the residence hall with him. Rocky was very eager to try this, but not sure how to proceed with getting Fitz officially permitted as an ESA on campus. Rocky was hopeful, but misinformed, and expected that once Fitz became an ESA, he would take the dog anywhere on campus, which is not the case. Rocky's therapist had heard of mental health professionals writing ESA letters for clients, but was not sure about the specifics of how to write such a letter, who was qualified to write such a letter, or how to get an emotional support dog permitted on a college campus.

EMOTIONAL SUPPORT ANIMALS: **TERMINOLOGY AND CONCEPTS**

An ESA is a companion animal who helps to reduce impairment experienced by an individual with a disability through simply being present and engaging in everyday interactions with that person; the need for an ESA should be verified in writing by a health care professional. While ESAs may be brought into campus housing as a housing accommodation, Rocky was incorrect in thinking that once Fitz became an ESA, he would be able to bring Fitz *everywhere* with him. Many people, like Rocky, confuse ESAs with service animals. While both ESAs and service animals have legally recognized roles in which animals help people with disabilities, there are tremendous differences in both the type of help provided by the animal and in the legal protections afforded to the person who needs an ESA versus the person who needs a service animal. The most widely known federal disability legislation, the Americans with Disabilities Act (ADA), does *not* recognize or protect the rights of individuals with ESAs (American Veterinary Medical Association, 2017); practically speaking, this means that even if Rocky does obtain verification of his need for Fitz to serve as an ESA, Rocky still will *not* have public access rights to take Fitz into spaces where pets are prohibited. The ADA strictly limits protection of public access rights to individuals with service animals, and narrowly defines service animals—exclusively dogs or miniature horses—as those who are trained to perform specific tasks to assist a person with aspects of that person's disability (Americans with Disabilities Act National Network, 2019). Examples of service animals would be a dog trained to provide guidance to a person with a visual disability or a dog trained to assist a person with a mobility disability by retrieving specific objects and opening and closing doors. In addition to training to perform specific tasks that assist with aspects of a person's disability, service animals typically undergo extensive training so that they can perform such tasks safely and reliably in a wide range of public settings.

ESAs, in contrast, are not trained to do specific tasks to assist people with aspects of a disability; rather, they help reduce distress and impairment related to a disability through their presence and everyday interactions with a person. The term *emotional support animal* is recognized in the United States in certain federal disability-related legislation. ESAs, while not recognized within ADA law, *are* recognized within two other disability-related federal laws: the Fair Housing Act (FHA) and Section 504 of the Rehabilitation Act (RHA) (AVMA, 2017). As summarized by Hoy-Gerlach, Vincent, and Lory Hector (2019):

> As per the FHA and RHA, individuals with ESAs in rental housing may not be charged a pet deposit or pet housing fee, nor may they be prohibited from having the ESA in housing that does not permit pets, as an ESA is considered a disability accommodation rather than a pet (AVMA, 2017). (unpaged)

At the time of writing this chapter, access for individuals with ESAs to public transportation and air travel was contested; the US Department of Transportation has just issued new regulations limiting animal-related air travel accommodation to service dogs only. For the purposes of understanding ESAs on college campuses, the Fair Housing Act is crucially important. As defined by the FHA, ESAs are considered a subtype of "assistance animals" for people with disabilities; an "assistance animal" can be a task-trained animal (such as those who meet the ADA definition of a "service animal") or an animal who provides "emotional support that alleviates one or more of the identified symptoms or effects of a person's existing disability" (US Department of Housing and Urban Development, 2013). Assistance animals falling into the latter category of FHA law are widely referred to as "emotional support animals." The FHA defines disability as "a physical or mental impairment that substantially limits one or more major life activities" (US Department of Housing and Urban Development, 2013, p. 3). In a federal notice released in January 2020, specific impairments were listed that will always be considered as meeting the FHA criteria for disability, including:

> Deafness, blindness, intellectual disabilities, partially or completely missing limbs, mobility impairments requiring the use of a wheelchair, autism, cancer, cerebral palsy, diabetes, epilepsy, muscular dystrophy, multiple sclerosis, Human Immunodeficiency Virus (HIV) infection, major depressive disorder, bipolar disorder, post-traumatic stress disorder, traumatic brain injury, obsessive compulsive disorder, and schizophrenia. (US Department of Housing and Urban Development, 2020, p. 10)

This list was not to imply that other conditions are not disabling; it just simplifies determining disability for those with conditions within the list. Because Rocky's diagnosis of social anxiety disorder is not included on the list, he is not *automatically* considered as disabled under the FHA.

In order for a person to qualify for an ESA as a housing accommodation under the FHA, the person requesting the accommodation must meet two criteria: (1) the person must have a disability that meets the FHA legal definition of disability (i.e., a physical or mental impairment that substantially limits one or more life activities); and (2) the animal must provide emotional support that alleviates one or more of the symptoms or impairment related to the person's disability (Wisch, 2015). A person seeking this accommodation "must submit reliable documentation of the disability and disability-related need for the assistance animal if the disability is not known or readily apparent" (Wisch, 2015, unpaged). According to the US Department of Housing and Urban Development (2013), reliable documentation for an emotional support animal accommodation is exemplified as documentation "from a physician, psychiatrist, social worker, or other mental health professional that the animal provides emotional support that alleviates one or more of the identified symptoms or effects of an existing disability" (p. 4). Rocky's social anxiety met the FHA legal definition of disability, as his anxiety and panic attacks were substantially impairing his ability to learn and function at school. Fitz, as reported by Rocky, provided comfort and a calming effect that helped alleviate his anxiety and panic attacks—symptoms of his social anxiety—that were impairing his ability to learn and function at school. As a licensed mental health therapist who was knowledgeable about Rocky's functional impairment related to his social anxiety disorder (Rocky's disability) *and* knowledgeable of how the presence of Fitz helped alleviate such (Rocky's disability-related need for an ESA), Rocky's therapist was legally qualified to provide verification of Rocky's need for an ESA as a disability accommodation.

THEORY OF *STRESS MEDIATION*: UNDERSTANDING *HOW* ESAS HELP

Unlike service dogs trained to do specific things to help people, Fitz helped Rocky with his social anxiety through the calming impact and emotional comfort of his presence. As an ESA, Fitz was not required to have special training to do specific things; rather, Fitz helped Rocky by being with him and interacting with him in natural, affiliative, human-dog ways.

Emotional support dog Bandit benefits University of Toledo student Ashton Graham through everyday interactions and presence. Photo Credit: Charles George

Fine et al. (2019) explain how support from ESAs can help to alleviate symptoms or effects of a person's disability as follows:

> The support that is provided by an ESA occurs through the benefits of everyday human-animal interactions. Although anyone can experience benefits as a result of human-animal interactions, *it is the impact of those benefits on the symptoms of a given person's disability that makes an ESA therapeutically appropriate* [emphasis added]. Such benefits include but are not limited to, physical (e.g., decreased heart rate, blood pressure, and respiration), social (e.g., direct benefits such as reduced loneliness and indirect benefits such as increased socialization with others resulting from the presence of the animal), and psychological (e.g., having a purpose and feeling needed) benefits ... an ESA does not need to have specific training to provide these benefits, and ESAs are generally indistinguishable from companion animals except in how they can ameliorate a person's disability symptoms. (pp. 199–200)

The term *support* is generally understood broadly when applied to ESAs and can be understood within the biopsychosocial dimensions of human functioning within which disability impairment can occur (Hoy-Gerlach & Wehman, 2017; Hoy-Gerlach et al., 2019). Rocky reported a pattern of "feeling better" and experiencing lessening of anxiety and panic symptoms when he was with Fitz. While there are not yet studies (Hoy-Gerlach and colleagues are currently engaged in a longitudinal ESA study) that explicitly examine how animals designated as ESAs may impact individuals living with mental health disabilities, related research literature indicates benefits of human-animal interaction can help to mitigate aspects of mental illness. In a seminal literature review, Beetz, Uvnäs-Moberg, Julius, and Kotrschal (2012) examined 69 studies of how human-animal interaction affected people, concluding:

> among the well-documented effects of HAI in humans of different ages, with and without special medical, or mental health conditions are benefits for: social attention, social behavior, interpersonal interactions, and mood; stress-related parameters such as cortisol, heart rate, and blood pressure; self-reported fear and anxiety; and mental and physical health, especially cardiovascular diseases. (p. 1)

Brooks et al. (2018) conducted a literature review of studies on individuals living with chronic mental illness who had companion animals; they located 17 studies meeting these criteria, and the findings of their review underscore how emotional, psychological, and social benefits of living with a companion animal (not formally designated as an ESA) can ameliorate mental illness symptoms and related impairment and distress.

The positive emotional, social, psychological, and physical benefits of human-animal interaction (HAI) do not occur in isolation from each other; rather, they can occur simultaneously and augment each other. The stress modulation effect refers to a combination of HAI benefits, resulting in an ameliorative impact on human physical and psychological indicators of stress and anxiety; the activation and impact of the "feel good" bonding hormone oxytocin—typically through physical contact and verbal interaction between a person and animal—triggers particular physical benefits (reduced heart rate, respiration rate, and blood pressure, among other things), which in turn can support the experience of psychological benefits (Beetz et al., 2012). Oxytocin has been found to increase in both humans and dogs when they are interacting; even gazing into each other's eyes has been found to increase oxytocin in both species, and is referred to as "the oxytocin gaze positive loop" (Nagasawa et al., 2015). (A cautionary note: this effect was found within bonded human-dog pairs; staring intently at and/or putting one's face close to a strange dog could be interpreted as a sign of aggression by the dog and hence is dangerous.) Beetz et al. (2012) proposed that the activation of the oxytocin system may explain many joint psychological and physiological effects of human-animal interaction, asserting "[a]s a common underlying mechanism, the activation of the oxytocin system does not only provide an explanation, but also allows an integrative view of the different effects of HAI" (p. 1). Several researchers and scholars have similarly linked oxytocin to human-animal interaction benefits (Handlin, Nilsson, Ejdebäck, Hydbring-Sandberg, & Uvnäs-Moberg, 2012; Odendaal & Meintjes, 2003; Yount, Ritchie, St. Laurent, Chumley, & Olmert, 2013).

As related to the stress modulation effect, health benefits derived through human-animal interaction can be divided into two categories: immediate, short-term benefits and longer-term health promotion and protective benefits. Immediate or short-term benefits are those that start directly upon interacting with an animal and end when one stops interacting with the animal. For instance, as described in the previous paragraph, the stress modulation effect could help to mitigate both Rocky's subjective feelings of anxiety and distress, and the physical symptoms related to anxiety such as heart palpitations, shortness of breath, and release of cortisol and alpha amylase. The HAI benefits related to the stress modulation effect also may be longer-term and persist beyond a single episode of interaction with an animal; an example of this is the long-term protective effects for cardiovascular health offered by HAI. In response to the emerging evidence, the American Heart Association (AHA) in 2013 issued a scientific statement indicating that living with a dog may be associated with decreased risk of cardiovascular disease, and may have a causal role in its reduction (Levine et al., 2013); increased activity related to having a dog was indicated as a likely mechanism. Exercise also has been linked to decreased stress and improved mental health among college students (VanKim & Nelson, 2013). It is reasonable to extrapolate that, in addition to short-term immediate beneficial effects (e.g., symptom relief) of having Fitz as an ESA when Rocky was having anxiety and panic attacks, there also were potentially long-term benefits to be had, such as a decrease in panic attack frequency due to less social anxiety after having Fitz in the dorm room with him.

Through having Fitz living on campus in his dorm room, Rocky would be able to experience the physical, psychological, emotional, and social benefits of HAI on an ongoing basis. While Rocky was not motivated to take walks on his own, he was willing to walk for Fitz's sake and looked forward to walking Fitz

University of Toledo student Jessica Funari and her emotional support dog Diago are likely sharing an "oxytocin gaze positive loop" (Nagasawa et al., 2015) moment. Photo Credit: Charles George

on campus; he felt more comfortable socially when the dog was walking with him, and the exercise of walking could help to reduce his anxiety. Psychologically, Fitz could motivate Rocky to be more active and structured in his routine, both of which can be helpful in managing anxiety. Emotionally, Rocky found comfort in Fitz when he was experiencing anxiety, and through their companionship, the college student found he had less anticipatory anxiety about leaving home; this would likewise help him when his dog moved on campus. Socially, Fitz also served as a bridge to others. Rocky was generally very self-conscious when people approached him; however, if people approached him to meet or ask about Fitz when they walked together at home in their neighborhood, he typically felt more at ease; this would likely hold true on campus as well. Having Rocky present as a focal point for conversations could help ease Rocky's anxiety about connections with other students.

RECOMMENDED PROCESSES AND PRACTICES FOR BRINGING AN ESA INTO CAMPUS HOUSING

In this section, we provide a step-by-step guide to support students in bringing their emotional support dogs to campus and successfully integrating the animal into the campus context.

STEP ONE: WRITTEN VERIFICATION OF NEED FOR AN ESA AS AN ACCOMMODATION

Rocky's therapist had already diagnosed Rocky with social anxiety disorder, and Rocky had already reported to Rocky's therapist that being with Fitz helped to reduce his symptoms of anxiety. Regarding how to best proceed in supporting Rocky, Rocky's therapist consulted a colleague knowledgeable about the different therapeutic roles of animals. The colleague correctly responded that, in order for a client to have an ESA in non-pet housing, that client would need written verification. This verification must explicitly state that: (1) the client met the FHA criteria for having a disability, and (2) having an ESA would alleviate that client's emotional distress and/or impairment related to the existing disability. The colleague explained that Rocky's therapist, as a mental health professional, could provide legally acceptable verification of need for an ESA as an accommodation; in FHEO Notice 2013-01, documentation from a physician, psychiatrist, social worker, or other mental health professional is explicitly exemplified as reliable documentation for an ESA verification (US Department of Housing and Urban Development, 2013). In order to qualify for an ESA accommodation, impairing mental health symptoms experienced by the person can be due to a primary mental illness disability or a related physical disability that causes ongoing mental health distress; ultimately, both can be understood as under the umbrella of mental health conditions. While a specific diagnosis is not legally required in an ESA verification letter, within the *Diagnostic and Statistical Manual of Mental Disorders* (DSM–5), the American Psychiatric Association does recognize ongoing mental health symptoms that do not meet full criteria for any mental disorder but "cause clinically significant distress or impairment in social, occupational, or other important areas" (2013, p. 708) as an "unspecified mental disorder." Rocky's therapist stated his client (Rocky) had been diagnosed with social anxiety disorder; the colleague cautioned that having a diagnosis was not synonymous with having a disability. While diagnoses are medical terms, disability is a legal term, and varies according to federal law; the colleague referenced meeting the FHA definition of disability as key to whether or not one could legally have an ESA as an accommodation.

Because Rocky's therapist had professional knowledge of how Rocky's anxiety disorder was impairing a major life activity—his ability to participate in school—he felt comfortable providing written verification of such as a disability according to the FHA criteria; the first criterion of ESA eligibility was hence met. Rocky's accounts in therapy of how Fitz helped reduced anxiety symptoms substantiated Rocky's therapist's conclusion that Rocky also met the second criterion of ESA eligibility—that the animal would alleviate disability-specific distress and/or impairment. Rocky's therapist also had recently completed an online webinar on the benefits of human-animal interaction, and felt he had a solid rationale for his professional opinion that an ESA would help alleviate Rocky's symptoms.

Fitz was Rocky's companion animal long before requesting the ESA verification letter; however, *having a specific animal identified to serve as an ESA prior to obtaining the ESA letter is* not *legally required*. Some people may obtain an animal specifically for the purpose of being an ESA; others may retrospectively recognize that interactions with current companion animals are helping to alleviate mental health-related symptoms and impairment, and request written verification of need for their current companion animals to serve as ESAs (Hoy-Gerlach et al., 2019). A person's history of beneficial interactions with their own and/or other people's animals can also be used to substantiate a mental health professional's opinion that obtaining an ESA would alleviate disability-specific distress and/or impairment, and the ESA may be obtained *after* the verification letter is written (Hoy-Gerlach et al., 2019). Based on his colleague's guidance, Rocky's therapist downloaded a template from Bazelon Center for Mental Health Law (2017) that contained generally agreed upon elements necessary for documented reasonable verification of ESA need from a mental health professional. Working from the template, Rocky's therapist prepared the letter shown in Figure 4.1 and gave it to Rocky at their next scheduled session.

Through this letter, Rocky now had written verification from a mental health professional verifying his need for an ESA (US Department of Housing and Urban Development, 2013; 2020). Rocky's therapist placed a copy of this letter in Rocky's chart, and Rocky kept the original letter.

Life Wellness Counseling Center
[Agency letterhead]

[Date]

To Whom It May Concern:

[Full Name of Patient] is my patient and has been under my care since September 15, 2018 **[date]**. I am very familiar with ____'s **[insert patient name]** history and with the functional limitations imposed by ____'s **[patient name's]** disability. **[patient name]** meets the Fair Housing Act definition of disability.

Due to his **[appropriate pronoun]** disability, **[client first name]** experiences **[list the symptoms alleviated by ESA presence and/or interactions]** that cause impairment in daily functioning. To help alleviate this impairment, **[client first name]** needs an Emotional Support Animal (ESA).

This ESA is necessary for the mental health of **[client name]**; the animal helps to reduce distress and impairment associated with____'s **[client name's]** disability.

Thank you,

Mental Health Professional, LISW, License ######
[name of clinician, license #: ######]

FIGURE 4.1 Template for the letter written by a mental health professional.

While not required to have an animal identified as an ESA prior to obtaining written verification of ESA need, Rocky knew that he wanted Fitz to serve in the ESA role. Until 2020, there were not specific species legal restrictions regarding which animal species could serve in an ESA role. In January 2020, the Department of Housing and Urban Development (HUD) released a new guidance memo known as the "Assistance Animals Notice," restricting species that can be used as ESAs to common household pets; the banning of specific breeds remains illegal (US Department of Housing and Urban Development, 2020). Common household pets are defined as "a dog, cat, small bird, rabbit, hamster, gerbil, other rodent, fish, turtle, or other small, domesticated animal that is traditionally kept in the home for pleasure rather than for commercial purposes" (US Department of Housing and Urban Development, 2020, p. 12).

Fitz was a gentle, friendly, three-year-old mixed-breed neutered dog, approximately 50 pounds, who was current on his vaccinations. The dog had not undergone any formal training—nor is such necessary for an animal to serve as an ESA. He walked calmly on his leash, was well behaved in the house, and enjoyed car rides and meeting new people at home or while out on walks. Fine et al. (2019) suggest that "friendly and outgoing animals are more likely to be suitable as ESAs" (p. 200), and underscore the importance of ascertaining an animal's health, temperament, and activity level in consultation with a veterinarian. Being in good health, easy-going, well-behaved, and very bonded with Rocky, Fitz fortunately was an excellent candidate to be an ESA within a residence hall setting.

Curious as to whether he needed anything else in order for Fitz to serve as an ESA, Rocky did an online search and quickly found numerous sites claiming to be the "official national registry" for emotional support dogs, offering costly certificates, vests, badges, bandanas, and other ESA-designation equipment for purchase. Rocky called Rocky's therapist, who again consulted with the colleague familiar with ESA and service dog qualifications. Rocky's therapist's colleague informed the therapist that such sites were not legitimate, and that there was no national registry for ESAs, as clarified within the "Assistance Animals Notice" (US Department of Housing and Urban Development, 2020). The colleague explained that because ESAs do not have public access rights under ADA law, the purchase of a vest or badge for Fitz was an unnecessary expense. Rocky was disappointed to learn he could not bring Fitz to movies and restaurants with him, but was relieved that he did not need to pay the fees he had seen online. Having obtained written verification of his need for an ESA as an accommodation from his therapist, Rocky next considered whether he needed to do anything else at the university to bring Fitz to campus to live with him.

STEP TWO: THE DISABILITY SERVICES OFFICE EVALUATES THE ACCOMMODATION REQUEST

Emotional support animals are permitted to be in a person's place of dwelling as a disability accommodation in accordance with the Fair Housing Act of 1988 and Section 504 of the Rehabilitation Act of 1973, and are recognized as falling under the umbrella category of assistance animals (which includes both ESAs and service animals in these legislative acts). Rocky's room in the residence hall is considered a dwelling, and hence falls under jurisdiction of these federal legislations. Under the FHA, a university is obliged review requests for reasonable accommodations within student housing and make necessary adjustments. Such adjustments include but are not limited to making an exception to a no pets policy to allow assistance animals in the dwelling, or modifications to the environment to remove barriers. The US Department of Housing and Urban Development is charged with enforcing the FHA, and defines reasonable accommodation as:

> a change in rules, policies, practices, or services so that a person with a disability will have an equal opportunity to use and enjoy a dwelling unit or common space. A housing provider should do everything s/he can to assist, but s/he is not required to make changes that would fundamentally alter the program or create an undue financial and administrative burden. (n.d., unpaged)

In the higher education setting, the person's "place of dwelling" would be the student's assigned room or suite in a residence hall. An ESA would support the student's use and enjoyment of the dwelling unit because of the therapeutic benefits an ESA provides. Requests for an ESA to reside with students are reviewed on a case-by-case basis, typically by a campus disability services office. Generally, fundamental alteration and undue burden do not apply to ESA requests.

Two major cases brought the issue of ESAs in the higher education setting to the forefront. In 2015, the US Department of Justice settled a lawsuit with the University of Nebraska at Kearney. This lawsuit was originally filed in 2011. This case involved two separate students who were denied the right to have their dogs, who were ESAs, reside with them in the university apartments. Several months after the University of Nebraska at Kearney case in early 2016, Kent State University in Ohio also entered into a settlement agreement with the US Department of Justice. This lawsuit was filed in 2014. A student and her husband alleged that they were denied the right to have a dog as an ESA reside with them in university apartments in 2010. The outcome of both lawsuits was that institutions of higher education put policies, processes, and procedures in place to allow students who qualify to have ESAs live with them in on-campus housing. In response, many colleges and universities established policies and procedures to govern decisions about dogs on campus generally and ESAs specifically. There are numerous institutions that have developed well-thought-out protocols for ESAs on campus; examples include the University of Toledo, The Ohio State University, Brown University, and Washington State University.

Let us return to our story with Rocky and Fitz. Fortunately, Rocky did not simply show up with Fitz—now legally considered an ESA—and insist on moving Fitz into his campus residence hall; he thought (correctly) that there was likely some campus process he needed to complete. Rocky contacted the Residence Life Office at his university; he was told he first needed approval from the Disability Services Office and was referred to staff there to start the approval process for having Fitz reside with him in the residence hall as an ESA. He spoke with a staff member of the Disability Services Office, who informed Rocky that they needed information from both him and his mental health therapist to assess the need for Fitz as a disability accommodation in the residence hall. Rocky provided the letter from Rocky's therapist, which verified his disability-related need for an ESA. In his meeting with disability services, Rocky explained his need for Fitz to come join him at college. He gave information about his psychological condition and provided a summary of how Fitz helps to alleviate the symptoms of his condition. He shared that, looking back, Fitz was instrumental in his well-being. Every day, Rocky looked forward to seeing Fitz after school and having him close by when completing homework. His parents and siblings often had people spend time in their home, and Fitz helped him to decompress. Rocky stated that Fitz would sit with him in his room at home, and that being able to pet and talk to Fitz lessened his anxiety. Similarly, in college, Rocky could return to his room in the residence hall throughout the day to interact with Fitz. He mentioned that he had already spoken to his roommate and anticipated no issues, as his roommate loves dogs. Having established a nexus between Rocky's disability and his disability-related need for Fitz as an ESA, the Disability Services Office approved Rocky's request for an ESA as a housing accommodation, and notified Rocky and the Residence Life Office of the approved accommodation via email.

In our story, the ideal situation occurred in that the student and mental health professional provided exactly what was required to process the request. There are other scenarios for which disability services would need to exercise professional judgment to determine whether the request for an ESA as an accommodation is approved, or if more information is needed to determine the nexus between disability and disability-related need for the ESA. One common issue encountered in doing such work is that students may provide a verification of ESA need from an online entity that mass markets provision of such for fees. Concerns regarding fraud and ethics have been widely raised across mental health professions about such entities (Fine et al., 2019; Hoy-Gerlach et al., 2019). It is our recommendation that disability services should ask for more specific documentation when presented with such online verification. The disability services office on a campus should ideally have an ESA verification form that a student can bring to their mental health professionals to be completed, or give specific guidelines for a letter to be provided, such as the letter Rocky's therapist provided for Rocky.

Another issue that may be encountered when the disability service office staff receives written verification of ESA need is that such verification may not include any diagnostic or symptom-related information. While diagnostic information is not legally required, this will likely necessitate the campus disability services provider asking for additional information to be provided by the mental health professional. Disability services professionals need to be able to draw a nexus between an accommodation as it relates to mitigating the individual's disability. In the case of an ESA, it should be clear that the animal would help to alleviate symptoms associated with the disability. For example, a student who experiences panic attacks would have a decrease in the frequency of panic attacks with continued interactions with the ESA. A student with depressive episodes, who experiences improved self-care from being on a regular schedule due to being vested in caring for the well-being of the ESA, is an additional instance of such. A third example would be a student like Rocky, who would return to his dorm room throughout the day to spend time with his ESA to decompress from all the anxiety-provoking social interactions in the classroom or other social activities such as student organization meetings, mandatory residence hall gatherings, study groups, and so forth.

STEP THREE: COORDINATION WITH THE RESIDENCE LIFE OFFICE

Once the Disability Services Office provided the email approval of an ESA as an accommodation for Rocky to the Office of Residence Life, the process of bringing the ESA to campus became an agreement between Rocky (the student) and the Office of Residence Life. Residence life staff contacted Rocky, emailed him information about the process entailed with moving an ESA into the residence hall (Box 4.1), and scheduled a meeting with a professional residence life staff member (not a resident assistant or other student-employed role).

> ## BOX 4.1 INFORMATION FOR STUDENTS
>
> ### PROCESS OF BRINGING AN EMOTIONAL SUPPORT ANIMAL INTO A RESIDENCE HALL
>
> Students may be permitted to have an emotional support animal within campus housing facilities if approved by the Disability Services Office and the animal is able to be accommodated within the residence halls.
>
> **A student may be permitted to have an emotional support animal in a campus housing unit as a reasonable accommodation if:**
> - The student has a verifiable disability; and
> - the animal is necessary to afford the student with a disability an equal opportunity to use and enjoy a dwelling; and
> - there is an identifiable relationship or nexus between the disability and the support the animal provides.
>
> **If a student is permitted to have an emotional support animal:**
> - There will be a minimum 10-business-day wait between approval of emotional support animal, starting at the day of the meeting with the associate director to review the agreement, and when the student can bring the animal to campus. During this time, roommates, suitemates, and appropriate staff will be informed of the approval of a pet.
> - The animal will be restricted to only housing areas. It may not be permitted to enter classrooms, recreational facilities, or other campus buildings. Requests for accommodations beyond the residential scope will be assessed on a case-by-case basis.
> - The student owner is responsible for controlling the animal and its behavior.
> - The student owner is responsible for the care and well-being of the animal, including appropriate inoculations.

- The student owner is responsible for all clean up and/or damages associated with the animal.
- The student owner is responsible for educating others in the campus community on how to appropriately interact with the animal.
- Animals need to be well cared for, clean, and hygienic.
- Animals must be in good health with regular check-ups and must comply with all state and local licensure and vaccination requirements.
- Documentation of vaccinations and licensure are required if the student and animal reside in campus housing facilities.
- Animals that may fundamentally alter the university's operations may not be allowed.
- Animals that may cause substantial physical damage may not be allowed.
- Animals cannot be a threat to the health or safety of others.
- Student must submit the signed emotional support animal agreement each year prior to move-in.
- Verification of examination and vaccines must be submitted on an annual basis prior to move-in.
- A sticker identifying that room as a room with an animal will be placed on the door to help staff know prior to entering the room that there is an animal in the room.
- If any roommate or suitemates have allergies or fear of the animal being brought into the room, they can move voluntarily.

Rocky and the residence life staff met to discuss the written ESA agreement (Figure 4.2) that Rocky needed to complete. The agreement outlines areas such as the expectation to control the dog, care for the dog, educate the community about their interaction with the dog, provide updated vet documentation for the dog, and to prevent the dog from negatively impacting the community.

After completing all university-required documents, discussing the expectations, and providing copies of all veterinary documents that showed that the ESA had a wellness exam within the last year and was up-to-date on all major vaccinations recommended by the vet, the ESA will be permitted by the Office of Residence Life to come to the residence halls as an ESA after a ten-day waiting period. Not all students seeking to move their ESAs into campus are as prepared as Rocky; there may be a delay in the start of the ten-day period while

Emotional Support Animal Agreement

Students may be permitted to have an emotional support animal within campus housing facilities if approved by the Office of Student Disability Services and the animal is able to be accommodated within the residence halls.

A student may be permitted to have an emotional support animal in a campus housing unit as a reasonable accommodation if:
- the student has a verifiable disability; and
- the animal is necessary to afford the student with a disability an equal opportunity to use and enjoy a dwelling; and
- there is an identifiable relationship or nexus between the disability and the support the animal provides.

If a student is permitted to have an emotional support animal, it will be restricted to only housing areas. It may not be permitted to enter classrooms, recreational facilities, or other campus buildings. Requests for accommodations beyond the residential scope will be assessed on a case by case basis.

Please initial below as an understanding of the agreement between you and University Housing:

____ The student owner is responsible for controlling the animal and its behavior.
____ The student owner is responsible for the care and well-being of the animal.
____ The student owner is responsible for all clean up and/or damages associated with the animal.
____ The student owner is responsible for educating others in the campus community on how to appropriately interact with the animal.
____ Animals need to be well cared for, clean, and hygienic.
____ Animals must be in good health with regular checkups and must comply with all state and local licensure and vaccination requirements.
____ Documentation of vaccinations, a flea prevention method, and licensure are required prior to student moving in each year if the student and animal reside in campus housing facilities.
____ Animals that may fundamentally alter the University of Toledo's operations may not be allowed.
____ Animals that may cause or have caused substantial physical damage may not be allowed.
____ Animals cannot be a threat to the health or safety of others.

Student name   Student signature

Student ID #   Residence Hall   Room Number

Document's submitted date

FIGURE 4.2 Emotional support animal agreement.

the Office of Residence Life staff waits on an ESA getting updated vaccines and/or on faxed or emailed veterinary records. Once approved by the Office of Residence Life for an ESA in the residence hall, the student is instructed to tell all roommates, as soon as possible within the ten-day period, that they would be bringing an approved ESA. In the case of Rocky, he had already informed his roommate, who was agreeable and excited about Fitz coming to campus. During the ten-day waiting period, the Office of Residence Life likewise notifies all roommate(s) in writing of the impending ESA presence within the dorm room, and offers an alternative space to the roommate(s) if not comfortable living with an ESA for any reason. Rocky's roommate declined the alternate space. The Office of Residence Life staff also will notify via email the hall director, maintenance supervisor, front desk clerical staff, graduate assistant, and resident adviser in the residence hall of the impending ESA presence and move-in date. Through this notification, key housing staff who could be impacted were proactively alerted to the ESA's arrival, *prior* to the ESA moving in. Such notification is important for the safety of the staff and the ESA when entering the student's room for things like routine maintenance or during a fire alarm.

If a roommate/student is not comfortable living with the emotional support dog, it is that student's responsibility to request a room change and move to a different space on campus. Since an ESA is an accommodation provided by the Disability Services Office, students with the accommodation would not be required to move, but could move if they chose to. Depending on the size of the ESA, there are times where a student may choose to move to a larger space to accommodate the ESA. Allergies are a common issue that might precipitate a student move; however, in some instances, allergy issues can be worked around. For instance, in a Greek house where two residents were approved for cats, and the heating and air conditioning system was interconnected throughout the residence, several students reported sensitivity to cat dander. Due to the nature of the Greek house being the primary residence for one Greek organization, comparable housing was not readily available for the students negatively affected by cat dander. All students were able to stay in the Greek house comfortably and enjoy the camaraderie through the installation of special filters, which ensured the cat dander wasn't impacting the other students. Such a solution could readily be applied in the instance of allergies to an emotional support dog.

Once an emotional support dog arrives on campus, it is the responsibility of the student to help the dog adjust to the new setting. An ESA may go through an adjustment period and struggle with the new environment, exhibiting stress behavior such as barking when left alone. Staff within the residence hall treat issues such as noise from the ESA the same as any other noise issue where it is documented; the hall staff work to educate and assist the student with this issue. Staff will meet with the student to develop a plan, and see how the staff can provide support to help the ESA and student to adjust to the residence hall environment. Often roommates will assist with the transition of the ESA by spending time with the ESA, walking the ESA if a dog, and feeding the ESA to help him or her adjust. It has been our experience that people in the room or on the floor typically greet ESAs with excitement and a willingness to assist with care of the ESA. In the case of an approved emotional support dog that does not adapt well to the residence hall and is causing a disruption to the community, the student is required to remove that ESA within a specified amount of time. The student still has a housing contract with the university and is still approved for an accommodation of an ESA, but the specific ESA disrupting the community would have to be removed from the residence hall through the university conduct process. The removal of the ESA would be based on policy violation that occurred based on that ESA's behavior. This occurrence is rare; every effort possible should be made to work with the student and the ESA to support them in their transition to college together. Residence life staff at The University of Toledo have helped students and their ESAs adjust to campus life in a variety of ways, including—but not limited to—linking the student and ESA to veterinary care; assisting with getting needed animal care/behavior information; and helping with obtaining needed animal care resources.

Dogs can provide the support that some students with mental health issues need to venture beyond the campus environment. Photo Credit: Mary Renck Jalongo

On a campus that is starting out bringing ESAs into residence hall settings, a clearly delineated policy for ESAs should be developed in collaboration between the disability services and housing offices. After a policy is developed, a specific procedure for handling ESA accommodation requests from students should be put in writing and be readily available online and in written housing and disability-related materials. An agreement between the student and campus housing regarding the ESA also should be used to specify student responsibilities related to the ESA. We have included sample materials from The University of Toledo (see Figure 4.1 and Box 4.1). Establishing relationships with local veterinary practices and dog trainers also may be helpful if a student needs extra support to transition an emotional support dog.

CONCLUSION

Fitz provided much needed and helpful support to Rocky in alleviating debilitating symptoms of his social anxiety disorder. Rocky was able to work with his therapist to obtain written verification of his need for an ESA, and Rocky was able to request having Fitz in his residence hall room as an ESA and housing accommodation. Although not clear on the process beforehand, Rocky experienced minimal stress in requesting the accommodation and bringing Fitz into the residence hall as an ESA. The process ran smoothly because there was a clearly delineated campus protocol, and cross-office collaboration and relationships had already been established to facilitate the accommodation process, not only for students requesting the accommodation, but also for others who might be impacted. Rocky's request for an emotional support dog as an accommodation was approved in a timely manner by disability services staff, and he subsequently met with residence life staff, completed the ESA agreement form (including provision of all veterinary records), and moved Fitz into the residence hall. He found himself able to relax more while in his room with Fitz, and experienced a reduction in his anxiety symptoms and panic attack frequency. Rocky is not an exception in benefiting from the presence of an ESA. We have had students with numerous debilitating mental health symptoms and disabilities, who, through the presence of their ESAs, have experienced alleviation of mental health symptoms and related impairment, and reported better overall functioning at the university. For instance, a female student with severe depression and post-traumatic stress disorder was approved to bring her emotional support dog onto campus. The young woman had been staying in her bed in her dorm room and missing class; although staying in bed, she also had been unable to sleep due to feeling nervous and hypervigilant. The presence of her emotional support dog and the dog's need for walks resulted in her forcing herself to get up and out for brief moments; she began to feel better once out, and the routine of caring for her dog reminded her to take her own medication. The presence of her dog also eased her fears at night, and she was able to sleep better. With the support of her ESA, this student was better able to cope with life on campus and started attending classes regularly.

Throughout this book, we have presented evidence that there are documented social, psychological, emotional, and physical benefits of living with a dog that can enhance the well-being of anyone who enjoys dogs. For someone living with a disability and related mental health symptoms, those benefits can be transformative, making the difference between being able to adequately function or not. As explicated in this chapter, the emotional support dog helps to mitigate disability not through special training to do tasks, but rather through the bonding and affiliative behaviors that dogs innately offer toward humans due to coevolving with us (Nagasawa et al., 2015). As the positive impact of dogs on human health and wellness is increasingly substantiated by research, we will likely see expanded recognition and leveraging of the everyday human-dog bond benefits within health care and education settings.

REFERENCES

American Psychiatric Association. (2013). *Diagnostic and statistical manual of mental disorders* (5th ed.). Arlington, VA: Author.

American Veterinary Medical Association (AVMA). (2017). *Assistance animals: Rights of access and the problem of fraud.* https://www.avma.org/KB/Resources/Reports/Pages/Assistance-Animals-Rights-of-Access-and-the-Problem-of-Fraud.aspx

Americans with Disabilities Act National Network. (2019). *What is the definition of disability under the ADA?* https://adata.org/faq/what-definition-disability-under-ADA

Bazelon Center for Mental Health Law. (2017). Right to emotional support animals in "no pet" housing. http://www.bazelon.org/wp-content/uploads/2017/04/2017-06-16-Emotional-Support-Animal-Fact-Sheet-for-Website-final.pdf

Beetz, A., Uvnäs-Moberg, K., Julius, H., & Kotrschal, K. (2012). Psychosocial and psychophysiological effects of human-animal interactions: The possible role of oxytocin. *Frontiers in Psychology, 3*, 234. https://pub.epsilon.slu.se/10563/1/uvnas_moberg_etal_130625.pdf

Brooks, H. L., Rushton, K., Lovell, K., Bee, P., Walker, L., Grant, L., & Rogers, A. (2018). The power of support from companion animals for people living with mental health problems: A systematic review and narrative synthesis of the evidence. *BMC Psychiatry, 18*(1), 31. https://doi.org/10.1186/s12888-018-1613-2

Fine, A. H., Knesl, O., Hart, B., Hart, L., Zenithson, N., Patterson-Kane, E., . . . Feldman, S. (2019). The role of veterinarians in assisting clients identify and care for emotional support animals. *Journal of the American Veterinary Medical Association*, *254*(2), 199–202. https://doi.org/10.2460/javma.254.2.199

Handlin, L., Nilsson, A., Ejdebäck, M., Hydbring-Sandberg, E., & Uvnas-Moberg, K. (2012). Associations between the psychological characteristics of the human-dog relationship and oxytocin and cortisol levels. *Anthrozoös, 25*(2), 215–228. https://doi.org/10.2752/175303712X13316289505468

Hoy-Gerlach, J., Vincent, A., & Lory Hector, B. (2019). Emotional support animals in the United States: Emergent guidelines for mental health clinicians. *Journal of Psychosocial Rehabilitation and Mental Health*, (Preprints), 1–10.

Hoy-Gerlach, J., & Wehman, S. (2017). *The relevance of human-animal interaction for social work practice*. Washington, DC: National Association of Social Work Press.

Levine, G. N., Allen, K., Braun, L. T., Christian, H. E., Friedmann, E., Taubert, K. A., . . . Lange, R. A.; on behalf of the American Heart Association Council on Clinical Cardiology and Council on Cardiovascular and Stroke Nursing. (2013). Pet ownership and cardiovascular risk: A scientific statement from the American Heart Association. *Circulation, 127*(3), 2353–2363.

Nagasawa, M., Mitsui, S., En, S., Ohtani, N., Ohta, M., Sakuma, Y., . . . Kikusui, T. (2015). Oxytocin-gaze positive loop and the coevolution of human-dog bonds. *Science, 348*(6232), 333–336.

Odendaal, J. S., & Meintjes, R. A. (2003). Neurophysiological correlates of affiliative behaviour between humans and dogs. *Veterinary Journal, 165*(3), 296–301. https://doi.org/10.1016/S1090-0233(02)00237-X

US Department of Housing and Urban Development. (n.d.). Reasonable accommodations and modifications. https://www.hud.gov/program_offices/fair_housing_equal_opp/reasonable_accommodations_and_modifications

US Department of Housing and Urban Development. (2013). *FHEO-2013-01 service animals and assistance animals for people with disabilities in housing and HUD-funded programs*. Washington, DC: Government Printing Office.

US Department of Housing and Urban Development. (2020). *FHEO-2020-01 assistance animal notice*. Washington, DC: Government Printing Office.

Vankim, N. A., & Nelson, T. F. (2013). Vigorous physical activity, mental health, perceived stress, and socializing among college students. *American Journal of Health Promotion, 28*(1), 7–15. https://doi.org/10.4278/ajhp.111101-QUAN-395

Wisch, R. (2015). FAQs on emotional support animals. https://www.animallaw.info/article/faqs-emotional-support-animals#s6

Yount, R., Ritchie, E. C., St. Laurent, M., Chumley, P., & Olmert, M. D. (2013). The role of service dog training in the treatment of combat-related PTSD. *Psychiatric Annals, 43*(6), 292–295. https://doi.org/10.3928/00485713-20130605-11

5

THERAPY DOGS AND FACILITY DOGS

Supporting Well-Being

MARY RENCK JALONGO, EDITOR, SPRINGER NATURE, INDIANA, PA, AND LORRAINE J. GUTH, DEPARTMENT OF COUNSELING, INDIANA UNIVERSITY OF PENNSYLVANIA, INDIANA, PA

INTRODUCTION

Three recently hired elementary school teachers write a proposal and submit it to the Board of Education for review. They are asking for approximately $1,000 to pay for their family pets to become therapy dogs. The teachers then want permission to bring their dogs to work with them daily as a way to support the children's learning. The board votes to table the discussion after two questions are raised: Are the dogs health checked and what is their level of training? and Have the teachers considered how the presence of dogs might affect the school's liability insurance premiums? When a summary of the board meeting is published in the newspaper without any names attached to the new proposal, it creates confusion. There is a local group affiliated with a respected, national therapy dog organization that has been doing a dog bite prevention program in the district for the past 20 years. Some people assume that they are the ones associated with the proposal when they are not. This results in a flurry of e-mails and telephone calls to people who are members of the well-established therapy dog group. Administrators and board members want to know:

A faculty member from the Department of Counseling provides service to the campus and surrounding community by volunteering with her bichon frise, a certified therapy dog. Photo Credit: Megan Higgins

Does it really cost that much to become a therapy dog?
Answer: No. The organization that the teachers referred to is not a recognized therapy dog group; it is a bogus "registry." According to the website, the group the teachers want to join does not conduct any evaluation of the handler/dog team, nor does it require a criminal record clearance from volunteers. Reputable therapy dog organizations are nonprofits that support community service, so the cost of joining is quite low—usually less than $40 a year.

Aren't the dogs that have been visiting for years health checked and trained?
Answer: Yes. Members of the Alliance of Therapy Dogs (ATD) must verify that their dogs' vaccinations are current and submit a health verification form from a veterinarian annually. Together, the handler and dog have to pass a test of basic obedience, dog temperament assessment tasks, and a simulated nursing home visit that includes orthopedic equipment. After that, the handler/dog team must successfully complete three visits out in the community that are observed and evaluated by an experienced therapy dog handler.

Aren't the handler/dog teams that have been visiting insured?
Answer: Yes. ATD provides liability insurance as a benefit of membership in the organization. A copy of the insurance letter that verifies this coverage is provided to the school administrator.

Additional issues surface as the proposal is discussed further. First, none of the three teachers has any experience with therapy dogs. Secondly, there is concern that the presence of three dogs might distract the teachers from adequately supervising the children and that being at school all day five days a week might be stressful for the animals. Ultimately, the request of the teachers is denied.

This situation in basic education illustrates some of the problems with bringing dogs into an educational environment without adequate knowledge, skill in dog training, careful preparation, and clear linkages to instructional objectives. It also clarifies the ways in which therapy dogs differ from a family pet. Therapy dogs also differ from service dogs and emotional support animals in important ways, as table 5.1 describes.

This chapter defines a therapy dog by citing the characteristics sought in these canines and the different roles that they often play in colleges and universities. It highlights the leading professional organizations that register and insure therapy dogs. Next, it will discuss contemporary views of wellness that consider not only physical well-being, but also psychological health and how the presence of therapy dogs can support human wellness. The third section of the chapter will review the research on animals' effects on human health and describe a wide array of activities in postsecondary institutions that involve therapy dogs in initiatives that promote college students' wellness and, at the same time, advocate for the welfare of the dogs. Chapter 5 concludes with recommendations for working effectively with handler/therapy dog teams in college events, projects, programs, and interventions.

DEFINITION OF A *THERAPY DOG*

In her book that calls for major changes in college teaching and learning, Weimer (2002) wrote these comments nearly twenty years ago that could have been written today:

Table 5.1 A Comparison of Therapy Dogs, Service Dogs, and Emotional Support Animals

TYPE OF DOG	DESCRIPTION	PUBLIC ACCESS RIGHTS UNDER ADA	COMMON MISCONCEPTIONS
Therapy dogs	Therapy dogs are working dogs who are "everybody's best friend." Unlike service dogs or ESAs, they are there for the express purpose of interacting with other people. Therapy dogs are working dog that are skilled at meeting and greeting lots of different people. Therapy dogs work to reduce stress, elevate positive mood, and encourage participation in activities. They are well-mannered, under control, and trained beyond basic obedience, but are not required to complete formal obedience classes.	Therapy dogs do not have public access rights through the Americans with Disabilities Act. They are visitors and guests who need to be invited to visit public places. On a college campus, therapy dogs are brought in by their volunteer owner/handlers at the request of faculty or staff.	Therapy dogs usually are at least one year old and have lived with their handlers for a minimum of six months. They are not homeless shelter dogs seeking to be adopted. They are not entertainers required to perform tricks. They are not assistance dogs that perform tasks to help a person with a psychological or physical disability. Therapy dog handlers volunteer and share their dogs with others as part of various community service activities. They are "*do* pet me" dogs.
Service dogs	Service dogs are individually trained to perform specific tasks for a person who has a disability. Usually, a professional service dog provider does the training rather than the dog's owner. Many service dogs have passed the rigorous Public Access Certification Test. Their level of training is high, often taking 1–3 years.	Service dogs do have public access rights. This means they can go places where dogs ordinarily are prohibited—on public transportation, in public buildings, and live in housing that ordinarily has a "no pets" policy. Increasingly, it is against the law to falsely represent an untrained dog as a service dog.	Service dogs should not be petted while they are working. People should speak to the person and ask before interacting with the dog. It is not permissible to ask what the dog's owner's disability is. It is acceptable to ask what tasks the dog performs.

Emotional support animals (dogs)	Emotional support dogs assist a person with a diagnosed disability that is listed in the American Psychiatric Association's manual and documented in a letter on letterhead by a licensed mental health professional. Emotional support animals are not required to have specialized training.	ESAs do not have public access rights according to the Americans with Disabilities Act. Everyone needs to understand that ESAs do not have the right to "go anywhere" on campus. Students can, however, apply to have their dog reside with them in the residence hall under the provisions of the Fair Housing Act.	Postsecondary institutions need to have clear policies about dogs on campus that are consistent with local, state, and federal legislation.
Facility dogs	The defining feature of a facility dog is that it is at the workplace on a regular basis. Usually, the dog is owned and handled by an employee who is responsible for it. Of course, everyone in the workplace needs to agree to this. An example of a facility dog is a registered and insured therapy dog that accompanies a university counselor to work.	This can be confusing because some facility dogs are trained at the service dog level while others are trained as therapy dogs. If the dog is not functioning as a service dog (i.e., performing helpful tasks for an individual with a disability) or if it is trained as a therapy dog only, then it needs permission to be in the workplace.	A facility dog is not a tool to be exploited. Dogs need rest, play, sleep, and time outdoors throughout the day. Expecting them to work constantly in pursuit of a professional's objectives is unfair to the animal. Dogs need to sleep 12 to 14 hours per day—perhaps more if they are older or a large breed dog (Clark, 2016). Overscheduling them disregards their requirements for good health.

How would you characterize today's college students? Empowered, confident, self-motivated learners? That is not how I would describe mine. The ones in my classes are hopeful but generally anxious and tentative. They want all classes to be easy but expect that most will be hard. They wish their major (whatever it might be) did not require math, science, or English courses. A good number will not speak in class unless called on. Most like, want, indeed need teachers who tell them exactly what to do. Education is something done unto them. It frequently involves stress, anxiety, and other forms of discomfort. (p. 23)

Self-report data gathered from college students highlights some of the mental health issues that predominate: they get homesick (Binfet & Passmore, 2016), feel the pressure of deadlines, and have to adapt to a new environment; in addition, about 75% of undergraduates are working at the same time they are attending college classes (Gallavan & Benson, 2014; Zivin, Eisenberg, Gollust, & Golberstein, 2009). Over 50% of college students report that they have moderate-to-severe depression, and 11% have suicidal thoughts (Crossman, Kazdin, & Knudson, 2015).

Why involve dogs in addressing mental health issues of students? Perhaps it is because canines, among all the animals, are particularly adept and giving human beings attention, demonstrating comfort-offering behaviors, and reciprocating affection (Miklosi, 2018). In many ways, dogs embody key characteristics of client-centered counselors, namely regard, empathy, and congruence (Jenkins, Laux, Ritchie, & Tucker-Gail, 2014). Therapy dogs are the animal of choice for most animal visitation programs on a college campus. The purpose of the dogs' presence is stress reduction, elevation of positive mood, and encouragement for people to participate in an activity, event, or interaction with a mental health professional. Ng et al. (2014) define a therapy dog-handler team as a dog with a consistent, nonfearful, and nonaggressive temperament, and a handler who is trained to minimize interactions that might be perceived as threatening by the dog. Among dog trainers, the term *bomb-proof* is used to refer to dogs that are amazingly unflappable and happy-go-lucky. To illustrate, if a person is looking for therapy dog potential in dogs at a shelter, it is advisable to find one that remains steady and calm when most other dogs are wildly racing around, highly reactive to sounds and other dogs, or immobilized by fear. Given that a therapy dog will be expected to interact with many different people, canines with greater therapy dog potential would tend to show interest in a stranger, perhaps by first studying the person's face and then approaching that person. Once out of the kennel, the dog might become even more relaxed and willing to interact. This is not to suggest that every future therapy dog will behave the same way, nor to suggest that dogs behave the same way in a shelter that they will in a home. However, there are some shared temperament characteristics of successful therapy dogs. If a dog can, as the saying goes, keep his head when others all around him are losing theirs, this holds promise for better training outcomes. When selecting a suitable canine candidate for therapy dog work, the following traits of a therapy dog are sought and developed through training:

- Not fearful or excessively shy
- Dependably nonaggressive toward people
- Eager to interact with people, yet not overexcited
- Accepting of strangers
- Willing to venture beyond home
- Capable of adapting to new environments
- Relatively calm and confident
- Not overly reactive to other dogs
- Eager to please the handler and responsive to training
- Able to bounce back quickly after being startled
- Well socialized to different contexts
- Looks to the handler for leadership and is bonded to that person

Even with all these capabilities in place, a successful handler/therapy dog team is something of a "perfect storm" because so many variables must align before arriving at a winning combination. Entire books have been devoted to describing the bond between the dog and the human being who is the animal's guardian, trainer, advocate, and cohabitant (Butler, 2013; Howie, 2015). As McConnell and Fine (2015) observe, "We are asking dogs to be absolutely bomb proof around other dogs, around a vast variety of people in a multitude of conditions, in stressful circumstances with weird, strange, noisy machinery. The dogs who are great at it are one in a million dogs" (p. 113).

Another way to define a therapy dog is to consider the main roles that they typically fulfill. The American Veterinary Medical Association (AVMA) (2019) has produced guidelines for animal-assisted interventions. Table 5.2 adapts and applies these guidelines to canine-assisted interventions in which therapy dogs often participate.

It is important to note that, in therapy dog work, "one size does not fit all." As Pet Partners, a highly respected therapy animal organization notes, it is the handler's job to advocate for his or her dog's welfare. This includes making

Table 5.2 Types of Canine-Assisted Interventions

TYPE OF INTERVENTION	DEFINITION	RESPONSIBLE PERSON	EXAMPLE
Activity (animal-assisted activity, AAA)	Dogs are used to motivate, educate, provide recreation, or enhance quality of life in a variety of environments.	Professionals, paraprofessionals, or volunteers working with dogs that meet specific criteria.	Registered and insured therapy dogs participate in a health fair for students and staff. Prospective and new students/families can opt to interact with the dogs during campus tours, freshman orientation, and move-in days for campus housing.
Therapy (animal-assisted therapy, AAT)	Dogs are part of a treatment process that is documented and evaluated. Designed to promote improvement in human physical, social, emotional, or cognitive function. May be group or individual.	Delivered or directed by health or human service providers working within the scope of their profession.	A university counselor partners with a therapy dog group to schedule monthly visits with dogs. Students' responses to the program are evaluated with a paper or online questionnaire. At a student's request, the dog also sits in during individual counseling sessions.
Education (animal-assisted education, AAE)	A planned and structured intervention directed and/or delivered by an educational and related service professional with specific academic or educational goals.	Educators work with other professionals, paraprofessionals, or volunteers and dogs that meet specific criteria.	A summer program for children who struggle with reading is staffed by experienced teachers who are earning a reading specialist certificate. Handler/therapy dog teams visit weekly, listen to the children read aloud, and ask questions to check the children's comprehension.
Facility dog or resident canine	The dog is at a facility all or most of the time and accompanies the owner/handler to work.	Personnel at the facility care for the dog and incorporate him or her into various activities.	A graduate student in counseling is the adviser at a dog-friendly residence hall. Her dog lives there with her. The dog is present—if the student wants the dog there—when the adviser meets with individual students or groups of students to discuss issues of concern. When she begins an internship and is away during the day, other students who are approved as foster pet parents through the university help to care for her dog.

thoughtful decisions about which activities the dog would enjoy, being alert to signs of stress, determining when to discontinue an activity, and deciding when the dog needs to retire from visiting. To illustrate, some therapy dogs thrive on fast-paced activities, such as meeting many different students at the library during exam week, while other therapy dogs are best suited for more quiet and subdued settings, such as individual sessions of a counselor with a university student seeking mental health services. To complicate matters further, some exuberant young dogs who initially appear to be unsuitable as therapy dogs become superlative therapy dogs after they mature, while others who have been wonderful therapy dogs for many years lose their zest for visiting with advanced age or health issues. There is also the influence of particular dogs on particular students. Some students may gravitate toward a big dog that immediately rolls over to get a belly rub, while others are captivated by a frisky little dog that can barely contain its enthusiasm. Everyone at the university who collaborates with therapy dogs and handlers needs to respect these dogs as sentient beings whose physical and emotional needs must be met. People also need to accept that each one of these animals is unique and irreplaceable with a value beyond measure to their person. They are not "just a dog," a representation of a breed (e.g., boxer), or category (e.g., "puppy mill rescue"). It is an impressive achievement to have a wonderful dog as your community service partner, and people are justifiably proud when their dog officially becomes a therapy dog. Keeping all these considerations in mind is the best way to incorporate therapy dogs into efforts to promote human wellness.

THEORY OF WELLNESS

There is an entire branch of psychology that focuses on positive human emotions called *positive psychology*. Happiness, for example, has received considerable attention among mental health professionals, yet it is difficult to define. One leader in the field of positive psychology is Mihaly Csikszentmihalyi. He has been the driving force behind a line of inquiry about optimal learning experiences, or "flow" (Csikzentmihalyi, 2014). This research studies how people act when they are doing the things that they love to do rather than the things they feel obliged to do. A former nurse, now a professional dog trainer, exemplified this when she commented: "You know, they tell you to do more of what you love during retirement and I told my family, I know what that is. I just want to teach puppy kindergarten classes for the rest of my life." This situation illustrates the characteristics of flow, or an optimal learning experience. If you observed this spry senior working with puppies and their handlers, you would think that she (1) has clear goals and purpose, (2) enjoys the task so much that she can lose track of time, (3) finds the work intrinsically rewarding, (4) appears to perform the task almost effortlessly, (5) has skills that are matched to the level of the challenge, (6) is uninhibited and not self-conscious, and (7) is capable of exercising control over a bouncy bunch of pups and their owners.

Tasks that college students are called upon to perform frequently do not meet one or more of these criteria. Instead, they might be thinking, "Why do we have to learn this?" while watching the clock, relying on grades as motivators, struggling with assignments, doubting their abilities, worrying about what others think of them, and feeling overwhelmed. Citing the American College Health Association's national survey data, articles in the *New York Times* report that nearly one in six college students has been treated for anxiety issues, that anxiety and depression are a major concern of college students, and that nearly 60% of them are taking more than four years to complete four-year programs (Hoffman, 2015; Wolverton, 2019). Given these statistics, it is not surprising that wellness is an issue for contemporary college students.

Wellness may be defined as "a way of life oriented toward optimal health and well-being in which mind, body, and spirit are integrated by the individual to live more fully within the human and natural community" (Myers, Sweeney & Witmer, 2000, p. 252). There are many different ideas and models of wellness. To illustrate, a book on wellness in postsecondary students categorizes the concept into five broad areas: (1) emotional, (2) social, (3) intellectual, (4) physical, and (5) spiritual (Anderson, 2016). Issues discussed within the context of these broad areas include topics as diverse as excessive use of technology, stress management, sexual decision making, social isolation, healthful sleep/nutrition/exercise, use of alcohol or recreational drugs, and relationships that jeopardize psychological health. On college campuses, developmental, preventive, and wellness-enhancing interventions frequently are offered to increase students' well-being (Binfet & Passmore, 2016). Various models of wellness have been developed (Granello, 2013; Hettler, 1980; 1984; Myers & Sweeney, 2004; Myers, Sweeney, & Witmer, 2000; Zimpher, 1992). These models have conceptualized wellness in different ways. For example, Hettler (1980) created the Six Dimensions of Wellness model that includes occupational, physical, social, intellectual, spiritual, and emotional wellness. In 2000, Myers, Sweeney, and Witmer

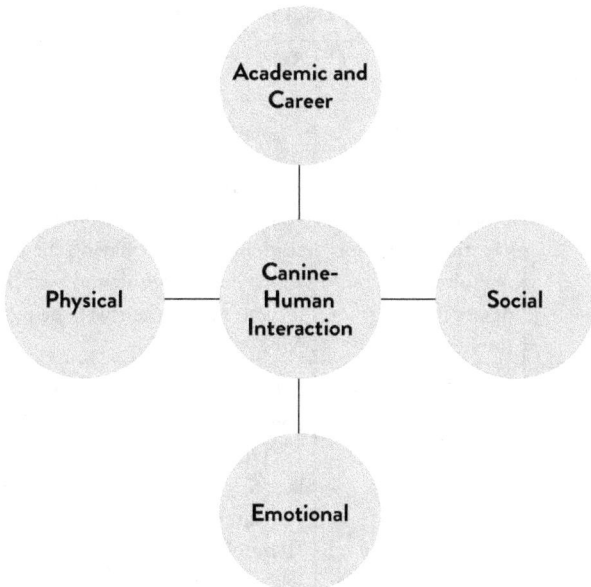

FIGURE 5.1 Model of wellness applied to human-canine interaction.

created the Wheel of Wellness model that included the wellness life tasks of spirituality, self-direction, work and leisure, friendship, and love. Then in 2008, Myers and Sweeney (2004) proposed the Indivisible Self Model of Wellness that conceptualized wellness as consisting of five components: creative, coping, social, essential, and physical. Figure 5.1 is a synthesis of these models of wellness applied to canine-human interaction. This model is comprised of four key components of wellness that are most impacted by the interactions between dogs and humans. Table 5.3 applies this model to research on the human-canine bond.

Bolstered by research findings such as those reported in table 5.3, many postsecondary institutions are now making a place for therapy dogs on campus.

RESEARCH AND INSTITUTIONAL INITIATIVES

Acceptance of therapy dogs on campus has increased dramatically in recent years. In 2015, Crossman et al. estimated that there were at least 925 animal visitation programs (AVPs) on college campuses in the United States. Over half of Canada's 98 universities had a dog program in place in 2015 (Dell et al., 2015).

Table 5.3 Research on the Role of Dogs in Student Wellness

WELLNESS COMPONENT	DEFINITION	RESEARCH ON HUMAN-CANINE INTERACTION
Academic and Career	Academic and career wellness refers to satisfaction in educational, vocational, and job pursuits. It encompasses learning, intellectual stimulation, creativity, and effective problem solving.	The presence of dogs often creates more positive perceptions of faculty (Wells & Perrine, 2001). In self-reported data gathered from students who attended library programs, students felt that having the dogs there showed that faculty and staff had a genuine interest in their well-being (Jalongo & McDevitt, 2015). Interactions with dogs prior to a test (Barker, Barker, McCain, & Schubert, 2016; McDonald, McDonald, & Roberts, 2017), before a presentation in class (Polheber & Matchock, 2014), or during exam week (Reynolds & Rabschutz, 2013) were associated with reductions in self-reported stress. Therapy dogs in the workplace have been found to lower stress, boost morale, and encourage teamwork (https://www.therapydogs.com/benefits-therapy-dog-workplace). Students also can learn about ways that dogs support wellness in their future careers, such as nurses learning about visiting therapy dogs in health care settings.
Social	Social wellness refers to having deep connections with others and includes friendships, family interactions, and intimate relationships. This dimension also includes the bond that is formed between humans and canines.	The presence of dogs in the workplace tends to increase positive social interactions (Foreman, Glenn, Meade, & Wirth, 2017). People are more likely to speak with a person who has a disability if that person has a service dog (Bould, Bigby, Bennett, & Howell, 2018). Pets have been found to provide social support and comfort (Adamle, Riley, & Carlson, 2009; McConnell, Brown, Shoda, Stayton, & Martin, 2011). Interactions with therapy dogs can help students to establish new relationships with others (Adamle et al., 2009). University students who participated in a single session therapy dog event also reported increases in a sense of school belonging (Binfet, 2017).

Emotional	Emotional wellness refers to the ability to be aware of emotions and use effective coping strategies to deal with life challenges. It also includes the ability to effectively communicate feelings with others.	Dogs give us permission to display emotions and cause us to be less self-conscious. Research also shows that therapy dogs can attenuate anxiety, stress, and depression (Adams et al., 2017; Folse, Minder, Aycock, & Santana, 2015). College students who participated in a therapy dog program reported that it made them happy, reduced stress (Wood, Ohlsen, Thompson, Hulin, & Knowles, 2017), and provided a sense of comfort (Daltry & Mehr, 2015; Lannon & Harrison, 2015).
Physical	The physical aspect of wellness includes optimal health and well-being. This dimension includes proper nutrition, healthy choices, physical exercise, mindfulness, and self-care strategies.	Dogs can exert a positive influence on human health (Casciotti & Zuckerman, 2016). A review of the literature concluded that dog ownership often increases physical activity (Christian et al., 2016). The American Heart Association found that dog owners are 54% more likely to get the recommended level of physical activity each day, which ultimately reduced their risk of heart disease (Ledoux, 2018). Elevated blood pressure associated with stress often returns to normal resting rates after college students pet a dog's fur (Muckle & Lasikiewicz, 2017). Research conducted with students indicates that therapy animals help to promote health (Lannon & Harrison, 2015). College students have also experienced decreases in diastolic blood pressure immediately after holding a dog (Somerville, Kruglikova, Robertson, Hanson, & MacLin, 2008). Vital signs of stress and salivary cortisol were reduced in nursing students who played with a dog for 15 minutes (Delgado, Toukonen, & Wheelter, 2018).

Although many postsecondary institutions now welcome trained, registered, and insured therapy dogs on campus, far fewer have gathered data on these initiatives (see chapter 9 for advice on evaluation). It is not all that difficult to collect information from students about their interactions with therapy dogs. At US institutions, the survey would have to be approved by the Institutional Review Board; however, the review would be expedited assuming that the students are 18 years or older, volunteer to participate, and have their responses kept confidential or anonymous. The easiest way to make evaluation part of therapy dog events is to contact others who have done this previously. You can obtain their permission to use or adapt the surveys they have developed or perhaps gather survey data at several different institutions. Another option for conducting research on therapy dog events is to partner with university faculty, staff, and students with an interest in AAA and AAT. They may be willing to design a study, collect, and analyze the data for a conference presentation, professional journal article, or thesis/dissertation. College students who are seeking service opportunities may be willing to assist with the data collection, and this can increase the likelihood that other students will participate. By far, the most common types

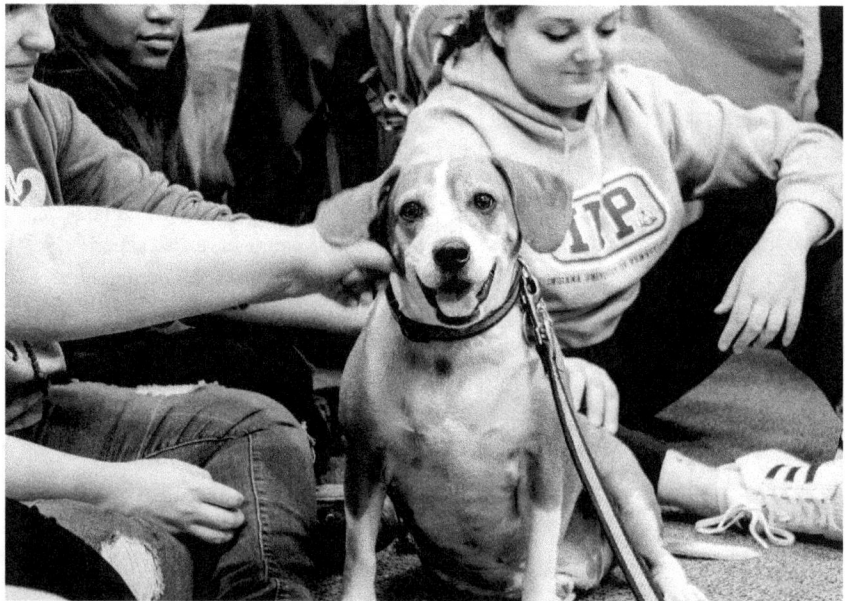

The codirector of the university's center for health and well-being secured permission to bring her registered and insured therapy dog to work on a regular basis. Photo Credit: Megan Higgins

of programs are those that bring dogs to campus during exam week or some other situation considered to be stressful, such as taking a test, making a presentation, or attending an orientation. Increasingly, mental health professionals have their own therapy dogs or partner with handler/dog teams as an alternative/adjunct form of therapy in counseling services for students. Less frequent, but growing in popularity, is access to a therapy dog on a more consistent basis as a facility dog.

TESTS AND EXAM WEEK

In one of the earlier studies of the effects of therapy dogs on students' test anxiety, a nursing professor gave her students the opportunity to interact with her dog prior to tests given in class (Young, 2012). Self-report data gathered from the students was so positive that she continued the program and expanded it. Kent State University (2020) in Ohio, for example, has a long-standing therapy dog program. During exam week, they had 22 handler/dog teams at the library. Numerous studies have used student self-report data as an indicator that interacting with therapy dogs reduces the stress associated with tests and exam week (Barker, Barker, & Schubert 2017). For more about university programs, check out BarkPost.com.

COUNSELING SERVICES AND VISITS

Therapy dogs are part of counseling services at some universities. Students can visit centers on campus and a facility dog or visiting dogs will be there to support the goals of the session or event. In addition, faculty or staff with advanced training in the mental health field sometimes volunteer with their therapy dogs to support students after some terrible event, such as incident of school violence, natural disaster, death of a member of the university community, or a fire that destroys student housing.

ORIENTATIONS, NEW EXPERIENCES, AND SCHEDULED EVENTS

Some colleges and universities incorporate therapy dogs into events that might otherwise be daunting to students, such as move-in days at the residence hall, freshman orientation meetings, or mixers that invite new students to interact.

Some institutions host or partner with community organizations to sponsor events that support survivors of abuse; raise funds for a domestic violence shelter; recognize wounded military veterans; hold a memorial service for member(s) of the university community who have died; and commemorate tragic events. Many times, the presence of therapy dogs is part of the plan.

FACILITY DOGS

Both the University of Southern California and the University of South Carolina, for example, have campus facility dogs. Students can stop by during "office hours" and follow the dogs' appearances at events on campus (Baranauckas, 2018). What people sometimes fail to understand is that the handler needs to be responsible for the dog, accompany it at all times, and keep it under control/on a leash. To do otherwise would violate the rules of all reputable therapy dog organizations and invalidate the liability insurance coverage. In addition, some handler/dog teams are covered by insurance only if they are volunteering, so an employee at work would not be covered. Animal welfare considerations need to figure prominently in any discussion of facility dogs on campus. Dogs are living beings, not inanimate tools. Facility dogs cannot be "on" 24/7; they need breaks, play, and rest. Even the most outgoing and energetic dogs get tired, may not be feeling well, or may find a specific context to be stressful. Sports events, for example, involve many unfamiliar and loud noises—whistles, buzzers, marching bands—and this may be overwhelming to a dog. Another thing to keep in mind is the age of the dog. Reputable therapy dog organizations require the dogs to be a minimum of one year old so, while it might seem like a good idea to those who do not understand the role of a therapy dog to bring puppies to campus, that is not an option with therapy dogs. This brings up another point—do not refer to adult dogs as pups or puppies in advertising as this will result in disappointment from participants who imagine 12-week-olds rather than mature adult dogs. Another concern is overscheduling a small group of therapy dogs. The most vital therapy dog programs on college campuses have a large pool of handler/therapy dog teams eligible to participate. It is possible for handlers and dogs to experience burnout if they are called upon too frequently. When issues such as these are considered, trained therapy dogs who are visiting with their handlers can enjoy the interaction as much as the human participants. In a study that examined the presence of the stress hormone cortisol in therapy dogs' saliva as well as observable behavioral indicators of stress in dogs, a well-planned animal-assisted

If the advertising for dogs visiting campus refers to them as pups or puppies, this is what students will expect. Photo Credit: Mary Renck Jalongo

activity did not appear to elevate stress levels in registered therapy dogs (Ng et al., 2014). It is important to continue research that examines effects of visiting on participants, handlers, and the dogs.

RECOMMENDATIONS FOR PRACTICE

The presence of therapy dogs on campus has become so popular that it can devolve into a bandwagon mentality. For example, there are now lists of the most "dog-friendly campuses" posted online as an aid to student recruitment (Pittman, 2019). People can be surprisingly uniformed or misinformed about dogs. For example, if they have seen adoption events hosted by shelters out in the community, they may think that therapy dogs are homeless animals. Remarks such as, "I love this dog. What do I have to do to adopt him and how much does it cost?" reveal this misconception. Some people who are eager to bring dogs to campus may erroneously assume that it is just a matter of recruiting family pets to participate. Expectations for the dogs' behavior vary widely as well, ranging from the terrifying Cujo to the beyond perfect Lassie—and all points in between. Mention bringing dogs to campus and some people will imagine wild barking, jumping, dog bites, dog-on-dog aggression, and extensive destruction of property. Others may base their expectations for therapy dogs on the behavior of their own family dogs. Still others might expect therapy dogs to be entertainers and inquire about what tricks the dogs can perform. In many ways, those who bring therapy dogs to campus are humane educators, defined by the Association for Humane Professional Educators (APHE) (2012) as "anyone who teaches and promotes humane attitudes toward people, animals and the environment" (p. 1). Their "Professional Guidelines for Humane Educators" states:

> APHE strongly recommends that all animals being considered as education partners be evaluated by a certified trainer, evaluator or behaviorist to ensure their physical and psychological well-being, as well as their comfort level in public settings. As a minimum, APHE recommends that dogs have their Canine Good Citizen certification or its equivalent. Domesticated and companion animals who accompany humane educators can be registered as therapy animals through national agencies such as Pet Partners. Local and regional organizations may exist in your area and may also serve as resources for training, evaluations and volunteers. APHE recommends that humane educators and volunteers only take animals that have met the recommendations listed to humane education programs. Taking an inexperienced, untested, unknown and/or untrained animal to an unfamiliar setting is stressful for the animal and could create a dangerous situation for the humane educator, the animal and the program participants. (APHE, 2012, p. 3)

Even after the role of therapy dogs is clarified, the point of view of therapy dog handlers and other university staff may be vastly different. The first thing that needs to occur is reciprocal trust and respect among the various partners. If that is lacking, there are just three alternatives—go along with whatever is requested, attempt to educate others about what is problematic, or be offended and refuse to cooperate. What follows are some situations that have surfaced for handlers of therapy dogs.

"I heard about the therapy dogs coming to campus and wondered if you could bring them to our Health Fair. We didn't have very good attendance at the last one. If a bunch of you could stand outside with your dogs, that might get more students to participate. We'd need the dogs there from 9 am to 4 pm."

Therapy dogs are not a gimmick, like a person in a plush animal costume holding a sign outside a local business to attract attention. The value in the activity comes from human-animal interaction, not just standing around. In one study, 84% of the students cited physical interaction (petting the dog, cuddling the dog, sitting close to the dog) as the greatest influence on reducing their anxiety (Stewart, Dispenza, Parker, Chang, & Cunnien, 2014). The person who made this request also needed know that the timeframe was unreasonable. Further, the requirement that they stand outside in the elements is not acceptable. Usually, people can understand these reservations and adjust accordingly. In this case, the solutions were to bring the handler/dog teams inside and give them a table, just like the other participants, where they could distribute literature about their program and answer questions; position the group so that the dogs had access to an outdoor area where they could take a break and eliminate; and schedule the group's participation in shifts so that no one dog/handler team was there for more than an hour or two.

This young whippet and her handler are certified and insured as a therapy team through Alliance of Therapy Dogs.
Photo Credit: Mary Renck Jalongo

Educated people can be surprisingly unaware of a dog's needs. For example, a librarian who had never owned a dog said, "There has been a lot of information lately about bringing dogs to academic library, particularly during exam week. Wouldn't it be fun for the students to 'check out' a dog and borrow it for a time?" The leader of the local therapy dog group said, "These dogs are very precious to us. They are our dogs and they are part of our families. Most of them have had over a year of training and we would never turn them over to strangers. We would have no idea about the students' knowledge, skill, and sensitivity to a dog's needs. It would be incredibly stressful, even for the most confident and happy dog, to get passed around like that." The librarian listened thoughtfully and understood, so they went on to discuss what would be more appropriate—an opportunity for students to visit the library during a two-hour event that would include six therapy handler/dog teams. The teams would be positioned throughout the main floor of the library so that students could sit on the carpeted floor or sofas and interact with the dogs. Volunteers from various student organizations could help to distribute surveys, take photos, and greet participants at the door. In recent years, there have been more studies to examine the effects of visiting on the dogs themselves, using such indicators as measures of cortisol, a hormone produced when dogs (and people) are stressed (Ng et al., 2014). Even though events are planned for people, the animals' welfare must be attended to just as assiduously as the potential benefits for human beings.

Service dogs in training can be part of dog visitation on campus, and this is something else that people do not necessarily understand. In a community that has a prison dog training program in which the inmates are responsible for raising and training service dog puppies, the pups visit campus at various times, accompanied by a prison staff member. During one such event, a university staff member was impressed by how well-behaved the puppies were and said, "We have a dog that is totally out of control His name is Taz, you know, like the Tasmanian devil. Can I put him into this prison program to get him trained?" The program director patiently explained several points: first, these dogs are being trained to work for a person who has a disability and needs help performing everyday tasks; second, the prison program does not train family dogs for the general public; third, the program is 18 months in duration; fourth, the dogs are participating in this event to increase their opportunities for socialization. She directed Taz's owner to other participants who were familiar with high-quality dog training resources in the area. College students often make comments about the dogs' good behavior and the behavioral issues that they have with their dogs at home. A student might say, "I could never get my dog to do this. Is it just their temperament or is it training?" when, of course, it is both. The great majority of therapy dog handlers trained their own dogs, and many have completed one or more obedience classes together, so they can share some of those insights. Excellent therapy dog hander/dog teams also are enthusiastic role models who can promote the "Enjoy your dog more; train it!" message.

Based on the information presented in this chapter on therapy dogs and facility dogs, we offer the following recommendations for practice.

1. The well-being of university staff, university students, and the dogs themselves has to be a priority in programs that bring them together. For each event under consideration, it is important to conduct a needs assessment, engage in planning that involves representation from all stakeholders, implement the event thoughtfully, and evaluate the outcomes.
2. When using therapy and/or facility dogs on campus, it is essential that the teams have the appropriate obedience training, evaluation, and therapy dog certification. For example, it would be important to ensure the therapy dog and handler be evaluated and currently registered/certified through a nationally recognized organization such as Alliance of Therapy Dogs, Love on a Leash, Pet Partners, or Therapy Dogs International.
3. When therapy dogs are incorporated into a professional's treatment plans, this is called animal-assisted therapy or AAT (Shelton, Leeman, & Ohara, 2011). The most common type of AAT in postsecondary institutions is the use of dogs in mental health interventions or animal-assisted therapy-counseling (AAT-C) (Chandler, 2005). It is important for counselors to be trained in AAT-C, be an appropriately credentialed mental health provider, have a specially trained/ evaluated animal, and be guided by Animal-Assisted Therapy in Counseling Competencies (Stewart, Chang, Parker, & Grubbs, 2016). Effective use of AAT-C has been shown to enhance the therapeutic alliance (Fine, 2015) and help clients talk about emotionally-charged topics (Shelton et al., 2011).
4. Positive relationships with counseling and educational facility staff must be established/maintained (Chandler, 2001). Proper authorizations must also be obtained from the campus leaders/administration to ensure that permission/support is given to have therapy dogs or facility dogs on campus. Many postsecondary institutions have a director of public safety who can be consulted on these matters. Comply with all campus policies as well as local/state/national laws.
5. Effective communication about visiting dogs is essential, not only for those who want to participate, but also for those who do not want to interact with the dogs. For example, arranging therapy dog teams to come to campus, publicizing events to students, alerting campus security, and notifying staff must be done in a timely manner (Reynolds & Rabschutz, 2013). Use signs and, if permitted, place arrows of tape on the floor to demarcate a clear pathway for people who want to avoid the dogs.
6. The campus locations for events involving dogs need to be carefully selected to accommodate dogs, handlers, and attendees. The location also must be accessible for people with disabilities. Particularly when sharing a workspace, everyone needs to agree upon the norms for canine and human behavior within that environment.

7. Handlers must attend to the animals' needs in general and at the campus location. This includes proper nutrition, exercise, grooming, veterinary care, resting time/space, regular bathroom breaks, and so forth. It also includes monitoring the dogs' stress indicators (e.g., panting, yawning, restlessness, cowering, trying to escape, turning away) and removing the dog from the situation when appropriate.
8. Educate the campus community about ways that interacting with a mellow dog can contribute to well-being. The programming and benefits of canine-assisted therapy on campus can be distributed via postings on the college website and other social media outlets (Reynolds & Rabschutz, 2013).
9. Formal and informal evaluation practices need to be implemented to explore the impact of campus programs on college students. Gathering data on participants' responses is valuable in making data-driven decisions about program improvement. It also serves as a resource when asking for support, justifying new program initiatives, or proposing expansion of an existing program.
10. Networking with other universities that have therapy and facility dogs can serve to share findings, insights, and programs. It also could lead to multisite research that strengthens the validity of findings and yields collaborative presentations/publications.

CONCLUSION

One of our college students was a former state police officer who decided to pursue certification as an elementary school teacher. He was a straight-A student as well as a very likeable and mature individual who was elected president of the student chapter of the Association for Childhood Education International. During his senior year, he and his wife were in a terrible auto accident on their way to a wedding. The young man suffered a traumatic brain injury that would forever alter his mental capabilities. When his classmates heard what had happened, several stopped by the professor's office to inquire about his recovery. Most of the students assumed that all would be well and that he would return to class before semester's end, fully healed. Sadly, that was not the outcome. When students heard this devastating news, many of them burst into tears. In the fall, after the student did return, he struggled to pass courses that he would have sailed through previously. His speech was slow and his manner was subdued. To his credit, he did complete the program and succeeded in securing a job in the education field. Each year, a student who has overcome great obstacles is the recipient of an award in his name at commencement. Looking back on this tragic event, how we wish that we had then what the university has now—a team of doctoral students in psychology, some of whom are also handlers of registered and insured therapy dogs. Together, they visit classes to help students and staff cope with grief and loss. Thirty years ago, involving a dog in a mental health professional's practice would have been viewed as strange, rather than as an alternative therapy designed to support wellness. Today, including the dog would be an option, both for the group visit and for individual students seeking services at the counseling center.

Making therapy dogs part of the wellness strategy for a college campus is gaining acceptance throughout the United States and in some other countries as well. At sessions designed to support students, many can be seen interacting with the dogs through touch, addressing comments directly to the dog, and, when coping with grief is the focus, burying their faces in the dog's fur. As Coren (2015) points out, there is groundswell of interest from "mainstream psychological, educational, and medical researchers and practitioners about ways to include animals—most frequently, dogs—into their practice" (p. xix). Bolstered by research and our collective wisdom, we can continue to learn about the human-canine bond and can put the accumulated evidence to work in canine-assisted interventions that support the wellness of humans.

REFERENCES

Adamle, K. N., Riley, T. A., & Carlson, T. (2009). Evaluating college student interest in pet therapy. *Journal of American College Health, 57*(5), 545–548.

Adams, T., Clark, C., Crowell, V., Duffy, K., Green, M., McEwen, S., . . . Hammonds, F. (2017). The mental health benefits of having dogs on college campuses. *Modern Psychological Studies, 22*(2), 50–59. https://scholar.utc.edu/cgi/viewcontent.cgi?article=1274&context=mps

American Veterinary Medical Association (2019). *Animal-assisted interventions: Guidelines.* https://www.avma.org/resources-tools/avma-policies/animal-assisted-interventions-guidelines

Anderson, D. S. (Ed.). (2016). *Wellness issues for higher education: A guide for student affairs and higher education professionals.* New York: Routledge.

Association for Professional Humane Educators (APHE). (2012). Professional guidelines for humane educators (version 6a2). https://www.aphe.org/Resources/Documents/APHE%20Professional%20Guidelines%20revised%202012%20March.pdf

Baranauckas, C. (2018, August 28). Therapy dogs ease the stress of transition for college students. *Huffington Post.* https://www.huffingtonpost.com/entry/therapy-dogs-ease-stress-college-students_us_5b84d6f3e4b0511db3d10b98

Barker, S. B., Barker, R. T., McCain, N. L., & Schubert, C. M. (2016). A randomized cross-over exploratory study of the effect of visiting therapy dogs on college student stress before final exams. *Anthrozoös, 29*(1), 35–46.

Barker, S. B., Barker, R. T., & Schubert, C. M. (2017). Therapy dogs on campus: A counseling outreach activity for college students preparing for final exams. *Journal of College Counseling, 20*(3), 278–288. https://doi.org/10.1002/jocc.12075

Binfet, J. (2017). The effects of group-administered canine therapy on university students' wellbeing: A randomized controlled trial. *Anthrozoös, 30*(3), 397–414.

Binfet, J., & Passmore, H. A. (2016). Hounds and homesickness: The effects of an animal-assisted therapeutic intervention for first-year university students. *Anthrozoös, 29*(3), 441–454.

Bould, B., Bigby, C., Bennett, P. C., & Howell, T. J. (2018). "More people talk to you when you have a dog": Dogs as catalysts for social inclusion of people with intellectual disabilities. *Journal of Intellectual Disability Research, 62*(10), 833–841. https://www.ncbi.nlm.nih.gov/pubmed/30125042

Butler, K. (2013). *Therapy dogs today: Their gifts, our obligations.* New York: Funpuddle Press.

Casciotti, D., & Zuckerman, D. (2016). The benefits of pets for human health. http://center4research.org/healthy-living-prevention/pets-and-health-the-impact-of-companion-animals

Chandler, C. (2001). Animal-assisted therapy in counseling and school settings. ERIC Document Reproduction Services No. ED 459 404. https://www.ericdigests.org/2002-3/animal.htm

Chandler, C. (2005). *Animal assisted therapy in counseling.* New York: Taylor & Francis.

Christian, H., Bauman, A., Epping, J., Levine, G. N., McCormack, G., Rhodes, R. E., . . . Westgarth, C. (2016, July). State of the art review: Promoting dog walking for healthy lifestyles. School of Nursing Faculty Publications. Paper 29. https://docs.lib.purdue.edu/cgi/viewcontent.cgi?article=1031&context=nursingpubs

Clark, H. (2016, August 23). Why do dogs sleep so much? https://www.akc.org/expert-advice/health/why-do-dogs-sleep-so-much

Coren, S. (2015). Foreword. In A. H. Fine (Ed.), *Handbook on animal-assisted therapy: Foundations and guidelines for animal-assisted interventions* (4th ed., pp. xix–xxii). Waltham, MA: Academic Press.

Crossman, M. K., Kazdin, A. E., & Knudson, K. (2015). Brief unstructured interaction with a dog reduces stress. *Anthrozoös, 28*(4), 649–659. https://doi.org/10.1080/08927936.2015.1070008

Csikzentmihalyi, M. (2014). *Flow and the foundations of positive psychology: The collected works of Mihaly Csikszentmihalyi.* New York: Springer.

Daltry, R. M., & Mehr, K. E. (2015). Therapy dogs on campus: Recommendations for counseling center outreach. *Journal of College Student Psychotherapy, 29*(1), 72–78.

Delgado, C., Toukonen, M., & Wheelter, C. (2018). Effect of canine play interventions as a stress reduction strategy in college students. *Nurse Educator, 43*(3), 149–153. https://doi.org/10.1097/NNE.0000000000000451

Dell, C. A., Chalmers, D., Gillect, J., Rohr, B., Nickel, C., Campbell, L., & Brydges, M. (2015). PAWSing student stress: A pilot evaluation study of the St. John ambulance therapy dog program on three university campuses in Canada. *Canadian Journal of Counselling & Psychotherapy, 49*(4), 332–359.

Fine, A. H. (2015). Incorporating animal-assisted therapy into psychotherapy: Guidelines and suggestions for therapists. In A. H. Fine (Ed.), *Handbook on animal-assisted therapy: Theoretical foundations and guidelines for practice* (4th ed., pp. 91–101). San Diego, CA: Academic Press.

Folse, E. B., Minder, C. C., Aycock, M. J., & Santana, R. T. (2015). Animal-assisted therapy and depression in adult college students. *Anthrozoös, 7*(3), 188–194.

Foreman, A. M., Glenn, M. K., Meade, B. J., & Wirth, O. (2017). Dogs in the workplace: A review of the benefits and potential challenges. *International Journal of Environmental Research and Public Health, 14*(5), 498–510. https://www.mdpi.com/1660-4601/14/5/498

Gallavan, N. P., & Benson, T. R. (2014). Getting on the same page: Expanding student support services to increase candidate success and educator accountability. *Action in Teacher Education 36*(5–6), 490–450.

Granello, P. (2013). *Wellness counseling.* Upper Saddle River, NJ: Pearson.

Hettler, B. (1980). Wellness promotion on a university campus. *Family and Community Health, 3*(1), 77–95.

Hettler, B. (1984). Wellness: Encouraging a lifetime pursuit of excellence. *Health Values: Achieving High Level Wellness, 8*(4), 13–17.

Hoffman, J. (2015, May 27). Anxious students strain college mental health centers. *New York Times.* https://static1.squarespace.com/static/576bf294d2b857d28be440ba/t/57b3a88159cc6834cfa2bfba/1471391873288/Anxious+Students+Strain+College+Mental+Health+Centers+-+NYTimes.com.pdf

Howie, A. R. (2015). *Teaming with your therapy dog.* West Lafayette, IN: Purdue University Press.

Jalongo, M. R., & McDevitt, T. (2015). Therapy dogs in academic libraries: A way to foster student engagement and mitigate self-reported stress during finals. *Public Services Quarterly, 11*(4), 254–269. https://doi.org/10.1080/15228959.2015.1084904

Jenkins, C. D., Laux, J. M., Ritchie, M. H., & Tucker-Gail, K. (2014). Animal-assisted therapy and Rogers' Core Components among middle school students receiving counseling services: A descriptive study. *Journal of Creativity in Mental Health, 9*(2), 174–187. https://doi.org/10.1080/15401383.2014.899939

Kent State University. (2020). Dogs on campus. https://www.kent.edu/tags/dogs-campus

Lannon, A., & Harrison, P. (2015). Take a paws: Fostering student wellness with a therapy dog program at your university library. *Public Services Quarterly, 11*(1), 13–22. https://doi.org/10.1080/15228959.2014.984264

Ledoux, A. (2018). Are dog owners more likely to be fit? *Houstonia.* https://www.houstoniamag.com/articles/2018/7/13/dog-owners-fitness

McConnell, A., Brown, C. M., Shoda, T. M., Stayton, L. E., & Martin, C. E. (2011). Friends with benefits: On the positive consequences of pet ownership. *Journal of Personality and Social Psychology, 101*(6), 1239–1252. http://allenmcconnell.net/pdfs/pets-JPSP-2011.pdf

McConnell, P., & Fine, A. H. (2015). Understanding the other end of the leash: What therapists need to understand about their co-therapists. In A. H. Fine (Ed.), *Handbook on animal-assisted therapy: Foundations and guidelines for animal-assisted interventions*, (4th ed., pp. 103–113). Waltham, MA: Academic Press.

McDonald, S., McDonald, E., & Roberts, A. (2017). Effects of novel dog exposure on college students' stress prior to examination. *North American Journal of Psychology, 19*(2), 477–484.

Miklosi, A. (2018). *The dog: A natural history.* Princeton, NJ: Princeton University Press.

Muckle, J., & Lasikiewicz, N. (2017). An exploration of the benefits of animal-assisted activities in undergraduate students in Singapore. *Asian Journal of Social Psychology, 20*(2), 75–85. https://doi.org/10.1111/ajsp.12166

Myers, J. E., & Sweeney, T. J. (2004). The indivisible self: An evidence-based model of wellness. *Journal of Individual Psychology, 60*(3), 234–245.

Myers, J. E., Sweeney, T. J., & Witmer, J. M. (2000). The wheel of wellness counseling for wellness: A holistic model for treatment planning. *Journal of Counseling and Development, 78*(3), 251–266. http://libres.uncg.edu/ir/uncg/f/J_Myers_Wheel_2000.pdf

Ng, Z. Pierce, B. J., Otto, C. M., Buechner-Maxwell, V. A., Siracusa, C., & Were, S. R. (2014). The effect of dog-human interaction on cortisol and behavior in registered animal-assisted activity dogs. *Applied Animal Behaviour Science, 159*,

69–81. http://accurateclinic.com/wp-content/uploads/2016/06/The-effect-of-dog-human-interaction-on-cortisol-and-behavior-in-registered-animal-assisted-activity-dogs-2014.pdf

Pet Partners (2020). Therapy animal program. https://petpartners.org

Pittman, O. (2019). 20 Pet-friendly colleges. *College Raptor.* https://www.collegeraptor.com/find-colleges/articles/student-life/20-pet-friendly-college-campuses

Polheber, J. P., & Matchock, R. L. (2014). The presence of a dog attenuates cortisol and heart rate in the Trier Social Stress Test compared to human friends. *Journal of Behavioral Medicine, 37*(5), 860–867. https://doi.org/10.1007/s10865-013-9546-1

Reynolds, J., & Rabschutz, L. (2013). Studying for exams just got more relaxing—animal-assisted activities at the University of Connecticut library. *College and Undergraduate Libraries, 18*(4), 359–367. https://doi.org/10.1080/10691316.2011.624934

Shelton, L. S., Leeman, M., & O'Hara, C. (2011). Introduction to animal assisted therapy in counseling. http://counselingoutfitters.com/vistas/vistas11/Article_55.pdf

Somerville, J. W., Kruglikova, Y. A., Robertson, R. L., Hanson, L. M., & MacLin, O. H. (2008). Physiological responses by college students to a dog and a cat: Implications for pet therapy. *North American Journal of Psychology, 10,* 519–528.

Stewart, L. A., Chang, C. Y., Parker, L. K., & Grubbs, N. (2016). *Animal-assisted therapy in counseling competencies.* Alexandria, VA: American Counseling Association, Animal-Assisted Therapy in Mental Health Interest Network. https://www.counseling.org/docs/default-source/competencies/animal-assisted-therapy-competencies-june-2016.pdf?sfvrsn=c469472c_14

Stewart, L. A., Dispenza, F., Parker, L., Chang, C. Y., & Cunnien, T. (2014). A pilot study assessing the effectiveness of an animal-assisted outreach program. *Journal of Creativity in Mental Health, 9*(3), 332–345.

Weimer, M. (2002). *Learner-centered teaching: Five key changes to practice.* San Francisco, CA: Jossey-Bass.

Wells, M., & Perrine, R. (2001). Pets go to college: The influence of pets on students' perceptions of faculty and their offices. *Anthrozoös, 14*(3), 161–168.

Wood, E., Ohlsen, S., Thompson, J., Hulin, J., & Knowles, L. (2017). The feasibility of brief dog-assisted therapy on university students' stress levels: The PAWS study. *Journal of Mental Health, 27*(3), 263–268. https://doi.org/10.1080/09638237.2017.1385737

Wolverton, B. (2019, February 21). As students struggle with stress and depression colleges act as counselors. *New York Times.* https://www.nytimes.com/2019/02/21/education/learning/mental-health-counseling-on-campus.html

Young, J. S. (2012). Pet therapy: Dogs destress students. *Journal of Christian Nursing, 29*(4), 217–221.

Zimpher, D. G. (1992). Psychosocial treatment of life-threatening diseases: A wellness model. *Journal of Counseling & Development, 71*(2), 203–209. https://eric.ed.gov/?id=EJ455382

Zivin, K., Eisenberg, D., Gollust, S. E., & Golberstein, E. (2009). Persistence of mental health problems and needs in a college student population. *Journal of Affective Disorders, 117*(3), 180–185.

6

SHELTER DOGS

Service-Learning Projects With Animal Welfare Organizations

MARY RENCK JALONGO, EDITOR, SPRINGER NATURE, INDIANA, PA, AND TUNDE SZECSI, COLLEGE OF EDUCATION, FLORIDA GULF COAST UNIVERSITY, FORT MYERS, FL

INTRODUCTION

Increasingly, college/university programs are requiring or recommending some sort of volunteer service hours before admitting students into professional schools. Effective service-learning can give students an irreplaceable opportunity to reflect on linkages among theory, research, and practice and, at the same time, make an important contribution to the community. One type of service-learning that is appealing to many postsecondary students with different backgrounds and college majors involves partnering with nonprofit animal welfare groups. The premise of this chapter is that direct experience with dogs in need can teach and transform college students. Chapter 6 begins by defining volunteerism and service-learning as well as identifying the elements of effective service-learning and its benefits for college students. Next, the chapter provides a brief overview of the theoretical base: identity formation and college student development. Accounts of experiences in shelters are used to illustrate how volunteerism challenges college students' assumptions, expands understanding, and shapes their values as animal advocates. Part three of the chapter reviews the literature on collaborations between postsecondary institutions and animal welfare groups that have provided effective service-learning opportunities for students. The chapter concludes with recommendations on ways to guide students in taking positive action that genuinely helps dogs in need, nonprofit animal welfare organizations, and the community at large.

DEFINITIONS OF *VOLUNTEERISM* AND *SERVICE-LEARNING*

"At first, I thought I might not be able to make it as a shelter volunteer. I get upset when I see animals suffering and have to change the channel when those commercials come on with the pets looking so miserable. I avoided shelters because I thought it would be too sad and that I would want to take all of them home. But I've learned that small things I do to help them to get good homes can be just as rewarding. When other students ask me about volunteering at the shelter, I say that the people who work here are crazy—and I mean that in a good way. I have met real animal rescuers who do things that I don't think I could do myself."

A police cadet volunteered to walk dogs and gave a little extra attention to this new arrival at the shelter. Photo Credit: Mary Renck Jalongo

"I knew nothing about handling dogs when I first started, but they taught me everything I needed to know. This is important to me because, in my country, street dogs are a problem. Some are feral. They can carry rabies. They are chased away, abused, and exterminated. A few people feed them or try to help but there are too many dogs. After I graduate and go back, I want to use what I have learned to help change things in my homeland."

"When we heard that the local humane society was in danger of closing its doors due to financial problems, our sorority decided to help. We volunteered at their fundraisers and adoption events. Then we organized collection boxes so that students and staff could make donations of materials on the shelter's 'wish list.' The whole community pitched in and the shelter managed to stay open. We were proud to do our part."

Each of these observations from students highlights the role of volunteerism and power of service-learning to influence beliefs, values, attitudes, dispositions, and behavior. *Volunteerism* has been defined as "a form of prosocial behavior that involves a freely chosen decision to commit a sustained amount of time and effort to helping another person, group, or cause, typically through a nonprofit organization" (Stukas, Snyder, & Clary, 2015, p. 450). According to the National and Community Service Trust Act of 1993, *service-learning* is a method under which volunteers learn and develop through active participation in thoughtfully organized service. To qualify as service-learning for college students, the experience is:

1. conducted in and meets the needs of a community
2. coordinated with the school, community service program, and the community
3. focused on fostering civic responsibility
4. integrated into the academic curriculum of the students and/or the educational components of the community service program
5. designed to provide structured time for the students to reflect on the service experience.

The checklist shown in figure 6.1, adapted from Youth Service California (2018), is a useful guide for postsecondary faculty members and their partners in nonprofit organizations when planning, implementing, and evaluating service-learning. A service-learning experience that has affirmative answers to all these questions holds the greatest promise for benefiting the various stakeholders.

BENEFITS OF SERVICE-LEARNING AT COLLEGES AND UNIVERSITIES

Most experts agree that a service orientation is related to altruism—the willingness to help others, even in the absence of a tangible reward. Altruism is particularly pertinent here because, based on national survey data, the self-reported altruism of postsecondary students declined significantly about 15 years ago (Hankinson & Rochester, 2005). In the mid-2000s, young adults were an underrepresented age group among the ranks of volunteers (Hankinson & Rochester, 2005). As a response to concerns about this downturn, more college/university programs began to require or recommend some sort of volunteer service hours from students (York & Fernandez, 2018). For undergraduates, community service often became a condition for admission to a professional school. For graduate programs, such as veterinary medicine, documentation of practical experience gained by volunteering in the community frequently is part of internships in the

Questions to Guide Service-Learning Projects: A Checklist

1. **Integrated Learning**
   Does the service-learning project have clearly articulated knowledge, skill or value objectives that are linked to course/program goals and institutional mission? Yes ☐ No ☐
   Does the service inform the academic content to be learned and does the learning content align with the service? Yes ☐ No ☐
   Are the life skills learned outside the classroom integrated back into professional preparation programs? Yes ☐ No ☐
2. **High Quality Service**
   Does the service respond to an actual community need that is recognized by the community? Yes ☐ No ☐
   Is the service activity appropriate and well-organized? Yes ☐ No ☐
   Does the design of the service achieve significant benefits not only for students and but also for the community? Yes ☐ No ☐
3. **Collaboration**
   Is there strong evidence of meaningful collaboration among all of the stakeholders (e.g., students, faculty, community-based organization staff, school administrators, and recipients of service)? Yes ☐ No ☐
   Did all partners contribute to the planning and benefit from the project? Yes ☐ No ☐
4. **Student Voice**
   Did the college students participate in choosing and planning their volunteerism? Yes ☐ No ☐
   Are students involved in implementing the reflection sessions, evaluation, and celebration? Yes ☐ No ☐
   Are college students taking on roles and tasks that are matched to their levels of experience? Yes ☐ No ☐
5. **Civic Responsibility**
   Did the service-learning project promote college students' responsibility to care for others and contribute to the community? Yes ☐ No ☐
   Were students aware of the impact of their volunteerism on the community and did they see the contributions of their efforts? Yes ☐ No ☐
6. **Reflection**
   Were structured opportunities for reflection built into the project before, during and after the service-learning experience? Yes ☐ No ☐
   Was reflection used to establish connections between postsecondary students' service experiences and the academic curriculum? Yes ☐ No ☐
7. **Evaluation**
   Were all the partners, especially students, involved in evaluating the service-learning project? Yes ☐ No ☐
   Were the results of the evaluation used to measure progress toward achieving the goals of the project and did the project organizers use the data to improve the project? Yes ☐ No ☐

FIGURE 6.1 Questions to Guide Service-Learning Projects: A Checklist (adapted from Youth Service California, 2018).

field (Lake, Berg, Kelly, & Patrick, 2016). Service-learning requirements were put in place, in part, to foster altruism and a service orientation in future professionals across the disciplines.

Service-learning has become an essential component in many higher education institutions and secondary schools. As a result, the number of young adults who complete service-learning is increasing, and young adults (aged 16–24) have become the most active group of volunteers in the United States (Lee & Won, 2011). According to Campus Compact, which is a coalition of universities and colleges representing more than 6 million students, 95% of member campuses have service-learning courses, and 62% of member campuses require service-learning as part of the curriculum (Re, 2015). Service-learning in postsecondary institutions is a high-impact pedagogical practice that infuses demanding academic studies with meaningful community service activities in ways that promote critical reflection and civic engagement of students (Kuh, 2008; Ngai, Chan, & Kwan, 2018).

Effective service-learning not only accrues benefits for the organizations in the community and the college students, but also for postsecondary institutions as a whole as they prepare the next generation of professionals. To illustrate, a small shelter was involved in community outreach activities in which they made presentations to schoolchildren about responsible pet ownership, animal sheltering, and dog bite prevention. However, none of the staff members had teaching experience and they felt their time with the students could have a greater impact if key concepts were presented more effectively, particularly during the sessions for young children. Through collaboration with faculty members in the college of education and students enrolled in early childhood teacher preparation programs, they were able to produce presentations that were developmentally appropriate and supported with high-quality instructional materials. The college students planned lessons with important purposes in the real world, all partners in the process reflected on what would be most effective, and all stakeholders gained from working together. At its best, this is what service-learning does: it contributes to the community and the economy (Lee & Won, 2011).

Table 6.1 summarizes the benefits of service-learning for students, highlights research that supports each benefit, and provides examples of service-learning activities with animal shelters.

Table 6.1 Contributions of Service-Learning

POTENTIAL BENEFITS (WANG & CALVANO, 2018)	EVIDENCE BASE	EXAMPLES
Cognitive development, academic learning, increased student engagement	Conway, Amel, & Gerwien, 2009; Kuh, 2008; Stevens & Gruen, 2014; Yorio & Ye, 2012	Pre-veterinary track students volunteer to assist at a free dog vaccination event and low-cost spay/neuter clinic. A mobile veterinary hospital goes to an underserved community, and students observe the surgeries and assist with monitoring the dogs' vital signs afterward.
Improved cultural knowledge and awareness	Boyle-Baise & Kilbane, 2000; Einfeld & Collins, 2008; Wood, 2011	Education majors volunteer to handle mellow dogs available for adoption at various events: a parade, a festival, and adoption days at two area pet stores. These efforts give the students opportunities to communicate effectively with families and children, an important skill in their professional preparation.
Enhanced skills to address social justice	Einfeld & Collins, 2008; Warren-Gordon & Graff, 2018; Yorio & Ye, 2012	Students majoring in social work volunteer to distribute donated dog food, free of charge. Their assumption that families in financial hardship are less committed to caring for their animals is challenged when they meet people who are doing everything possible to keep their dogs.
Civic-mindedness and citizenship outcomes	Conway et al., 2009; Garcia & Robinson, 2005; Holzman, Horst, & Ghant, 2017; Huda, Mat Teh, Nor Muhamad, & Mohd Nasir, 2018	Rather than taking a beach vacation over spring break, students sign up for an alternative spring break at the local animal shelter. They help by cleaning kennels, feeding/watering, and exercising/socializing dogs. Students with skills in photography and graphic design create posters to promote adoptions and distribute them via social media.

Personal growth and insights	Conway et al., 2009; Yorio & Ye, 2012	Shelter staff and college student volunteers attend a workshop that is copresented by the kennel manager who is a certified dog trainer. The goal is to achieve greater consistency in how the dogs are handled and to teach the dogs behaviors that make them more appealing to prospective adopters (see Herron, Kirby-Madden, & Lord, 2014; Howard & DiGennaro Reed, 2014). The students' evaluations indicate that they are eager to try some of these techniques with the family dogs they know.
Leadership skills of planning, organizing, decision making, and managing (Kuh, 1995)	Grace & Seemiler, 2016; Karr-Lilienthal, Norwood, & Morstad, 2013	Various student groups organize fundraisers to benefit the local shelter: a car wash, a pancake breakfast, and a 5K run. They plan, implement, and evaluate these events and make donations to the shelter.

THEORETICAL BASE: IDENTITY FORMATION, COLLEGE STUDENT DEVELOPMENT, AND SERVICE-LEARNING

Identity refers to a self-constructed definition of self ("Who am I?). Identity is affected by personal priorities ("What do I believe?") and influenced by aspirations and accomplishments ("How do I fit into society?") (McDevitt & Ormrod, 2020). Adolescence and early adulthood are "prime time" for exploring career options, membership in groups, and choosing a course in life. As students pursue college study, they engage in the ongoing process of intentionally aligning actions and behaviors with their evolving sense of identity (Johansson & Felten, 2014). In the literature, there is some agreement that the progression in college students' thinking is to move away from simple, "one right answer" perspectives to a growing acceptance that situations are complex and that multiple perspectives on issues exist (Jones & Abes, 2013). From a cognitive developmental perspective, 18 years of age is the average age at which the human brain is fully myelinated and functioning at an adult level; of course, this can vary considerably, depending upon the individual (Gilbert, 2002), so many of the traditional-age undergraduates may not yet be reasoning at what is regarded as a mature level.

The theoretical base for exploring college students' involvement in service-learning activities is college student development (Patton, Renn, Guido, & Quaye, 2016). College courses with a service-learning component offer students expanded opportunities to act on their values and on their commitments in real-life situations. Through service to others, students increase their critical-thinking, communication, problem-solving, and reflective skills. As students form personal/professional identities, they experience cognitive dissonance, which is disruption of their current understanding about the world. Given that there is great diversity among college students in terms of age, ethnicity, gender, and other variables, it is important to emphasize contexts for learning that transcend the boundaries of the typical college classroom (Patton et al., 2016). Venturing out into the community expands a range of experiences that support social, cognitive, and psychological development in postsecondary students. Research suggests that the process of reflection affords students the opportunity to experiment with different perspectives, which often serves to broaden and build their worldviews. With these newly established insights in place, students can then act on their new understandings, fully integrate them into their knowledge, and demonstrate what they have learned through their behavior. This gradual and thoughtful transformative process contributes to identity growth in young adults (Mezirow, 2000).

In William Perry's (1988) classic theory of college student development, there are four levels, which we apply here to situations encountered while working with homeless dogs.

1. *Dualism—the student thinks in more simplistic terms and absolutes—either right or wrong.* One compelling example of an issue that challenges simple yes/no answers is euthanasia of dogs. Students may state that no dog should be "put down" ever, for any reason. When students volunteer at a shelter, they find out that such decisions are complex and agonizing. For many shelters, inadequate funding is a constant reality and the number of animals needing help is staggering. Some communities have no shelter at all (English, 2018). In addition, each state has different dog laws that come into play, such as mandatory quarantine of the dog following a bite incident, and professional guidelines for categorizing a dog as dangerous, such as those developed by the American Society for the Prevention of Cruelty to Animals (2019). A dog with a bite history that later severely mauled a young child fell into this category. The dog warden deemed the dog to be unadoptable and ordered it to be euthanized. Everyone was upset by the situation. Some students felt sorry for the dog because it did not behave aggressively when they passed by the glass door of its isolation room. Others were angry and said that the decision was just another instance of breed bias because the dog was a bully breed. A few searched desperately, yet unsuccessfully, for a different rescue that would take the dog. The one area of agreement was that feelings were very raw about this situation. Nevertheless, it caused most of the volunteers to think less in terms of absolutes and to consider the safety of both humans and animals.
2. *Relativism—students' repeated encounters with multiple interpretations can result in the attitude that knowledge is just an opinion, with everyone's interpretation just as valid as the next.* A new student volunteer at the shelter had completed an orientation but violated several of the rules in a single incident. A large sign on the door read: "NO ADMITTANCE WITHOUT A STAFF MEMBER PRESENT." A sign on each kennel read: "Caution. No fingers or hands inside kennels. I might bite." During the orientation, student volunteers were told to speak in a quiet voice (or not at all) and to avoid sudden movements. The kennel manager also demonstrated how to feed a treat from an open palm, rather than between

thumb and forefinger to avoid injury. She reminded them that these were not their pet dogs and emphasized that the dogs might be frightened or quickly snap up a treat. The student went back to the kennels, unaccompanied, sat down on the floor with her face pressed up against the bars, and had her entire arm wedged between the bars so that she could reach a dog that was keeping his distance. After the dog was on a leash, she put a treat inside her fist and kept pushing it all around the dog's mouth without allowing it to get the treat while repeating, in a loud voice, "Sit!" "Sit!" This illustrates relativism because she evidently thought that her opinions about how to work with dogs were just as valid as those of a person who had worked with shelter dogs for thirty years.

3. *Multiplicity—requests for evidence and authoritative sources lead students to appreciate that some forms of knowledge are more valid than others. They begin to acknowledge complexity, the influence of the context, and build a greater tolerance for ambiguity.* As the reasoning of college students develops, they move away from unsubstantiated opinions and place greater faith in evidence and expertise. An injured dog that came into the local shelter prompted many volunteers to rethink their assumptions. After a German shepherd dog was struck by a car on the highway, she suffered a shattered hip socket and was at the shelter for months being rehabilitated. The surgery was extremely complex, had to be performed by a specialist, and intensive care afterward cost $1,500 per day. Shelter staff decided to manage the dog's care themselves and the dog kennel manager, a retired nurse, had the know-how to do this. The staff went above and beyond to save this dog, providing her with pain medication, creating a soft space for her to rest, and giving frequent, short exercise breaks with a sling for support to prevent her muscles from atrophy during the long recuperation. The dog was very vocal and some of the volunteers winced at her cries, convinced that she was in terrible pain and suffering. Yet after the dog was healed, walking well, and had an adoption pending, students who had disapproved of the dog's treatment noticed that she continued to vocalize in the same way. Now they had to reexamine some of their objections. The kennel manager's access to professional guidance from the dogs' surgeon, extensive experience with dog rehabilitation, and awareness of the dog's quirks were more accurate than students' assumptions and opinions.

4. *Commitment—students recognize the need to make well-informed decisions, commit to those choices, and apply what is being learned. They integrate logical processes with their own experiences and emotions.* When college students frequent a shelter, they encounter many people with a strong commitment to the welfare of animals.

A good example is the situation of a lost or stray dog that is on the run and in total panic mode. Misconceptions abound. Many people assume that if the owner calls a lost dog's name or a stranger brings along a bag of treats or chases the dog, that will work when, usually, it does not. Even when people know about humane traps, they may not realize that you first need some indicator of where the dog is located and that frequent monitoring of the trap is essential, particularly in harsh weather conditions. A group of community volunteers in a rural area that humanely traps stray dogs heard that a dog had been spotted several times in the same general area. Then an employee at a farm supply store discovered that the dog been sleeping next to the dumpster where expired dog foods were discarded. The rescuers made a trail of stinky cat food leading up to the trap and placed a blanket from the dog's brother's bed inside. That worked. When the volunteers carried the captured dog into the shelter, several

A terrified stray dog that had been on the run for days was caught in a humane trap and brought to the shelter. The college volunteers were concerned about him and had many questions for the rescuers. Photo Credit: Mary Renck Jalongo

college students were there volunteering. Students wanted to know how the rescuers got started doing this, how it was accomplished, and why a dog would need to be trapped. A few students wanted to pet the dog and show it affection, but the rescue group's leader said, "He's too flipped out to want that right now; maybe next time you visit." Instead, students looked on as the rescuers carried the large crate back to the doorway of an isolation kennel and gently ushered the dog inside so that he could calm down and get comfortable. No one claimed the dog, and it was adopted. Several students later mentioned that they were really impressed by the rescuers' determination to help this animal; they had worked for several days, around the clock. Some college students also got online and investigated what services their own communities had for tracking and humanely trapping lost or stray animals, and expressed interest in helping these groups in the future.

At its best, higher education prepares students for an ongoing change and personal/professional improvement. Student development theories guide our understanding of how students grow and develop holistically during their years in higher education. An integrated perspective that includes consideration of college students' identity formation, psychosocial development, and cognitive functioning helps college faculty members and staff at nonprofit organizations who work with them (Patton et al., 2016). Some key points based on developmental theory are:

- The period of young adulthood often is characterized by a search for identity, decisions about making commitments, and forging close relationships with others (Erikson, 1974).
- Complexity is a distinguishing feature of college student development because learning is affected by culture, values, the context, power relationships, institutional norms, and professional standards (Abes, 2009; Reason & Kimball, 2012).
- Successful service-learning experiences match the tasks/environment with students' personality types (Holland, 1996) and signature strengths.
- College student development theory provides a foundation for service-learning projects as well as conceptual framework for research (see Whitley, 2014 for a review).

RESEARCH AND INSTITUTIONAL INITIATIVES: INFLUENCES ON THE DECISION TO VOLUNTEER

Greater insights into college students' interest and motivation for service-learning can further increase student involvement and commitment to volunteer. Numerous studies have examined young adults' motivation for volunteering. Strigas (2006) proposed five motivational factors that influence the decision to engage in service-learning, which we apply to college students as follows:

1. *social function of leisure*—volunteerism provides opportunities for social interaction, so students may suggest to a friend or partner that they volunteer together or may hope to form a new network of like-minded individuals during the experience
2. *material/expected gain*—work at a shelter can provide direct benefits, such as getting the daily 10,000 steps in by walking dogs or the possibility that volunteer service will enhance a résumé and prospects for employment
3. *egoistic/self-actualization*—college students may identify themselves as animal advocates or rescuers and volunteering at a shelter supports this self-concept; they may want to demonstrate their seriousness of purpose to others, including university faculty who will be called upon later for letters of recommendation
4. *purposive*—college students who plan to work with animals in their future professions as veterinary assistants, technicians, or veterinarians may volunteer primarily to gain practical skills and hands-on experience; for example, they may get familiar with infection control protocols and post-surgical care while volunteering at a shelter
5. *external influences*—students may volunteer because their institution, major, or a course that they enroll in requires a prescribed number of hours of volunteer service

Studies of college student volunteers suggest that motivational factors such as altruism, affiliation/connectedness, and personal improvement exert a powerful influence on decisions about volunteering (Boz & Palaz, 2007). Students who are more academically secure, rather than struggling, are also more likely to volunteer. Shields (2009) found that college students with higher grade point averages were more likely to volunteer on a consistent basis because they felt better able to take on responsibilities in addition to those associated with their academic programs.

College students consider various reasons for selecting the specific organization or site for their service-learning. Shields (2009) found that young adults were more likely to develop and maintain interest in volunteering for organizations that were local, with which they had some personal connection, or that were nationally renowned. Moore, Warta, and Erichsen (2014) concluded that students' decisions often are driven by altruistic reasons, selflessness of volunteering, and the intention to gain new knowledge. This study indicated that participants were mainly interested in volunteering in health-related settings, although 13.7% of the participants expressed animal care and rescue-related organizations as their main interest. College students were more likely to select a volunteering opportunity if they were attracted to the mission of the agency, referred by friend or colleagues, responsible for direct service, have flexible hours, and the volunteer site was located within a 15-minute driving distance (Lee & Won, 2011). Opportunities to work with animals were identified by both males and females as particularly interesting and worthwhile (Shields, 2009).

Motivation is apt to decrease if the student is disappointed by the assignment, so it is essential to understand variables that keep volunteers away initially or cause them to quit. Allen and Mueller (2013) surveyed 151 volunteers in an animal shelter about intention to quit and burnout. Their research concluded that volunteers were more likely to complete volunteer service when they perceived that their voices were heard and had clear job/role descriptions. Although participants in this study were older, lack of voice is an issue for all volunteers.

The motivation of faculty members to initiate, maintain, and enhance service-learning experiences for students is another issue. Overall, the primary motivator that encouraged faculty to promote service-learning was seeing their students' engagement in community service. Faculty are critical actors in the service-learning partnership between the community and the university (Darby & Newman, 2014). Faculty members control the curriculum as well as the instructional strategies in specific courses, so their decisions about service-learning are highly influential. Garcia and Robinson (2005) reported that faculty at colleges with a service-learning office and staff were more likely to perceive the coordinators of these programs as the primary resource. While faculty members regarded professional development as the main benefit of service-learning for college students, they also noted other benefits, such as learning about the community and practical work experience.

There is a critical, persistent, and growing need for volunteers in nonprofit animal welfare groups. To illustrate, although there has been some decline in the number of dogs entering shelters during the past 7–8 years, an estimated 3.3 million dogs every year become shelter dogs, but only about half of them—1.6 million dogs—get adopted (American Society for the Prevention of Cruelty to Animals, 2017). In addition to the possible neglect and abuse that these dogs might have experienced before entering the shelter, life in the shelter exposes the dogs to stressors such as confined spaces, frequent barking, and minimal human interaction. Ultimately, shelter dogs need compassion from those who take care of them, both staff and volunteers (Davis, 2013). One of the factors that significantly increases the adoptions of homeless dogs is socialization and the absence of behaviors that are unacceptable to many adopters, such as jumping up, mouthing, excessive barking, and resource guarding. However, animal shelters seldom have enough funds to hire staff beyond those necessary to provide basic care for dogs. Shelters are in dire need of volunteer service to teach dogs basic "house manners" (Bright & Hadden, 2017). Volunteers are needed to improve the dogs' well-being. The more that qualified and reliable volunteers participate in the daily care and basic training of the dogs, the better the chances that homeless dogs will find a forever home (Davis, 2013).

Furthermore, empirical studies suggest that even brief positive interactions with humans can benefit shelter dogs. For example, Coppola, Grandin, and Enns (2006) used measures of cortisol, the hormone associated with stress, to document that positive interaction with humans decreased cortisol levels in dogs. They noted that human contact has the potential to contribute to animal welfare and to promote successful adoptions. College students, both in conjunction with college coursework and as an out-of-class volunteer activity, can provide a service that shelters otherwise could not afford.

Although the benefits of service-learning for college students are well documented, a limited number of recent research studies have focused on gains for the community organization and/or partners. For example, Allen and Mueller (2013) noted that volunteer work was valued at nearly $173 billion in 2010. Lee and Won (2011) estimated the value of college students' service to be $4.45 billion. Bright and Hadden (2017) reported on the effectiveness of Safewalk training to prepare volunteers for more effective interaction with dogs. They noted the adoption rate for pit bull-type dogs increased after the training—something that not only represents a financial savings for the shelter, but makes space to help additional homeless dogs.

Two volunteer dog walkers comfort an owner-surrendered dog during her first days at the shelter. Photo Credit: Mary Renck Jalongo

Overall, the published literature has given scant attention to the impact of college student volunteers on nonprofit animal welfare organizations. This is an important area for future research.

SERVICE-LEARNING WITH SHELTER DOGS

There are many different courses and out-of-course initiatives that bring students and animal welfare groups together. Animal shelters sometimes highlight the potential benefits for students as way to recruit them to become volunteers. For example, Central California Society for the Prevention of Cruelty to Animals (2015) identified seven benefits of volunteering at a shelter. Volunteers can: (1) socialize dogs and make them more adoptable; (2) see immediate results and the difference volunteering makes; (3) perform an essential job—dog

When college students volunteer at the shelter, they meet community members who share their commitment to animals.
Photo Credit: Mary Renck Jalongo

walking—that reduces the emotional and physical stress on the dogs; (4) use their interactions with dogs to improve their own mental health; (5) explore future careers; (6) exercise civic responsibility; and (7) learn responsibility and time management. In fact, these positive effects are supported by the evidence published in empirical research on the outcomes of service projects involving college students and shelters. A good example is a project that gave veterinary medicine students experiences in several different animal shelters (Stevens & Gruen, 2014). The students committed to traveling longer distances because this approach enabled them to compare/contrast the various facilities. Students' projects were tailored to support the specific needs of each organization. It was particularly gratifying for students to see their ideas implemented when the rotation returned them to a previously visited site. One student, for example, had designed a whelping room that was based on research about how best to meet the needs of pregnant and nursing mothers with puppies. She was pleased to see the area in use on a subsequent visit and to know that her project had been of direct benefit to shelter staff and the animals.

What follows is a review of some institutional initiatives organized by colleges and universities to engage students in service with dogs off campus. The initiatives range from direct services for dogs (e.g., exercising them, teaching them simple commands, handling them at an adoption event) to indirect services (e.g., creating advertising, participating in fundraisers, meeting with prospective adopters, conducting library research to support a shelter's grant writing). These examples indicate the broad spectrum of college courses for various majors that could incorporate service for dogs.

In a physical activity course, college students completed approximately 40% of the daily recommended physical activity requirement (2.2 miles in 28 minutes) as volunteer dog walkers at the animal shelter (Sartore-Baldwin, Das, & Schwab, 2020). Reciprocity existed because the dogs gained from being physically active as well. In a subsequent study, the impact of a dog walking service-learning course was evaluated with a logic model that examined inputs, activities, outputs, outcomes, and impacts (Das & Sartore-Baldwin, 2019). (See chapter 9 on evaluation for more on logic models and how they can be used to evaluate projects and programs.) The evaluation design used multiple data sources—including observations, student journal entries, and pedometer counts—to study the service-learning project. Results underscored the importance of institutional support from both the university and the shelter as well as the need for effective interprofessional relationships between department and shelter personnel. Das and Sartore-Baldwin (2019) identified two key outcomes of a successful dog walking service-learning project: (1) physical and psychological benefits for humans and dogs and (2) increased visibility of a "town and gown" partnership.

The Reading Buddies program in Fort Myers, Florida, organized by a university student, involved local school children in reading aloud to shelter dogs on the weekends (Szecsi & Meehan, 2018). Inspired by media reports of such programs, the student responded to a course assignment that required students to study child/dog interaction. She designed, implemented, and evaluated a program in the local shelter that simultaneously addressed the socialization needs of shelter dogs and the reading practice needs of young children. The event was scheduled on Saturday mornings. The findings indicated that there were positive outcomes for all stakeholders: the children, parents, shelter personnel, and university students. While most parents emphasized the academic and social/emotional benefits for their children, some also elaborated on the community service aspects their child experienced. Shelter personnel highlighted the change in dogs' behavior as they adjusted to human interaction and sometimes became more comfortable around children. In addition, the shelter director noted that this project influenced the next generation of prospective adopters as children developed knowledge about shelter dogs, pet overpopulation, and compassion for and empathy toward homeless animals. Similarly, children's perception of benefits mainly focused on the dogs' well-being. As one child said: "I think they [dogs] like it [reading to them] because they don't get to interact with people a lot and some like the company" (Szecsi & Meehan, 2018, p. 312). Both the university and the surrounding community benefited from this project.

Another example of direct service to dogs is a university course in Singapore in which psychology majors were responsible for designing and teaching new behaviors to dogs as way to increase the dogs' adoptability (McConnell, 2016). After a few weeks of in-classroom preparation, students spent three hours daily for two weeks in the shelter teaching the dogs basic prosocial behaviors. During this time, the students and their instructors reflected together on how to deal with dog behavioral issues. Data for evaluating the effectiveness of the intervention included student feedback, evaluation of the course assignments, and the instructor's direct observations. In particular, the students appreciated the real-life application of their new knowledge on learning and behavior, which ultimately enhanced their understanding of the course content. This experiential learning situation also encouraged students to engage in future research to test hypotheses. In addition, students found it rewarding to see the dogs' new behavior due to the training. Evaluation of the course assignments indicated a moderate increase in students' learning, although not to the extent the instructor had hoped. McConnell (2016) reported on the logistics and the impact of the course on students' learning; however, the benefits that shelter personnel might have perceived from the students' service were not explored at this stage of the research. It will be interesting to pursue reciprocal benefits in subsequent studies of this type (see Edwards, Mooney, & Heald, 2001; Yorio & Ye, 2012).

The course Research and Service in Humane Education combined a service-learning project with an action research component for undergraduate students (Szecsi, 2015). The service included a seven-week long implementation of KIDS: Kids Interacting with Dogs Safely package (Deming, Jones, Caldwell, & Phillips, 2009) in kindergarten classrooms. College students were responsible for designing and teaching lessons on safe interaction with dogs to 5-year-old children. (For a detailed description of the service-learning project, see Szecsi, 2014.) In addition to teaching seven lessons to kindergarten students, these education majors participated in the design and implementation of research. They aimed to measure the change in kindergartners' knowledge about dogs as well as children's empathy, responsibility, and respect for dogs. Participation in this service-learning project afforded opportunities for students to practice pedagogical skills, engage in interdisciplinary collaboration, consider new professions as careers, develop emerging research skills, and disseminate their research findings at professional events (Szecsi, 2015).

Another service-learning project for students involved them in dog-training classes taught by a professional dog trainer and offered to the members of the community (Karr-Lilienthal & Norwood, 2013). The students' service included preclass preparation such as advertising the dog training class, registering participants, setting up the facility, and communicating with attendees. During the training, students assisted with checking in the participants, practicing basic obedience and dog handling skills, and supporting the professional dog trainer who evaluated the handlers and dogs using the American Kennel Club's Canine Good Citizen (CGC) test at the end of the experience. On the exit survey administered to students they credited the experience with (1) building greater skill as a responsible dog owner, (2) developing a deeper understanding of the challenges of dog training, and (3) gaining greater insight into the complexity of the human-animal bond. They also made connections between the course materials and real life, developed communication and organization skills, and felt better prepared for their future profession, because working with animals was part of their careers. The professional dog trainers indicated that they enjoyed working with the college students and found this class even more worthwhile than other dog training classes in which they had participated previously. The project organizers also noted the long-term benefit for shelters, which could enlist the more skilled and educated students in their volunteer programs (Karr-Lilienthal & Norwood, 2013). This study demonstrated the interconnection between universities and communities.

A variety of indirect service projects to shelters were completed by students at Auburn University Montgomery (Lucy-Bouler & Lucy-Bouler, 2012). First, for eight years as out-of-class projects, students in a leadership alliance assisted shelter personnel in locating hundreds of homes for dogs. Students collected donation items for shelters, advertised and marketed adoption events in the media, and assisted shelter workers with the development of better forms, such as dog intake forms. Another project was an embedded service-learning component in a Web Application course in which students developed and submitted their designs for the Humane Society's website. The outcome was a completed website.

The preceding service-learning experiences, projects, and courses are just a few of the possibilities. We would go so far as to say that there are either direct or indirect opportunities to work with shelters that could align with most majors and/or professional and service organizations to which students belong. In the next section, we offer some recommendations to guide such practices.

RECOMMENDATIONS FOR PRACTICE

A group of college students visits the local animal shelter. They are members of a service club who have volunteered to participate in an evening program that provides dogs with exercise in the fenced area and/or walks outside, commencing at 7:30 p.m. and lasting until about 9:00 p.m., one night per week. The regular meeting time is Sunday nights, but students can come on a different evening or during the day if that suits their schedules better. Goals for the dog walking volunteer program are to provide vigorous physical activity for dogs housed in the shelter, socialize the dogs as a route to increasing adoptability, give the dogs a chance to eliminate outside, and (for the few students willing to do this) clean the kennels that are soiled. The volunteer supervisor is the originator of the dog walking program that has been in operation for over twenty years now; she also serves on the Board of Directors for the shelter. When students come to the kennels, she tells them to work with dogs that are easy to control, at least at first. She shows them how to get the dogs out of their kennels and check the security of their collars/leashes. She reminds them that they need to take one dog through the kennel at a time and that, once they are outside, they should try to get the dog to "go," record it on the chart posted outside the dog's kennel, note any problems, and pick up/dispose of any excrement. Responses from volunteers after the first evening of volunteering differ dramatically. Even though the students were advised to wear comfortable, old clothing and shoes, one young woman worries aloud about her clothes being ruined and says that she "nearly threw up" when she was expected to pick up after a dog with loose stools during the walk. Her friend is surprised and displeased to hear that they cannot be on their cellphones or texting while walking dogs; she was planning to multitask. In contrast to these reactions, two enthusiastic young women in university sweatshirts walk the calmer dogs at first and then ask if they can take the strong, high-energy ones on a run if they double leash them and work as a team. After they return from a run with a big, young redbone coonhound, he still has plenty of energy, looks out the door longingly, and bays. They laugh, exchange a knowing smile, and take him out again because "He probably gets passed over a lot by other walkers." An elderly volunteer photographer says "You ladies are doing so much good for the dogs. I'm sure that they appreciate you!" and the students begin to talk about how much they love dogs. A few more weeks into the semester, this dynamic duo is still going strong, but the two others who started with them have dropped out.

As these very different outcomes for college students suggest, the overall success of service-learning experiences can vary considerably. We offer the following recommendations to maximize program effectiveness.

1. *Build on the work of other successful initiatives.* Before beginning a service-learning project with animals, review some of the well-established programs and their materials. Pennsylvania State University, for example, has a site called Penn State Animal Volunteers (https://sites.psu.edu/pennstateanimalvolunteers). Make use of resources such as implications of the research for practice that are reported in the literature (Kronick & Cunningham, 2013; Terry, Smith, & McQuillin, 2014).

2. *Make thoughtful choices at the planning stage.* If the service-learning component is embedded in a course, which course is the most appropriate and how will the experience mesh with the course objectives, as well as with state and national professional standards used to evaluate the program? Establishing clear objectives and setting precise goals not only addresses the needs of the college students, but also the needs of the shelter or other agency sites (McElravy, Matkin, & Hastings, 2018). In terms of personnel, the faculty members who partner with shelters need to have a commitment to helping animals, to build mutual trust and respect with shelter staff, and to be service-learning savvy. The site for the students' service-learning should be relatively easy to access with schedules that are not excessively demanding of students' time; otherwise, volunteer attrition rates can be high (McConnell, 2016). When initiating a service-learning project that involves dogs, it is imperative to (1) make a plan for recruiting students, (2) establish ways to communicate and schedule meeting times, (3) clarify the roles and responsibilities of each stakeholder, (4) set realistic timelines for completion of tasks and goals, and (5) include opportunities for debriefing and critical reflection as a way to support continuous program improvement.

3. *Place human and animal welfare and safety as top priorities.* Students are sometimes so eager to show their compassion for animals that they want to shower a frightened dog with affection. Before students interact with any dogs, they need to be taught how to recognize signs of stress in dogs and advised to be slow, steady, and quiet. There is no need to invent resources to teach this; the posters about how to read dog body language and interact safely with dogs from Dr. Sophia Yin and Lili Chin are a good resource, as are others that will come up from a search of "posters canine body language." Any dog can bite when it feels threatened, and students need to be cautioned about getting too familiar too fast with dogs. Sometimes college students overstep. In one memorable situation, a dog kennel manager was shocked to see that two students, oblivious to the danger, had decided to take a puppy without its vaccinations into an area outside where the dogs still in isolation were walking by. Fortunately, everyone stayed healthy,

but the students needed to fully appreciate that they could have done harm to the puppy. It is not pleasant to have such conversations with students whose reaction can range from embarrassed silence to indignation that they "got yelled at"—even when no raised voices were heard. However, it must be done to keep everyone safe. Such messages need to be delivered diplomatically and privately, yet clearly and firmly. In this instance, the kennel manager took the two students aside and began with, "I think you may have forgotten something important from your orientation, so I wanted to remind you that . . ." He then concluded with a vote of confidence, saying, "I'm sure that this won't happen again because you both love animals so much and want to protect those little puppies."

4. *Insist on adherence to the rules.* A simple "golden rule" such as "ask first," even when the answer seems obvious, can avoid many problems. Things can change in between students' visits to the shelter. For instance, the dog that ran with them a few days ago now needs to be leash walked after spay surgery or a dog who was fed treats from the jar now must be on a restricted diet per the veterinarian's instructions. These things need to be said as well as reinforced by signage that ideally includes words and bright, colorful images that attract attention, such as photo of a toy that has been destroyed, a red circle with a line through it, and the words "No stuffed toys!" Habits that protect dogs and people—such as hand sanitizing—need to be fully ingrained and modeled for the students. Rules and the reasons behind them need to be restated frequently to students.

5. *Set students' expectations appropriately.* The initial reaction of some students as they sign up to volunteer at a shelter is "Yay! I'm going to get to play with puppies!" First, there may not be a litter of puppies at the shelter for several months. Second, dogs do some disgusting things—smear feces all over their kennels, roll in incredibly smelly stuff, and try to eat all kinds of substances. Successful shelter volunteers like dogs enough to calmly accept that these things happen. Dogs also come in emaciated, neglected, ill, injured, and with parasites. Working with dogs in desperate circumstances can be emotionally draining. It is hard not to get angry when someone has neglected or abused a helpless dog. It is doubly infuriating when shelter personnel checked an adopter's references but the animal "bounces back" to the shelter in poor condition. And it is depressing when, even though everyone did their very best to help, a sick or injured dog does not survive. Once, when a young child entered the shelter, she asked, "Mom, is a shelter a happy place or a sad place?" The only truthful answer is that it is both. College students need to understand this harsh reality. Life at a shelter is characterized by extreme emotional highs and lows.

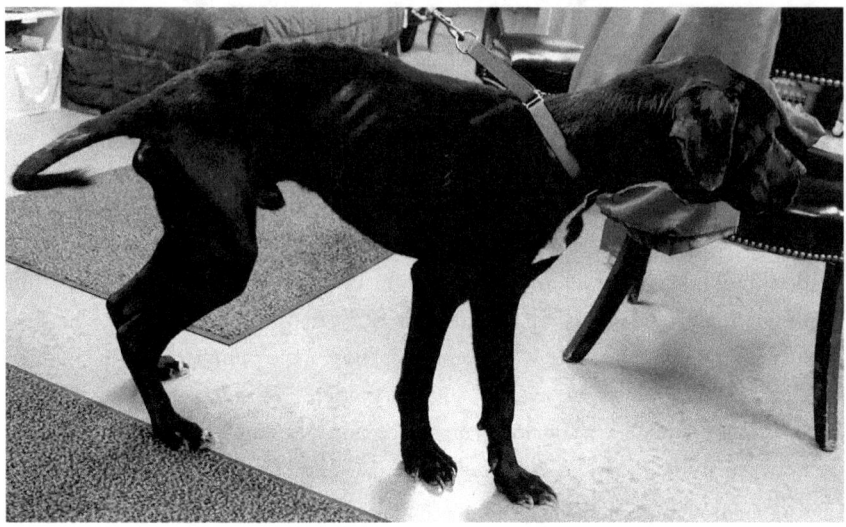

Students followed the progress of this emaciated dog as he was restored to health. He had been so starved that he ate sticks, leaves, rocks, and pieces of a food bowl. Photo Credit: Mary Renck Jalongo

6. *Teach students to respect expertise and experience.* Reciprocal trust and respect between the partners are foundational to effective service-learning (Kane, 2012). Team-building activities between college students and shelter staff before starting the development and implementation phase of the project can strengthen the collaboration. Most shelter personnel are working for minimum wage or, if they are part-time employees, even less. If college students look down on them or think that they are being bossed by them, this undermines success. For instance, where dog walking is concerned, college students sometimes approach it with more enthusiasm than good sense; they will need to follow the advice of the more experienced. For example, "OK, but it's not a good idea to wrap the leash tightly around your hand like that because, if he takes off, you'll get dragged. It's better to hold it in two places—the looped handle and down farther. We even have some double loop leashes and I would recommend trying the no-pull harness with the more powerful dogs, or the two of you can walk a dog that is really strong on lead together."

7. *Require students to behave in a responsible manner and demonstrate their commitment.* The best volunteers have a sense of obligation to the animals and do not miss the appointed time without good reason. They notify others if they cannot

be there as expected and plan to make up hours that were missed. When college students volunteer at a shelter, they are bound to see examples of commitment from others: a box of donations collected by the scouts, an old park bench outside the building beautifully refinished and restored, or a child who gave up presents for himself at his birthday party and requested gifts for the animals instead. Postsecondary students will need to mirror this type of commitment in order to maximize the benefits from their volunteer service. Another way of showing their commitment is to pursue interests beyond the scheduled time. The best volunteers do such things as seek out additional information, follow the shelter's social media, inquire about the dogs' status, watch animal rescue shows on TV, and investigate dog training methods.

8. *Take a gradual approach.* Too often, volunteers are not adequately prepared for their roles and, in the interest of saving time, it is "sink or swim" rather than actual training. Having students interact with easygoing shelter dogs who are not stranger-shy can ease the process of becoming familiar with and accustomed to the dogs before the service activity begins (McConnell, 2016). A well-researched approach to teaching a task is the gradual release of responsibility model (Fisher & Frey, 2013). It can be summarized as a cycle that begins with "I do" (demonstrating the skill), "we do" (guided practice with the experienced person working alongside the novice), "you do it together" (performing the task together with a peer), and "you do it alone" (the novice demonstrates independent mastery of the skill). A good example of this is the process of taking the dog out of the kennel before a walk and placing it back inside afterward. There are many things that can go wrong; the dog can be shy and not want to come out, resist being put back inside, get loose, or even start a fight with another dog through the bars. Students need guided practice in order for this process to run smoothly.

9. *Respect students' preferences.* Shelter personnel need to resist the urge to ask student volunteers to do anything and everything that needs to be done at a busy shelter. If the students volunteered to socialize and walk dogs, take photographs that help dogs get adopted, work on social media, or submit designs for an outdoor exercise area, these preferences need to be respected. Students need to do what they signed on to do (Lambright & Lu, 2009). Salaried staff can sometimes be resentful that they are relegated to the "hard jobs" and get little praise while the volunteers get all the "fun things" to do and are recognized for their service. Strive to cultivate a staff attitude of "we appreciate everything you do for us because we are so busy doing direct care of animals that we probably would not have time to do some of these things that help the dogs to get adopted." It is also important

for nonprofit organizations to expect that there are times when college students' academic work must take precedence, such as during exam week or an internship at another location. Reminding shelter staff that college students' primary job is to succeed in their academic programs helps to avoid the sense that students are unreliable and to defuse grumbling about them not being around as much.

10. *Approach tasks with good humor.* A college student volunteered to walk dogs at the shelter, completed the orientation, and arrived at the shelter at the appointed time. The dog kennel manager chatted with her briefly and then said, "OK, since it is your first night, let's get you a really easy-to-walk dog to start out with." He then led the student, who surely weighed not more than 100 pounds, to an outdoor kennel and showed her a rambunctious young Alaskan malamute that weighed 140 pounds. As the dog placed his front paws on top of the 7-foot high fence and stretched to his full length, the student looked a little concerned. He then quickly added, "Just kidding—we'll save him for later." Then they walked off together, laughing, and got a shy little beagle ready for the student's first official shelter dog walk. As the student prepared to leave and sign out on the volunteer log, she was animatedly telling others about the good-natured teasing and how she had been "pranked." The kennel manager's show of a sense of humor helped to build a positive working relationship with the student volunteers.

11. *Provide clear guidance about reflection.* Incorporating reflection activities in service-learning courses and opportunities can enhance the college students' learning outcomes (Cress, Collier, & Reitenauer, 2013; McElravy, Matkin, & Hastings, 2018). Too often students are given a vague assignment about keeping a journal and the faculty members are disappointed by the level of reflection in the students' work. It is more important to have a few entries—such as critical incidents—that are thoughtfully analyzed than daily entries that are perfunctory. Consider providing more guidance on how, exactly,

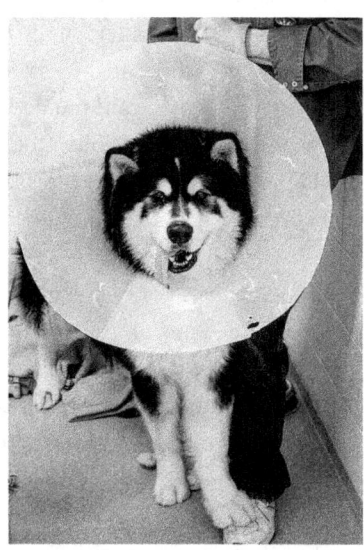

This was the dog that was jokingly suggested for a new college student/shelter volunteer's first try with dog walking—notice the paw in relation to a size 13 shoe. Photo Credit: Mary Renck Jalongo

to reflect (Sturgill & Motley, 2014). Ash, Clayton, and Moses (2007) suggest a template that uses the acronym DEAL and follows the sequence in figure 6.2.

12. *Evaluate comprehensively.* Make an evaluation plan to assess needs at the outset, get stakeholders' perspectives during the experience, make adjustments as necessary, and determine the impact after the experience has been completed. The evaluation should be inclusive for all stakeholders, such as college students, faculty, and shelter personnel, to ensure the exploration of effectiveness from all angles and to use data for further program improvement. For accountability, it is important to systematically collect and interpret data, as this is the best way to understand and document the effectiveness of the service-learning project for all stakeholders (Eames-Sheavly & Miller, 2008; Gelmon, Holland, & Spring, 2018). Researchers will find it helpful to review some of the published scales that have been used to assess service-learning (Bringle, Philips, & Hudson, 2004; Waters & Anderson-Lain, 2014).

DEAL: A Tool for Promoting Student Reflection

D—Describe the experience objectively:
What? Where? Who? When? Why?

E–Examine the experience in terms of three categories:

- *personal growth* (examples: Your strengths/weaknesses skills/assumptions that emerged? Effect of your service on others? Need to change? How to change?)
- *civic engagement category* (examples: Trying to accomplish what? Approaches taken? Why? Need to change to more systemic approach? How?)
- *academic enhancement category* (examples: Academic concept that applies? Same/different from experience? Why? Need to rethink concept? How?)

AL—Articulate Learning (AL) by responding to: What did I learn? How did I learn it? Why is it important? What will I do because of it?

For more strategies that support student reflection, see Hatcher and Bringle, 2012; Hatcher, Bringle and Muthiah, 2004; and Sturgill and Motley (2014). Students' written reflections also can serve as a documentation of critical thinking and personal/professional growth (Ash & Clayton, 2009).

FIGURE 6.2 DEAL: A Tool for Promoting Student Reflection.

CONCLUSION

A severely emaciated bull mastiff was found in a ditch by the side of the road, placed on a blanket in the back of a pick-up truck, and carried into the shelter by a community member. The dog looked like a skeleton with a hide stretched over it and could neither walk nor stand. One college student volunteer suggested preparing a giant bowl of food for the mastiff when a staff member gently explained that the dog's system could not tolerate that; he would need frequent, small meals instead. Even so, the dog was too weak to eat. Another one of the college student volunteers attempted to feed the dog bits of savory food by hand. The next morning, a veterinarian examined the dog. He said it was close to the end of the lifespan for a giant breed—probably about 9 years old. The mastiff also had debilitating arthritis so, even if he managed to gain the 80 pounds necessary to reach a normal weight, his bone structure might not be able to support it. Still, it was possible that there could be an obstruction in the intestines that explained the dog's horrific body condition. The board and staff decided to move forward with exploratory surgery to make sure there was no blockage. Some people felt that the dog's chances of survival were so slim that he should not have been put through an operation and that this decision would needlessly prolong the animal's suffering. Others saw it as giving this gentle giant the one last chance that he deserved. Still others were of the opinion that surgery on such a weakened and old dog was a waste of scant resources, given the shelter's precarious financial situation. Sadly, the dog did not survive. Most of the college student volunteers were stunned by this outcome. They had assumed that with love, care, and food the dog would recover. Staff and veteran volunteers tried to comfort the college students with, "At least he was safe, warm, dry, and cared for at the end instead of suffering and dying in a ditch" and, "We gave him every chance but he just was not strong enough to make it."

Living through the life and death drama of this animal caused students to see that it is not always possible to make it all better, that there are strong differences of opinion about an appropriate response, and that someone will always object to whatever is decided. People need to support one another through these difficult circumstances rather than criticize or blame. As this example illustrates, service-learning experiences can be unforgettable and have a major impact on beliefs, attitudes, values, dispositions, and behavior. That is why service-learning

Some students find it rewarding to participate in rehabilitating an animal and seeing it adopted. Photo Credit: Mary Renck Jalongo

is regarded as a high-impact educational practice. It became a widely infused pedagogy in postsecondary curricula due to its potential for engaging college students in real-life experiential learning as well as exerting a positive effect on the community.

This chapter focused on theory, research, and practice that can serve to guide college students' service-learning opportunities with dogs. In each collaboration, the needs of the nonprofit organizations were identified as the first step. After these needs were matched to the postsecondary institution's mission, the purposes for the professional preparation program, and the specific course objectives, faculty members used creative approaches to design an appropriate service-learning opportunity for students.

Although the initiatives reviewed here are promising, a dire need for dedicated volunteers and their service to nonprofit animal welfare organizations persists (English, 2018; Neumann, 2015). That need can be expected to intensify as even the most well-funded shelters and entire states strive to meet the criterion of "no-kill," defined as saving at least 90% of dogs that come into their care. At the same time, shelters are working hard to change their institutions in ways that make them less stressful for the animals and more appealing to prospective adopters and volunteers. When possible, shelters are replacing the stark chain link kennels, cement floors, dank spaces, and poor lighting with aluminum or glass doored kennels, beds that raise dogs off the floor, fresh air, and sunlight. Efforts to give the dogs time outdoors, teach them some basic manners, and promote them for adoption beyond the shelter environment are more common now. Indeed, these are some ways that college student volunteers can help—providing exercise outdoors, practicing simple training behaviors, and taking a dog they've formed a bond with to adoption events. Students also can engage in indirect activities that support shelters, such as designing a quiet area where adopters can meet with candidates to adopt as family pets, organizing a donation room that has spun out of control, or assisting with grant writing activities. The tasks that students take on as volunteers may differ considerably, but the worth and value of the experience must be assured for all participants. Yorio and Ye (2012) refer to the "3 Rs" of service-learning: (1) reality—involvement in authentic tasks that have a positive impact; (2) reflection—intentional efforts to take the needs of all stakeholders into account and reassess perspectives, based on evidence and experience; and (3) reciprocity—engaging in activities that are beneficial for everyone involved in the process.

Not all volunteer service is created equal. Poorly planned, implemented, and evaluated initiatives fail to fulfill the promise of service-learning (Moely & Ilustre, 2014). Experts in the service-learning field have noted that inadequate service-learning experiences can have negative consequences, not only for the students, but also for organizations (Cate & Russ-Eft, 2017; Waterman, 2014). It is essential that service-learning in shelters focuses squarely on animal welfare, college student learning, and support for organizations so that our communities become safer, better informed, and more humane.

REFERENCES

Abes, E. S. (2009). Theoretical borderlands: Using multiple theoretical perspectives to challenge inequitable power structures in student development theory. *Journal of College Student Development, 50*(2), 141–156.

Allen, J. A., & Mueller, S. L. (2013). The revolving door: A closer look at major factors in volunteers' intention to quit. *Journal of Community Psychology, 41*(2), 139–155.

American Society for the Prevention of Cruelty to Animals. (2017). ASPCA releases new data showing remarkable progress for homeless dogs & cats. https://www.aspca.org/about-us/press-releases/aspca-releases-new-data-showing-remarkable-progress-homeless-dogs-cats

Ash, S. L., Clayton, P. H., & Moses, M .G. (2007). *Teaching and learning through critical reflection: An instructor's guide*. Sterling, VA: Stylus Publishing.

Boyle-Baise, M., & Kilbane, J. (2000). What really happens? A look inside service-learning for multicultural teacher education. *Michigan Journal of Community Service-Learning, 7*, 54–64.

Boz, I., & Palaz, S. (2007). Factors influencing the motivation of Turkey's community volunteers. *Nonprofit and Voluntary Sector Quarterly, 36*(4), 643–650.

Bright, T. M., & Hadden, L. (2017). Safewalk: Improving enrichment and adoption rates for shelter dogs by changing human behavior. *Journal of Applied Animal Welfare Science, 20*(1), 95–105.

Bringle, R. G., Philips, M. A., & Hudson, M. (2004). *The measure of service-learning: Research scales to assess student experiences.* Washington, DC: American Psychological Association.

Cate, R., & Russ-Eft, D. (2017). A review of current methods to develop empowering service-learning programs for Latina/o college students. *Journal of Hispanic Higher Education, 17*(3), 216–228.

Central California Society for the Prevention of Cruelty to Animals. (2015). Seven benefits of being an animal shelter volunteer. https://www.ccspca.com/blog-spca/benefits-animal-shelter-volunteer

Conway, J. M., Amel, E. L., & Gerwien, D. P. (2009). Teaching and learning in the social context: A meta-analysis of service-learning's effects on academic, personal, social, and citizenship outcomes. *Teaching of Psychology, 36*(4), 233–245.

Coppola, C. L., Grandin, T., & Enns, R. M. (2006, March). Human interaction and cortisol: Can human contact reduce stress for shelter dogs? *Physiology & Behavior, 87*(3), 537–541.

Cress, C. M., Collier, P. J., & Reitenauer, V. L. (2013). *Learning through serving: A student guidebook for service-learning and civic engagement across academic disciplines and cultural communities* (2nd ed.). Sterling, VA: Stylus Publishing.

Darby, A., & Newman, G. (2014). Exploring faculty members' motivation and persistence in academic service-learning pedagogy. *Journal of Higher Education Outreach and Engagement, 18*(2), 91–119.

Das, B. M., & Sartore-Baldwin, M. L. (2019). Development of logic model of a service-learning, dog walking course for college students. *Evaluation and Program Planning, 76,* 1–8.

Davis, R. (2013). *Understanding volunteerism in an animal shelter environment: Improving volunteer retention.* Marquette University College of Professional Studies Professional Projects (Paper 54). https://epublications.marquette.edu/cgi/viewcontent.cgi?article=1053&context=cps_professional

Deming, J., Jones, K., Caldwell, S., & Phillips, A. (2009). *Kids interacting with dogs safely.* Englewood, CO: American Humane Association.

Eames-Sheavly, M., & Miller, M. (2008). Recommendations for engaging undergraduate students in community-based extension field experiences. *Journal of Extension, 46*(6), 1–4.

Edwards, B., Mooney, L., & Heald, C. (2001). Who is being served? The impact of student volunteering on local community organizations. *Nonprofit and Voluntary Sector Quarterly 30*(3), 444–461.

Einfeld, A., & Collins, D. (2008). The relationships between service-learning, social justice, multicultural competence, and civic engagement. *Journal of College Student Development, 49*(2), 95–109.

English, C. J. (2018). *Rescue matters: Four years. Four thousand dogs. An incredible true story of rescue and redemption*. Middletown, DE: English House.

Erikson, E. H. (1974). *Dimensions of a new identity*. New York: Norton.

Fisher, D., & Frey, N. (2013). *Better learning through structured teaching: A framework for the gradual release of responsibility* (2nd ed.). Alexandria, VA: Association for Supervision and Curriculum Development.

Garcia, R. M., & Robinson, G. (2005). Transcending disciplines, reinforcing curricula: Why faculty teach with service-learning. https://digitalcommons.unomaha.edu/slcehighered/190/

Gelmon, S. B., Holland, B. A., & Spring, A. (2018). *Assessing service-learning and civic engagement: Principles and techniques* (2nd ed.). Boston: Campus Compact.

Gilbert, I. (2002). *Essential motivation in the classroom*. London: Routledge/Falmer.

Grace, M., & Seemiler, C. (2016). *Generation Z goes to college*. San Francisco, CA. Jossey-Bass.

Hankinson, P., & Rochester, C. (2005). The face and voice of volunteering: A suitable case for branding. *International Journal of Nonprofit and Voluntary Sector Marketing, 10*(2), 93–105.

Herron, M. E., Kirby-Madden, T. M., & Lord, L. K. (2014). Effects of environmental enrichment on the behavior of shelter dogs. *Journal of the American Veterinary Medical Association, 244*(6), 687–692. https://doi.org/10.2460/javma.244.6.687

Holland, J. L. (1996). Exploring careers with a typology. *American Psychologist, 51*(4), 397–406.

Holzman, S. S., Horst, S. J., & Ghant, W. A. (2017). Developing college students' civic-mindedness through service-learning experiences: A mixed-methods study. *Journal of Student Affairs Inquiry, 3*(1), 1–22.

Howard, V. J., & DiGennaro Reed, F. D. (2014). Training shelter volunteers to teach dog compliance. *Journal of Applied Behavior Analysis, 47*(2), 344–359. https://doi.org/10.1002/jaba.120

Huda, M., Mat Teh, K., Nor Muhamad, N., & Mohd Nasir, B. (2018). Transmitting leadership based civic responsibility: Insights from service-learning. *International Journal of Ethics and Systems, 34*(1), 20–31. https://doi.org/10.1108/IJOES-05-2017-0079

Johansson, C., & Felten, P. (2014). *Transforming students: Fulfilling the promise of higher education*. Baltimore, MD: John Hopkins University Press.

Jones, S. R., & Abes, E. S. (2013). *Identity development of college students: Advancing frameworks for multiple dimensions of identity* (1st ed.). San Francisco, CA: Jossey-Bass.

Kane, E. W. (2012). Student perceptions of community-based research partners and the politics of knowledge. *Michigan Journal of Community Service-learning, 19*(1), 5–17.

Karr-Lilienthal, L. K., Norwood, K., & Morstad, J. (2013). Student organization sponsored dog training classes provide experiential learning opportunity for students and community participants. *NACTA Journal, 57*(1), 10–15.

Kronick, R. F., & Cunningham, R. B. (2013). Service-learning: Some academic and community recommendations. *Journal of Higher Education Outreach and Engagement, 17*(3), 139–152.

Kuh, G. D. (1995). The other curriculum: Out-of-class experiences associated with student learning and personal development. *Journal of Higher Education 66*(2), 123–155.

Kuh, G. D. (2008). *High-impact educational practices: What they are, who has access to them, and why they matter.* Washington, DC: Association of American Colleges and Universities.

Lake, V. E., Berg, T., Kelly, L., & Patrick, S. (2016). Connecting preservice teachers with diverse families through service-learning experiences. In C. Winterbottom & V. E. Lake (Eds.), *Praxeological learning: Service-learning in teacher education* (pp. 225–244). New York: Nova Publishers.

Lambright, K. T., & Lu, Y. (2009). What impacts the learning in service-learning? An examination of project structure and student characteristics. *Journal of Public Affairs Education, 15*(4), 425–444.

Lee, Y., & Won, D. (2011). Attributes influencing college students' participation in volunteering: A conjoint analysis. *International Review on Public and Nonprofit Marketing, 8*(2), 149–162.

Lucy-Bouler, T., & Lucy-Bouler, T. (2012). Service-learning positively impacts student involvement, retention and recruitment. *Journal of Higher Education, 8*(1), 19–24.

McConnell, B. L. (2016). Teaching with dogs: Learning about learning through hands-on experience in dog training. *Psychology Learning and Teaching, 15*(3), 310–328.

McDevitt, T. M., & Ormrod, J. E. (2020). *Child development and education* (7th ed.). Upper Saddle River, NJ: Pearson.

McElravy, L. J., Matkin, G., & Hastings, L. J. (2018). How can service-learning prepare students for the workforce? Exploring the potential of positive psychological capital. *Journal of Leadership Education, 17*(1), 35–55.

Mezirow, J. (2000). *Learning as transformation: Critical perspectives on a theory in progress.* San Francisco, CA: Jossey-Bass.

Moely, B. E., & Ilustre, V. (2014). The impact of service-learning course characteristics on university students' learning outcomes. *Michigan Journal of Community Service-learning, 21*(1), 5–16.

Moore, R. W., Warta, S., & Erichsen, K. (2014). College students' volunteering: Factors related to current volunteering, volunteer settings, and motives for volunteering. *College Student Journal, 48*(3), 386–396.

National and Community Service Trust. (1993, September 21). Public Law 103-82 [H.R. 2010] https://www.nationalservice.gov/pdf/cncs_statute_1993.pdf

Neumann, S. L. (2015). Animal welfare volunteers: Who are they and why do they want to do what they do? *Anthrozoös, 23*(4), 351–364.

Ngai, G., Chan, S., & Kwan, K. (2018). Challenge, meaning, interest, and preparation: Critical success factors influencing student learning outcomes from service-learning. *Journal of Higher Education Outreach and Engagement, 22*(4), 55–79.

Patton, L. R., Renn, K. A., Guido, F. G., & Quaye, J. (2016). *Student development in college: Theory, research and practice.* San Francisco, CA: Jossey-Bass.

Perry, W. G. (1988). Different worlds in the same classroom. In P. Ramsden (Ed.), *Improving learning: New perspectives* (pp. 148–159). London: Kogan Page.

Re, M. L. (2015). Service-learning community: A win for students, community, and faculty. In V. Jagla, A. Furco, & J. Strait (Eds.), *Service-learning pedagogy: How does it measure up?* (pp. 155–177). Charlotte, NC: Information Age Publishing.

Reason, R. D., & Kimball, E. W. (2012). A new theory-to-practice model for student affairs: Integrating scholarship, context, and reflection. *Journal of Student Affairs Research and Practice, 49*(4), 359–376.

Sartore-Baldwin, M., Das, B. N., & Schwab, L. (2020). Undergraduate students' physical activity levels and experiences in a service-learning walking class: an exploratory pilot study. *Journal of American College Health*, 1-8.

Shields, P. O. (2009). Young adult volunteers: Recruitment appeals and other marketing considerations. *Journal of Nonprofit & Public Sector Marketing, 21* (2), 139–159.

Stevens, B. J., & Gruen, M. E. (2014). Training veterinary students in shelter-medicine: A service-learning community classroom-based technique. *Journal of Veterinary Medicine Education, 41*(1), 83–89. https://doi.org/10.3138/jvme.0813-105R

Strigas, A. (2006). Research update: Making the most of volunteers. *Parks & Recreation, 41*(4), 26–29.

Stukas, A. A., Snyder, M., & Clary, E. G. (2015). Volunteerism and community involvement: Antecedents, experiences and consequences for the person and the situation. In D. A. Schroeder & W. G. Graziano (Eds.), *The Oxford handbook of prosocial behavior* (pp. 459–493). New York: Oxford University Press.

Sturgill, A., & Motley, P. (2014). Methods of reflection about service-learning: Guided vs. free, dialogic vs. expressive, and public vs. private. *Teaching and Learning Inquiry, 2*(1), 81–93. https://files.eric.ed.gov/fulltext/EJ1148685.pdf

Szecsi, T. (2014). Teaching pre-service early childhood educators about humane education. In M. R. Jalongo (Ed.), *Teaching compassion: Humane education in early childhood* (pp. 49–66). New York: Springer.

Szecsi, T. (2015). Undergraduate student research in humane education: Benefits gained in action research. *Council on Undergraduate Research Quarterly, 35*(4), 42–46.

Szecsi, T., & Meehan, M. (2018). Dogs are great listeners: A university course project leads to young children's reading to shelter dogs. In M. R. Jalongo (Ed.), *Children, dogs, and education.* (pp. 299–320). New York: Springer Nature.

Terry, J. D., Smith, B. H., & McQuillin, S. D. (2014). Teaching evidence-based practice in service-learning: A model for education and service. *Journal on Excellence in College Teaching, 25*(1), 55–69.

Wang, L., & Calvano, L. (2018). Understanding how service-learning pedagogy impacts student learning objectives. *Journal of Education for Business, 93*(5), 204–212.

Warren-Gordon, K., & Graff, C. S. (2018). Critical service-learning as a vehicle for change in higher education courses. *Change: The Magazine of Higher Learning, 50*(6), 20–23.

Waterman, A. S. (Ed.). (2014). *Service-learning: Applications from the research.* New York: Routledge.

Waters, S., & Anderson-Lain, K. (2014). Assessing the student, faculty, and community partner in academic service-learning: A categorization of surveys posted online at Campus Compact member institutions. *Journal of Higher Education Outreach and Engagement, 18*(1), 89–122.

Whitley, M. A. (2014). A draft conceptual framework of relevant theories to inform future rigorous research on student service-learning outcomes. *Michigan Journal of Community Service-learning, 20*(2), 19–40.

Wood, C. H. (2011). Institutional ethos: Replicating the student experience. *New Directions for Higher Education, 155*, 29–39. https://doi.org/10.1002/he.442

Yorio, P. L., & Ye, F. (2012). A meta-analysis on the effects of service-learning on the social, personal, and cognitive outcomes of learning. *Academy of Management Learning and Education, 11*(1), 9–27.

York, T. T., & Fernandez, F. (2018). The positive effects of service-learning on transfer students' sense of belonging: A multi-institutional analysis. *Journal of College Student Development, 59*(5), 579–597.

Youth Service California. (2018). https://www.ydnetwork.org/documents/Service%20Learning/YSCal%207%20Elements%20of%20Service-Learning.pdf

PART THREE

Involving Canines Across the Disciplines

7

INCREASING STUDENT ENGAGEMENT

Roles for Dogs in College Courses

MARY RENCK JALONGO, EDITOR, SPRINGER NATURE, INDIANA, PA,
AND LORRAINE J. GUTH, DEPARTMENT OF COUNSELING,
INDIANA UNIVERSITY OF PENNSYLVANIA, INDIANA, PA

INTRODUCTION

Undergraduate and graduate criminal justice majors have been invited to a panel discussion that will report on a dog training program housed in a federal prison not far from campus. In this ongoing program, shelter dogs are prepared for life in a home by being house-trained and mastering basic obedience. Members of the panel are a diverse and interesting group. The project director is an alumnus of the program that is hosting the event. Another key person in the project is a professional dog trainer; she not only conducts temperament tests on the dogs, but also teaches the inmates how to work with them and evaluates the dogs prior to placing them for adoption. A third person on the panel is a former inmate who was in the correctional facility's dog training program for three years. He was paroled and now operates a successful dog training business. The fourth and final member of the panel is a young mother. Her family adopted one of the dogs trained by the inmates, and she has brought the dog—a pit bull mix—along for the students to meet.

A group of therapy dog handlers and their dogs have been invited to make a presentation to a group of master's degree students in counseling who are enrolled in a course on wellness. The presenters consist of a retired college of education professor, school counselor, elementary school principal, and a middle school teacher. As they arrive for class, students are greeted by the handler/dog teams. The presentation is a synthesis of the research on physiological and psychological effects of positive human-canine interactions. Students discuss a case study that describes an episode of school violence and the process that mental health professionals use to determine why, how, and when therapy dogs might become part of the healing process for students and staff. Afterward, the instructor and one of the students inquire about their family dogs' potential as therapy dogs.

A group of undergraduate nursing majors is assembled in a meeting room at a nursing home. The professor is reviewing expectations for their roles during the internship. At that moment, four members of Therapy Dogs International and their registered and insured therapy dogs arrive and gather in the hallway, something that grabs the students' attention. The faculty member pauses to acknowledge the distraction and gets a unanimous "Yes!" when she asks her students if they would like to meet the handler/dog teams. The leader of the group briefly explains what they do and why. The professor is captivated by the gentle sweetness of one of the dogs, a retired racing greyhound. Later, when students are selecting topics for class papers, several choose to review research related to human-animal interaction in health care facilities. One nursing major, for example, investigates research on live dogs versus robotic dogs in nursing homes, while another investigates zoonotic diseases and infection control. In the years to come, the professor adopts two greyhounds through the local greyhound adoption group.

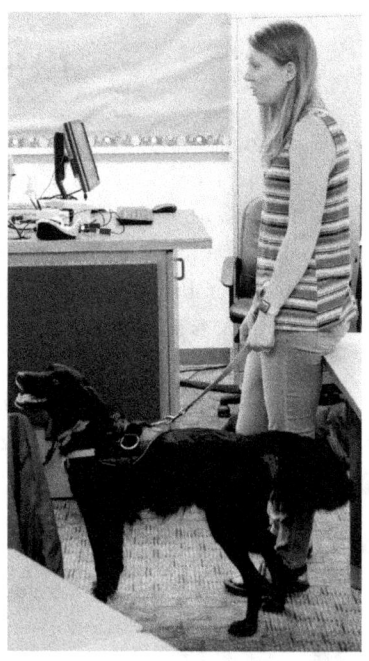

A doctoral candidate in psychology makes a presentation on therapy dogs to undergraduates. Her dog was returned to the shelter twice before she trained him to be a therapy dog. Photo Credit: Haley Romanko

Among psychologists, learning often is defined as an enduring change in behavior that is shaped by experience. Within the context of the postsecondary population, that change needs to take students in a positive direction, one that is consistent with the goals and roles that students are pursuing through their major area of study. It is important to note that cognitive psychology further describes learning as a process that begins with a motivated individual. College students may feel that they have been pushed into attending college by others' expectations for them. They are sometimes disaffected, preoccupied, and bored despite the efforts of their instructors to engage them in course material. This chapter begins by defining learning and describing the learning process, based on research on the human brain. It outlines a theory of student engagement; in other words, the conditions that need to be met for learning to occur. Next, it explores key attributes of powerful and enduring learning experiences capable of transforming the learner in some significant way—a premise that is widely accepted among experts on college learning (Abrahams, 2016; Bain, 2012). The third part of the chapter examines ways in which dogs can contribute to students' learning during classes—typically as these canines accompany guest speakers whose expertise makes a unique contribution consistent with the mission of the program. It underscores the importance of linking these events to course objectives rather than treating them as a pleasant diversion from class routines. Chapter 7 provides guidelines for college course instructors seeking to connect dogs with the content of their classes. It suggests ways of contacting handlers/dogs, offers a checklist for faculty members to prepare for the visit, and endorses evaluating the event with the students. The chapter concludes with a discussion of expanded roles for dogs in a wide variety of courses across disciplines.

DEFINITION OF *LEARNING*

Albert Einstein once said that "Learning is experience. Everything else is just information." As the preceding vignettes suggest, interactions with canines can be linked with course objectives, program purposes, and institutional missions. Although learning is a widely agreed upon goal of a college education, there is less agreement about a definition of learning. Nevertheless, many experts from various fields would concur that, at its most basic, learning is an enduring change in behavior that is acquired through experience. If, for example, a person dreams of volunteering in the community with a registered and insured therapy dog but has never done more than teach a dog basic "house manners," both the handler's and the dog's behavior will need to change for it to qualify as learning. A second area of some agreement is that learning is influenced by "within the learner" variables (e.g., prior experience, cognitive ability, and emotional state) as well as "outside the learner" variables (e.g., social support, the task demands, the types of materials available, and teaching behaviors) (Ormrod, 2015).

Taken as a group, college students can be less than enthusiastic about the learning experiences that others plan for them. They sometimes find higher education to be a passive, alienating, and burdensome experience that is part of a "paper chase" to earn a degree (Cook-Sather & Bovill, 2014). Ideally, college teaching would produce "deep, integrative learning." Evidence of this type of learning includes such things as:

- Integrating ideas or information from various sources
- Including diverse perspectives in class discussions/writing
- Putting together ideas from different courses
- Seeking additional information about topics and issues outside of class
- Discussing ideas with others
- Analyzing the basic elements of an idea, experience, or theory
- Synthesizing and organizing ideas, information, or experience
- Making judgments about the value of information
- Applying theories to practical problems or in new situations
- Examining the strengths and weaknesses of their position on an issue
- Trying to better understand others' perspectives
- Correcting misconceptions based on evidence
- Learning something that changes how they understand an issue (American Association of Colleges and Universities, 2008; Laird, Shoup, Kuh, & Schwarz, 2008).

THEORY OF STUDENT ENGAGEMENT

Engagement is the word that cognitive psychologists use to describe learning at its best. Shernoff (2013) conceptualizes learner engagement as an admixture of three elements:

1. *Interest*: the individual's attention, concern, and curiosity about a particular topic or task.
2. *Concentration*: the ability to focus on the topic, task, or skill and filter out distractions.
3. *Enjoyment*: feelings that encourage the learner to try again, despite the initial awkwardness that is frequently associated with doing something new and to persist at a task long enough to master the requisite skills.

The most effective college instructors engage students in meaningful tasks and are successful in motivating students to produce high-quality work. For example, an academic librarian transformed her routine assignment into something more engaging through a community outreach approach:

> An academic librarian is the instructor for a course called "Introduction to Information Literacy." The purpose of the course is to teach undergraduates the research skills that they need to succeed in college study. The students' major assignment is to investigate a topic using authoritative sources and, rather than completing it as an exercise, the instructor decides to use the results of their library research to support community organizations. She invites faculty members to suggest topics and, by far, the ones involving dogs are the most frequently selected. Two criminal justice majors choose to investigate dog training programs in prisons; their community partner is a state correctional facility. A nursing major chooses to investigate vaccination policies and procedures for dogs; her partner is the animal shelter. A student pursuing a degree in counseling reviews the research on counselors who incorporate a registered and insured dog into their practice; her partner is a mental health facility. After the students submit their projects, faculty members who do community outreach with organizations report back on how the information supported their efforts. The work on dog training in correctional facilities was used to write a proposal for an edited book that was awarded a contract; the nursing major's work on vaccinations was used to plan a professional development session for shelter staff; and the work on dogs in counseling was used to get board approval to expand the program. Linking the students' library research to community service in such concrete ways builds students' skills in information literacy and their appreciation for the power of authoritative information to persuade.

In the preceding example, the topic of dogs is used to foster student engagement, but there is no direct interaction with canines. When dogs visit and interact with students, those exchanges may be categorized as four basic types.

INVOLVING CANINES TO MAXIMIZE LEARNING

Because *learning* can be difficult to define adequately, one alternative strategy is to identify characteristics of effective learning experiences. Eyler (2018) identifies some themes in the literature that we apply to interactions with canines in college classes.

1. *Capitalize on curiosity.* When a plan is made to bring dogs into the college classroom, it tends to spark curiosity. Why did our instructor decide to do this? Who will be speaking? Will dogs actually be present? How will this experience relate to my professional goals? Having questions such as these affects motivation. Motivation is "a theoretical construct to explain the reason or reasons we engage in a particular behavior. It is the feeling of interest or enthusiasm that makes somebody want to do something" (Barkley, 2010, p. 9). Motivation also refers to "the level of enthusiasm and the degree to which students invest attention and effort in learning" (Brophy, 2004, p. 4). Novelty is a great tool for generating interest, enthusiasm, and motivation to learn—and dogs represent a departure from the routine in college classes. Furthermore, there is some research evidence that interaction with animals results in higher levels of alertness and mental stimulation (Palley, O'Rourke, & Niemi, 2010).

2. *Create a sense of social belonging.* Completing a course of study in college requires persistence, but that determination is difficult to summon unless students believe that they belong there. Becoming socialized to a professional role, acquiring the skill set necessary to fulfil that role, and internalizing the ethics of the profession—these outcomes are essential to effective higher education across the disciplines. College instructors accomplish more with student learners when they invite them into the professional dialogue. Students need experience in formulating questions that require higher-order thinking skills (application, analysis, synthesis, and evaluation). Examples of effective questions include:
   - What research evidence supports ____?
   - What else may account for ____?
   - If ____ occurred, how might that change your thinking about the issue?
   - Who are the stakeholders in this situation? How might their perspectives differ—and why?
   - From all that we have discussed, what do you consider to be the most important? Why?

   Another way to invite students into the professional conversation is to ask them to generate questions for the guest speakers well in advance and share them with the presenters. This helps to familiarize the presenters with the audience and makes the material more relevant to the class.

3. *Allocate time for students to interact physically with dogs.* There is a growing body of research to document that gentle touch is important, both for the college student

(Stewart, Chang, Parker, & Grubbs, 2016; Stewart, Dispenza, Parker, Chang, & Cunnien, 2014) and for the dog (McGowan, Bolte, Barnett, Perez-Camargo, & Martin, 2018). This tactile interaction releases endorphins in both species (see Matuszek, 2010, for a review). Interacting with a dog for seven to ten minutes led to significant reductions in state anxiety as measured by the State-Trait Anxiety Inventory, while no such change was observed in the control group (Crossman & Kazdin, 2015; Crossman, Kazdin, & Knudson, 2015). Physical contact between a person and a mellow dog can elevate positive mood in college students (Binfet, 2017), including those who are experiencing homesickness (Binfet & Passmore, 2016).

4. *Recognize the role of emotions in learning.* Contrary to the old "right brain/left brain" dichotomy, we now know that emotions exert a powerful influence on learning (Tyng, Amin, Saad, & Malki, 2017). Powerful emotions command the brain's attention. If the learning experience is positive, endorphins—the "feel-good hormones"—are increased in the blood (Zak, 2015). This tends to increase learner engagement, supports students in putting forth their best effort, and aids in the retention of material (Barkley, 2010). On the other hand, if a learning experience is negative, anxiety interferes with the ability to focus and learn. The learner can feel "swamped" by emotion and logical reasoning suffers because the learner is too overwhelmed. Anxiety and a mismatch between a learner's skill level and the task are threats to student engagement (Brophy, 2004).

When students face challenging tasks but do not think they possess the necessary skills, they experience anxiety; conversely, when the students' skill level is high but the task is not challenging, students become bored; when both challenge and skill level are low, students become apathetic. Any time that college students are called upon to perform a task, appraisal emotions are activated as they "size up" whether they can experience success. A dissatisfying learning experience activates appraisal emotions and students may decide that it isn't worth it to try because they aren't "good at" it. Generally speaking, people pursue a learning task when they expect to succeed and when they perceive some benefit from making that effort: "The effort that people are willing to expend on a task is the product of the degree to which they expect to be able to perform the task successfully (expectancy) and the degree to which they value the rewards as well as the opportunity to engage in performing the task itself (value)" (Barkley, 2010, p. 11).

One important task in college is test-taking. There is a growing body of literature to suggest that the opportunity to interact with a mellow dog helps to address test anxiety. Dell and Poole (2015) reported that over half of all 98

Canadian universities offered therapy dog programs during exams. Others have offered opportunities for students to interact with therapy dogs immediately prior to exams and then used self-report measures of student stress (Barker, Barker, McCain, & Schubert, 2016; Chapell et al., 2005; McDonald, McDonald, & Roberts, 2017; Young, 2012). So this is another way to involved dogs in class—as visitors prior to an exam.

5. *Use case studies.* Cases are used across the disciplines to show how professionals in a field think about trends, issues, challenges, and controversies. In fact, one hallmark of the differences between expert and novice practice is that experts have a rich reservoir of cases they can draw upon when approaching a new situation, while novices have comparatively few. Some of the features of effective cases are:

After the therapy dog handlers made a presentation at a faculty retreat on wellness, this instructor invited them to speak with a group of early childhood education majors. Photo Credit: Mary Renck Jalongo

- Tells a true, powerful, and memorable story
- Points up common misconceptions, issues, or controversies
- Is concise yet includes sufficient details to understand the situation
- Examines an important issue from multiple perspectives
- Relies on higher-order thinking skills (i.e., application, analysis, synthesis, evaluation) for a response
- Reinforces professional dispositions and ethical practices
- Invites reflection through thought-provoking questions
- Does not provide easy answers
- Encourages student sharing of other experiences related to the case

Box 7.1 is an example of a case used with a group of graduate students enrolled in a master's degree program in counseling (Jalongo & Petro, 2018).

BOX 7.1 THERAPY DOGS AND SCHOOL COUNSELING

A horrifying episode of school violence occurred when a 16-year-old male student arrived at school with two large kitchen knives. As his classmates crowded together in the hallway at the start of the school day, the attacker began slashing furiously at anyone within reach. Even though he was quickly subdued by the principal, many students were severely injured. The school was closed for several days and the building was cleaned by a restoration company. A committee consisting of district administrators, counselors, psychologists, parents, and students knew that returning to the scene of this event would cause strong emotional reactions, so they reached out to the local therapy dog group for support. When the school reopened, students and staff were greeted by a group of calm and beautiful dogs, eager to greet them. Interacting with the dogs and their volunteer handlers introduced a fresh topic of conversations and was an alternative to dwelling on the deeply disturbing episode of school violence. Professional staff were there to speak with students and help them to cope with the aftermath of the tragedy. In the days that followed, nearly 30 different therapy dogs visited the school, and their handlers devoted many hours to bringing comfort and calm to the scene of so much distress and emotional upheaval.

Questions
1. If you had been on the committee, would you have supported this plan? Why or why not?
2. What objections might be raised to bringing the therapy dogs to school? How could you address these concerns?
3. As it turned out, there was tremendous community support for the dogs' presence. They were featured in a television documentary about the incident. What elements are important in the success of such interventions?

The discussion of this case was followed up with important considerations in animal-assisted therapy (AAT) for counselors seeking to include therapy dogs in their practice. Some questions raised were:

- How would you decide, in advance, which clients might benefit from a dog's presence?
- Might the animal become more of a distraction rather than a route to better communication?
- If you thought that a client was using the dog to avoid the more difficult work of addressing mental health issues in themselves, how might you handle this?
- What precautions, policies, and procedures could address issues of trust and confidentiality if the dog is handled by someone other than the counselor? (MacNamarra, Moga, & Pachel, 2015).

PREPARING TO BRING DOGS INTO THE CLASSROOM

A group of college students organizing a 5K run as a fundraiser for the local animal shelter sent out a flyer that read "Pets welcome!" There are several problems with this. First, it leaves both the type of animal and its behavior wide open, so the potential for an incident of aggression between animals or between animals and humans is great. Second, higher education institutions have policies governing the presence of animals on campus and may have specific requirements for dogs because they are the animal that is most commonly proposed as a campus visitor. Before inviting anyone to class with a dog, it is important to consult those documents. This is not one of those situations where it is better to "ask for forgiveness rather than ask for permission." Table 7.1 highlights common concerns about bringing canines to class and strategies for addressing each one.

At the other end of the leash is the human who is handling the dog. Much of the time, they are guest speakers. Some practical advice on planning to include them is in Box 7.2.

Table 7.1 Ways of Addressing Concerns About Dogs Visiting a College Class

OBJECTION	WAYS OF ADDRESSING THE CONCERN
Allergies	The source of most people's allergic reactions to dogs is dander. Some ways of diminishing dander include keeping dogs well-groomed, holding the event outside where the dander is more dispersed into the air, wiping the dog down with anti-dander wipes, using a HEPA filter unit, providing disposable gloves if a person with allergies wants to touch the dog, allowing a person with severe allergies to participate in the class on the computer in an office away from the dog. Some people, if they are notified in advance, will take medication to prevent an allergic reaction so that they can join the class.
Fears, phobias, and disgust toward dogs	Not everyone is accepting of dogs in the workplace. It is important to allow people to disclose this privately rather than simply ask the entire class if anyone is afraid of or dislikes dogs. Some neighborhoods keep aggressive dogs to protect property. Individuals may have had a traumatic experience involving a dog. In a culture/community where feral dogs are present, they may be viewed as vermin. Be respectful of such differences and give everyone an opportunity to opt out of the interaction with dogs if they wish. Designate a "no dog" pathway when students arrive for class and a place within the room where they can keep their distance. Many times, the presence of well-groomed and well-behaved animals begins to change students' ideas about dogs.
Dog bites	Dogs must always be on leash and under the owner/handler's control. Dogs visiting a class should be obedience trained and have their temperaments assessed by an independent evaluator. At the very least, the dogs should earn as the American Kennel Club's Canine Good Citizen. Better still would be the AKC's Community Canine title. For therapy dogs, testing/registration with a reputable therapy group that includes liability insurance is recommended. For service dogs, successful completion of the public access test is recommended.

Transmitting disease, unpleasant odors, shedding fur	Dogs with sores or bandages should not visit. They should not be encouraged to lick or "kiss" people, particularly on the face/mouth, nor to lick bandages on a person. Dogs should not "high five" or "shake/give paw" because their feet are more likely to be unclean. Participants should not feed dogs treats because this can put saliva on the person's hands. The single most effective way to prevent a dog from acting as a carrier of disease to humans (referred to as zoonotic diseases), is through thorough proper handwashing (Centers for Disease Control, 2016; Stull, Brophy, & Weese, 2015). If soap and water are not available, supply antibacterial pump sanitizer or wipes. Any visiting dogs should be well-groomed. This would help to minimize odors and shedding. Provide rollers with sticky tape so that participants can remove fur from their clothing. See guidelines for health care facilities (Murthy et al., 2015) for additional recommendations.
Barking	When a group of therapy dogs visits, they typically meet outside first for a few minutes so that the dogs get to greet one another. This is a time when dogs are more likely to bark because they see their canine friends. In general, therapy dogs and service dogs are trained to be calm and quiet. Nevertheless, something unusual might cause them to bark and the owner/handler would correct the dog.
Dog feces, urine, or vomit; tracking in mud/water; damage to property	Plan for an outdoor area where the dogs can go if they need to eliminate or are ill. Responsible dog handlers carry a towel to wipe rain, snow, and mud off the dog's body and paws or drool off the dog's face. Visiting dogs should be reliably house-trained; however, accidents may occur, particularly if the dog becomes ill suddenly. In the case of an accident, it is the owner/handler's responsibility to clean up and dispose of it properly, not the custodian's. The dogs that visit should not be out of control or grabbing things they see.
Fall, slip, or trip hazards	Visiting dogs should not exhibit behaviors that might throw someone off balance, such as jumping up or "hugging" people. Owner/handlers should wipe up any water that is spilled from the dog getting a drink and be alert to where the leash is at all times to avoid a tripping hazard.

Note: For further details on the management of safety risks, see Foreman, Glenn, Meade, & Wirth, 2017.

BOX 7.2 PREPARING FOR HANDLER/DOG TEAMS TO VISIT

Before You Begin
Check campus policies. Some institutions may require a criminal record check for anyone interacting with students, particularly students who are still minors. This is sometimes accomplished by scanning a valid driver's license. Handlers may be required to provide evidence that their dogs' vaccinations are current. The rules pertaining to regular volunteers may differ from those that apply to a guest speaker. For instance, if therapy dogs will be visiting the library or counseling center regularly, their handlers may need to attend an orientation or training first.

Set the Purpose
The most common reason for inviting guest speakers is that they have specialized expertise that the instructor does not possess. Make sure that what is planned aligns with course objectives and the mission of the program. Share this with the handlers and their dogs prior to the visit so that they can adapt accordingly. This helps to prepare a presentation that is suited for the audience.

Well in Advance
Agree on a date, time, and location. Determine if any audiovisual equipment is necessary or materials are to be copied and who will be responsible. Request a very brief biographical sketch so that you can prepare an appropriate and enthusiastic introduction that energizes the speaker and prepares the class for the learning opportunity. Invite the students to generate good questions. Share them with the speaker well in advance to focus the presentation and help the speaker to know the audience better. Plan for how the students will interact with the dog(s) if they wish. Give the speaker a copy of the evaluation form that will be used and let them know that the students' (anonymous) responses will be shared with them after the presentation or event.

A Few Days Prior
Clarify again the time parameters, the focus, and the audience. Several days in advance, confirm the guest speaker or volunteer's participation and the

materials necessary. Reconfirm the date, time, and location. For those unfamiliar with campus, provide a map that designates where to park; supply a parking permit if necessary. Indicate where the speaker can take the dog to eliminate prior to the presentation and how to dispose of any solid waste appropriately. Let the speaker know you will be signaling five minutes before the presentation is to conclude and to reserve a few minutes for questions. Develop a contingency plan in case there is an equipment malfunction, or the guest speaker cannot be there. Prepare a brief introduction and share it with the speaker to make sure it is accurate.

On the Day of the Presentation
Use the introduction that you agreed upon. Model effective listening skills for the students by maintaining eye contact with the speaker. Resist the urge to use this time to check text messages, perform other routine tasks, or go back to the office. Put your hand up to signal the five-minute warning. If a speaker continues to talk anyway, move toward the front of the room, and stand there. Allocate some time for questions. At the conclusion of the presentation, thank the speaker aloud, reinforce the "takeaway" message, and state how the presentation links to course objectives. Ask the students to evaluate the presentation. It could be relatively informal, written responses on a note card to questions such as:

- Three important things that I learned from this presentation were . . .
- The most helpful activity in class today was:
- Today, I changed the way I think about ___ because . . .
- One question that I still have is . . .
- The thing that helped me to understand ___ was ___
- The most difficult concept for me continues to be:
- In future presentations of this type, I would like to do more of ___ and less of ___

Figure 7.1 is an example of a rating scale that was developed to evaluate a session on therapy dogs in counseling. It uses a Likert scale (ranging from strongly agree to strongly disagree) so that students can respond to a series of statements.

Session Evaluation: Therapy Dogs

Our group is registered and insured with the Alliance of Therapy Dogs, a national group headquartered in Cheyenne, WY. We are an all-volunteer organization committed to community service in the Indiana, PA area. You can help us improve our effectiveness by completing the brief survey below. Please mark the box on the right-hand side that best describes your response to each statement at left.

Statement	Strongly Agree	Agree	Neutral	Disagree	Strongly Disagree
Overall, the session was of high quality.					
Presentation					
The presenters were knowledgeable about the topic.					
There was evidence of careful preparation.					
Research and the implications for practice were included.					
Content					
The information was relevant to the audience.					
The material followed a logical progression.					
The resources provided were authoritative.					
Learning					
I learned from this presentation.					
The questions raised were answered thoughtfully.					
I would recommend this presentation to colleagues.					

FIGURE 7.1 Session evaluation: Therapy dogs.

Bam-Bam, a veteran therapy dog, joins his handler during a panel discussion for education majors about dogs in the lives of children. Photo Credit: Haley Romanko

RESEARCH AND INSTITUTIONAL INITIATIVES

When dogs are effectively incorporated into the college curriculum, this practice is called animal-assisted education or AAE (Cirulli, Borgi, Francia, & Alleva, 2011; see chapter 5). The International Association of Human-Animal Interaction Organizations (IAHAIO Task Force, 2018) has published a white paper that provides useful guidelines to protect the wellness of the animals when conducting animal-assisted activities and interventions (see chapter 2). Recommended practices are frequently referred to as "one health, one welfare," a concept dating back to the 1800s that recognized the interconnectedness of wellness across species and the environment (Jordan & Lem, 2014; Pinillos, Appleby, Manteca, Scott-Park, & Smith, 2015). (For more on One Health, see www.onehealthinitiative.com and chapter 2.) Table 7.2 highlights some of the strategies that tend to increase learner engagement.

Table 7.2 Strategies to Promote Learner Engagement in College Classes

WAYS TO INCREASE LEARNER ENGAGEMENT	EXAMPLE	RESOURCES
Provide enthusiastic role models of professionalism	Graduate students in child and family psychology work alongside a play therapist who has incorporated her well-trained dogs into her private practice with families.	Family Enhancement and Play Therapy Center, http://play-therapy.com Van Fleet, R., & Faa-Thompson, T. (2017). *Animal-assisted play therapy*. Sarasota, FL: Professional Resources Press.
Focus attention and generate interest	Students in a Reserve Officer's Training Corp (ROTC) learn about the preparation of military working dogs (MWDs) from a professional dog trainer and a retired military veteran/dog handler.	Ritland, M., & Brozek, G. (2015). *Team dog: How to train your dog—the Navy SEAL way*. New York: G. P. Putnam. *SEAL Dog* (DVD)
Invite interaction and relationship building in the larger community	Social work majors meet justice workers who support child victims of abuse, violence, and crime and the courthouse dog/handler team.	Courthouse Dogs: Official Site, https://courthousedogs.org Courthouse Service Dogs (PowerPoint), https://www.slideserve.com/bryce/courthouse-dogs Courthouse Dogs Programs, http://assistancedogsofthewest.org/courthouse-dogs-teamwork-supports-families-generates-better-outcomes-for-children

Give students guided practice to increase self-efficacy	Students pursuing teacher certification volunteer at two events involving dogs. The first is a club for junior high school students who love animals, and service dogs in training will visit. The second is a summer reading program at the public library in which children can make an appointment to practice reading aloud with a handler and dog. In the second event, the public library offers opportunities for children to practice reading aloud with handlers and their therapy dogs during the summer months.	Rivera, M. (2004). *Canines in the classroom: Raising humane children through interactions with animals.* Herndon, VA: Lantern Books. Jalongo, M. R. (Ed.). (2018). *Children, dogs, and education.* New York: Springer Nature.
Help students to identify with their future students/clients	Professional trainers of hearing assistance dogs make a presentation to students who are pursuing teacher certification in deaf education. They discuss the Americans with Disabilities Act, the rights of the person and the service dog, and bring a trained dog to demonstrate how hearing assistance dogs provide support to their owners.	Assistance Dogs International: Hearing Dogs, https://assistancedogsinternational.org/about-us/types-of-assistance-dogs/hearing-dog NEADS World Class Service Dogs, https://neads.org/service-dog-programs/hearing-dogs-deaf-and-hearing-loss Healthy Hearing, https://www.healthyhearing.com/report/52637-Hearing-assistance-dogs-are-changing-lives
Support students as they attempt challenging tasks	Registered and insured therapy dogs and their handlers are available to students prior to taking an exam or other stressful task, such as making a presentation to peers.	Several studies have found that the presence of dogs can reduce stress and anxiety prior to exams (Barker et al., 2016; Chapell et al., 2005; Crossman, 2017; Daltry & Meher, 2015; Dell & Poole, 2015; Islam, Spruin, & Hernandez, 2017; McDonald et al., 2017)

RECOMMENDATIONS FOR PRACTICE

Given the information that was shared in this chapter, we offer nine recommendations for how to appropriately involve dogs in college courses.

1. Work only with dogs that are trained, tested, health checked, and insured. Although it may be tempting to bring some homeless animals from the shelter to class, this is taking a huge risk. Many times, shelter animals are under considerable stress and taking them out into unfamiliar territory can result in some unanticipated behaviors. Dogs that visit need to be reliably house-trained, nonaggressive toward people and other animals, current on all vaccinations and vet checked, clean and well-groomed, and covered by liability insurance.
2. Invite therapy dogs or service dogs to the classroom only if the experience helps to meet course objective(s). A good example is including laws that pertain to dogs in the professional preparation of lawyers. Increasingly, the ownership of a family dog is a very contentious issue in divorces and dogs are sometimes included in wills. In one terrible example of what can happen when these plans are not part of a legal document, a person who was given a large sum of money to care for her friend's dog spent the money and brought the dog to the shelter instead. It is not surprising, then, that people want a binding contract that that will ensure the dog's proper care. After Leona Helmsley, the wealthy owner of hotels and other real estate died in 2007, she left the remainder of her estate—$12 million—to her Maltese dog, making it the richest dog in the world (James, 2011). Another area of the law has to do with protecting the rights of dogs that are emotional support animals (ESAs) and service dogs. Furthermore, more states have added laws to the books that deal with dog welfare, such as limits on the amount of time and the weather conditions in which a dog can be tethered outside, the removal of dogs from inside an overheated car, and prosecution for animal cruelty/abandonment. As a result of these trends, these topics are more often included in paralegal and lawyers' professional training, so knowledge of "dog law" definitely meshes with course objectives.
3. Announce the presentation ahead of time so students can voice any potential issues such as allergies or fears. This should be done confidentially out of respect for individual students. Students may be reluctant to announce, in front of a group, that they have an irrational fear (phobia) (McCabe, 2015) or had a traumatic experience involving a dog. If most or all other students are eager to have the dogs come to class, they also may not want to be the one who creates an issue. Figure

out a way for them to be included—perhaps by being seated at a distance from the dogs during the presentation or observing the session using video equipment.
4. Establish group norms at the beginning of the presentation such as when students can interact with the dogs, expected level of class participation, and so forth. Faculty members need to work with guest speaker(s) so that the presenter not only conveys information verbally, but also gives students practice in applying what they have learned, facilitates teamwork, hones students' analytical skills, and leads them to high-quality visual/print/online resources. Remind them that students retain 31% of information when they teach others and put learning to immediate use, 27% from guided practice, 18% through visual and verbal group processing, 11% from demonstration, 7% from audiovisual, 4% from reading, and 2% from lecturing (Barkley, 2010). Suggest that presenters afford opportunities for a large group discussion, small group activity, and individual responses from students.
5. Tailor therapy dog presentations to the students and course content. This may require the instructor of record to work with the presenters as they plan. It is unrealistic to expect everyone who works with dogs to be an effective presenter. Many times, they have seen others in the community doing the least effective type of presentation—totally impromptu or the same "canned" presentation, no matter who the audience might be. Many presenters feel honored to be asked to speak with college students and are proud to tell others that they are doing this; however, professional development should be reciprocal. Faculty cannot assume that people from other fields have teaching expertise. Rather, they need to work *with* their guests to assure the best possible outcome. The faculty member should support effective teaching of the particular student group as needed and the guest speaker should be educating the community about the dog part of the subject matter. Encourage presenters to bring the real world into college classes. A case study, a series of photos, a short film clip, a brief news item—all of these can become the basis for discussion. As with all satisfying interpersonal relationships, reciprocal trust and respect are the foundation and, at the university, providing role models of professionalism is just as important as mastering course content.
6. Integrate evidence-based research to support the use of therapy dogs in the discipline being discussed. Suggest developing a one-page list of resources that the instructor can copy and distribute. For example, there is a large body of research on the role of dogs and physical health. Quotations from leading experts that "sum up" the research are concise and memorable ways of communicating. To illustrate, in terms of the benefits of walking with a dog, Rebecca Johnson, a researcher University of Missouri College of Veterinary Medicine, said "Exercise

is good for both ends of the leash" (Novello & Graves, 2019, p. 86) while Carri Westgarth, from the University of Liverpool, England, stated that "Our studies have shown that the number one reason people walk their dogs is because it makes them—the *humans* happy.... In this age of information and work overload, we have our dogs to thank for getting us outside, letting us share their abundant joy and providing a sense of balance and well-being" (Novello & Graves, 2019, p. 88).

7. Make the session interactive. For example, instead of telling students why therapists include animals in their practice, ask the group to write their ideas on self-adhesive notes. This gets them to invest in the discussion and breaks the ice. The presenters can then categorize the students' contributions using a list from experts in the field, such as the following:

- Rapport-building
- Engagement
- Meaning-making
- Skill development
- Assessment
- Motivation to change (MacNamarra et al., 2015).

An administrative assistant trained her Pomeranian/Australian cattle dog mix puppy as a therapy dog. Photo Credit: Megan Higgins

8. Encourage questions and plan for time when students can speak with handlers individually. Students may have questions but be reluctant to ask them in front of the entire group. If a portion of the time is reserved for them to interact with handler/dog teams, this can provide an opportunity to discuss their individual interests and concerns. For example, a graduate student in counseling had adopted a shelter dog recently and wondered about the process of getting the dog tested as a therapy dog. The leader of the visiting therapy dog group also happened to be a tester/observer for therapy dog teams seeking to join the Alliance of Therapy Dogs. In addition, she volunteered weekly at the shelter, so she already knew the dog who was adopted from the time she spent at the shelter. This resulted in an animated conversation about the little Brussels griffon mix's potential as a therapy dog and how a therapy dog could be incorporated into the student's future practice in the discipline.
9. Have participants complete an evaluation at the end of the presentation and share these results with the presenters. Everyone involved in teaching the college students needs to strive for continuous improvement. Asking students to evaluate gives them practice in assessment. When the presenters review the students' comments, they can begin to think about ways to make the session even more effective the next time it is offered.

CONCLUSION

The presence of canines in the college classroom should not be approached as a break from routine or perhaps a way to relieve the instructor of record of some class responsibility; instead, these events should be viewed as learning opportunities from which everyone comes away with enhanced knowledge, skill, and insight. According to the Self-Determination Theory set forth by Deci and Ryan (2000), human beings have three central psychological needs: (1) autonomy, (2) competence, and (3) relatedness. The most effective learning experiences incorporate all three. When instructors bring dogs into a class, each of these elements ought to be considered. Doing so makes "what the best college teachers do" a touchstone for practice. Bain (2012) suggests that highly effective instructors focus more on goals for students and less on what they will do. In his research, transformative learning was occurring when there was evidence that students were developing multiple perspectives and the ability to think about their own thinking; striving to understand the ideas for themselves; attempting to reason with the concepts and information they encountered; using material widely; and relating what they were learning to previous experience and education. Highly effective professors created a challenging yet supportive learning environment in which students grappled with significant problems and engaged in authentic tasks that caused them to rethink their assumptions (Bain, 2012). This chapter began by defining learning, discussing learner engagement, and advocating for transformative learning in college classes. Ultimately, "Transformative learning involves experiencing a deep, structural shift in the basic premises of thought, feelings and actions. It is a shift that dramatically and irreversibly alters our way of being in the world. Such a shift involves our understanding of ourselves . . . our relationships with other humans and with the natural world" (O'Sullivan & Morrell, 2002, p. 18).

REFERENCES

Abrahams, L. (2016). The spiral road of transformative learning: Through the lens of college students with learning differences. *New Directions for Teaching and Learning, 147*, 11–18.

American Association of Colleges and Universities. (2008). *High-impact educational practices: What they are, who has access to them, and why they matter.* Washington, DC: Author.

Bain, K. (2012). *What the best college students do.* Boston: Belknap/Harvard University Press.

Barker, S. B., Barker, R. T., McCain, N. L., & Schubert, C. M. (2016). A randomized cross-over exploratory study of the effect of visiting therapy dogs on college student stress before final exams. *Anthrozoös, 29*(1), 35–46.

Barkley, E. F. (2010). *Student engagement techniques: A handbook for college faculty.* San Francisco, CA: Jossey-Bass.

Binfet, J. (2017). The effects of group-administered canine therapy on university students' wellbeing: A randomized controlled trial. *Anthrozoös, 30*(3), 397–414.

Binfet, J., & Passmore, H. A. (2016). Hounds and homesickness: The effects of an animal-assisted therapeutic intervention for first-year university students. *Anthrozoös, 29*(3), 441–454.

Brophy, J. E. (2004). *Motivating students to learn.* Mahwah, NJ: Lawrence Erlbaum.

Centers for Disease Control. (2016). Healthy pets, healthy people: Dogs. https://www.cdc.gov/healthypets/pets/dogs.html

Chapell, M. S. B., Benjamin, Z., Silverstein, M. E., Takahashi, M., Newman, B., Gubi, A., & McCann, N. (2005). Test anxiety and academic performance in undergraduate and graduate students. *Journal of Educational Psychology, 97*(2), 268–274. https://doi.org/10.1037/0022-0663.97.2.268

Cirulli, F., Borgi, M., Berry, A., Francia, N., & Alleva, E. (2011). Animal-assisted interventions as innovative tools for mental health. *Annali dell'Istituto superiore di sanita, 47*(4), 341–348.

Cook-Sather, A., & Bovill, C. (2014). *Engaging students as partners in learning and teaching: A guide for faculty.* San Francisco, CA: Jossey-Bass.

Crossman, M. K. (2017). Effects of interactions with animals on human psychological distress. *Journal of Clinical Psychology, 73*(7), 761–784.

Crossman, M. K., & Kazdin, A. E. (2015). Animal visitation programs in colleges and universities: An efficient model for reducing student stress. In A. Fine (Ed.), *Handbook on animal-assisted therapy: Foundations and guidelines for animal-assisted interventions* (pp. 333–337). New York: Elsevier.

Crossman, M. K., Kazdin, A. E., & Knudson, K. (2015). Brief unstructured interaction with a dog reduces distress. *Anthrozoös, 28*(4), 649–659.

Daltry, R. M., & Mehr, K. E. (2015). Therapy dogs on campus: Recommendations for counseling center outreach. *Journal of College Student Psychotherapy, 29*(1), 72–78.

Deci, E. L., & Ryan, R. M. (2000). The "what" and "why" of goal pursuits: Human needs and the self-determination of behavior. *Psychological Inquiry, 11*(4), 227–268.

Dell, C. A., & Poole, N. (2015). Taking a PAWS to reflect on how the work of a therapy dog supports a trauma-informed approach to prisoner health. *Journal of Forensic Nursing, 11*(3), 167–173. https://doi.org/10.1097/JFN.0000000000000074

Eyler, J. R. (2018). *How humans learn: The science and stories behind effective college teaching.* Morgantown, WV: West Virginia University Press.

Foreman, A. M., Glenn, M. K., Meade, B. J., & Wirth, O. (2017). Dogs in the workplace: A review of the benefits and potential challenges. *International Journal of Environmental Research and Public Health, 14*(5). https://doi.org/10.3390/ijerph14050498

International Association of Human-Animal Interaction Organizations (IAHAIO) Task Force. (2018). The IAHAIO definitions for animal assisted intervention and guidelines for wellness of animals involved in AAI. http://iahaio.org/iahaio-white-paper-updated-april-2018

Islam, S., Spruin, E., & Hernandez, A. F. (2017). The benefits of therapy dogs on student wellbeing within a UK university. *Psychology and Behavioral Science International Journal, 7*(1), 555–702. https://doi.org/10.19080/PBSIJ.2017.07.555702

Jalongo, M. R., & Petro, J. (2018). Promoting children's well-being: Therapy dogs. In M. R. Jalongo (Ed.), *Children, dogs, and education: Caring for, learning alongside, and gaining support from canine companions* (pp. 179–209). New York: Springer Nature.

James, S. D. (2011, June 10). Leona Helmsley's little rich dog Trouble dies in luxury. https://abcnews.go.com/US/leona-helmsleys-dog-trouble-richest-world-dies-12/story?id=13810168

Jordan, T., & Lem, M. (2014). One health, One welfare: Education in practice veterinary students' experiences with community veterinary outreach. *Canadian Veterinary Journal, 55*(12), 1203–1206. https://www.ncbi.nlm.nih.gov/pmc/articles/PMC4231813

Laird, T. F. N., Shoup, R., Kuh, G. D., & Schwarz, M. J. (2008). The effects of discipline on deep approaches to student learning and college outcomes. *Research in Higher Education, 49*(6), 469–494.

MacNamarra, M., Moga, J., & Pachel, S. (2015). What's love got to do with it? Selecting animals for animal-assisted interventions. In A. H. Fine (Ed.), *Handbook on animal-assisted therapy: Foundations and guidelines for animal-assisted interventions* (4th ed., pp. 91–101). Waltham, MA: Academic Press.

Matuszek, S. (2010). Animal-facilitated therapy in various patient populations: Systematic literature review. *Holistic Nursing Practice, 24*(4), 187–203. https://doi.org/10.1097/HNP.0b013e3181e90197

McCabe, R. (2015). *Phobias: The psychology of irrational fear.* Westport, CT: ABC-CLIO.

McDonald, S., McDonald, E., & Roberts, A. (2017). Effects of novel dog exposure on college students' stress prior to examination. *North American Journal of Psychology, 19*(2), 477–484.

McGowan, R. T. S., Bolte, C. B, Barnett, H. R., Perez-Camargo, G., & Martin, F. (2018). Can you spare 15 min? The measurable positive impact of a 15-min petting session on shelter dog well-being. *Applied Animal Behaviour Science, 203*, 42–54. https://doi.org/10.1016/j.applanim.2018.02.011

Murthy, R., Bearman, G., Brown, S., Bryant, K., Chinn, R., Hewlett, R., . . . Weber, D. (2015). Animals in healthcare facilities: recommendations to minimize potential risks. *Infection Control and Hospital Epidemiology, 36*(5), 495–516. https://doi.org/10.1017/ice.2015.15

Novello, C., & Graves, G. (2019). *Mutual rescue: How adopting a homeless animal can save you, too.* New York: Grand Central Publishing.

Ormrod, J. E. (2015). *Human learning* (7th ed.). Upper Saddle River, NJ: Pearson Education.

O'Sullivan, E., & Morell, A. (Eds.). (2002). *Expanding the boundaries of transformative learning: Essays on theory and praxis.* New York: Palgrave

Palley, L. S., O'Rourke, P. P., & Niemi, S. M. (2010). Mainstreaming pet therapy. *ILAR Journal, 51*(3), 199–207.

Pinillos G., Appleby, M., Scott-Park, F., & Smith, C. (2015). One welfare. *Veterinary Record, 177*(24), 629–630. http://dx.doi.org/10.1136/vr.h6830

Shernoff, D. J. (2013). *Optimal learning environments to promote student engagement.* New York: Springer.

Stewart, L. A., Chang, C. Y., Parker, L. K., & Grubbs, N. (2016). *Animal-assisted therapy in counseling competencies.* Alexandria, VA: American Counseling Association, Animal-Assisted Therapy in Mental Health Interest Network.

Stewart, L. A., Dispenza, F., Parker, L., Chang, C. Y., & Cunnien, T. (2014). A pilot study assessing the effectiveness of an animal-assisted outreach program. *Journal of Creativity in Mental Health, 9*(3), 332–345. https://doi.org/10.1080/15401383.2014.892862

Stull, J. W., Brophy, J., & Weese, J. S. (2015). Reducing the risk of pet-associated zoonotic infections. *Canadian Medical Association Journal, 187*(10), 736–743. https://doi.org/10.1503/cmaj.141020

Tyng, C. M., Amin, H. U., Saad, M. N. M., & Malik, A. S. (2017). The influences of emotion on learning and memory. *Frontiers in Psychology, 8*(1454). https://doi.org/10.3389/fpsyg.2017.01454

Young, J. S. (2012). Pet therapy: Dogs destress students. *Journal of Christian Nursing, 29*(4), 217–221.

Zak, P. J. (2015, February 2). Why inspiring stories make us react: The neuroscience of narrative. *Cerebrum, 2.* https://www.dana.org/article/why-inspiring-stories-make-us-react-the-neuroscience-of-narrative

8

MEETING PROFESSIONAL EXPECTATIONS

Practica, Internships, Volunteerism, and Collaborative Research With Faculty

JEAN P. KIRNAN, PSYCHOLOGY DEPARTMENT, THE COLLEGE OF NEW JERSEY, EWING, NJ, AND TAYLOR SCOTT, GRADUATE COLLEGE OF SOCIAL WORK, UNIVERSITY OF HOUSTON, HOUSTON, TX

INTRODUCTION

An elementary education/psychology double major completed his senior-level capstone project in a faculty-led research lab. The focus was on assessing the effectiveness of a dog-assisted literacy program implemented by a local elementary school. In his own words, the student reflected on the work he completed, the paper he wrote, and the perspectives he gained:

> Specifically, I wrote about the effects of animal-assisted therapy (AAT) on struggling readers. After I graduated, I assisted in writing a paper on the positive effects that AAT has on oral fluency. My section of the paper focused exclusively on the positive outcomes of AAT on young ESL/ELL students. I gained a great deal of knowledge in the area of students with limited English proficiency and the struggles they suffer when learning to read in school. I also learned about many different animal-assisted therapy programs in educational and noneducational formats, and how they aim to address critical needs of patients from abuse and trauma victims to struggling readers in a school setting. I gained many skills while writing the paper as well. I learned firsthand what it takes to get a paper published in the field of psychology and the inner workings of an archival study. I learned how to research relevant information and how to extract valuable information for my own thesis.

My perspective on reading literacy on the whole changed as well. This was critical for me as an educator and proved to be very valuable in the first few years of my career. I learned that while reading is certainly about phonemes and phonics and other assorted literacy terms, it is also important that students feel confident in their ability to read. A common theme among struggling readers, and especially ESL students who struggle to read, is low self-confidence, a lot of which stems from a perceived inability to read aloud (oral fluency). This is why AAT was so helpful for these students. Dogs do not judge and do not care if you slip up on words. They are friendly and attentive no matter what. This bolsters student confidence. So all and all, I learned the importance of keeping all of my students confident in their abilities as readers.

This student's practical skills and leadership qualities have been developed during five years of volunteering at an animal shelter. Photo Credit: Mary Renck Jalongo

One of the great achievements of university study is students' knowledge of and adherence to the ethical principles and practices that are used to accredit professional programs. The leading associations in each field require evidence that students have acquired the requisite skills and dispositions that lead to distinguished performance in the discipline and that program graduates are prepared to become practicing professionals. In response to these trends, college/university faculty and administrators have created programs with multiple opportunities for postsecondary students to put what they are learning into practice through an internship, volunteer experience, or collaborative research with a more experienced professional. This chapter focuses specifically on campus experiences that incorporate canines and contribute to student professional development. In the opening vignette, a future teacher working in a faculty research lab gained knowledge about English language learners and AAT, developed skill in research and professional writing, and gained insights into the limitations that low confidence causes in young students. Student nurses completing an internship at a medical facility might encounter a therapy dog visitation program at a hospital, a dog at a physical therapy facility that is used to encourage patients to comply with a treatment program, or a facility dog at a residential health care facility for the elderly. A student organization may partner with the counseling center on a college campus coordinating Welcome Week and final exam AAT destress events while learning about the mental health benefits of human-animal interactions. This chapter begins with a definition of professionalism and next identifies the theoretical basis and practices employed on college campuses to prepare students to enter their professions. The third section of the chapter presents research specifically on professional development via canine-campus experiences and describes an exemplary postsecondary program that incorporates human-animal interaction into students' professional preparation. The fourth and final portion of the chapter suggests future directions for bringing college students into contact with dogs as part of the process whereby they develop the skill set of a professional in their chosen fields.

DEFINITION OF *PROFESSIONALISM*

What is "professionalism"? In the discussion of professions and professionalism, several writers reference early definitions by sociologists who noted that working in a profession required a specific body of knowledge and skills (Arnold, 2002; van Mook et al., 2009). In her discussion of the pharmaceutical profession, Hammer (2000) extended this definition beyond traditional cognitive and technical skills, referencing the "professional attitudes and behaviors—the 'As and Bs' of professionalism" (p. 455). Hammer points to the upholding of professional ideals that include attributes such as teamwork, integrity, and respect for clients. Thus, in defining "professionalism," there is not only a focus on acquiring discipline-specific knowledge of "how to do something," but also the need to learn what one "ought to do." Both academic and business sources agree that discipline-specific knowledge and adherence to established codes of conduct are essential components of becoming a professional.

DESCRIPTION AND THEORY OF PROFESSIONAL DEVELOPMENT

While the knowledge and skills considered as essential for professionalism vary across academic disciplines and roles, there are many areas of commonality. In this section we review the knowledge, skills, and dispositions considered to be essential for postsecondary students, both by professional organizations and by employers. We next consider the courses, programs, and campus experiences by which these skills and dispositions are acquired.

HARD SKILLS, SOFT SKILLS, AND DISPOSITIONS

In preparing students for entry into the workforce and their professions, academics and employers have long agreed upon the need for discipline-specific or domain knowledge and technical competency, often referred to as "hard skills" (Sethi, 2014). Indeed, these are the foundation of the early definition of professionalism cited above. More recently, academics, accrediting agencies, and employers have focused attention on the need for "soft skills". In 2005, Shuman, Besterfield-Sacre, and McGourty reported on changes in the criteria used by engineering accrediting agencies (i.e., American Board for Engineering and Technology, ABET) to add process skills or soft skills to the existing attributes of knowledge and technical skill. The hard skills of knowledge and technical expertise that ensured success years ago will no longer suffice in work environments that have shifted to more service-based jobs (National Business Education Association, 2000; Zehr, 1998). Additional skills and competencies have been identified as essential for success: "More than ever before, merely being technically competent is not sufficient. To be successful in the global and diverse workplace, students must develop human relations, self-management, and workplace enhancement skills" (NBEA, 2000, p. 1). Most desirable are skills that are broad-based and apply to multiple job and career settings. Termed "crosscutting" skills, these attributes are highly valued by employers (Hart Research Associates, 2015, p. 1).

While there is some variability in the specific soft skills desired by accrediting agencies, academic departments, and employers, there is a strong consensus on the most critical attributes. A review of scholarly research and professional publications revealed that the three commonly cited soft skills were (1) communication, (2) teamwork, and (3) ethical conduct or integrity (American Board for Engineering and Technology, n.d.; American Psychological Association,

2013; Hart Research Associates, 2015; National Association of Colleges and Employers, 2017; Robles, 2012). Other frequently referenced skills included a broad, often global, perspective of the profession in a larger context (ABET, n.d.; APA, 2013; NACE, 2017) and a strong work ethic (NACE, 2017; Robles, 2012).

Soft skills have not only been identified in the United States, but also by academics and business professionals in other countries. Shakir (2009) reported that the Ministry of Higher Education in Malaysia identified seven core soft skills deemed essential for human capital development, which are now required in the undergraduate curriculum. Similarly, Sethi (2014) surveyed business professionals enrolled in the Indian Institute of Management and identified soft skills essential for obtaining a job and continuing professional development.

Interestingly, several of the soft skills cited in the literature might be better defined as dispositions, values, or perspectives. These include developing a positive attitude, becoming a lifelong learner, understanding one's profession in a global context, developing a sense of responsibility, and general professional development.

Along this line, Wilson et al. (2013) differentiated between the acquisition of specific knowledge and skills and the transformation of the student into a professional. In their study of undergraduate and graduate students in psychology, pharmacy, public relations, and international studies, these researchers identified a developmental trajectory, where less sophisticated students held a simplistic view of professionalism as the acquisition of knowledge and skills, while more mature students understood that it also included a personal transformation of values and identity. Wilson et al. (2013) thus extend the definition of professionalism to encompass more than skills—hard or soft. Rather, it is the transformation of students as they become part of a broader community shaped by shared values and attitudes about the profession as a whole as well as themselves as individuals operating within the broader societal and global context.

A review of prior literature reveals an expansion to the discipline-specific knowledge and hard skills historically identified as necessary for professional development. Academics and employers have now added soft skills, recognized as transferrable across a broad range of careers. Increasingly, we see the addition of dispositions and values that go beyond skill acquisition to transformation of the individual. For our purposes, we will consider knowledge, hard skills, soft skills, and dispositions as components of student professional development as portrayed in figure 8.1. Next, we investigate the methods by which students acquire these various components.

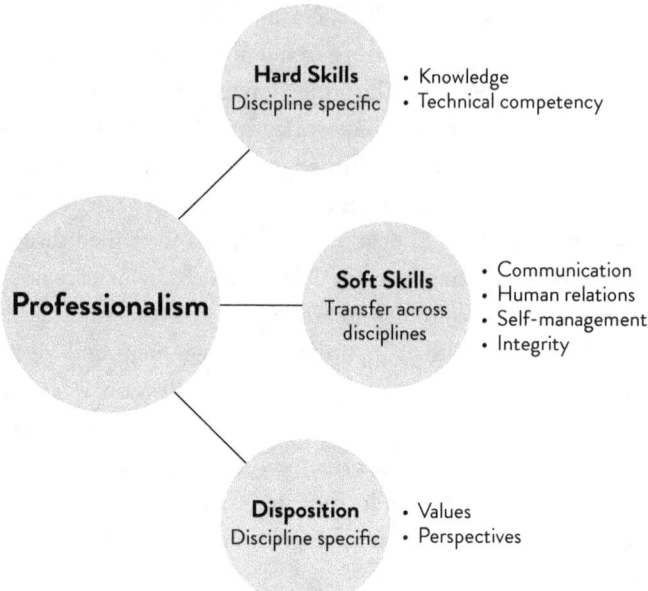

FIGURE 8.1 Influences on the development of professionalism.

DEVELOPING PROFESSIONALISM IN THE COLLEGE LEARNER

Reflecting on the process of learning in a postsecondary environment, what usually comes to mind are the traditional classroom and laboratory courses as college faculty have long been the primary source for knowledge and hard skills. However, the acquisition of knowledge, skills, and dispositions occurs in a wide array of settings, ranging from traditional coursework to volunteer opportunities and internships. Indeed, the recent literature demonstrates a strong focus on experiential learning as a method to ensure the transfer of learning from the classroom to the real world (Eyler, 2009) as well as offering opportunities to gain soft skills and professional values (Washor, 2015).

A common and much researched experiential learning opportunity is the internship, practicum, or cooperative experience. These experiences are quite varied in terms of work tasks, but generally a student is placed in an appropriate professional setting and performs specific tasks under the guidance of a workplace supervisor. Such experiences conform well to learning models (skill acquisition model, Dreyfus & Dreyfus, 2005; experiential learning theory, Kolb, 1984) in that they provide concrete experiences where students learn through feedback and self-reflection and are able to progress to higher levels of expertise. Depending on the tasks assigned and the work environment, college students can develop many of the soft skills as well as professional values and dispositions in conjunction with practical work experiences. Research on cooperative education and internship programs found strong support for the gain of knowledge (Griffin, Lorenz, & Mitchell, 2010; Jaekel et al., 2011), development of hard skills (Jaekel et al., 2011), development of soft skills (Griffin et al., 2010; Jaekel et al., 2011; Wanless, 2013), and acquisition of professional values (Sides & Mrvica, 2007; Wanless, 2013).

Students studying veterinary medicine provide excellent examples of learning professionalism while working alongside an experienced mentor. Clinical experience is often gained working in local animal clinics or shelters that provide service at no-cost or low cost to pet owners (Cummings School, n.d.). Students not only develop knowledge and technical skills, but also learn the importance of civic responsibility and volunteerism. Furthermore, they may gain new perspectives by interacting with people and animals who have lives very different from that of a university student. While volunteering, students may meet, for example, people who are homeless and assert "my dog always eats first" (Irvine, 2015; Lem, 2016). Contrary to social stigma and expectations, the companion dogs of people without homes frequently are in better physical condition and more contented than the supposedly pampered pets who live in luxurious homes, yet spend most of their days isolated and crated, overfed and underappreciated

In addition to workplace experiences, students engage in experiential learning via faculty-led research (Washor, 2015). Lopatto (2010) described the various methods by which students can be involved in research, including intensive summer research programs and research that occurs during the academic year (independent study, honors programs, and paid research positions). Regardless of the timing of the research opportunity, the benefits appear to be comparable. Similar to internship, involvement in research yields hard and soft skills (research design, data collection and analysis, information literacy, self-management, and communication), but also adds several aspects of professional development (relationships with mentors and peers, being part of a learning community, and scholarly publication). The opening vignette, as well as the exemplary program detailed in the following section, provide examples of the professional development gained by student participation in faculty-led research.

While it stands to reason that one of the most effective methods to develop professionalism in students is to have them work side-by-side with professionals, there are learning strategies other than experiential learning. While traditional courses convey knowledge and hard skills, they can be imbued with more active learning as well to incorporate soft skill development. Existing courses can transition the learning process from abstract to concrete by the addition of problem-based learning, research projects, case study, role play, or simulations (Lopatto, 2010; NBEA, 2000; Shakir, 2009). Alternatively, standalone courses can be developed that specifically focus on a professional component such as communication (Shakir, 2009) or ethics (Hammer, 2000). An undergraduate course on applied behavior analysis (ABA) incorporated canines both in the classroom and as part of a course assignment. A handler visited the class with her certified therapy dog, explaining the dog's training process and providing examples of different clients that they visited. Students thus gained an understanding of the application of psychological learning principles in dog training, the therapeutic value of animal-assisted programs in senior centers and elementary schools, and the benefits of volunteerism in one's community. As part of their course assignments, students visited a dog training facility that employed ABA techniques, observed at least two different levels of ability (puppy, beginner, intermediate, advanced), and wrote a reflection paper linking theory learned in class with its application in the field.

College campuses also offer less conventional avenues for professional development. Student organizations, faculty-led activities, and community-based experiences (NBEA, 2000; Shakir, 2009), can provide an environment to develop many professional skills such as leadership, collaboration, communication, and interpersonal skills.

Hammer (2000) adds to this peer and professional mentorship, forums, and seminars presented by professionals as additional mechanisms where students can develop professionalism. In the photograph, Bob, a certified therapy dog, copresents a talk on animal-assisted interventions with his human handler. Undergraduate students learned about various canine- and equine-assisted therapeutic interventions and had a chance to personally experience the benefits of human-animal intervention (HAI) by petting Bob.

On-campus employment was investigated by Fede, Gorman, and Cimini (2018) as another potential avenue for professional skill development. Students working in paid positions for an on-campus program, the Supplemental Nutrition Assistance Program Outreach, reported similar professional development as noted in off-campus positions. Fede et al. reported growth in transferrable skills (communication, problem solving, personal ethics), dispositions

Bob, Dr. Jean Kirnan's therapy dog, attends an informational talk for undergraduate psychology students about his work in elementary schools. Photo Credit: Grace Gottschling

(empathy and appreciation of diversity), as well as gains in civic engagement and social responsibility.

Students can develop professionalism through a variety of traditional and nontraditional experiences during their postsecondary careers. While one tends to think of internships and faculty-led research as experiences that develop professionalism, other venues are available as well, including traditional courses revised to include simulations and experiential components, skill-focused courses, on-campus work and volunteer opportunities, and one-time events and professional talks. We next turn our attention to canine-campus events available to students that mirror both the wide range of activities noted above and also provide for similar professional development in hard skills, soft skills, and dispositions.

RESEARCH AND INSTITUTIONAL INITIATIVES

In this section, we describe how institutions capitalize on the professional development opportunities that are possible when dogs are part of the campus culture. We use the results of a survey distributed to professionals to highlight key points.

CANINE-CAMPUS EVENTS

Despite the recent increase in canine-campus events, there is little published information on the professional development for students resulting from these types of activities. Most of the literature remains focused on the benefits for individuals attending such events, rather than the students involved in their delivery or analysis. For this reason, we conducted a brief survey to collect examples of such events and the reported benefits for student professional development.

Using purposeful sampling, we identified professionals who are active in canine-campus events and emailed a short online survey. Further using a snowballing technique, these professionals were asked to forward the survey to other individuals working in this area, and also to forward a student version of the survey to any students who had been involved in these events (not as participants, but as active partners in planning, implementation, or assessment). The initial outreach included 33 professionals and 12 students (known to the chapter authors). The final sample was comprised of 16 professionals and 22 students, of which 17 participated in these events as undergraduates, 3 as graduate students, and 2 at both academic levels. The bulk of the survey allowed for open-ended responses where the participant described one or more events and the professional development that ensued. Additional demographic data was collected to describe the samples.

The most common majors in the student sample were psychology (8 or 36%) and science or health (5 or 23%). The remaining students were from varied disciplines of which many had no obvious connection to the HAI field (e.g., management, economics, mechanical engineering). This is a real strength of these programs. Students from a variety of disciplines and backgrounds benefit from participation in canine-campus events and these programs are likewise enriched by the diversity of their student volunteers. The college campuses where the students were involved were less diverse than observed with the professional responses, with 15 (68%) students participating in a series of programs at the University of British Columbia. The remaining 7 students were involved in programs at four different schools.

Most of the professionals responding to the survey were faculty (9 or 56%), with most being in psychology and the remainder in education or animal sciences. Five (31%) were professionals working either in counseling or some other wellness support for students on campus. The remaining professionals were a librarian and an elementary school principal. Over half of the professionals worked with undergraduates, about 40% worked with students at the graduate level, and one worked at both levels. The locations of the professionals were much more far-ranging than that reported by the students. Within the United States, professionals were from 9 different states, including New York, New Jersey, Pennsylvania, Tennessee, Ohio, Wisconsin, Michigan, Minnesota, and Colorado. Professionals outside the United States were working in Canada and Brazil.

TYPES OF EVENTS/ACTIVITIES

Professionals and students were overwhelmingly in agreement on the types of activities and events that allowed students to develop professionally. The most frequently cited experiences of students were assisting in AAT events (75%) or as part of a research team analyzing data related to AAT outcomes (25%), with several students citing both. For professionals, the most frequently cited activities were events (50%), followed by research (36%), but also included animal training, off-site placements or visits, and classes.

On-campus AAT events were sponsored by the counseling center, library, or individual faculty and students participated by volunteering individually (as peer educators with counseling or health and wellness offices) or as part of larger student organizations (e.g., sorority, service club). Student tasks included planning and coordinating, publicizing (website, social media, flyers), reception (sign-in, scheduling participants), set-up and clean-up, and collecting data (tracking attendance and administering surveys). Events ranged from one-time occurrences, such as exam period doggy destress and a health and wellness expo, to weekly or monthly regularly scheduled events where participants interacted with visiting therapy dogs and their handlers. While most events occurred on campus, some took place in the local community; for example, at a Boys and Girls Club. The next photograph presents an example of an annual wellness expo where therapy dogs facilitated conversations about student mental health issues.

Most research opportunities stemmed from faculty projects and students participated as research assistants, as part of a capstone course, or senior honors thesis, and were often credit-bearing. Their tasks were primarily data collection (survey, observation, and interview) and analysis, but also included research design, as well as writing and preparation of results for conferences or journal publication.

Professionals mentioned extended off-campus experiences where students were involved in a semester-long practicum or internship such as training shelter

Tricia Baker (cofounder and volunteer with Attitudes in Reverse, a nonprofit that raises awareness regarding mental health issues) and her therapy dog, Misha Silver Lining, attend a health and wellness expo on a college campus. Photo Credit: William R. Petrick

dogs or working at a local humane society. A few faculty members also noted that select classes introduced students to human-animal bond (HAB) concepts. These courses applied general learning and behavioral theories to the training and behavior of therapy animals. Additionally, several had assignments that required observation at external facilities or sponsored guest speakers who spoke of their AAT experiences. For example, a faculty member who was a therapy dog volunteer in her community visited the class with her dog. She demonstrated aspects of the certification test, discussed dog training, and shared experiences from visiting senior centers and elementary schools. A faculty member in physical education had their students design exercise programs that utilized therapy dogs. Two different client groups were targeted—children on the autism spectrum and clients struggling with obesity—and students had to develop separate activities and exercises for each.

A unique hands-on experience was reported by a staff adviser to a companion animal club and a guide dog puppy raising club, both on a university campus. They describe how the students foster service animals-in-training within on- and off-campus housing. The students learn about the different tasks service dogs can be trained to perform and how those tasks benefit the eventual recipient of the service dog. The students gain knowledge and experience in training practices, care of the animals, and socialization of the animal, and members pass this knowledge on to other students through weekly lectures and other activities on campus. Students also visit local schools and other organizations to educate the community about service animals. Members of both organizations take part in outreach initiatives such as volunteer work on and off campus to spread knowledge and awareness of service animals and how they can benefit individuals with disabilities.

The survey responses confirmed that canine-campus events facilitate the professional development of students. This development can be achieved through credit-bearing courses of traditional lectures (enhanced by guest speakers or focused professional assignments) as well as experiential courses (internship, research, co-op, and practicum). Additionally, many students develop professionally through noncredit-bearing opportunities, such as volunteerism through on- or off-campus events or programs.

PROFESSIONAL DEVELOPMENT OUTCOMES

Given the nature of our data collection, a comparison of the percent indicating any given outcome would be misleading (often multiple students were referred by one professional and at other times no students were referred or they were unable to respond, giving greater and lesser weights to specific types of events and outcomes). However, even given such limitations there appear to be patterns in the outcomes, as shown in table 8.1. Respondents reported a wide array of hard skills related to research (data collection, data analysis, scientific procedures, and professional writing) and campus events (event coordination, publicity, skill application).

Soft skills of teamwork and communication noted in the literature also were reported by our participants, as well as leadership and interpersonal skills. Skills related to knowledge dissemination were noted and included professional writing, creation of tables and graphs to convey research findings, speaking at on-campus and off-campus venues, and preparing results for journal submission or conference presentation. In the photo, a senior-level student learns interviewing, gaining hard skills in data collection and analysis, as well as soft skills in communication and interpersonal competence.

Taylor Scott (right), an undergraduate student, interviewing Kristen Klein, a case manager at the college about her experience working with dogs on campus to help students. Photo Credit: Jean Kirnan

The three most frequently cited outcomes by professionals were knowledge of HAI, data collection, and skill application, while those for students were event coordination, interpersonal skills, and empathy. A review of the outcomes presented in table 8.1 further reveals that students identified more soft skill development than professionals, and were also the only ones to report professional opportunities such as networking and changes in personal perspective by developing empathy for program participants. This difference seems reasonable when one considers that relationships and attitudes are not easily observed by others. Students will be aware of these changes, but their supervisor(s) may not be. An example can be found in the opening vignette where the narrator describes how the research project sensitized him to the impact of low confidence on young readers. His story further suggests that the impact of this insight was not fully realized until a few years into his career when he had a classroom and students of his own.

UNIVERSITY OF BRITISH COLUMBIA, AN EXEMPLARY PROGRAM

One exemplary program discovered through our research is the Building Academic Retention through K9s therapy dog program (BARK, n.d.), created and run by John-Tyler Binfet, a professor of education at the University of

Table 8.1 Professional Development Outcomes Reported by Professional Staff/Faculty and Students

		PROFESSIONAL STAFF/FACULTY	STUDENTS
KNOWLEDGE	HAI/education/etc.	×	×
HARD SKILLS	Data collection	×	×
	Data analysis	×	×
	Event coordination	×	×
	Publicity		×
	Scientific procedures	×	×
	Skill application	×	×
	Writing skills (academic course writing)	×	×
SOFT SKILLS	Communication		×
	Interpersonal skills		×
	Leadership	×	×
	Teamwork	×	×
PROFESSIONAL OPPORTUNITIES	Knowledge dissemination (conferences, journals, theses, spreading word to campus)	×	×
	Networking		×
PERSPECTIVES	Empathy		×

British Columbia's Okanagan campus. BARK brings therapy dogs to the UBC Okanagan campus to relieve the stress and homesickness felt by the students, especially those in their first year attending college. Beginning in 2012 with 12 dogs, the program has expanded to now include 55 dogs and 30 student volunteers who orchestrate over 4,000 student visits per year. As there is currently little research on the effects of animal-assisted activities (AAAs), Binfet then studies the participants at these events to determine how visiting with the dogs impacts student well-being. While programs on other campuses are increasingly including an evaluative component to their programs, BARK is unique in that it also includes intervention studies—formal research programs that employ randomized controlled trials allowing for a more rigorous scientific test of the effects of AAAs. (Several publications stemming from the program appear in the reference list [Binfet, 2017; Binfet & Passmore, 2016; Binfet, Passmore, Cebry, Struik, & McKay, 2018; Binfet & Struik, 2018; Binfet, Trotman, Henstock, & Silas, 2016].) In addition, BARK has expanded beyond the UBC campus and is involved in the community providing AAA at the Boys and Girls Club in a program to teach confidence and social skills to 5- to 12-year-old children. Not only is Binfet at the forefront of AAA research, he also has created a leading professional development program of student volunteers who assist in running the program and collaborators who work with him on his research.

Binfet identified his encouragement of student-learning for skills such as event coordination, data collection, teamwork, and knowledge dissemination. However, his students also stated that, through working with him on events and projects for BARK, they gained interpersonal skills, empathy for program participants, and the ability to handle responsibility. One student wrote that volunteering with BARK "allowed [them] to develop the skill of being exceptionally extroverted and personable, as many clients come in feeling more closed and introverted, so aiding them to be more relaxed and chat has a huge impact on their mood and experience." Students typically begin volunteering with the

Therapy dog Meesha spends time with students while attending a canine-assisted event sponsored by Dr. John-Tyler Binfet's program, Building Academic Retention through K9s (BARK) on the University of British Columbia's Okanagan Campus. Photo Credit: Freya Green

program by helping with event set-up and clean-up. They may also monitor events by ensuring that the animals and handlers have everything that they need and address any issues that may arise. Students interested in research help with data collection and some may even assist with analysis. More advanced students assist in preparation of research for conferences and journal submissions and can earn authorship. After gaining experience, student volunteers may be offered employment opportunities to plan events or promote the program through posters and other forms of media. Students can advance to leadership positions within the program, not just remain volunteers throughout their time at UBC. The willingness of Binfet's students to answer questions about their experiences with BARK also was notable in that such a great number of them described their work and appreciation for Binfet. Another student stated, "Dr. John-Tyler Binfet, taught me to always push the boundaries, be innovative, and come up with creative solutions to problems." It is evident that the opportunities that Binfet provides help to shape young professionals and provide students with experiences to aid their success after college.

RECOMMENDATIONS FOR PRACTICE

A review of the published literature as well as professional writings reveals the expectation that students entering their professions will have acquired discipline-specific knowledge and hard skills, as well as soft skills applicable in a wide array of positions and careers. Beyond the traditional classroom, student professional development can be achieved via experiential learning by involvement in internships, co-ops, research, and various volunteer opportunities both on and off campus. A survey of faculty, professional staff, and students active in canine-campus events revealed that courses and experiences involving dogs provide opportunities for student professional development. Further insights from the literature and survey responses follow.

PROGRAM STRUCTURE

Faculty and professional staff involved in canine-campus events and research can adapt the practices noted above on their campuses. Existing canine events and research initiatives can be reviewed with an eye to adding student roles that would enhance professional development. When new events or initiatives are in the development phase, tasks and roles can be built in that engender student professionalism. Faculty and staff are encouraged to think beyond the traditional research assistant and internship paths for professional development and consider tasks related to event planning and execution, as well as student organization involvement, and one-time talks or workshops as ways to further involve students and add to their professional development.

PROGRAM PARTICIPANTS

In their study of on-campus employment as a means of student professional development, Fede et al. (2018) noted the benefit for students who were not able to pursue off-campus experiential learning such as internships or service-learning. Off-campus opportunities often are unpaid and require transportation, factors that may preclude students with differing abilities or of lower economic means from pursuing them. Most faculty research opportunities and college-canine events take place on campus and likely would appeal to students with such limitations. Additionally, faculty and professionals should consider recruiting students from a wide array of academic disciplines. Forty percent of the student respondents in our survey were from majors that are not directly related to physical or mental health professions. Yet these students also benefited personally and professionally from the programs, often citing the general soft skills identified as critical in today's workforce and applicable across professions.

PROGRAM OUTCOMES

In preparing this chapter, we found ourselves reflecting on the professional development opportunities afforded in our own practices. We hope the information presented here inspires the reader to similarly consider ways in which the canine-campus activities they are involved in could be used as vehicles to expand student professional development. Professionalism opportunities can be added to existing programs by creating leadership opportunities where experienced volunteers train newcomers, asking students to develop lab manuals or event procedures, and charging students with communication tasks such as developing and implementing publicity or emailing/phoning dog handlers or speakers. Even for topics where students may not be able to directly participate, explanation—sharing and discussion of procedures and protocols (i.e., IRB or funding/grant applications)—would be beneficial.

STUDENT ASSESSMENT

We further encourage professionals and faculty to consider assessing the professional development in the students who work with them. As has been shown in the survey data presented here, students perceived additional soft skills as well as professional opportunities and perspectives of which faculty and professional staff were unaware. Giving students "voice" and obtaining their perspective is critical. A simple open-ended survey similar to that used in this research that asks for detail on the tasks performed and the outcomes would shed light on the development that is occurring. Comparison to the literature and research presented in this chapter might reveal areas where future development could be explored. While interviews and focus groups provide alternative means of collecting such information, the anonymity of a survey may garner more honest responses. We further suggest obtaining feedback from both current students and alumni as often the benefits of professional development are not realized until later in one's career.

Documentation of professional outcomes should prove helpful at many levels. This information can be used to modify existing programs to increase professional development, develop new programs with specific professional outcomes, recruit students to participate in programs, garner funding, and contribute to assessment of academic programs where outcomes include professional growth and development.

CONCLUSION

Postsecondary institutions strive to identify opportunities for students to develop professionally. Canine-campus events provide unique experiences for student learning through internships, engagement in faculty research, event coordination, observation, professional talks, and applied projects. Students can develop hard skills (data collection, analysis, writing, event planning, and delivery), soft skills (leadership, teamwork, communication, and interpersonal), as well as take advantage of professional opportunities (networking and dissemination of results). We further see the transformation of students' attitudes and dispositions (development of empathy), suggesting the more sophisticated level of professional development proposed by Wilson et al. (2013). The wide array of activities with varied tasks attracts students from disciplines that are conceptually related to HAI, but also those who are not, resulting in benefit for all.

A mechanical engineering major participated in a program where college students could alleviate stress and homesickness by interacting with therapy dogs visiting their campus. This student eloquently describes the personal and professional benefits that they derived from volunteering in the program even though they were not studying a discipline that focused on mental health or wellness:

> I was involved with a K9 therapy program that had two main goals: to increase student retention and to use the K9s as a "social lubricant" to help facilitate long-lasting and meaningful relationships. I was surprised just how popular this program was and how effective it was at accomplishing these goals. I was asked to volunteer as a media person to photograph and document some of these interactions for publicity and research purposes. I was an engineering undergraduate, and not at all related to the field of psychology. I took this opportunity because it was a diverse volunteering opportunity for me (away from the normal technical events associated with engineering). Through this experience, I was able to enhance my knowledge and skill set in photography, videography, and media documentation (a hobby I thoroughly enjoy). In addition, it allowed my creative work to be featured within the university campus and even at a conference. In addition, as someone who did not grow up with a pet in the family, I saw firsthand the benefits that K9s can have on humans, especially students, who are dealing with many personal challenges associated with attending university for the first time. It also enabled me to learn about another field outside of engineering, which broadened my perspective on the scientific and research processes. Lastly, it enabled me to develop my own personal relationships with new people, both volunteers and participants in the program, which was a very fulfilling aspect of my time with the program. As an engineer-in-training, there are many colleagues of mine who do not have the same level of communication required to be effective, and in my opinion, this lack of social skills is extremely frustrating to other project stakeholders. I learned how to find common ground with a person through a conversation and understand the meaning of "active listening"—as opposed to just asking a question and nodding along. I feel my ability to network effectively has grown immensely from this experience, regardless of the age, social status, race, or gender of another person.

REFERENCES

American Board for Engineering and Technology (ABET). (n.d.). General criteria for baccalaureate programs: General criterion #3: Student outcomes. http://www.abet.org/accreditation/accreditation-criteria/criteria-for-accrediting-engineering-programs-2018-2019/#GC2

American Psychological Association (APA). (2013). APA guidelines for the undergraduate psychology major. http://www.apa.org/ed/precollege/about/psymajor-guidelines.pdf

Arnold, L. (2002). Assessing professional behavior: Yesterday, today, and tomorrow. *Academic Medicine*, 77(6), 502–515.

Binfet, J. (2017). The effects of group-administered canine therapy on university students' wellbeing: A randomized controlled trial. *Anthrozoös*, 30(3), 397–414. https://doi.org/10.1080/08927936.2017.1335097

Binfet, J., & Passmore, H. A. (2016). Hounds and homesickness: The effects of an animal-assisted therapeutic intervention for first-year university students. *Anthrozoös*, 29(3), 441–454. https://doi.org/10.1080/08927936.2016.1181364

Binfet, J. T., Passmore, H. A., Cebry, A., Struik, K., & McKay, C. (2018). Reducing university students' stress through a drop-in canine-therapy program. *Journal of Mental Health*, 27(3), 197–204.

Binfet, J. T., & Struik, K. (2018). Dogs on campus: Holistic assessment of therapy dogs and handlers for research and community initiatives. *Society & Animals*, 28(5–6), 489–501. https://doi.org/10.1163/15685306-12341495

Binfet, J., Trotman, M. L., Henstock, H. D., & Silas, H. J. (2016). Reducing the affective filter: Using canine assisted therapy to support international university students' English language development. *BC TEAL Journal*, 1(1), 18–37. https://doi.org/10.1163/15685306-12341495

Building Academic Retention through K9s (BARK). (n.d.). The University of British Columbia, Okanagan Campus, Faculty of Education. http://bark.sites.olt.ubc.ca

Cummings School of Veterinary Medicine at Tufts University. (n.d.). Shelter medicine program. http://vet.tufts.edu/shelter-medicine-at-cummings-school/for-students/clinical-program/rotations

Dreyfus, H., & Dreyfus, S. (2005). Peripheral vision: Expertise in real world contexts. *Organization Studies*, 26(5), 779–792. https://doi.org/10.1177/0170840605053102

Eyler, J. (2009). The power of experiential education. *Liberal Education*, 95(4), 24–31.

Fede, J. H., Gorman, K. S., & Cimini, M. E. (2018). Student employment as a model for experiential learning. *Journal of Experiential Education*, 41(1), 107–124. https://doi.org/10.1177/1053825917747902

Griffin, J. E., Lorenz, G. F., & Mitchell, D. (2010). A study of outcomes-oriented student reflection during internship: The integrated, coordinated, and reflection-based model of learning and experiential education. *Journal of Cooperative Education & Internships, 44*(2), 42–50.

Hammer, D. P. (2000). Professional attitudes and behaviors: The "A's and B's" of professionalism. *American Journal of Pharmaceutical Education, 64*(4), 455–464.

Hart Research Associates. (2015). Falling short? College learning and career success. https://www.aacu.org/sites/default/files/files/LEAP/2015employerstudentsurvey.pdf

Irvine, L. (2015). *"My dog always eats first": Homeless people and their animals.* Boulder, CO: Lynne Rienner.

Jaekel, A., Hector, S., Northwood, D., Benzinger, K., Salinitri, G., Johrendt, J., & Watters, M. (2011). Development of learning outcomes assessment methods for co-operative education programs. *Journal of Cooperative Education and Internships, 45*(1), 11–33.

Kolb, D. A. (1984). *Experiential learning: Experience as the source of learning and development.* Englewood Cliffs, NJ: Prentice-Hall.

Lem, M. (2016). Street-involved youth and their animal companions: Stigma and survival. In C. Blazina and L. R. Kogan (Eds.), *Men and their dogs: A new understanding of man's best friend* (pp. 73–96). New York: Springer.

Lopatto, D. (2010). Undergraduate research as a high-impact student experience. *Peer Review, 12*(2), 27–30.

National Association of Colleges and Employers (NACE). (2017). Career readiness for the new college graduate: A definition and competencies. http://www.naceweb.org/uploadedfiles/pages/knowledge/articles/career-readiness-fact-sheet.pdf

National Business Education Association (NBEA). (2000). This we believe about teaching soft skills: Human relations, self-management, and workplace enhancement (policy statement no. 67). http://www.nbea.org/newsite/curriculum/policy/no_67.pdf

Robles, M. M. (2012). Executive perceptions of the top 10 transferrable skills needed in today's workplace. *Business Communication Quarterly, 75*(4), 453–465. https://doi.org/10.1177/1080569912460400

Sethi, D. (2014). Executive perceptions of top ten soft skills at work: Developing these through SAIF. http://dspace.iimk.ac.in/bitstream/handle/2259/706/2014-HLA-018.pdf?sequence=1

Shakir, R. (2009). Soft skills at the Malaysian institutes of higher learning. *Asia Pacific Education Review, 10*(3), 309–315. https://doi.org/10.1007/s12564-009-9038-8

Shuman, L. J., Besterfield-Sacre, M., & McGourty, J. (2005). The ABET "professional skills"—Can they be taught? Can they be assessed? *Journal of Engineering Education, 94*(1), 41–55. https://doi.org/10.1002/j.2168-9830.2005.tb00828.x

Sides, C. H., & Mrvica, A. (2007). *Internships: Theory and practice.* Amityville, NY: Baywood Publishing.

van Mook, W. N., de Grave, W. S., Wass, V., O'Sullivan, H., Zwaveling, J. H., Schuwirth, L. W., & van der Vleuten, C. P. (2009). Professionalism: Evolution of the concept. *European Journal of Internal Medicine, 20*(4), e81–e84. https://doi.org/10.1016/j.ejim.2008.10.005

Wanless, D. (2013). Perspectives from internships and co-ops with industry. American Society for Engineering and Education Annual Conference, Atlanta, GA, 2013 paper ID#8186.

Washor, K. S. (2015). *Bridging the soft-skill gap from education to employment through internships* (Doctoral Dissertation). http://digitalcommons.uri.edu/cgi/viewcontent.cgi?article=1336&context=oa_diss

Wilson, A., Åkerlind, G., Walsh, B., Stevens, B., Turner, B., & Shield, A. (2013). Making "professionalism" meaningful to students in higher education. *Studies in Higher Education, 38*(8), 1222–1238.

Zehr, M. A. (1998). New office economy putting greater demands on schools. *Education Week, 17*(23), 7.

PART FOUR

Future Directions

9

EVALUATING OUTCOMES: EVENTS, PROJECTS, AND PROGRAMS INVOLVING DOGS

MARY RENCK JALONGO, EDITOR, SPRINGER NATURE, INDIANA, PA, AND THERESA MCDEVITT, ACADEMIC LIBRARIAN, INDIANA UNIVERSITY OF PENNSYLVANIA, INDIANA, PA

INTRODUCTION

A university librarian has been reading about the initiatives of various postsecondary institutions designed to get students to visit the library, interact with staff, and support the students' growth in information literacy. An idea that captures her imagination is the practice of inviting registered and insured therapy dogs to campus during exam week to help students "de-stress." She discovers that a colleague is involved with the local therapy dog group and they decide to collaborate and offer an event of this type. They work with the director of public safety at the university to comply with the institution's rules about bringing dogs on campus. At first, there are some objections raised by staff who fear that a group of out-of-control animals will descend upon the library. A compromise is made, and the dogs are permitted to be outdoors under a small tent in a grassy area located to the left of the library entrance. At first, students are puzzled by the presence of the dogs, so the dog handlers start greeting the students and inviting them to meet the dogs if they wish. Heavy rains dampen spirits a bit, but the students' responses to the dogs encourage the librarian and the therapy dog group to try again next semester. Worries about the dogs' behavior have subsided and the handler/dog teams are stationed in the lobby. Signage is used to direct those who do not wish to interact with dogs to avoid the group. One volunteer uses a handheld counter to keep track of the number of participants. A short survey, developed for this purpose, is distributed and collected by student volunteers with clipboards and pencils.

Data collected from the participants are overwhelmingly positive. Many of the respondents mention how much they miss their dogs and one student writes, "I haven't touched a dog in months." Other written comments include:

"It indicates that the university cares about stress during finals."

"It makes the library a more welcoming place and it makes me feel not as stressed with all I need to accomplish."

"Great idea! Keep it 'pup.'"

A bulletin board that reads "Leave your stress here" is filled with post-it

Gibbs, a chocolate Labrador retriever and therapy dog, is handled by a retired teacher who has visited with her dogs for over 20 years. Photo Credit: Mary Renck Jalongo

notes on which students have written the sources of their stress. There is also a graffiti wall where students can respond to the question "How do you feel after interacting with the dogs?" What began rather tentatively as a single event is now progressing to a project because "de-stress with dogs" will be offered consistently during exam week each fall and spring semester. The planners evaluate the outcomes in terms of (1) participation, defined as a head count of the number of students/staff attending each session; (2) perceptions of well-being, based on students' self-reports of the dogs' influence on their stress and mood on a survey; and (3) effectiveness of publicity, based on survey questions about how students became aware of the activity. In reviewing students' written comments, the most common recommendation for improvement is that the dogs be brought on campus more frequently than once at the end of each semester. Staff from the university's Center for Health and Well-Being have collaborated with the library staff at these events. The center's staff now offer bimonthly afternoon and evening sessions that include the therapy dogs; they also evaluate the students' responses using an online survey. A third venue for the therapy dogs is Welcome Weekend. This is when the freshmen arrive one week prior to the other students to complete their orientation and get settled into on-campus housing. The therapy dogs become part of move-in day for the regular students and visit the residence halls periodically. Handler/therapy dog teams also participate in (1) the university's health fair for students and staff; (2) a gathering called Take Back the Night for survivors of violence and sexual abuse; and (3) an annual fundraiser cosponsored by the animal shelter and domestic violence center called "Bark Against Violence." It was the evaluation data that helped to "win over" staff and administrators who were initially skeptical. Attendance at the "de-stress with dogs" typically ranged from about 200 to as many as 500, and responses from students who elected to participate were overwhelmingly positive. Therapy dogs are becoming a part of university life as the connection between university personnel and local members of the Alliance of Therapy Dogs has been strengthened through reciprocal trust and respect. Their relationship is now approaching the level of a program, defined as multiple events, activities, and projects that are consistent with the university's mission, tied to key goals for students, and subjected to systematic evaluation.

One persistent criticism of programs involving dogs is that the effectiveness of these initiatives is based on individual enthusiasm for the project and anecdotal information rather than research. Chapter 9 is a helpful guide to evaluation design. It guides program developers and participants in gathering both qualitative and quantitative data to document program effectiveness. Contemporary evaluation design uses what are frequently referred to as *logic models* to map out the goals, inputs, activities, and outcomes for an event, project, or program. Logic models can be represented concisely and visually. This frequently is helpful when attempting to gain support for the continuation and expansion of programs. It can be particularly useful when seeking internal or external funding sources as well. The coauthors of this chapter have gathered data on a "de-stress with dogs" event hosted by the university library for five years (Jalongo & McDevitt, 2015). What began with having a few therapy dogs stationed outside the library has evolved into an end-of-semester gathering inside the library attended by hundreds of students. This would not have been possible without the student survey data collected. Results of the survey were used to persuade others that events involving dogs were well attended, supported, and appreciated by the students. It also helped to pave the way for other opportunities for students to interact with registered and insured therapy dog/handler teams during their college experience.

Institutions of higher education are putting greater emphasis on assessing outcomes to document their progress toward important goals that have been agreed upon by various stakeholders. The expectation is that those proposing, planning, and implementing new initiatives will link them to strategic plans and other campus-wide objectives. Dog-assisted events, projects, and programs are a relatively new phenomenon at postsecondary institutions that have several sources of appeal: they are generally well-attended by students, are easy to set-up, and are affordable because they rely on volunteers (Crossman, 2016; Daltry & Mehr, 2015; Haggerty & Mueller, 2017; Jalongo & McDevitt, 2015). Thoughtful evaluation planning prior to involving dogs in events, projects, and programs enlists greater "buy-in" from the campus community, averts many common pitfalls, and provides direction for designing interactions that are the safest, most positive, and most effective for all involved. Evaluation is also a response to the persistent criticism of human-animal interaction (HAI) efforts; namely, that decisions are based on individual enthusiasm rather than propelled forward by data. We begin this chapter by defining evaluation and evaluation models. Next, we provide an overview of the major strategies that go into an evaluation design, followed by a discussion of data collection tools. After that, we discuss research at various institutions that has documented the attainment of important outcomes for college students. The chapter concludes with recommendations for practice.

DEFINITION OF *EVALUATION*

Although there are many definitions of the word *evaluation*, most of them touch upon five concepts. First, an evaluation is a planned and structured process that involves the various stakeholders. Second, evaluation is tied to predetermined goals and appraises success toward attaining those goals. Third, evaluation gathers data and makes modifications based on evidence. Fourth, evaluation takes place not only at the conclusion of the project (summative evaluation), but also during the project or program as a tool for monitoring progress (formative evaluation). Fifth, evaluation is a tool for reflection that can then support continuous improvement of projects and programs (Evaluation Toolbox, 2010).

There are many different designs for conducting an evaluation study that are sometimes referred to as *logic models* in the literature. The University of

Wisconsin Extension (2013) defines a logic model as "a simplified picture of a program, initiative, or intervention that is a response to a given situation. It shows the logical relationships among the resources that are invested, the activities that take place, and the benefits or changes that result" (unpaged). They go on to say that the logic model is not only valuable for communicating the results of an initiative, but also for planning, designing, and managing a project or program. Whenever a project or program is initiated, the developers have an idea in mind of what it will accomplish. Evaluation models are a "roadmap" of sorts that display, in abbreviated and visual ways, the interconnections among at least three things:

1. *Inputs:* The resources that go into a program.
2. *Outputs:* The activities the program undertakes.
3. *Outcomes/impact:* The changes or benefits that result.

Usually, these items are arranged as three columns so that it is possible to look at a table and get a visual representation of the entire evaluation plan. An example of a logic model used to assess a service-learning/dog walking project for college students was published recently by Das and Sartore-Baldwin (2019). It shows how dogs are prepared to support people with autism spectrum disorder (ASD), post-traumatic stress disorder (PTSD), and with seizures from epilepsy.

These therapy dog teams volunteer regularly at Indiana University of Pennsylvania's Center for Health and Well-Being. Photo Credit: Megan Higgins

EVALUATING DOG-ASSISTED EVENTS, PROJECTS, AND PROGRAMS INVOLVING COLLEGE STUDENTS

Thousands of scholarly and popular publications have discussed the impact of human-dog interaction (Crossman, 2016; Hooker, Freeman, & Stewart 2002; Maujean, Pepping, & Kendall 2015; Morrison, 2007; Shubert, 2012). Studies of beneficial aspects of human-dog interactions are often found under the heading of "pet therapy," "animal-assisted therapy," "animal-assisted intervention," "animal-assisted activities," or other similar broad terms. In most HAI studies, canines are the animal of choice in the intervention. A history of the use of "pet therapy" listed dogs most often (Hooker et al., 2002). (For more on the history of animal-assisted therapy, see charts listing major events from prehistoric periods to the modern day in Fine, Beck, & Ng, 2019; Morrison, 2007; and O'Haire, 2010). Ein, Li, and Vickers (2018) examined the literature relating to therapeutic interactions between humans and animals. Although they searched under terms such as "animal-assisted therapy," "animal-assisted intervention," "animal-facilitated therapy," or "pet-facilitated therapy," dogs dominated HAI research. Another meta-analysis reviewed nearly 1,000 randomized controlled trials on the impact of animal-assisted therapy (Kamioka et al., 2014). As was the case with analyses already mentioned, dogs were the animal of choice in most studies. Similarly, Souter, and Miller's (2007) meta-analysis of animal-assisted activities used to treat depression found that dogs were the animal used exclusively in research that met their criteria for methodological rigor.

Many writings document attempts to evaluate the outcomes of human-animal interactions or HAI. Studies come from diverse disciplines, including psychology, child development, library science, public health, sociology, business, education, and nursing. The impact of human-dog interaction has been the subject of popular news reporting, scholarly journal articles, dissertations, and full-length monographs. The type of evaluation that is found in these works varies. Some studies are primarily anecdotal and rely on descriptive statistics applied to survey or interview data. Other researchers, perhaps in response to the criticism that human-animal interaction studies frequently are flawed, have chosen experimental or quasi-experimental designs that rely on randomized sampling, control groups, and standardized measures to collect physiological and/or psychological data.

Academic librarians posted this photo after a therapy dog visit to encourage students to come to the reference desk with their questions. Photo Credit: Bobbie Zapor

When canines are brought on campus, it is often with key goals in mind, for instance:

- counteracting feelings of loneliness and isolation
- familiarizing students with key support services on campus
- increasing student retention and program completion
- building a sense of community and belonging
- fostering wellness by reducing unhealthy levels of stress
- supporting students' academic success and progress toward professional goals

Therapy dog events are offered at hundreds of colleges and universities. They are inexpensive, easy to plan, able to reach hundreds of students, and viewed by many as beneficial to the university community. Increasingly, those responsible for programs are being urged to consider the hard questions. Just as students may like a college class but learn little from it, students might participate in canine-assisted activities yet not derive much value from their participation.

If the college student-canine interaction is beneficial, for whom and in what ways? Does human-dog contact calm students, facilitate social interaction, relieve feelings of loneliness, and help students do their best on exams? Will participation in these events have a positive impact on student persistence at their studies? If so, how should these animal-assisted activities be structured? What "dosage" is necessary—how often and for how long—to yield the best results? Are the interactions between postsecondary students and canines only of immediate benefit or do they have long-term impacts? Can they have negative consequences and, if so, what are they and how can they be avoided? These are just a few of the many research questions that bear further investigation.

EVALUATION STRATEGIES AND TOOLS

After those responsible for the event decide that evaluation is worth pursuing, they need to consider the range of data collection tools available to them. Published studies provide examples of evaluation models and often use a combination of qualitative and quantitative measures to strengthen the study design.

FREQUENCY COUNTS.

Numerical data, such as the number of individuals involved, the number of therapy dog teams providing services, or how long and how often subjects spent time interacting with dogs often are reported in evaluation studies. It is beneficial for studies to report the way numbers were obtained (i.e., event sign-in, gate-counts, counts made periodically by an observer, etc.). Counting is easier when there is a structure in place. If, for example, students are volunteering at the local animal shelter to participate in a dog walking program, the sign-in sheets can call for them to check a box that differentiates them from other community volunteers. The sign-in sheet also can be used to tabulate the number of hours of service logged individually, by a student service organization, or by all university student volunteers during a designated time. In large open events, with hundreds of people coming and going, accurate numbers may be more difficult to obtain. If the objective is to involve as many students as possible, such as a freshman orientation event designed to familiarize students with counseling and library services, then the number of individuals who interacted with dogs is an important piece of information. A small, handheld counter clicked as students enter the meeting room may suffice. When selecting a way of gathering frequency counts, it is best to avoid things than might discourage participation and, in that case, an estimate of the number attending an event or program may be enough (Adams et al., 2017). Other types of counts can also be useful. Binfet's (2017) article includes a chart that compares the amount of time spent with dogs, the number of sessions per week, how many weeks sessions were offered, and the number of participants served across thirteen different studies.

NATURALISTIC OBSERVATIONS.

Studies often use an observer to record field notes during a planned activity. Observers of the event can gather qualitative as well as quantitative data, and the type of observations they complete can be structured or more open-ended (Guest, Namey, & Mitchell, 2013). Observers may also document the event with photos and recordings. In these cases, privacy rights of the participants should be considered and respected. If there is any plan to post or publish photographs, it will be necessary to obtain a model release from everyone pictured. For example, Charles and Wolkowitz (2018) reported on a recent study that used the participant observer method to conduct naturalistic observations of staff, students, and volunteers.

GATHERING INFORMAL FEEDBACK.

Some studies will report informal feedback gathered during or after an event. This could be in response to questions posed to participants on whiteboards or graffiti walls or through feedback booths set up at the events (see Charles & Wolkowitz, 2018). Analysis of media postings in newspapers and social media is another means of informal evaluation. Lannon and Harrison (2015), for example, included a chart in their descriptive article that listed media coverage of their therapy dog events on campus via newspaper, radio, and Twitter. Brief individual interviews with just a few key questions are another informal evaluation strategy.

FOCUS GROUPS.

A group interview with selected individuals about a topic is referred to as a *focus group* (Liamputtong 2011). Usually there is a script or structured interview protocol that the interviewer follows with a group of 6–12 people. The purpose of such groups is to better understand the perspective of the participants on a presented topic. This strategy has been used extensively in the business field to get customer input on products. Although focus group interviewees are volunteers, they are sometimes compensated for their participation. A small token of appreciation—such as a gift card for the campus bookstore—is a common choice. Focus groups are preferred when interaction among the respondents is seen as useful; for example, the comments of one person can stimulate additional input from others. Marks and McLaughlin (2005) used focus groups to collect suggestions on how to increase attendance at counseling center outreach events and Binfet and Passmore (2016) used focus groups to complement their quantitative findings.

SURVEYS.
Surveys are frequently used to measure outcomes. The most common form involves gathering participants' responses to statements scored on a Likert scale (i.e., a five-point scale ranging from strongly disagree to strongly agree). Surveys can be print or online in format. Researchers can administer them before an event to measure interest, during an event to assess attitudes on the spot, or sometime after students have participated. There also are many different online survey tools (e.g., SurveyMonkey, Qualtrics) that offer the convenience of tabulating results as they come in. Questionnaires can be standardized measures that have been tested for reliability and are used again and again, or researcher-developed instruments used for a particular event and purpose. Decisions about surveys include not only the design of meaningful questions, but also who to survey, how to survey them, and strategies for improving response rates (Joye, Wolf, Smith, & Fu, 2016).

Locally designed paper face-to-face surveys are frequently administered by researchers during or immediately after dog therapy events because response rates are higher (see House, Neal, & Backels, 2018; Jalongo & McDevitt, 2015). Rose, Godfrey, and Rose (2015) sent online surveys to all students on their Canadian campus, and Haggerty and Mueller (2017) sent online surveys to personnel at randomly chosen institutions across five regions of the United States to collect data to address their research questions. Bell (2013) collected data in several ways, including paper and electronic surveys. One limitation of self-report data is that respondents may not be candid and respond in ways that they infer to be the more socially accepted response. To illustrate, an international student from a place that does not have a culture of keeping animals as companions or viewing dogs as kin may be surprised by the presence of therapy dogs at the library but respond to the statement "Do you feel that interacting with the dogs today allowed you to relax and focus during exam week?" affirmatively because they are in the minority and see that others are enthused about the activity. In addition, the sample may be biased. Those who agree to respond to a survey may be more enthusiastic about dogs and support the presence of dogs on campus in comparison with those who opted not to complete a questionnaire (Foreman, Allison, Poland Meade, & Wirth, 2019). Furthermore, if surveys are anonymous and distributed multiple times—such as at the end of each semester when therapy dogs visit to reduce stress during exams—some of the same respondents will be included in the samples, even if they are collected at different events. For all these reasons, questionnaires are not perfect, but this is a reason to combine them with other methods of evaluation (e.g., attendance counts, focus group interviews, naturalistic observations) rather than not use them at all. By design, a survey solicits information and opinions from many people. It accomplishes this in a cost-effective, less work-intensive fashion than many other data collection methods, and this makes the questionnaire a valuable component of an evaluation plan.

PSYCHOMETRIC TOOLS.

A variety of psychometric tools are sometimes used in HAI research. They can be both psychological and physiological measures. Some psychological states that are commonly evaluated in studies of the human-animal bond are listed in Box 9.1. For additional resources on psychological measures, see the American Psychological Association's (2019) PsychTESTS database that is continuously updated, and the Mind Garden (2019) site where you can search by topic. Most academic libraries have copies of reference tools, such as the annual publication *Handbook of Psychological Assessment* (Groth-Marnat & Wright, 2016). The Buros Center for Testing (2019) is an impartial source for reviews of the various psychological measures in the annual *Buros Mental Measurement Yearbook* in print and online. An article by Beidas et al. (2015) offers a review of free, brief, and validated measures for researchers with limited resources. Collaborating with professionals in psychology can provide the expertise necessary to administer some of the formal instruments available.

Physiological tests may also be used if (1) the participating students are adult volunteers; (2) there are medical professionals qualified to conduct these assessments; and (3) the research has been reviewed and approved by the Institutional Review Board. Grajfoner et al. (2017) and McDonald, McDonald, and Roberts (2017) used physiological measures such as student participants'

BOX 9.1 SELECTED PSYCHOLOGICAL TRAITS AND MEASURES USED IN HAI STUDIES

Anxiety
State-Trait Anxiety Inventory (STAI) for Adults (Spielberger, 1983; 1989).
Burns Anxiety Inventory (Stewart, Dispenza, Parker, Chang, & Cunnien, 2014),
Beck Anxiety Inventory (Beck & Steer, 1993; Beck, Steer, & Brown, 1996).

Bonds With Animals
Emotional and Supportive Attachment to Companion Animals Scale (ESACA) (Meehan, Massavelli, & Pachana, 2017).
Assessing the Human-Animal Bond: A Compendium of Actual Measures (Anderson, 2007)

Depression
Beck Depression Inventory (Beck et al., 1996)
Hospital Anxiety and Depression Scale (Hall, 2018)

Loneliness
Philippines Loneliness Assessment Scale (Stewart et al., 2014)

Mood
Brief Mood Introspection Scale (Mayer & Gaschke, 1988)
The Four Mood Introspection Scale (Mayer, Allen, & Beauregard, 1995)

Stress
Perceived Stress Scale (Cohen, Kamarck, & Mermelstein, 1983; Lee, 2012)

Well-Being
The Warwick-Edinburgh Mental Well-Being Scale (Grajfoner, Harte, Potter, & McGuigan, 2017)

Worry
Penn State Worry Questionnaire (Brown, Antony, & Barlow, 1992; Meyer, Miller, Metzger, & Borkovec, 1990)

A therapy dog team meets a future elementary school teacher following a presentation to the class. Photo Credit: Haley Romanko

salivary cortisol and blood pressure to measure the impact of dog therapy sessions on student well-being, mood, and anxiety. Measures of this type obviously are more intrusive, so this needs to be considered and the research protocol must be approved by the university's committee for the ethical treatment of human subjects.

Randomized controlled trials are synonymous with the experimental method and frequently are regarded as the "gold standard" in research. The hallmarks of experimental design are random selection and random assignment to the control and treatment groups—something that seldom is feasible for many dog-assisted activities. Nevertheless, many recent meta-analyses of research have noted that experimental and quasi-experimental studies are needed in HAI research (Crossman, 2016; Kamioka et al., 2014; Vogt, 2005).

RESEARCH AND INSTITUTIONAL INITIATIVES

In this section, we review the research conducted at various postsecondary institutions to evaluate the success of their respective programs.

STUDENT PARTICIPATION AND TYPES OF PROGRAMS

Where are programs involving dogs being held, what are they like, and what kind of policies have been established to help them run smoothly and address liability issues? Haggerty and Mueller (2017) attempted to measure the prevalence, structure, and policies affecting animal-assisted programs in postsecondary institutions. They sent a survey to randomly sampled personnel who worked in colleges and universities in five regions of the county and in departments most likely to be involved in such programs. Their survey gathered information about the presence of animal-assisted programs, how they were structured, and what policies had been designed to guide them. Their survey design allowed them to demonstrate that programs were present in 62% of the institutions surveyed, and that those responding to the questionnaire were able to provide data on frequency of the events, size of the crowds, length of programs, and location of events (most often the library). Based on the data gathered from the different sites, the authors developed a chart of safety precautions that schools required for such events such as health certifications and age limits for the dogs, number of dog teams, duration of visits, and location of programs. Their survey questions are included in the article and reviewing them can serve to highlight some of the points to be considered when evaluating animal visitation programs on campus.

PROGRAM IMPROVEMENT AND OUTCOMES ASSESSMENT

If the goals are to increase student attendance at outreach events as well as to assess how satisfied attendees are with the programs, the design of Marks and McLaughlin (2005) is instructive. They used four methods of gathering data, which included focus groups, a survey of the general student body, evaluations taken after presentations, and comparison of the number of attendees at sessions. Two focus groups were held with students who volunteered to participate. Facilitators led a discussion with students about attendance at/satisfaction with their outreach initiatives, a strategy that yielded ideas and suggestions from students' perspectives. Later a survey was used to determine what factors influenced students' decision to participate, the activities that they preferred, and their recommendations for improvement. Students completed the survey in exchange for extra credit in classes—something that would need to be handled carefully to avoid any hint of coercion. Questions focused on the value of the presentations, topics for future sessions, and effectiveness of the event in which they participated. The research team used multiple assessment methods to strengthen the study design. Results aided not only in planning for the next academic year, but also in increasing student participation.

EFFECTS ON STUDENT STRESS AND WELL-BEING

The methods used to measure the impact of dog therapy on college student stress and well-being can be simple or complex. We administered short paper surveys to students who had dropped by a dog therapy session in a public area of the university library before finals (Jalongo & McDevitt, 2015). Questions included on the survey related to how they found out about the event, whether they had heard of therapy dogs previously, whether the event was calming for them, why they stopped to interact with dogs, why they came to the library that day, and whether the activity made them more likely to visit the library in the future. A copy of the survey used appears in this chapter's appendix. Similarly, Daltry and Mehr (2015) wished to provide stress relief and to promote their counseling center, and used a survey to measure outcomes of their dog therapy event. House et al. (2018) measured the impact of their dog therapy event for finals at Millersville University Student Center with a short survey administered after the event that invited students to provide self-report data about possible influences of the event on their homesickness and stress. It also evaluated whether participation in the event increased student awareness of mental health services on campus. They found that the event was highly successful in reducing perceived levels of stress and homesickness, and increasing awareness of campus mental health support services.

Adamle, Riley, and Carlson (2009) administered a questionnaire to first-year university students who chose to attend a wellness session at a student orientation that included therapy dogs. The questionnaire was given at the beginning of a session, which included a lecture on the benefits of pet therapy and an opportunity to visit with pets, and measured students' relationship to pets and their interest in pet therapy on campus. Rose et al. (2016) distributed an online survey they developed to the entire population of undergraduate students on their campus. Questions asked students to rate how effective each of the library-sponsored programs (including those involving therapy dogs) were in helping them to lower their level of stress. Survey questions are included in the article.

Students interact with a nine-year-old golden retriever during Just PAWS—a regularly scheduled time to visit with therapy dogs. Photo Credit: Megan Higgins

Bell (2013) collected data in several ways, including paper and electronic surveys and a tally of the number of participants. Paper survey responses were collected at a dog therapy event; the researcher printed bookmarks with the electronic survey URL and posted it on social media as well. Staff members also observed the event, wrote down feedback shared there, and counted numbers of attendees. Survey questions are included in the chapter's appendix. Dell et al. (2015) also used a researcher-developed survey to evaluate students' responses during dog therapy events and then sent out a follow-up survey to measure students' perception of the event after some time had elapsed. Their article includes the survey questions.

STANDARDIZED PSYCHOLOGICAL OR PHYSIOLOGICAL MEASURES

Inspired by some of the published research on the calming effects of dogs on students taking exams, a doctoral student in the Nursing Department has a designed a multisite dissertation study. Volunteer undergraduate nursing students at three different colleges who are scheduled to take an exam later that morning will complete a print survey and have their vital signs recorded before and after interacting with handler/therapy dog teams. The students' blood pressure and heart rate will be measured. Students also will provide self-report data on their perceptions of whether the interaction with the dogs helped them to feel less stressed when taking the exam. Orchestrating this study is a challenge. First, the student must contact therapy dog groups to see if they are willing to help with the study, pending its approval. She will need many handler/dog teams. Even though no laboratory animals are involved, the Institutional Animal Care and Use Committee at this university has requested two letters. The first comes from the leader of the therapy dog group and the second from the researcher. These letters must describe, in detail, how the welfare of the dogs will be ensured. Finally, the study must be approved by the Institutional Review Board for the ethical treatment of human subjects.

As this brief description suggests, conducting research involving students and dogs can be daunting, yet doing these studies can be of benefit not only to the local institution, but to other institutions as well. Reviewing the published research offers many benefits: it can stimulate thinking about lines of inquiry, frame important research questions, identify instruments that can be used or adapted, avoid replicating research that had major flaws, put researchers in contact with others willing to collaborate, and advance thinking on a topic of importance to those involved with HAI.

To illustrate, Stewart et al. (2014) studied a counseling center outreach program that was offered in residence halls and involved dogs. They administered the University of the Philippines Loneliness Assessment Scale and the Burns Anxiety Inventory to measure well-being and loneliness of students who attended the session, and the institution's Session Rating Scale to measure attendees' opinion of program effectiveness and gather additional feedback. Other researchers have used a battery of five different standard psychological scales and a student writing exercise that describes a traumatic experience to measure student responses to a dog's presence (Hunt & Chizkov, 2014). Still other research teams have focused on physiological measures, such as Somervill, Kruglikova, Robertson, Hanson, & MacLin (2008), who found a significant decrease in diastolic blood pressure in students after they had the opportunity to hold a dog or cat. Some researchers have combined psychological and physiological assessment strategies. Barker, Barker, McCain, and Schubert (2016) assessed the impact of dog therapy sessions held the week before finals. They used two standardized test scales that collected self-reported perceived stress levels as well as two noninvasive physiological tests to compare groups of students who did and did not interact with the dogs. They also gathered demographic information on participants, the degree to which they had interacted with the dogs, and whether they were pet owners. Students in a graduate physical therapy program were randomly assigned to one of two groups prior to an examination (Williams, Emond, Maynord, Simpkins, Stumbo, & Terhaar, 2018). The "dog group" visited two researchers and a therapy dog for 15–20 minutes before the test while the "nondog group" visited with two researchers but no therapy dog. Afterward, both groups were given psychological and physiological tests that measured blood pressure or a standardized measure of state anxiety level and a post-participation questionnaire. The study found that state anxiety scores were lower for participants who interacted with a therapy dog (Williams et al., 2018).

In other instances, researchers opt to use qualitative research methods. Charles and Wolkowitz (2018) designed a study to examine the social interactions and impact of a "de-stress with dogs" library event on students, therapy dog handlers, library staff, and the dogs themselves. The participant observer method often used in ethnographic research was the primary data collection tool, and this method resulted in a "multi-species ethnographic approach by being open to how animals as well as humans shape the interactions." (p. 3). The event was held in a private area in the library that facilitated collection of data. In addition to observing the interaction and the outward manifestations of human and animal reactions to the event, facilitators invited student participants to leave feedback on a whiteboard when they exited the event. Finally, post-interaction interviews were held with 16 individuals representing library staff, guardians (dog handlers), and students.

RANDOMIZED CONTROLLED TRIALS

Kamioka et al. (2014) reviewed nearly 1,000 studies in a meta-analysis of randomized controlled trials on the impact of animal-assisted therapy. They found very few studies that qualified as randomized controlled trials. For those interested in pursuing experimental and quasi-experimental research, their article contains useful charts that provide a summary of key study characteristics, outcome variables, and moderators. Crossman's (2016) review article, which focused on the quantitative evidence relating to the effects of interactions with animals on human psychological distress, is another helpful resource. Although not limited to dogs, it provides extensive guidance on quality research design and features useful charts, including one that lists the common methodological issues encountered in the literature. Their article also offers suggestions on how to improve research for those who wish to work further on the topic. Similarly, an article by Kamioka et al. (2014) examined randomized controlled trials and makes recommendations for future research. *The Handbook of Animal-Assisted Therapy: Foundations and Guidelines for Animal-Assisted Interventions* (Fine, 2015) is a valuable reference tool for those seeking conducting rigorous research in the HAI field.

RECOMMENDATIONS FOR PRACTICE

Based on this literature review of canine-college student events, projects, and programs, we offer the following recommendations to those seeking to implement new initiatives as well as those striving to maintain and enhance existing ones.

USE CAMPUS RESOURCES

When conducting research, adhere to the principles of informed consent as well as the guiding principles published by the American Evaluation Association (2018). Their professional journal, *New Directions for Evaluation*, reports on exemplary evaluations of programs and can be a helpful resource. Work with your local Institutional Review Board to design studies that adhere to the principles of informed consent, treat human participants ethically, and protect the welfare of the dogs. Many campuses have offices that offer support for research and assessment, so take advantage of the help. Counseling centers and libraries may need assessment data as a condition of continuing a project or program. Individual faculty members from across the disciplines with an interest in HAI and research/publication experience can be enlisted as project supporters as well. Students in many disciplines might gain valuable professional experience by assisting in evaluation of events. Nursing majors, for example, may want to practice taking blood pressure and helping with a study could represent valuable experience for them. Sociology or anthropology students might volunteer to write field notes during an event, thereby giving them practice in this skill. Students majoring in education and psychology need to learn how to write low-inference behavioral observations, and this is yet another practical skill that can be developed through HAI research. For graduate students who will be completing a research project, thesis, or dissertation, participation in HAI research can provide an apprenticeship as they collaborate with more experienced researchers. The direct experience with a research project may also assist them in narrowing a general area of interest into a researchable question.

REVIEW THE LITERATURE FIRST

Reviews of existing research provide an overview of what has been done and suggest ways to conduct more effective evaluations. Expert reviews are more than a condensed version of research. A high-quality review of the literature synthesizes and critiques the literature, both classic and current (Jalongo & Heider, 2014). Many times, the result is clustered around themes or strands that create a landscape of what has been learned thus far through investigation. Literature reviews include information about the research questions, different populations/samples, variables of interest, ways of gathering data, methods of analyzing data, strengths and weaknesses of the studies, challenges encountered in the research, and recommendations for future inquiry. Researchers seeking to study the human-animal bond can strengthen their research designs by reviewing such studies before they begin. Proceeding in this way can be particularly helpful in identifying the best quality assessment instruments available. Many times, researchers can use or adapt existing psychometric tools with permission from the developers, thereby saving time and enhancing the reliability/validity of the proposed research.

MATCH ASSESSMENT METHODS TO RESEARCH QUESTIONS

Under optimal conditions, outcomes demonstrate that purposes for an event, project, or program were fulfilled; however, even disappointing outcomes can be instrumental in modifying and improving initiatives that bring college students and dogs together. Therefore, considering outcomes is paramount in the evaluation process. Evaluation designs will vary, depending upon the nature of the objectives sought or research question addressed. For example, after a crisis such as a bombing or a mass shooting, specially trained dogs and handlers may be brought on campus to help the community cope. Such assistance efforts need to be launched immediately, so evaluation should be as seamless as possible (Shubert, 2012). "Drop-in" animal-assisted activities—held, for example, in in the lobbies of libraries or student unions—sometimes attract hundreds of students, but their outcomes may be difficult to evaluate. If promoting positive attitudes toward the university is an objective, asking students during a busy time of the semester to stop and take a survey or wait to have their blood pressure taken before and after the event may be counterproductive because few students may agree to do this.

CONSIDER TIME, STAFFING, AND FUNDING

Although dog therapy events usually rely on volunteers and are no or low cost, the evaluation piece may require resources. In evaluation studies, both the timing of the data collection and the amount of time required from respondents should be considered. Those collecting data may need specialized skills, specific training, or professional credentials, such as when a saliva sample is collected to test cortisol levels or when a psychometric tool to evaluate stress is protected, meaning that it must be administered by a licensed professional and may require specific training in how to give the test or interpret the results. It takes time to plan objectives, formulate research questions, design an evaluation, and conduct the evaluation. Identifying staff or volunteers to gather data, analyze the results, and disseminate the findings in ways that are appropriate for individuals or groups is another consideration. Payment may be necessary to obtain copies of standardized tests, use an online version of an instrument, or have the tests electronically scored and results tabulated. If part of the evaluation involves physiological signs of stress (e.g., heart rate, galvanic skin response) recorded before, during, and after interaction with a therapy dog, this would require a level of expertise and specialized equipment that might not be available. All this must be taken into consideration before setting the evaluation plan in motion.

CONCLUSION

There are several misconceptions that get in the way of systematic evaluation efforts. The first is the "anecdotal impressions" mentality that assumes these events, projects, and programs are good in their own right without any effort to gather evidence of effectiveness. Administrators who agree to modify the environment need to see data on the consequences of those decisions to feel that the changes were warranted. Attendance alone is not enough to persuade others about the continuation of canine-assisted interventions; evaluation models take a cost/benefit perspective. Even with all volunteer staffing, those participating need to feel that it is worthy of their time and effort. If, for example, six volunteer therapy dog handlers give of their time, groom their dogs, and travel to campus at their own expense, they need to see that their efforts are contributing to students' well-being. Another impediment to evaluation is the assumption that, if such experiences are offered to students at "ivy league" institutions, then other institutions should follow their examples without much forethought or consideration of their institutional mission and goals. Actually, the colleges and universities that have emerged as leaders in HAI frequently are campus cultures with a strong commitment to animal welfare, such as those with schools of veterinary medicine, with research centers that focus on HAI, or with laboratories where canine behavior and/or training is studied in nonintrusive ways. As we have argued throughout this book, the best HAI initiatives on a college campus are linked to the institutional mission and goals as well as the program/course objectives and professional development of students. Comparatively speaking, HAI research is a relatively new, yet burgeoning, area of inquiry that spans many of the traditional disciplinary boundaries. It will require intelligent and imaginative inquiry into its effectiveness to realize—and document—its full potential.

REFERENCES

Adamle, K. N., Riley, T. A., & Carlson, T. C. (2009). Evaluating college student interest in pet therapy. *Journal of American College Health, 57,* 545–548.

Adams, T., Clark, C., Crowell, V., Duffy, K., Green, M., McEwen, S., ... Hammonds, F. (2017). The mental health benefits of having dogs on college campuses. *Modern Psychological Studies, 22*(2), 50–58.

American Evaluation Association. (2018). Guiding principles for evaluators. https://www.eval.org/p/cm/ld/fid=51

American Psychological Association. (2019). PsychTESTS: An unparalleled resource for psychological measures, scales, and instrumentation tools. https://www.apa.org/pubs/databases/psyctests

Anderson, C. (Ed.). (2007). *Assessing the human-animal bond: A compendium of actual measures.* West Lafayette, IN: Purdue University Press.

Barker, S. B., Barker, R. T., McCain, N. L., & Schubert, C. M. (2016). A randomized cross-over exploratory study of the effect of visiting therapy dogs on college student stress before final exams. *Anthrozoös, 29*(1), 35–46.

Beck, A. T., & Steer, R. A. (1993). *Beck Anxiety Inventory: Manual* (2nd ed.). San Antonio, TX: The Psychiatric Corporation.

Beck, A. T., Steer, R. A., & Brown, G. K. (1996). *Manual for the Beck Depression Inventory* (2nd ed.). San Antonio, TX: The Psychological Corporation.

Beidas, R. S. Stewart, R. E., Walsh, L. Lucas, S. Downey, M. M. Jackson, K., . . . Mandell, D. S. (2015). Free, brief, and validated: Standardized instruments for low-resource mental health settings. *Cognitive Behavioral Practice, 22*(1), 5–19. https://doi.org/10.1016/j.cbpra.2014.02.002

Bell, A. (2013). Paws for a study break: Running an animal-assisted therapy program at the Gerstein Science Information Centre. *Partnership: The Canadian Journal of Library and Information Practice and Research, 8*(1), 1–14.

Binfet, J. T. (2017). The effects of group-administered canine therapy on university students' wellbeing: A randomized controlled trial. *Anthrozoös, 30*(3), 397–414.

Binfet, J. T., & Passmore, H. A. (2016). Hounds and homesickness: The effects of an animal-assisted therapeutic intervention for first-year university students. *Anthrozoös, 29*(3), 441–454.

Brown, T. A., Antony, M. M., & Barlow, D. H. (1992). Psychometric properties of the Penn State Worry Questionnaire in a clinical anxiety disorders sample. *Behaviour Research and Therapy, 30*(1), 33–37. https://doi.org/10.1016/0005-7967(92)90093-V

Buros Center for Testing. (2019). Test reviews and information. https://buros.org/test-reviews-information

Charles, N., & Wolkowitz, C. (2018). Bringing dogs onto campus: Inclusions and exclusions of animal bodies in organizations. *Gender, Work & Organization, 26*(2–3), 303–321 ttps://doi.org/10.1111/gwao.12254

Cohen, S., Kamarck, T., & Mermelstein, R. (1983). A global measure of perceived stress. *Journal of Health and Social Behavior, 24*(4), 385–396. https://pubmed.ncbi.nlm.nih.gov/6668417

Crossman, M. K. (2016). Effects of interactions with animals on human psychological distress. *Journal of Clinical Psychology, 73*(7), 761–784. https://doi. 10.1002/jclp.22410

Daltry, R. M., & Mehr, K. E. (2015). Therapy dogs on campus: Recommendations for counseling center outreach. *Journal of College Student Psychotherapy, 29*(1), 72–78.

Das, B. M., & Sartore-Baldwin, M. L. (2019). Development of a logic model for a service learning, dog walking course for college students. *Evaluation and Program Planning, 76*. https://doi.org/10.1016/j.evalprogplan.2019.05.002

Dell, C. A., Chalmers, D., Gillett, J., Rohr, B., Nickel, C., Campbell, L., ... Brydges, M. (2015). PAWSing student stress: A pilot evaluation study of the St. John ambulance therapy dog program on three university campuses in Canada. *Canadian Journal of Counselling and Psychotherapy/Revue Canadienne de Counseling et de Psychothérapie, 49*(4), 332–359.

Ein, N., Li, L., & Vickers, K. (2018). The effect of pet therapy on the physiological and subjective stress response: A meta-analysis. *Stress and Health, 34*(4), 477–489. https://onlinelibrary.wiley.com/doi/abs/10.1002/smi.2812

Evaluation Toolbox. (2010). http://evaluationtoolbox.net.au/index.php?option=com_content&view=article&id=11&Itemid=17

Fine, A. H. (2015). *Handbook of animal-assisted therapy: Foundations and guidelines for animal-assisted interventions* (4th ed.). New York: Academic Press.

Fine, A. H., Beck, & Ng, Z. (2019). The state of animal-assisted interventions: Addressing the contemporary issues that will shape the future. *International Journal of Research in Public Health, 16*(20), 3997. https://doi.org/10.3390/ijerph16203997

Foreman, A. M., Allison, P., Poland, M., Meade, B. J., & Wirth, O. (2019). Employee attitudes about the impact of visitation dogs on a college campus, *Anthrozoös, 32*(1), 35–50. https://doi.org/10.1080/08927936.2019.1550280

Grajfoner, D., Harte, E., Potter, L. M., & McGuigan, N. (2017). The effect of dog-assisted intervention on student well-being, mood, and anxiety. *International Journal of Environmental Research and Public Health, 14*(5), 483. https://www.mdpi.com/1660-4601/14/5/483

Groth-Marnat, G., & Wright, A. J. (2016). *Handbook of psychological assessment* (6th ed.). New York: Wiley.

Guest, G., Namey, E. E., & Mitchell, M. L. (2013). *Collecting qualitative data: A field manual for applied research*. Thousand Oaks: Sage.

Haggerty, J. M., & Mueller, M. K. (2017). Animal-assisted stress reduction programs in higher education. *Innovative Higher Education, 42*(5–6), 379–389.

Hall, D. (2018). Nursing campus therapy dog: A pilot study. *Teaching and Learning in Nursing, 13*(4), 202–206.

Hooker, S. D., Freeman, L. H., & Stewart, P. (2002). Pet therapy research: A historical review. *Holistic Nursing Practice, 17*(1), 17–23.

House, L. A., Neal, C., & Backels, K. (2018). A doggone way to reduce stress: An animal assisted intervention with college students. *College Student Journal, 52*(2), 199–204.

Hunt, M. G., & Chizkov, R. R. (2014). Are therapy dogs like Xanax? Does animal-assisted therapy impact processes relevant to cognitive behavioral psychotherapy? *Anthrozoös, 27*(3), 457–469.

Jalongo, M. R., & Heider, K. (2014). Re-examining the literature review: Purposes, approaches, and issues. In O. N. Saracho (Ed.). *Handbook of research methods in early childhood education, Volume I* (pp. 753-782). Charlotte, NC: Information Age Publishing.

Jalongo, M. R., & McDevitt, T. (2015). Therapy dogs in academic libraries: A way to foster student engagement and mitigate self-reported stress during finals. *Public Services Quarterly, 11*(4), 254–269.

Joye, D., Wolf, C., Smith, T. & Fu, Y. (2016). Survey methodology: Challenges and principles. In C. Wolf, D. Joye, T. W. Smith & Y. Fu (Eds.)., *The Sage handbook of survey methodology* (pp. 3–15). London: Sage.

Kamioka, H., Okada, S., Tsutani, K., Park, H., Okuizumi, H., Handa, S., . . . Honda, T. (2014). Effectiveness of animal-assisted therapy: A systematic review of randomized controlled trials. *Complementary Therapies in Medicine, 22*(2), 371–390.

Lannon, A., & Harrison, P. (2015). Take a paws: Fostering student wellness with a therapy dog program at your university library. *Public Services Quarterly, 11*(1), 13–22.

Lee, E. (2012). Review of the psychometric evidence of the Perceived Stress Scale. *Asian Nursing Research, 6*(4), 121–127.

Liamputtong, P. (2011). *Focus group methodology: Principles and practice*. London: Sage.

Marks, L. I., & McLaughlin, R. H. (2005). Outreach by college counselors: Increasing student attendance at presentations. *Journal of College Counseling, 8*(1), 86–96.

Maujean, A., Pepping, C. A., & Kendall, E. (2015). A systematic review of randomized controlled trials of animal-assisted therapy on psychosocial outcomes. *Anthrozoös, 28*(1), 23–36.

Mayer, J. D., Allen, J., & Beauregard, K. (1995). Mood inductions for four specific moods: Procedure employing guided imagery vignettes with music. *Journal of Mental Imagery, 19*(1–2), 133–150.

Mayer, J. D., & Gaschke, Y. N. (1988). The experience and meta-experience of mood. *Journal of Personality and Social Psychology, 55*(1), 102–111.

McDonald, S., McDonald, E., & Roberts, A. (2017). Effects of novel dog exposure on college students' stress prior to examination. *North American Journal of Psychology, 19*(2), 477–484.

Meehan, M., Massavelli, B., & Pachana, N. (2017). Using attachment theory and social support theory to examine and measure pets as sources of social support and attachment figures. *Anthrozoös, 30*(2), 273–289. https://doi.org/10.1080/08927936.2017.1311050

Meyer, T. J., Miller, M. L., Metzger, R. L., & Borkovec, T. D. (1990). Development and validation of the Penn State Worry Questionnaire. *Behaviour Research and Therapy, 28*(6), 487–495. https://doi.org/10.1016/0005-7967(90)90135-6

Mind Garden. (2019). List of psychological assessments. https://www.mindgarden.com/14-our-products

Morrison, M. L. (2007). Health benefits of animal-assisted interventions. *Complementary Health Practice Review, 12*(1), 51–62. https://www.uclahealth.org/pac/Workfiles/PAC/ReviewofBenefits_Morrison.pdf

O'Haire, M. (2010). Companion animals and human health: Benefits, challenges, and the road ahead. *Journal of Veterinary Behavior, 5*(5), 226–234.

Rose, C., Godfrey, K., & Rose, K. (2015). Supporting student wellness: "De-stressing" initiatives at Memorial University Libraries. *Partnership: The Canadian Journal of Library and Information Practice and Research, 10*(2), 1–21.

Shubert, J. (2012). Therapy dogs and stress management assistance during disasters. *US Army Medical Department Journal, 2*, 74–78.

Somervill, J. W., Kruglikova, Y. A., Robertson, R. L., Hanson, L. M., & MacLin, O. H. (2008). Physiological responses by college students to a dog and a cat: Implications for pet therapy. *North American Journal of Psychology, 10*(3), 519–528.

Souter, M. A., & Miller, M. D. (2007). Do animal-assisted activities effectively treat depression? A meta-analysis. *Anthrozoös, 20*(2), 167–180. http://patastherapeutas.org/wp-content/uploads/2015/07/Depressa%CC%83oMetaAnalise.pdf

Spielberger, C. D. (1983). Manual for the state-trait anxiety inventory STAI (form Y) ("self-evaluation questionnaire"). Palo Alto, CA: Consulting Psychologists Press.

Spielberger, C. D. (1989). *State-Trait Anxiety Inventory: Bibliography* (2nd ed.). Palo Alto, CA: Consulting Psychologists Press.

Stewart, L. A., Dispenza, F., Parker, L., Chang, C. Y., & Cunnien, T. (2014). A pilot study assessing the effectiveness of an animal-assisted outreach program. *Journal of Creativity in Mental Health, 9*(3), 332–345. https://doi.org/10.1080/15401383.2014.892862

University of Wisconsin Extension. (2013). Enhancing program performance with logic models. https://fyi.extension.wisc.edu/programdevelopment/files/2016/03/lmcourseall.pdf

Vogt, W. P. (2005). *Dictionary of statistics and methodology*. Thousand Oaks, CA: Sage.

Williams, C., Emond, K., Maynord, K., Simpkins, J., Stumbo, A., & Terhaar, T. (2018). An animal-assisted intervention's influence on graduate students' stress and anxiety prior to an examination. *Open Access Library Journal, 5*, e4831. https://file.scirp.org/pdf/OALibJ_2018091915361329.pdf

APPENDIX

THERAPY DOGS AT THE LIBRARY QUESTIONNAIRE

Q1 Below are some reasons for coming to the library. Please indicate how influential each was in making your decision to visit the library today.

	Extremely important	Very important	Neither important nor unimportant	Very unimportant	Not at all important
To work on class assignments	○	○	○	○	○
To have a quiet place to study	○	○	○	○	○
To borrow or return materials	○	○	○	○	○
To use the computer	○	○	○	○	○
To connect with a friend	○	○	○	○	○
To see the dogs	○	○	○	○	○

Q2 How did you find out the dogs were here?
- ○ Newspaper
- ○ Twitter
- ○ Posters or flyers
- ○ A friend told me
- ○ Did not know in advance

Q3 Below are some reasons for interacting with the dogs. Please indicate how important each reason is to you.

	Extremely important	Very important	Neither important nor unimportant	Very unimportant	Not at all important
I'm just a "dog person" and enjoy dogs	○	○	○	○	○
I needed a break	○	○	○	○	○
I miss my dog	○	○	○	○	○
Interacting with a dog lowers my stress	○	○	○	○	○

Q4 Do you feel that interacting with the dogs today allowed you to relax and focus during exam week?
- ○ Definitely yes
- ○ Probably yes
- ○ Maybe
- ○ Probably not
- ○ Definitely not

Q5 Are you aware of any reports in the media about the effects of dogs on stress reduction in human beings?
- ○ Definitely yes
- ○ Probably yes
- ○ Maybe
- ○ Probably not
- ○ Definitely not

Q6 Does this event with the dogs influence your view of the library?
- ○ Definitely yes
- ○ Probably yes
- ○ Maybe
- ○ Probably not
- ○ Definitely not

Q7 If there were other library-sponsored and campus events that gave you an opportunity to interact with the dogs, how likely would you be to attend?
- Very unlikely
- Unlikely
- Undecided
- Likely
- Very likely

Q8 Do you believe that this sort of event with the dogs will influence your use of library resources, spaces, and services in the future?
- Definitely yes
- Probably yes
- Maybe
- Probably not
- Definitely not

Q9 Comments:

10

POSSIBLE FUTURES: MOVING TOWARD A MORE DOG-FRIENDLY CAMPUS CULTURE

MARY RENCK JALONGO, EDITOR, SPRINGER NATURE, INDIANA, PA

INTRODUCTION

"Regarding Animals" is a liberal studies elective course that meets in an auditorium to accommodate the large number of students who enroll in it annually. The students select a focus for their studies and, this year, they have agreed upon the theme of animal rescue. Until very recently, the only option for a homeless dog in this rural community was a dilapidated barn with chain link cages containing multiple dogs. This evening's guest speakers represent a group of citizens who have planned and built the first no-kill shelter after a local animal advocate donated a piece of property for that purpose in her will. The four presenters are accompanied by their dogs, all adopted from shelters. During the presentation, the college students give their full attention. Afterward they ask good questions and relish the opportunity to interact with the dogs. Several sign up to volunteer at the new facility.

This presentation was made in 1990. Today, college students are an integral part of the shelter's operations. Although students can volunteer during the day, most opt for evenings and weekends during times when the shelter is closed to the public. For students without a car, a community service club provides transportation. Under the supervision of a board member/volunteer program coordinator, local college students help by walking (or running) with dogs, comforting the ones who are frightened, or sanitizing kennels, if the student is willing to do this. Some help to administer medications and injections to the animals as an apprentice to the dog kennel manager who is a retired nurse, thereby providing a learning experience in a "real-world" context (Lave & Wegner, 1991).

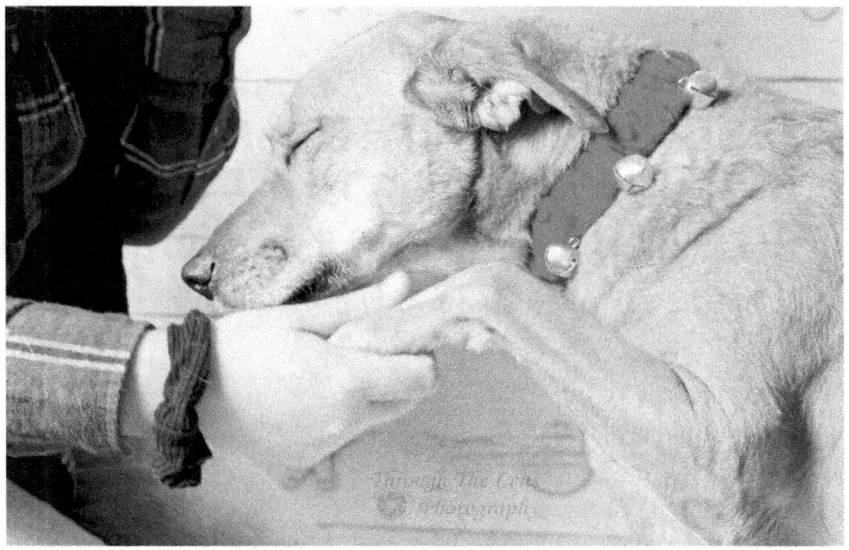

Bringing college students and dogs together needs to be a mutually positive experience. Photo Credit: Haley Romanko

Student volunteers also reinforce canine behaviors that might tip the scales in a dog's favor with a potential adopter (Thorn, Templeton, Van Winkle, & Castillo, 2006). They practice getting the dog to sit before exiting the kennel or getting a treat. College students handle the dog during a photo shoot so that the volunteer photographers can publicize the animals up for adoption via social media. Typically, the first thing that students do after signing in is to go and check the dry erase board in the hallway. It lists the names of dogs who have been adopted as well as those with an adoption pending and, particularly for animals who have been kenneled for a long time, the promise of a loving, forever home is cause for celebration. The whiteboard also indicates which dogs are at the veterinarian for routine or emergency treatment. Sadly, it sometimes includes RTS (returned to shelter) dogs who did not work out for a family or, sadder still, RIP (rest in peace) notifications when, despite everyone's best efforts, a dog does not survive. New dogs—owner surrendered, found as strays, or transferred from an overcrowded shelter—are a topic of discussion as students read the kennel cards for the backstory on each one. For example, a half-grown puppy jumped into the open door of a parked United Parcel Service (UPS) delivery truck, so the driver brought him to the shelter. So far, no one has claimed the pup. An old and overweight terrier mix's owner went into a nursing home and passed away; the overindulged lap dog looks so sad and scared. Buddy, an emaciated black Labrador retriever mix, about a year old, generates great sympathy and comments about how cruel people can be. Beka, a bulldog/pit bull mix, has been returned. She has severe separation anxiety and jumped through the screen on a second story window to follow her adopter's car to work. Disappointment and inspiration, dramatic and funny rescues, literal matters of life and death—all are part of volunteering at the animal shelter. Students make comments that highlight the psychological, emotional, and physical influence of their involvement, such as "I forget about the pressures at school while I'm here," "When I see that a dog got adopted, it makes my day!" "Walking and running with dogs *is* my exercise program."

As the previous chapters have discussed, when college/university personnel bring students and dogs together in well-planned ways that are linked to the institutional mission, professional standards, and program goals, this can improve the quality of life for students. This chapter begins with a contemporary definition of Quality of Life or QoL. QoL includes not only physical health, but also psychological and social well-being. The theoretical base for this chapter is a concept that has been fundamental in evaluating the college experience—namely "value-added." It refers to the idea that it is not sufficient to log hours in classes and plod through a program; rather, the successful completion of a course of study needs to demonstrate that there is a substantive, positive difference between groups of students with similar characteristics who have successfully completed a college program and those who have not. The third section describes innovative practices and research that offer opportunities for college students to interact with canines, both on and off campus. The chapter concludes with recommendations on ways to make campuses more dog-friendly as a route to improving the quality of life for college students.

DEFINITION OF *QUALITY OF LIFE*

The concept of *quality of life* has been the focus of study in the field of psychology since the 1980s. It attempts to answer the question, "What makes it possible, not just to survive and exist, but to thrive and flourish in life?" It includes physical and mental health, cognitive functioning, social support, competence in work, and positive emotions such as optimism, wisdom, resilience, and so forth

(Efklides & Moraitou, 2013). Although QoL was originally developed in the field of human health, today it has expanded to include not only physical health, but also psychological and social well-being (Friedmann, Son, & Saleem, 2015; Perea-Mediavilla & López-Cepero, 2017). Many college students are just beginning to answer QoL questions. They may have careers in mind but are unsure about the intermediate steps to get there. If time-to-graduation rates are any indication, it is taking longer for them to decide on a career path and complete their studies. In the United States in 2016—the most recent year for which data are available—it took, on average, 5.1 years to earn what is designed as a 4-year program, and 3.3 years to earn a 2-year associate's degree (Shapiro et al., 2016). Variables such as changing majors, taking a time-out, or enrolling in less than full-time study frequently contribute to that statistic.

The high school to college group born between 1995 and 2010 is sometimes referred to as "Generation Z"; it constituted about one-third of the US population in 2020 (Grace & Seemiler, 2016). Their world has been shaped by the Internet and their telephones. Their sense of security has been shaken by 9/11, economic recession, war, and high unemployment rates. For the more traditional age undergraduates—those in the 18- to 24-year-old age bracket—the idealism that is characteristic of adolescents has led to big dreams about solutions to global issues. Taken as a group, they tend to be thoughtful, open-minded, determined, compassionate, and responsible (Grace & Seemiler, 2016). Although today's college students often have more in the way of material resources to support their education than their predecessors—such as well-equipped residential spaces and increased access to technology—they also report greater dissatisfaction, higher rates of substance abuse, and greater need for mental health support services. Mental health issues that are increasing among young adults in the United States are:

- Over 50% of college and university students experience moderate to severe depression.
- The suicide rate among 15- to 24-year-olds in the United States has increased moderately but steadily since 2007. Up to 11% of college students report having suicidal thoughts.
- A survey of college counseling centers has found that more than half their clients have severe psychological problems, an increase of 13% in just two years.
- Anxiety and depression, in that order, are now the most common mental health diagnoses among college students.

- Nearly one in six college students has been diagnosed with or treated for anxiety.
- Females, first-year students, and international students may be at greater risk for loneliness and homesickness (Center for Collegiate Mental Health, 2018; Crossman, Kazdin, & Knudson, 2015; Crump & Derting, 2015; Elore, 2016; Hoffman, 2015).

Issues that contribute to these mental health problems include unrealistic portrayals of life on social media, inadequate skills in self-assessment of mistakes or failures, and lofty expectations, such as expecting immediate and dramatic changes from their efforts (Elore, 2016).

At the same time, demographic trends suggest that the population of students transitioning directly from high school to college will decline by 15% over the next decade (EAB Daily Briefing, 2018). Over half of the college student population is now what used to be considered "nontraditional": adults who are married, have their own families, and are living independently of parents (Berman, 2018). Balancing all of those responsibilities can be a source of considerable stress, particularly since many of them are the first in their families to pursue college study. As a result, they may have few college-savvy individuals in their network of social supports to turn to for advice.

Psychology suggests that one of the great achievements of human beings during late adolescence and early adulthood is identity formation. Given that the age span of the traditional undergraduate student bridges this period of the life trajectory, the college years are an irreplaceable opportunity for personal growth. To a considerable extent, personal growth during college study will be influenced by students' ability to mesh their "signature strengths" (Seligman, 2012) with their chosen career paths. Attention to their QoL is essential in that process.

Martin Seligman (2012), a prominent researcher in the field, developed a theory of well-being with five elements, using the acronym PERMA. Table 10.1 uses his model, applies it college student/canine interactions, and provides an evidence base.

Positive interactions with dogs have the potential to support student well-being in at least three important ways. First, conversations about dogs can put feelings of social awkwardness aside to some extent. Studies conducted in nursing homes have a long history of testing different catalysts for conversation. When presented with a plant, a bottle of wine, or a dog, the most effective in initiating and sustaining dialogue is the dog, presumably because it

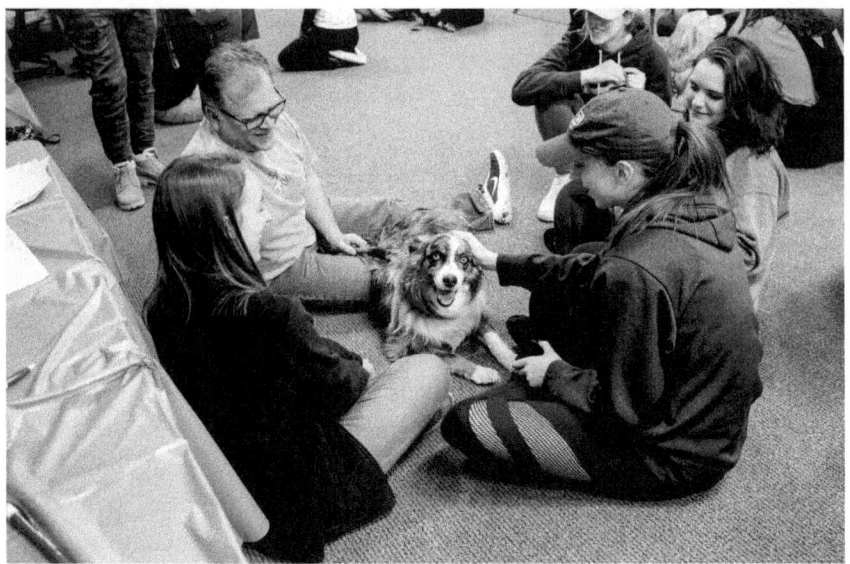

An Australian shepherd and therapy dog and her handler are "sharing smiles and joy"—
the motto of Alliance of Therapy Dogs. Photo Credit: Megan Higgins

generates more of an emotional response and stimulates memory formation (Robb, Boyd, & Pristash, 1980). In institutional settings, such as nursing homes (Lutwack-Bloom, Wijewickrama, & Smith, 2005; Phelps, Miltenberger, Jens, & Wadeson, 2008) and hospitals (Matuszek, 2010), a dog is more likely to elicit talk, awaken memories, and evoke a positive emotional response than other types of stimuli. A similar effect has been observed when dogs are brought to campus (Wood et al., 2015). The hesitancy and social awkwardness that is sometimes observed at other gatherings on campus is far less evident. In addition, dogs can temporarily suspend absorption in technology. When dogs are present, phones and tablets are seldom a distraction; rather, the use of these devices is relevant to the goings on. If students do access technology, the purpose often is to share a photo of a family dog, sadly tell the story of a dog that has passed on, or to get a photo with the visiting dogs that will be sent to family or friends. Furthermore, there is a growing body of research from various fields to suggest that positive interactions with canines can ameliorate physiological and psychological stress (Polheber & Matchok, 2014) and provide a break from the pressure to perform well in college (Wood, Ohlsen, Thompson, Hulin, & Knowles, 2018).

Table 10.1 The PERMA Model Applied to College Student-Canine Interactions

ELEMENTS OF WELL-BEING (SELIGMAN, 2012)	STUDENTS' WRITTEN COMMENTS	EVIDENCE BASE
Positive emotions	"Loved seeing these dogs. I am less stressed!"	Feelings of contentment, reduced anxiety, and less irritability were associated with as few as 10 minutes of human-animal interaction (Crossman & Kazdin, 2015). Animals can help to moderate stress responses (Friedmann & Gee, 2017; Muckle & Lasikiewicz, 2017; Stewart, Dispensza, Parker, Chang, & Cunnien, 2014), reduce distress (Crossman, 2017), and reduce depression (Folse, Minder, Aycock, & Santana, 1994). Even brief interactions with animals can contribute to the emotional health of college students (Pendry, Carr, Roeter, & Vandagriff, 2017; Thelwell, 2019).
Engagement	"Dogs rule! :)" "My girlfriend knew I was stressed so she texted me 'get over here—the dogs are at the library!'"	Reservations about expressing emotions can be moderated by interactions with dogs (Bryan et al., 2014). International students who spoke a different language were more likely to interact in English when dogs were present (Binfet, Trotman, Henstock, & Silas, 2016).
Relationships	"Love when the dogs come! We get to interact with community members and take a break from finals stress! Thank you!"	The presence of dogs facilitates getting to know other college students (Wood et al., 2015). Thinking about dogs (or cats) can reduce feelings of social rejection (Brown, Hengy, & McConnell, 2016). Dogs appear to function as "ice breakers" that stimulate conversation (Kim, Hong, Lee, Chung, & Lee, 2015; Knight & Edwards, 2008).
Meaning	"Best day ever!" "It always needs to be here. It really helps with depression."	Just looking at photographs of dogs can reduce college students' self-reported levels of stress (Torres, Arnold, & Shutt, 2016).
Accomplishments	"I was feeling really stressed out with all the projects due and tests coming up. Now I'm ready to push through it all."	Companion animals can moderate stress responses during challenging cognitive tasks (see Friedmann & Gee, 2017, for a literature review).

A student meets a therapy dog during an evening event that brings students, handlers, and dogs together. Photo Credit: Megan Higgins

THEORETICAL BASE: VALUE-ADDED

Traditionally, the quality of colleges and universities has been assessed by reputational rankings, alumni survey data, and the achievements of their graduates. The difficulty here is that the premier institutions frequently are the most expensive and selective, so they tend to remain at the top. Another, less prestigious institution may be doing excellent work in taking students from where they are to where they aspire to be, yet never get recognition. The argument—ongoing since the 1980s—is that we need to look more at value-added. Value-added would assess quality by the degree to which a postsecondary institution develops the abilities of its students. Simkovic (2017) explains a value-added approach in higher education by comparing it to the evaluation of hospitals. If differences in patient health prior to admission were not considered, the "best" hospitals would be those that treated the healthiest people. As applied to postsecondary education:

> Elite institutions—those that serve primarily students with high standardized test scores, excellent primary and secondary schooling, strong motivation, and rich, powerful, and well-connected families—are assumed to

add the most value. This is because their students have the best outcomes: the highest completion rates, the best chances of finding a job, the highest pay, the lowest debt burdens, and the lowest chances of defaulting on their debts.... Conversely, many institutions' graduates have less attractive outcomes—lower completion rates, lower employment rates, lower pay, higher debt burdens, and higher student loan default rates. These institutions are often assumed to do less to help their students, even though these institutions typically serve students who faced many challenges before they arrived at college or graduate school—lower standardized test scores, weaker academic preparation, lower levels of motivation, and less educated and wealthy families ... because poor outcomes for these students are perceived to be caused by the institutions they attend, the institutions that serve them have a harder time attracting students and must offer their services at a lower price—lower tuition, or higher discount, rates. As a result, these institutions have fewer resources and struggle to improve the quality of services they can provide.... It does not necessarily make sense for institutions with the best incoming students and the best outcomes to charge the highest prices and have the most resources because those institutions may not always add the most value. (pp. 124–125)

Thus, value-added is an attempt to measure the portion of success that is attributable to college rather than judging a university to be excellent because it enrolls a wealthy, well-prepared student body (Supiano, 2015). In order to document value-added, institutions first establish an "expected" level of performance for students fitting a particular "profile" and then compare/contrast that with what alumni actually achieved using indicators such as midcareer earnings, student-loan repayment, and the average salary of occupations in which alumni work. Another important way of documenting value-added is to look for evidence beyond time spent in classrooms. For example, over 80% of employers want graduates with leadership skills and the ability to work on a team, while 70% want new employees with written communication skills and the ability to solve problems (Grace & Seemiler, 2016). As verification of such skills, employers want to see more than a transcript; they expect to see evidence that students have accomplished these things out in the world. Admission to a school of veterinary medicine offers a good example. The University of California, Davis School of Veterinary Medicine, for example, has the following requirements for admission to the program:

A minimum of 180 hours of *veterinary experience* are required by the application deadline (September 17 of current application year) to have your application considered for admission; however, admitted applicants have an average of 1,475 hours of quality "hands-on" experience in the veterinary field. You are expected to have a realistic and appropriate perspective of the responsibilities of the veterinary profession. Your experience may come from a job or volunteer service. You may acquire experience by working with veterinarians in private practice, farms, ranches, animal shelters, zoos, aquaria, etc.

Expectations for other majors—even those not focused on a career working with animals—also are relying more on real-world experience as a marker of competence and commitment. To illustrate, positions for elementary school teachers and graduate assistantships at the master's level can be highly competitive. One applicant had volunteered with the local therapy dog group. When the therapy dog teams visited the public library, children could sign up for a 15-minute appointment to read aloud with one or more of the dogs. The student volunteer greeted the children and their guardians upon arrival, helped each child to get settled in with a dog and handler for their time slot, distributed a short survey to the adults, and suggested other books and audiovisual materials that families could borrow from the library. She participated in tabulating the survey information and helped a professor who volunteered with her therapy dog in preparing a conference presentation on the project. The student also worked with the local chapter of the International Reading Association on a special "Literacy Day" program at the library during the summer. She helped to plan seven different learning activities from which the children could choose. Later, when this student sought a position as a classroom teacher and later still, when she wanted to begin work on her master's degree, those experiences distinguished her from the other applicants. The fact that she had demonstrated leadership skills, worked successfully in teams of professionals, solved problems in order to offer a successful event or program, and applied skills in writing and mathematics all spoke to her ability to fulfill the role of a teacher and a graduate student.

The next section describes some value-added strategies that provide students with practical experience and new skill sets by bringing them together with dogs on and off campus.

RESEARCH AND INSTITUTIONAL INITIATIVES

Most of the time, when college students interact with canines other than their own dogs and network of known dogs owned by family and friends, it is during exam week or in conjunction with counseling services. Visiting therapy dogs are nearly always the animals that are included (see chapters 5 and 7). This section highlights some innovative practices that are just beginning to gain acceptance. All of them will require a more dog-friendly campus in order to operate. Currently, the most common policy at postsecondary institutions is that no dogs are permitted in residences or other buildings on campus, other than service dogs and invited therapy dogs.

UNIVERSITY SERVICE DOGS OR THERAPY DOGS

As more and more people request to bring their dogs to campus, postsecondary institutions will need to consider the best ways to keep people safe and, at the same time, consider the dogs' welfare (Humane Society of the United States, 2010; Tepper, 2010). When dogs are selected as education partners, a kindly family pet is not enough. Insurance for therapy dog handler/dog teams often does not cover employees, and only the handler who tested with the dog can be in charge for the policy to be in effect. Universities also tend to have longer breaks between semesters and during the summer, so this must be considered as well. One strategy that has been used in public schools is for the principal to have a dog trained at the service dog level. Dogs sometimes go through extensive training to become service dogs but are not placed with an individual with a disability. The dog might, for example, be unable to physically perform the work because of a health condition, such as hip dysplasia. That physical limitation would make the dog unsuitable for tasks such as aiding a person's balance when climbing stairs, pulling open a heavy door, serving as a brace when the person rises from a chair, and so forth. Sometimes, the dog's disposition is not a good match. A particularly gregarious dog, for example, may be a better fit for interaction with many people. This sets extremely high standards for the dog's behavior, makes certain that the person responsible for the dog is there, and provides care for the dog during times when school is not in session. The best advice here is to work with a reputable service dog provider—ideally, one that is accredited by Assistance Dogs International.

The other option for a facility dog at the university is a registered and insured therapy dog team with insurance coverage that extends, not only to volunteers, but also to employees. Alliance of Therapy Dogs recently made that option available to members so that additional insurance coverage can be purchased to cover the therapy dog team in the handler's workplace. The employee who tested with the dog has to be in control of the dog at all times. The insurance coverage would not apply if someone else was left in charge of the dog and an incident occurred. The most common situation is for a university counselor to be the owner/handler of a certified therapy dog, to have the dog on site, and to incorporate the dog into events and individual counseling sessions with students who are receptive to the dog's presence.

RETHINKING MASCOTS

Some universities have a long history with a canine mascot. For example, when Lewis and Clark set out to map the Louisiana Purchase in 1804, they purchased a Newfoundland, Seaman, for $20 to accompany them on their journey. The dog was greatly admired by the Native Americans and saved the explorers on more than one occasion from a bull buffalo and bears (National Park Service, 2015). Today, the Lewis and Clark College mascot is a Newfoundland dog. In 1931, a mixed-breed dog named Reveille became the official mascot of Texas A&M University. More recently, collies have filled this role. At least 18 different breeds of dogs have been identified as the college or university mascot (Lebowitz, 2015). Usually, these dogs are owned and live with a university staff member. Nevertheless, a sports competition, such as a football game, is very often the context in which these dogs are trotted out. Stadium and arena settings can be exceptionally stressful for a dog with crowds of people shouting, marching bands, and the like. It is asking too much of most dogs to tolerate these conditions. If dogs' presence is sought on campus, it would be preferable to opt for dogs trained at the therapy or assistance dog level that would actually interact with students and staff in positive ways rather than exploited as an emblem for the university, even though these dogs may not be the same breed as the mascot. As noted in chapter 2, if the goal is to feature the dog as mascot, a plush representation of the breed is a better choice.

Several universities have a trained therapy dog as their official mascot and working dog for the campus safety department (Kelly, 2020). A staff member is the owner/handler of the dog and they report that the dog's presence is helpful to many students who have experienced some difficult personal incident or want to report a crime. At Iowa State University, the police department hired a former student with a degree in psychology and animal science to provide additional support to students. She inquired about the possibility of incorporating her golden retriever/therapy dog into her role and the handler/dog team became part of the campus safety program (Keren, 2019). This approach is similar to the Courthouse Dogs program, in which therapy dogs are present during forensic interviews or during court testimony to mitigate stress (Courthouse Dogs Foundation, 2019).

DESIGNATED DOG-FRIENDLY STUDENT HOUSING

Given concerns about allergies to dogs, fears/phobias about dogs, disapproval of canines on campus, cultural differences in views about appropriate roles for dogs, or simply disliking dogs, it may be necessary to work with campus housing to create on-campus residential facilities that are dog-friendly. Both indoor and outdoor spaces have to be considered. At Wright State University, for example, the service dogs have their own dog park. Of course, instituting these options requires collaboration with staff responsible for housing as well as careful consideration of how breaks will be handled and who will have responsibility for the dogs. Self-described as one of the "most pet-friendly campuses on the planet," Stephens College (2019) in Columbia, Missouri, has been welcoming dogs to campus for over 10 years. Their Pet Program Agreement and Pet Fostering Application are good examples of the types of documentation that is necessary. Their site also includes some videos that explain how the programs operate and the benefits that these experiences offer to students.

Another advantage of designated dog-friendly housing is that college students can acquire skills in dog care and training by partnering with service dog providers to become puppy raisers. Some institutions that have service dog puppy raising in campus residence halls include East Central Illinois, Rowan University, Rutgers University, University of Redlands, and University of Illinois at Champaign-Urbana. When students have responsibility for a puppy, it is particularly important to consider how to handle emergencies. An online survey of 53 white, female, able-bodied college student puppy raisers concluded that they needed more information and training about safety, risk, preparedness, and disaster response (DeYoung, Farmer, Callaro, & Naar, 2020).

OPPORTUNITIES TO ACQUIRE SKILLS IN DOG TRAINING

The country of Iceland has earned international recognition for its dramatic improvements in reducing alcohol and drug abuse in adolescents. Harvey Milkman (2017), a psychologist from Metropolitan State University of Denver, designed a comprehensive, community-wide program that changed perspectives on what to do about the groups of teens roaming the streets while under the influence of alcohol and drugs. One strategy was to promote teenagers' engagement in learning something that they found particularly appealing—sports, music, anything within reason. In addition, families were urged to rethink the "quality time" assumption and increase the quantity of time that they spent with their children. Parents were provided with financial support to get their teens involved in learning activities (for more details, see Milkman & Wanberg, 2012). The outcomes were particularly impressive. During the period from 1998 to 2016, the percentage of 15- to 16-year-old Icelandic youth drunk in the past 30 days declined from 42% to 5%; daily cigarette smoking dropped from 23% to 3%; and the use of cannabis one or more times fell from 17% to 5%.

Learning about and interacting with dogs is something that interests many college students. University-sponsored dog training classes that students enroll in voluntarily or for a nominal fee through noncredit courses represent interesting learning opportunities. These experiences not only build a more dog-friendly campus, but also educate the next generation of responsible dog owners. An eight-week dog training program that culminated in completing the Canine Good Citizen test at University of Nebraska-Lincoln is a good example of how to plan and deliver this course to interested college students (Karr-Lilienthall, Norwood, & Morstad, 2013). Some of these students were preparing for careers in veterinary medicine, so the dog training classes added value to their professional preparation. Even for those students in other majors, learning to train dogs was something that they genuinely wanted to learn. The project planners not only involved the students in the dog training activities, but also in planning and coordinating the project to build their leadership skills. Survey data gathered from students suggested that the program was highly effective, and the survey instrument is included in the publication. Even if providing a project of this type is not feasible, it may be possible to plan internship opportunities with dog-savvy institutions in the community (see chapter 6).

THERAPY DOGS TO ADDRESS HOMESICKNESS

When a big, tough-looking football player's grades began to slide, his instructor set up an appointment to talk. This young man was from an urban environment and was now enrolled in a rural state college. "So, what's going on with you?" the professor inquired. "I'm concerned that you started out so strong but now seem to be struggling." As his eyes filled with tears, the student replied, "I miss my mother. That food at the cafeteria is nasty. I don't know how people can sleep here—it's just too quiet. I want to sleep in my own bed."

Making the transition to college life sometimes can be difficult. Even students who began with enthusiasm to break away from home and become independent may surprise themselves by yearning for home. Some campuses have begun bringing therapy dogs to campus on "move-in" days or making visits to residence halls as a way to normalize the environment, reduce stress, and mitigate homesickness (Biliczky, 2010; Fox, 2010; Messina, 2007). Opportunities to interact with therapy dogs are emerging in the research as an important way to help students cope with homesickness and to prevent them from dropping out of college (Binfet & Passmore, 2016).

POST-TRAGEDY DOG VISITS

When the university community comes together to support one another following a tragic incident, it is increasingly likely to see therapy dogs as part of these gatherings (Felix, Dowdy, & Greif, 2018; Siebert et al., 2017). The tragedy can be a natural disaster, such as a flood, blizzard, hurricane, or tornado so severe that students have to be evacuated or campus is shut down. At other times, the tragedy is caused by a human being. Northern Illinois University, for example, brought therapy dogs to campus following a shooting incident that resulted in multiple casualties. Classmates can sustain terrible injuries or die. On a dog-friendly campus, the university has formed partnerships with handler/dog therapy teams who can be called upon to visit campus after a tragedy or disaster. Skilled mental health professionals with therapy dogs also could visit individual classes to support students who are experiencing grief and loss. The Florida State University Counseling Center, for example, includes therapy animals in its outreach programs and in crisis response situations (Kronholz, Freeman, & Mackintosh, 2015). Outreach efforts such as these are important because students who need emotional support may not use the available services for a variety of reasons. They might view working with a mental health professional as a sign of weakness or worry about the possibility of a social stigma. They may assume that only those who are severely traumatized need support, be uninformed about what services are available, or think that they must pay to access services that are provided free of charge. The presence of dogs addresses many of these reservations, helps students to see staff as approachable, and increases the likelihood that students will make use of available mental health resources.

ALTERNATIVE SPRING BREAKS

When the university is on break, students who have few financial resources and international students who live great distances may remain in on- or off-campus housing with little to occupy themselves. This can intensify feelings of loneliness, depression, and homesickness. For students with money, friends, and family nearby, breaks frequently are times for fun-filled vacations, something that underscores the divide between them and the students who remain behind during breaks. On a dog-friendly campus, faculty can collaborate with animal welfare organizations to plan service-learning opportunities during the "downtime" of breaks. International students may be available for an alternative break activity. Their native country's general attitudes toward, resources for, and treatment of homeless animals may be very different from what is widely accepted in the United States, so they have many questions as they make cross-cultural comparisons of beliefs, values, and practices. Beatrice Humane Society (2019) in Nebraska, for example, offers many suggestions for ways that college students can help animals as part of an alternative break, while University of Central Florida (2020) has partnered with an animal shelter as an alternative spring break for their students.

This dog was left by the side of the road in a cardboard box sealed with duct tape. After she heard the dog's story, this volunteer immediately wanted to comfort him. Photo Credit: Megan Higgins

RECOMMENDATIONS FOR PRACTICE

Public safety and animal welfare are the two top priorities, both when bringing dogs to campus and when planning off-campus opportunities for student-canine interactions. Interactions with dogs need to be thoughtfully planned, carefully monitored, and regularly evaluated (Huss, 2012).

REDUCE RISKS OF INFECTION

Zoonotic diseases are those that can be transmitted from animals to humans. A dog can be asymptomatic and still pass along infection to people or other dogs. It is also possible for the animals themselves to contract a disease from people or for the handlers to become infected by a pathogen that their dog picked up while visiting. There are several ways of managing risks; some focus on the dogs' health while others rely on the handlers' practices. In terms of dog health, no unvaccinated animals should be permitted on campus. This is one advantage to using dogs that are registered, certified, and insured with a national therapy dog organization, because they typically require the following health checks of dogs for active membership: (1) proof of current vaccinations; (2) annual veterinary check; (3) fecal flotation test to determine the dog is free of intestinal parasites; and (4) on flea/tick and heartworm preventative medication.

In addition to the veterinarian's check, all reputable therapy dog groups and service dog providers direct handlers to keep dogs well-groomed with nails trimmed (to avoid accidental scratches). Some groups, such as Alliance of Therapy Dogs (ATD), specify that the dog cannot be on a raw diet due to the possibility of transmitting disease, mainly salmonella. They also test handlers on ATD's rules, one of which is that their dogs should not be permitted to lick a person's face. Allowing people other than the handler to give the dog treats is another practice that is forbidden by many therapy dog groups, not only because the dog's saliva would be on the person's hands, but also because it increases the risk of an accidental scratch or bite. Other groups, such as Therapy Dogs International, require a physical barrier, such as a towel, between the person and a small dog if it is placed on a lap at the person's request. The reason for this is that, as with the soles of people's shoes, the bottoms of a dog's feet may have *E. coli* present. The trick of teaching the dog to "give paw" or "shake" should be avoided for the same reason. As we have learned during the COVID-19 pandemic, the behavior that is most effective in reducing the risk of disease transmission is thorough and frequent hand washing with soap and water and, if that is unavailable, hand sanitizer wipes or gel pumps. Many therapy dog handlers carry hand sanitizer with them. For further helpful details on infection control, visit the Centers for Disease Control and Prevention's (2019) National Center for Emerging and Zoonotic Infectious Diseases (NCEZID) and Healthy Pets, Healthy People websites. See also Boyle, Corrigan, Buechner-Maxwell, and Pierce (2019) and Linder, Siebens, Mueller, Gibbs, and Freeman (2017). Pet Partners (2017), another national therapy dog organization, offers guidelines and training on infection control as well.

In terms of humans' allergies, there are some strategies that can reduce this problem that is present in approximately 10% of the population (American Kennel Club, 2019). Technically, there is no such thing as a perfectly "hypoallergenic dog," because most people react to the dander rather than the fur. When a dog sheds fur—to which dander is attached—this can cause a reaction in people with allergies. Some dogs have low-shed hair coats—breeds such as poodles, shih tzus, Yorkshire terriers, bichon frises, and Portuguese water dogs. For a complete list, see the American Kennel Club's (2019) article on the topic. Note that breed mixes—for example, a poodle/Labrador or poodle/golden retriever—may or may not shed hair; it depends on whether their coats are more like the poodle's or more like that of Labrador's and golden retriever's.

If a person with allergies still wants to interact with the dogs, some strategies that can be used include:

- a face mask to reduce inhalation of dander, such as those used when painting or in hospital settings
- wearing plastic gloves and washing or sanitizing hands immediately afterward
- taking allergy medication in advance of the visit
- holding the event in large, well-ventilated areas or outdoors (where dander would be widely dispersed)
- bathing and/or wiping the dog down with anti-dander wipes prior to the interaction
- meeting in an area with HEPA air filters or installing them

REVISE TERMINOLOGY

Becoming more enlightened about human-animal interaction also requires some attention to the words that campus personnel use when talking about dogs. During conversations among the coauthors of this book, we agreed that we have issues with terminology that objectifies dogs and refers to them as if they were inanimate, such as using the pronoun "it" or describing a service dog as a "tool." Likewise, the word "owner" has limitations, suggesting that the dog is property. There are some issues with referring to pet dogs as well, because it places them in a precarious position. By definition, the status of a pet is contingent upon being pleasing to the person, as this is what results in preferential treatment. So, if the dog chews up the TV remote, he can easily lose that privileged status. Thus, when describing canines that belong to students, reside with them, and are viewed as kin, it is more accurate to call them "family dogs." Even the Biblical phrase about having "dominion over" animals has been challenged; contemporary scholars have argued that it would be better translated as responsibility or guardianship for animals rather than bending them to our will or exploiting them to suit humans' purposes. The terminology "animal guardian" does a better job of capturing the role of an animal advocate. Although it is in wide use, the word "handler" is not a particularly satisfying as way to characterize the relationships between people and their therapy dogs or service dogs. A further personal objection to that word is that it is associated with the now practically defunct circuses that used harsh training methods with wild animals (think whips, chairs, and tigers) rather than the enduring bond between person and dog. A therapy dog team or service dog partnership seem to describe these relationships better.

APPRECIATE DOGS' EMOTIONAL LIVES

When we argue that dogs are sentient, this does more than state the obvious; namely, that dogs are living, breathing creatures. That is evident. *Sentient* means that dogs have a psychological existence as well as a physiological one; in other words, they experience a range of emotions. While experience and observation of dogs would suggest that dogs do indeed have emotional lives, it is only recently that research—such as studies to "map" the canine brain using functional magnetic resonance imaging (fMRI) or analysis of samples that show the presence of various hormones associated with emotions—has provided empirical support that dogs experience emotions. Although there are areas of disagreement, leading experts such as Marc Bekoff (2008) and Franz de Waal (2020) do agree that animals experience at least basic emotions, such as excitement/arousal, contentment, distress, joy, fear, anger, disgust, and love. There is emerging evidence that dogs have a basic sense of fairness where rewards are concerned (Essler, Marshall-Pescini, & Range, 2017). Dogs have long been credited with loyalty and there is some interesting data there also. When a stranger failed to help their person, most dogs would not interact with the stranger afterward—even though a treat was offered (Chijiiwa, Kuroshima, Hori, Anderson, & Fujita, 2015). One area of disagreement between popular opinion, some dog trainers, and researchers is the presence of guilt in dogs. Although a person might say that their dog felt guilt or shame after destroying the new sofa, many dog trainers would say it is more likely that the dog is reacting to the person's anger, frustration, or disappointment rather than any sense of guilt or shame. Ditto for being "spiteful"—this presupposes that the dog has devised a way to make the human suffer. So, the misguided person who is gone all day and comes home to a puddle or pile on the carpet attributes it to the dog getting even for being left behind when it is more likely attributable to the dog being physically uncomfortable from "holding it" that long. The argument here is that, first, the dog has no idea about the value of property. Further, dogs are guileless. That is one of the sources of their appeal—they are innocent rather than conniving. Dogs almost never invite another dog to frolic with a "play bow" (i.e., front paws down, hind end raised, tail wagging, mouth relaxed and slightly open) and then follow with anything other than play behavior (Bekoff, 2008). Unlike some people, they do not trick others by pretending to be nonaggressive and then betray that trust.

ESTABLISH A DOG COUNCIL AND PET POLICIES

Important decisions at respected universities are typically built on committees with representation from various stakeholders. Dogs on campus merit the same consideration. At least some members of this group need to be knowledgeable about dogs well beyond having a family dog. A dog-friendly campus culture can be supported by clear guidelines that minimize risks to humans and animals. At the very least, dogs on campus need to be licensed and have current rabies vaccinations. Increasingly, campus personnel have set higher standards for members of the postsecondary community seeking to bring their dogs on campus. Some campuses, such as the Maryland Institute College of Art (MICA), require dogs who are owned by members of the campus to obtain a photo ID, supply a vet verification form, and sign a liability waiver. They also have the policy in Box 10.1.

Additional examples of pet policies at other institutions are in table 10.2.

BOX 10.1 MARYLAND INSTITUTE COLLEGE OF ART PET POLICY

All pets must be registered with the Environmental Health and Safety Office before they are allowed to come to campus. By bringing your pet to campus, you are assuming all culpability releasing MICA of any liability.

- All pets must be leashed at all times, even when inside buildings. It is the responsibility of the owner to keep the animal under control at all times.
- Campus lawns and gardens are an extension of the classrooms and an important relaxation space for the MICA community. They are not to be used for walking pets or as pet waste areas. All owners are must pick up their pet's waste.
- No exotic animals, insects, rodents, or reptiles (including but not limited to snakes, lizards, and ferrets) of any kind are allowed on campus unless preapproved for a class project by an instructor and prior written approval from the Environmental Health and Safety Office.
- Certain areas of the campus are designated as "pet-free" zones, and all animals (except service animals) are prohibited. Current prohibited areas include:
    - any room with a "no pets" sign
    - all food service areas
    - college-owned/college-managed housing
    - computer and print labs
    - Art/Tech Center
    - all performance spaces; including Falvey Hall, A-Box, and B-Box
    - Decker Library
    - all galleries
    - all studio and shops
- All pet owners are responsible for making sure that their animals are up to date on required vaccinations. Failure to do so may result in being banned from bringing pets to campus.
- Once approved and granted an ID tag, that tag must be worn by the animal whenever it is on campus.
- If a fight occurs between animals, do not attempt to separate them. Call 311 to request a Baltimore City First Responder, and then notify Campus Safety immediately.

Please note that the MICA's Pet Program is applicable only to members of the MICA community: No guests/visitors may bring animals on campus unless it is a service animal (such as a seeing-eye dog).

Table 10.2 Examples of Universities' Policies on Pets

TYPE OF POLICY	INSTITUTION	DOCUMENT
Pet Policy	University of Nebraska	https://bf.unl.edu/policies/animal-pet-policy#policy-statement
Emotional Support Animal Policy	Shenandoah University, Virginia	https://q8rkuwu1ti4vaqw33x41zocd-wpengine.netdna-ssl.com/learning-support/files/2018/06/Emotional-Support-.pdf
Service Animal Use on Campus	Wright State University, Ohio	https://policy.wright.edu/policy/13650-service-animal-use-campus

Eckerd College (2019) in St. Petersburg, Florida, is identified as one of the most pet-friendly campuses in the United States, with 14 residence halls that allow animals. They have a committee that includes representation from students, and their policy covers:
- glossary of terms
- large and small pets permitted on campus
- number of large and small pets
- registration and inoculation
- rules of conduct
- owner responsibility
- visitors, faculty, and staff
- appeals to the Pet Life staff
- complaints
- emotional support animals and service animals
- Florida laws
- hurricane evacuations and campus breaks

Some other institutions with detailed pet policies pertaining to dogs include Stetson University in DeLand, Florida; University of Northern Colorado in Greeley, Colorado; and Clarion University of Pennsylvania in Clarion, Pennsylvania. A few postsecondary institutions have extensive experience with dogs on campus, and reviewing their materials can inform and improve the initiatives of other colleges and universities.

As with other dog initiatives, campuses will need to be aware of the consequences of a single, negative incident. One dog bite or fight between dogs can result in the discontinuation of long-standing programs or more restrictive policies. Many times, the dogs permitted on campus already know one another. Therapy dogs and their handlers typically volunteer together, and their dogs sometimes play together. Likewise, when a group of three service dog puppies being trained at the local prison came to campus, they already knew one another. As dogs become more accepted and have a greater presence on campus in various roles, however, the probability of interactions between canines who are not familiar with one another increases. The situation at nursing homes offers an example of this dynamic. Some residential health care centers now have facility dogs that accompany an employee to work on a regular basis. In addition, more of these groups—particularly assisted living programs—are permitting residents to own small dogs if they are trained, registered, and insured.

When postsecondary institutions are establishing a policy about dogs on campus, it is not necessary to "reinvent the wheel" or be pressured by people who claim to "know their rights" when they actually do not understand the Americans with Disabilities Act at all. Many institutions have given these matters extensive consideration. It is not enough to specify which dogs are permitted on campus. It also is important to have a clear policy about when to intervene to remove a dog, how to handle a dog bite incident, and who will be held liable if property damage occurs. Even a service dog can be removed from campus if the animal bites another person. Assistance Dogs International and the International Guide Dog Federation are highly respected organizations that have set standards for service dogs. Note that these standards exclude many of the dogs that people are falsely claiming to be service animals (Von Bergen, 2015). Misrepresenting a dog as a service dog has become such an issue that several states have enacted law to penalize people who do this. Claiming that a dog is a service animal when it is not is fraud. It also undermines the work that real service dogs and their trainers do to support people with disabilities who genuinely need the assitance of a service dog.

RAISE TRAINING LEVELS FOR DOGS

If dog training were conceptualized as a pyramid with the highest levels of training at the apex, most people would place a guide dog for the blind or a Navy SEAL dog in that position for two reasons. First, people are literally trusting these animals with their lives. Second, dogs in these roles need to make judgment calls and intelligently disobey a command if they sense danger. At the bottom of the dog training pyramid would be many puppy mill dogs with substandard care, no socialization, and zero training. Some stray shelter dogs and dogs that live indoors yet have no "house manners" whatsoever would also be positioned at the lowest levels of training. It is a truism in education that, as attainment levels increase for the top tier, it has a ripple effect on expectations for those below. Therapy dogs offer an excellent example of rising expectations for dogs. It soon became apparent that many dogs visiting nursing homes, schools, and libraries in their communities were not necessarily equipped to handle a disaster situation, so Therapy Dogs International instituted a more rigorous training/evaluation called Disaster Stress Relief (TDI DSR). A second example of higher training expectations is the American Kennel Club's (2020) Canine Good Citizen Advanced (CGCA) test, commonly referred to as the Community Canine. It is more rigorous than the Canine Good Citizen (CGC) because it evaluates the dog in a distracting environment out in the community, such as a park or shopping mall. There is a definite trend toward higher standards for dogs in public places, particularly if they are working dogs. To illustrate, most of the first courthouse dogs that supported victims during interviews and in-court testimony were therapy dogs with volunteer handlers who had specialized training. However, the courthouse dogs in Canada are trained at the assistance dog level and now are handled by the Royal Canadian Mounted Police.

In the interest of public health and safety, postsecondary institutions cannot afford to welcome random dogs to campus. If a student, faculty member, or administrator is serious about bringing their family dog into the campus community, the dog needs to be healthy, well-mannered, house-trained, and tolerant of other dogs. It would not be unreasonable, then, to expect the dog to successfully complete the American Kennel Club's basic Canine Good Citizen (CGC) test. The test is conducted by an experienced trainer, affordable (currently $20), widely available, and yields a CGC title and tag. Items on the test include, for example, basic obedience (sit, down, stay, heel, come), acceptance of a friendly stranger, and passing by a nonreactive dog.

EDUCATE THE CAMPUS COMMUNITY

Several years ago, a residential student who was legally blind attended college with his guide dog and made the difficult decision to return the dog to the service dog provider. The problem was that students wanted to interact with the dog as they did with their own dogs at home and "felt sorry" for the animal

A rescued collie passed the American Kennel Club's Canine Good Citizen test and her therapy dog test with Alliance of Therapy Dogs. Photo Credit: Megan Higgins

because it had a working role. Rather than respecting when the dog was working and when it was not, some of the students tried to distract him from his work. If the well-trained dog resisted, they resorted to using scraps of whatever food they were eating to get its attention. The treats not only undermined nearly three years of training, but also wreaked havoc with the dog's digestive tract because he was a Labrador retriever who needed to be on a special diet since puppyhood.

Many, if not most, college students today could be expected to be more enlightened than these individuals because society has learned more about the general protocol for interacting with service dogs. Although it frequently is referred to as "service animal etiquette," it has more to do with respecting persons with disabilities.

Nevertheless, there will be people who are completely uniformed or misinformed about assistance dogs or therapy dogs. Postsecondary institutions need to work with their public information people to get important messages out, such as the protocols for interacting with service dogs. A search using the terminology "service dog etiquette" will yield many useful print and video resources. Students with skills in art, photography, and advertising can partner with groups who represent the dogs to produce high-quality posters, flyers, public service announcements, and posts on Facebook, Instagram, and Twitter to educate others about service dog etiquette.

RETHINK ASSUMPTIONS

Twenty years ago, few people would have imagined that shopping malls would be in decline and largely replaced with online shopping. In a similar fashion, many of the faculty and staff members who experienced libraries as quiet places of study might be shocked to see the multipurpose and far-from-quiet atmosphere that they encounter in libraries today. Yet changes in the communication environment change human behavior in dramatic, sweeping ways—from the invention of the printing press to the widespread use of smartphones. Some college faculty, staff, and students may believe very strongly that dogs do not belong in work environments or on college campuses, although they likely represent the minority view at most college campuses in the United States (Foreman, Allison, Poland, Meade, & Wirth, 2019). Some, even those who are studying animal care as a career, may also oppose dogs—even assistance dogs—being anywhere near where people are preparing or consuming food (Miura, Bradwha, & Tanida, 2015). Yet it is not unusual these days for coffee shops that serve beverages and food to be in or near the library. Nevertheless, the desire of many academic librarians to remain connected with the students, their main clientele, have led them to make the decision to explicitly include therapy dogs in their statement of purpose. A good example is the Cushing/Whitney Medical Library of Yale University. Their statement of purpose is that the library:

> provides the healthcare community with the information services critical to training students and informing doctors. While they have seen their clients' dependence on print materials decline, they have also seen the role of the library as a place to study, socialize, and relax increase in importance. Research shows that healthcare professionals experience significantly higher levels of stress anxiety and depression than the general population. In response to this need, the library has reinvented itself not only as a place to study and socialize, but also a place that provides opportunities for relaxation and stress reduction through opportunities such as a therapy dog program. (Norton, Funaro, & Rojani, 2018, p. 203)

REDUCE DOG HANDLERS' STRESS

Generally speaking, therapy dogs and trainer/handlers form a particularly strong bond (Cohen, 2015; Wanser & Udell, 2019). The same holds true for the bonds between a service dogs, their trainers, and the person with a disability (O'Haire & Rodriguez, 2018). In Serpell's biaxial perspective on dogs that includes utility (work roles) and affect (emotional ties), therapy dogs and service dogs include both types of relationships. It is to be expected that, if handlers are stressed, this will be communicated to the dogs. Dogs selected for therapy and service roles generally would score high on what Schoen (2001) refers to as attunement to human beings. Dogs that are attuned to people pick up on and respond appropriately to human emotions more than many other dogs, just as dogs that are used to track missing people have a keener sense of smell and persistence than the average dog. Research that assesses the stress levels not only of college students, but also in the therapy dog/handler teams is just emerging. Initial findings suggest that handler stress has consequences for the dogs (Silas, Binfet, & Ford, 2019). It is important, then, to attend to issues that might raise the stress levels of the handlers and, subsequently, affect the dogs. Parking on campus is a good example. If a handler is worried about being late and must drive around several parking lots before finding a parking space, the handler may arrive at a therapy dog event flustered. The simple courtesy of letting visitors know where they are permitted to park or, better yet, providing a temporary parking pass, can reduce this worry and avoid transmitting the anxiety to the dog.

Therapy dog handlers know their dogs well and want them to feel at ease in the environment. Communicating clearly, in advance, the physical set up of the room is helpful in setting expectations appropriately. For example, when seven handler/dog teams were on campus to interact with students, the program planners explained that each handler would have a clean blanket or quilt on the floor for the dogs to sit on and a chair for the handler, in case sitting on the floor would be difficult for them (many of them were retirees with arthritis or some orthopedic issues). All reputable therapy dog organizations teach their members to protect their dogs and remove them from situations if they see signs of stress. Knowing where they can go just to give the dog a break, which areas are available for the dog to relieve itself, and where they can dispose of any waste is important. Thoughtful program organizers also point out the location of the bathrooms or hand sanitizing stations so that handlers can access them as needed. Handlers are expected to bring water and a bowl for their dogs, so there is no need to do this.

Another source of stress for handlers may have to do with their dogs ingesting something that jeopardizes their health. Most dogs have been taught the "leave it" command to prevent this, but bits of enticing food items might be on the floor or a participant in the activity may think it is acceptable to feed something to the dogs when it is not. Some dogs are on very restricted diets and even a couple pieces of greasy snack food items can cause severe digestive upset. People who are not aware of this may think that making little doggy bags of dollar store types of treats and chews for the dogs would be a nice way to thank the handlers for participating, but few handlers of therapy and service dogs would allow their dogs to have these questionable items. Furthermore, not everyone is aware that certain foods, such as raisins or chocolate, are toxic to dogs. In one therapy dog group, a tiny dog that accidentally ingested just a few raisins from a snack box became critically ill and required extensive medical treatment. It may be helpful to post some "dos and don'ts" for participants online, on signage, and as single pages distributed to those who attend to prevent inappropriate behavior such as screaming, squeezing a dog tightly, kissing the dog, or rough handling. Particular dogs may have things that make them nervous, such as being patted on the head or having their feet touched, and students need to respect this and comply with the handers' requests.

CONCLUSION

The president at a state university is asked to leave amid controversy. The university community wants to choose a replacement carefully, so a well-respected university president who just retired is asked to be the interim for a year. When she arrives at her new workplace, her cocker spaniel accompanies her. Her reasoning is that this is an exceedingly difficult transition for many administrators and faculty with emotions running high. When she meets with staff, parents, or students, the presence of the dog defuses tension and helps others to see her as more approachable. If they have an issue with dogs, they meet in the board room instead but, so far, her calm, friendly canine companion has been a great asset in her challenging new role.

In this situation that occurred back in the 1990s, one person in authority decided to bring an untrained and untested dog on campus. At the time, the general rule was that dogs—other than service dogs—were not permitted on campus. The idea that groups of dogs would be permitted in the library or that a student could reside in a dog-friendly residence hall would have been viewed as outlandish, at best. The presence of dogs on campus has come a long way since this situation occurred. Nevertheless, postsecondary institutions need to avoid a bandwagon mentality about bringing dogs on campus. These decisions must be made thoughtfully and with input from various stakeholders so that college campuses can accommodate the presence of various types of dogs. In many ways, college students can become "dog deprived," particularly when they leave home, family, and dogs behind to become residential students. While other people's dogs obviously cannot fill the void created by this, the research indicates that, for many students, dogs on campus can exert a positive influence on staff members' and students' perceptions of the quality of life in postsecondary institutions. Furthermore, when students get involved in working with various types of dog programs as volunteers or as part of an internship and develop leadership and communication skills, these activities can contribute to the value-added, both by their programs of study and the overall college learning experience.

REFERENCES

American Kennel Club. (2019). Hypoallergenic dogs. https://www.akc.org/dog-breeds/hypoallergenic-dogs

American Kennel Club. (2020). AKC community canine. https://www.akc.org/products-services/training-programs/canine-good-citizen/akc-community-canine/test-items

Beatrice Humane Society. (2019). Get involved! Volunteer today. https://www.beatricehumanesociety.org/get-involved/get-involved.html

Bekoff, M. (2008). *The emotional lives of animals: A leading scientist explores animal joy, sorrow, and empathy—and why they matter*. Novato, CA: New World Library.

Berman, J. (2018, February 25). Today's college students probably aren't who you think they are. *Market Watch*. https://www.marketwatch.com/story/todays-college-students-probably-arent-who-you-think-they-are-2018-02-20

Biliczky, C. (2010, February 16). Dogs on campus sniff out students in need of hugs—volunteers visit Kent residence halls with goal of reducing stress. *Akron Beacon Journal*, B1

Binfet, J., & Passmore, H. A. (2016). Hounds and homesickness: The effects of an animal-assisted therapeutic intervention for first-year university students. *Anthrozoös, 29*(3), 441–454.

Binfet, J. T., Trotman, M. L., Henstock, H. D., & Silas, H. J. (2016). Reducing the affective filter: Using canine assisted therapy to support international university students' English language development. *BC TEAL Journal, 1*(1), 18–37.

Boyle, S. F., Corrigan, V. K., Buechner-Maxwell, V., & Pierce, B. J. (2019). Evaluation of risk of zoonotic pathogen transmission in a university-based animal assisted intervention (AAI) program. *Frontiers in Veterinary Science, 6*, 167. https://www.frontiersin.org/articles/10.3389/fvets.2019.00167/full

Brown, C. M., Hengy, S. M., & McConnell, A. R. (2016). Thinking about cats or dogs provides relief from social rejection. *Anthrozoös, 29*(1), 47–58.

Bryan, J. L., Quist, M. C., Young, M., Steers, M. N., Foster, D. W., & Lu, Q. (2014). Canine comfort: Pet affinity buffers the negative impact of ambivalence over emotional expression on perceived social support. *Personality and Individual Differences, 68,* 23–27. https://www.ncbi.nlm.nih.gov/pmc/articles/PMC4423613

Center for Collegiate Mental Health. (2018). *2018 annual report.* https://ccmh.psu.edu/publications

Centers for Disease Control and Prevention. (2019). National Center for Emerging and Zoonotic Infectious Diseases (NCEZID). https://www.cdc.gov/ncezid

Chijiiwa, H., Kuroshima, H. Hori, Y., Anderson, J. R., & Fujita, K. (2015). Dogs avoid people who behave negatively toward their owner: Third-party affective evaluation. *Animal Behaviour, 106,* 123–127. https://www.sciencedirect.com/science/article/abs/pii/S0003347215001979

Cohen, S. P. (2015). Loss of a therapy animal: Assessment and healing. In A. Fine (Ed.), *Handbook on animal-assisted therapy* (4th ed., pp. 341–355). Waltham, MA: Academic Press.

Courthouse Dogs Foundation. (2019). https://courthousedogs.org

Crossman, M. K. (2017). Effects of interactions with animals on human psychological distress. *Journal of Clinical Psychology, 73*(7), 761–784.

Crossman, M. K., & Kazdin, A. E. (2015). Animal visitation programs in colleges and universities: An efficient model for reducing stress. In A. H. Fine (Ed.), *Handbook on animal-assisted therapy: Foundations and guidelines for animal-assisted interventions* (4th ed., pp. 333–357). Waltham, MA: Academic Press.

Crossman, M. K., Kazdin, A. E., & Knudson, K. (2015). Brief unstructured interaction with a dog reduces distress. *Anthrozoös, 28*(4), 649–659.

Crump, C., & Derting, T. L. (2015). Effects of pet therapy on the psychological and physiological stress levels of first-year female undergraduates. *North American Journal of Psychology, 17*(3), 575–590.

de Waal, F. (2020). *Mama's last hug: Animal emotions and what they tell us about ourselves.* New York: W. W. Norton.

DeYoung, S. E., Farmer, A. K., Callaro, Z., & Naar, S, (2020). Disaster preparedness among service dog puppy-raisers (human subject sample). *Animals, 10*(2), 246. https://doi.org/10.3390/ani10020246

EAB Daily Briefing. (2018, Sept 25). Traditional student population will fall 15% over the next decade. https://www.eab.com/daily-briefing/2018/09/25/traditional-student-population-will-fall-15-percent-over-the-next-decade

Eckerd College. (2019). Pet life. The privilege of pets living on campus. http://www.eckerd.edu/housing/petlife/petpolicy.php

Efklides, A., & Moraitou, D. (Eds.). (2013). *A positive psychology perspective on quality of life*. New York: Springer.

Elore, T. (2016). What's happening to college students today? I have a sad story to tell you. *Psychology Today*. https://www.psychologytoday.com/blog/artificial-maturity/201511/what-s-happening-college-students-today

Essler, J. L., Marshall-Pescini, S., & Range, F. (2017). Domestication does not explain the presence of inequity aversion in dogs. *Current Biology, 27*(12), P1861–1865E3.

Felix, E. D., Dowdy, E., & Greif, J. (2018). University student voices on healing and recovery following tragedy. *Psychological Trauma: Theory, Research, Practice, and Policy, 10*(1), 76–86.

Folse, E. B., Minder, C. C., Aycock, M. J., & Santana, R. T. (1994). Animal-assisted therapy and depression in adult college students. *Anthrozoös, 7*(3), 188–194. https://doi.org/10.2752/089279394787001880

Foreman, A. M., Allison, P., Poland, M., Meade, B. J., & Wirth, O. (2019). Employee attitudes about the impact of visitation dogs on a college campus. *Anthrozoös, 32*(1), 35–60. https://doi.org/10.1080/08927936.2019.1550280

Fox, E. (2010, September 15). Sonoma State welcomes therapy dogs to campus, *Sonoma State Star*. http://www.sonomastatestar.com/features/sonoma-state-welcomes-therapy-dogs-to-campus-1.1598761

Friedmann, E., & Gee, N. R. (2017). Companion animals as moderators of stress responses: Implications for academic performance, testing, and achievement. In N. R. Gee, A. H. Fine & P. McCardle (Eds.), *How animals help students learn: Research and practice for educators and mental health professionals* (pp. 98–110). New York: Routledge.

Friedmann, E., Son, H., & Saleem, M. (2015). The animal-human bond: Health and wellness. In A. H. Fine (Ed.), *Handbook on animal-assisted therapy: Foundations and guidelines for animal-assisted interventions* (4th ed., pp. 73–88). Waltham, MA: Academic Press.

Grace, M., & Seemiler, C. (2016). *Generation Z goes to college*. San Francisco, CA. Jossey-Bass.

Hoffman, J. (2015, May 27). Anxious students strain college mental health centers. *The New York Times*. https://static1.squarespace.com/static/576bf294d2b857d28be440ba/t/57b3a88159cc6834cfa2bfba/1471391873288/Anxious+Students+Strain+College+Mental+Health+Centers+-+NYTimes.com.pdf

Humane Society of the United States. (2010, July 28). Pets at college: An idea that might not make the grade. http://www.humanesociety.org/news/news/2010/07/pets_at_college_072810.html

Huss, R. (2012). Canines on campus: Companion animals at postsecondary educational institutions. *Missouri Law Review, 77*(2), Article 5. https://scholarship.law.missouri.edu/cgi/viewcontent.cgi?referer=https://www.google.com/&httpsredir=1&article=1288&context=mlr

Karr-Lilienthal, L. K., Norwood, K., & Morstad, J. (2013). Student organization sponsored dog training classes provide experiential learning opportunity for students and community participants. *North American Colleges and Teachers of Agriculture (NACTA) Journal, 57*(1), 10–15.

Kelly, J. (2020, January 10). Meet Cooper, a therapy dog working alongside his owner in UVA's police department. https://news.virginia.edu/content/meet-cooper-therapy-dog-working-alongside-his-owner-uvas-police-department

Keren, L. (2019, May 10). ISU police department's mental health advocate has a therapy dog sidekick. https://www.amestrib.com/news/20190510/isu-police-department8217s-mental-health-advocate-has-therapy-dog-sidekick

Kim, O., Hong, S., Lee, H., Chung, Y., & Lee, S. (2015). Animal assisted intervention for rehabilitation therapy and psychotherapy. https://www.intechopen.com/books/complementary-therapies-for-the-body-mind-and-soul/animal-assisted-intervention-for-rehabilitation-therapy-and-psychotherapy

Knight, S., & Edwards, V. (2008). In the company of wolves: The physical, social, and psychological benefits of dog ownership. *Journal of Aging and Health, 20*(4), 437–455. https://doi.org/10.1177/0898264308315875

Kronholz, J. F., Freeman, V. F., Mackintosh, R. C. (2015). Animal-assisted therapy: Best practices for college counseling. *Vistas Online.* https://www.counseling.org/docs/default-source/vistas/article_7525cd23f16116603abcacff0000bee5e7.pdf?sfvrsn=bbdb432c_8

Lave, J., & Wegner, E. (1991). *Situated learning: Peripheral participation.* New York: Cambridge University Press.

Lebowitz, B. (2015, June 28). 18 most popular dog breeds that double as college mascots. https://www.business2community.com/sports/18-most-popular-dog-breeds-that-double-as-college-mascots-01261047

Linder, D. E., Siebens, H. C., Mueller, M. K., Gibbs, D. M., & Freeman, L. M. (2017). Animal-assisted interventions: A national survey of health and safety policies in hospitals, eldercare facilities, and therapy animal organizations. *American Journal of Infection Control, 45*(8), 883–887. https://doi.org/10.1016/j.ajic.2017.04.287

Lutwack-Bloom, P., Wijewickrama, R., & Smith, P. (2005). Effects of pets versus people visits with nursing home residents. *Journal of Gerontology and Social Work, 44*(3), 137–159.

Matuszek, S. (2010). Animal-facilitated therapy in various patient populations: Systematic literature review. *Holistic Nursing Practice, 24*(4), 187–203. https://doi.org/10.1097/HNP.0b013e3181e90197

Messina, J. (2007, November 1). Helping students cope with homesickness: It's a job that administrators are taking on in various ways, *University Business, 80.* https://www.questia.com/magazine/1G1-171658713/helping-students-cope-with-homesickness-it-s-a-job

Milkman, H. (2017, December 6). Iceland succeeds at reversing teenage substance abuse: The U.S. should follow suit. https://www.huffpost.com/entry/iceland-succeeds-at-rever_b_9892758

Milkman, H., & Wanberg, K. (2012). *Pathways to self-discovery and change: Criminal conduct and substance abuse treatment for adolescents—provider's guide and participant's workbook.* Thousand Oaks, CA: Sage.

Miura, A., Bradshaw, J. W. S., & Tanida, H. (2015). Attitudes towards assistance dogs in Japan and the U.K. *Anthrozoös, 15*(3), 227–242. https://doi.org/10.2752/089279302786992496

Muckle, J., & Lasikiewicz, N. (2017). An exploration of the benefits of animal-assisted activities in undergraduate students in Singapore. *Asian Journal of Social Psychology, 20*(2), 75–84. https://doi.org/10.1111/ajsp.12166

National Park Service. (2015, April 10). Seaman. https://www.nps.gov/jeff/learn/historyculture/seaman.htm

Norton, M. J., Funaro, M. C., & Rojiani, R. (2018). Improving healthcare professionals' well-being through the use of therapy dogs. *Journal of Hospital Librarianship, 18*(3), 203–209. https://doi.org/10.1080/15323269.2018.1471898

O'Haire, M. E., & Rodriguez, K. E. (2018). Preliminary efficacy of service dogs as a complementary treatment for posttraumatic stress disorder in military members and veterans. *Journal of Consulting and Clinical Psychology, 86*(2), 179–188.

Pendry, P., Carr, A. M., Roeter, S. M., & Vandagriff, J. L. (2017). Experimental trial demonstrates effects of animal-assisted stress prevention program on college students' positive and negative emotion. *Human-Animal Interaction Bulletin, 6*(1). https://www.apa-hai.org/human-animal-interaction/haib/experimental-trial-demonstrates-effects-of-animal-assisted-stress-prevention-program-on-college-students-positive-and-negative-emotion

Perea-Mediavilla, M. A., & López-Cepero, J. (2017). Expectations towards animal-assisted interventions and improvement on quality of life: Triangulating information from different actors and levels of analysis. In A. Maturo, S. Hošková-Mayerová, D. Soitu, & J. J. Kacprzyk (Eds.), *Recent trends in social systems: Quantitative theories and quantitative models* (pp. 399–406). New York: Springer.

Pet Partners (Producer). (2017). *Infection prevention and control: Therapy animal visitation in healthcare settings* [Online Module]. https://petpartners.org/learn/online-education

Phelps, K. A., Miltenberger, T. J., Jens, T., & Wadeson, H. (2008). An investigation of the effects of dog visits on depression, mood, and social interaction in elderly individuals living in a nursing home. *Behavioral Intervention, 36*(3), 181–200. https://doi.org/10.1002/bin.263

Polheber, J. P., & Matchok, R. I. (2014). The presence of a dog attenuates cortisol and heart rate in the Trier Social Stress Test compared to human friends. *Journal of Behavioral Medicine, 37*(5), 860–867. https://doi.org/10.1007/s10865-013-9546-1

Robb, S. S., Boyd, M., & Pristash, C. L. (1980). A wine bottle, plant and puppy: Catalysts for social behavior. *Journal of Gerontological Nursing, 6*(12), 721–728. https://doi.org/10.3928/0098-9134-19801201-07

Schoen, A. M. (2001). *Kindred spirits: How the remarkable bond between humans and animals can change the way we live.* New York: Broadway Books.

Seligman, M. E. P. (2012). *Flourish: A visionary new understanding of happiness and wellbeing.* New York: Atria Press.

Seibert, E. C., Stewart, D. G., Hu, E. M., Estoup, A. C., Underbrink, E. G., & Moore, L. S. (2017). Post-traumatic stress and alcohol-related problems following a college shooting: Effect of help-seeking. *Journal of School Violence, 17*(2), 180–193. https://doi.org/10.1080/15388220.2017.1292918

Shapiro, D., Dundar, A., Wakhungu, P. K., Yuan, X., Nathan, A., & Hwang, Y. (2016, September). *Time to degree: A national view of the time enrolled and elapsed for associate and bachelor's degree earners* (Signature Report No. 11). Herndon, VA: National Student Clearinghouse Research Center.

Silas, H. J., Binfet, J., & Ford, A. T. (2019). Therapeutic for all? Observational assessments of therapy canine stress in an on-campus stress-reduction program. *Journal of Veterinary Behavior, 32*, 6–13. https://doi.org/10.1016/j.jveb.2019.03.009

Simkovic, M. (2017). A value-added perspective on higher education. *UC Irvine Law Review, 7*, 123–132. https://www.law.uci.edu/lawreview/vol7/no1/Online_Simkovic.pdf

Stephens College. (2019). The most pet-friendly campus on the planet. https://www.stephens.edu/student-life/pet-program

Stewart, L. A., Dispensza, F., Parker, L., Chang, C. Y., & Cunnien, T. (2014). A pilot study assessing the effectiveness of an animal-assisted outreach program. *Journal of Creativity in Mental Health, 9*(3), 332–345.

Supiano, B. (2015, April 29). New rankings gauge colleges' "value-added" by measuring alumni outcomes. https://www.chronicle.com/article/New-Rankings-Gauge-Colleges-/229745

Tepper, N. (2010, October 20). Students (try to) fit pet adoption into their college lifestyle, *Indiana Daily Student*. http://www.idsnews.com/news/story.aspx?id=778 43

Thelwell, E. L. R. (2019). Paws for thought: A controlled study investigating the benefits of interacting with a house-trained dog on university students' mood and anxiety. *Animals, 9*(10), E846. https://doi.org/10.3390/ani9100846

Thorn, J. M., Templeton, J. J., Van Winkle, K. M. M., & Castillo, R. (2006). Conditioning shelter dogs to sit. *Journal of Applied Animal Welfare, 9*(1), 25–39.

Torres, A., Arnold, K. L., & Shutt, E. M. (2016). The effects of visual pet stimuli on stress and math performance. *College Student Journal, 50*(1), 112–120.

University of California, Davis Veterinary Medicine. (2019). Criteria for admission. https://www.vetmed.ucdavis.edu/admissions/criteria-admission

University of Central Florida. (2020). UCF students spend spring volunteering at animal shelter. https://hospitality.ucf.edu/ucf-students-spend-spring-break-volunteering-at-animal-shelter

Von Bergen, C. W. (2015). Emotional support animals, service animals, and pets on campus. *Administrative Issues Journal: Connecting Education, Practice, and Research, 5*(1), 15–24. https://doi.org/10.5929/2015.5.1.3

Wanser, S. H., & Udell, M. A. R. (2019). Does attachment security to a human handler influence the behavior of dogs who engage in animal-assisted activities? *Applied Animal Behaviour Science, 210*, 88–94. https://doi.org/10.1016/j.applanim.2018.09.005

Wood, E., Ohlsen, S., Thompson, J., Hulin, J., & Knowles, L. (2018). The feasibility of brief dog-assisted therapy on university students stress levels: The PAwS study. *Journal of Mental Health, 27*(3), 263-268.

Wood, L., Martin, K., Christian, H., Nathan, A., Lauritsen, C., Houghton, S.,...McCune, S. (2015). The Pet Factor: Companion animals as a conduit for getting to know people, friendship formation and social support. *PLoS ONE, 10*(4), e0122085. https://doi.org/10.1371/journal.pone.0122085

AFTERWORD

AS THIS BOOK goes into production, the world is in turmoil due to the COVID-19 pandemic. During such desperate times, dogs are both winners and losers. Some fortunate canines are treasured more than ever and play a larger role in the daily lives of their humans. A photo on Facebook showed a dog perched on top of a kitchen wall cabinet captioned with, "No way. I've already had five walks today," and posts about dogs' positive spin on having everybody at home all of the time were frequent. In a few communities, there was even an uptick in dog adoptions as people decided that a canine companionship could lessen their sense of isolation. Meanwhile, shelter personnel worried that some of the dogs who adapted readily to a stay-at-home environment would be less well-adjusted when people returned to work. When interpersonal contact is disrupted and disallowed, there is a human tendency to form social bonds with dogs (Palmer & Custance, 2008; Stoeckel, Palley, Gollub, Niemi, & Evins, 2014). Still, some rescuers worry that these same dogs will bounce back to shelters with the already common excuse that the dog has separation anxiety or that some people will seek to rehome dogs when they become less convenient.

For many other dogs, things are getting much worse. Early on, there were people who believed, in the absence of any evidence, that dogs were carriers of the virus and wanted them to be destroyed. Some people with old or infirm dogs decided to have the dogs euthanized and, as unemployment skyrocketed, many dogs became homeless when people could no longer afford to keep them.

Prior to the stay-at-home order, student volunteers took shelter dogs to gatherings such as this parade to help them get adopted. Photo Credit: Haley Romanko

Dogs frequently bear the brunt of peoples' problems. During a global pandemic, many of the major reasons for giving up family dogs increase: death, illness, financial hardship, and changes in living arrangements. Shelters that were barely remaining operational, already experiencing staffing problems, and overcrowded with stray animals before the crisis, are buckling under the weight. The volunteers who they relied on heavily are complying with stay-at-home orders. Low-cost spay/neuters have been discontinued in many places because they involve gathering people together. Many veterinarians have been forced to concentrate on ill or injured animals only during these difficult times. The temporary cessation of spay/neuter surgeries can be expected to increase the population of strays and unwanted litters, dragging many areas back to the way it was decades ago, with the no-kill movement losing traction.

Animal visitation programs that had been in place for years were among the first to be suspended as colleges and universities mobilized to "flatten the curve" and finished the semester online. Those of us who volunteer with therapy dogs remained in limbo. The vulnerable people who were the focus of our visits, such as nursing home residents or children with special needs, were prohibited from interactions—college students included. The process of evaluating

Some of the local students followed the COVID-19 safety protocols but continued to walk shelter dogs outdoors and took photos to post online. Photo Credit: Mary Renck Jalongo

The hope is that the new normal involves bringing college students and dogs together. Photo Credit: Megan Higgins

new dogs for therapy dog work came to a halt. Service dogs in training were losing a critical period for socialization as weeks of quarantine became months. Emotional support animals of college students fulfilled their roles in the home setting only, rather than using their hard-won privilege of being permitted to reside on campus. Student service-learning opportunities to volunteer or complete professional internships with animal welfare groups ceased as shelters closed to the public. Students' plans to engage in collaborative HAI research with faculty have been disrupted, diminished, or even dismantled. People with a commitment to integrate dogs into the campus community continue to collectively hold our breath, fearful that a misinformation campaign could undo years of progress in HAI.

Given this situation on and off campus, it is anybody's guess what the new normal will be for us and our canine companions. Yet there is hope. Dogs, the first domesticated species, remain steadfast in their hypersocial affiliation with humans and integration into human ecology (Cook, Prichard, Spivak, & Berns, 2016). They are always available and their interaction with humans is not prohibited as is person-to-person contact. Dogs remain joyful, playful, in the moment, grounded in the natural world, and oblivious to Draconian measures.

Meanwhile, their human partners are busy with applications of technology intended to serve as stopgap measures. University administrators, staff, and faculty quickly convert courses and experiences to online formats. Personnel at postsecondary institutions with a commitment to HAI scramble to find inventive ways to keep students in virtual contact with the therapy dog teams by posting photos, videos, dialogue, and presentations online. Students who volunteered at the shelter follow social media to see which of the animals that they know have been placed in homes. Scholarly writers and researchers collaborate using various platforms to share and edit documents or hold individual conferences and group meetings online. Academic publishing goes on as planned, orchestrating almost everything from afar. The life vest of hope buoys us up while our dogs remind us, if only we allow them to, that they will remain loyal and loving even when humankind is preoccupied with a global struggle to keep our species alive.

REFERENCES

Cook, P. F., Prichard, A., Spivak, M., & Berns, G. S. (2016). Awake canine fMRI predicts dogs' preference for praise vs food. *Social Cognitive and Affective Neuroscience, 11*(12), 1853–1862. https://doi.org/10.1093/scan/nsw102

Palmer, R., & Custance, D. (2008). A counterbalanced version of Ainsworth's Strange Situation Procedure reveals secure-base effects in dog–human relationships. *Applied Animal Behaviour Science, 10*(2), 306–319.

Stoeckel, L. E., Palley, L. S., Gollub, R. L., Niemi, S. M., & Evins, A. E. (2014). Patterns of brain activation when mothers view their own child and dog: An fMRI study. *PLoS ONE 9*(10), e107205. http://dx.doi.org/10.1371/journal.pone.0107205

INDEX

Page numbers in italics indicate figures, tables, and photos.

AAA. *See* animal-assisted activities
AAE. *See* animal-assisted education
AAII. *See* Animal Assisted Intervention International
AAIs. *See* animal-assisted interactions
AAT. *See* animal-assisted therapy
ABA. *See* applied behavior analysis
abilities: of dogs, 3–5; 4 Paws for Ability, 22; with seven roles, 11–14
abuse: animal, 10, 17, 73, 186, 199; drug and alcohol, 318; with ESA request denied, 73; Five Freedoms and, 60; survivors, 172
academic enhancement, students and, *211*
academic librarians, 17, 20, 227, *281*, 330
accommodation request evaluation, Disability Services Office with, 146–48
accreditation, by ADI, 315
ADA. *See* Americans with Disabilities Act
Adamle, K. N., 289
Adams, A. C., 67
ADI. *See* Assistance Dogs International
adoptions: of dogs rehabilitated, *213*; of homeless dogs, *51*; increased, 341; of shelter dogs, 304, 306
aesthetic, as biophilic approach, 63
Afghan hounds, 35–36
aggression model, ladder of, 70
AHA. *See* American Heart Association
Ainsworth, M. D., 38
AL. *See* Articulate Learning
alcohol, drugs and, 318
Allen, J. A., 198, 199

allergies, 74, 103, 110, 241, 317; children with decrease in, 37; filters, 152; food, 5; humans and, 23, 322
Alliance of Therapy Dogs (ATDs): with certifications, 177; equipment requirements, 81; health checks, 158, 321; insurance coverage and, 17, 158, *175*, 237, 316; motto, *310*; program, 277; tester/observer for, 244; therapy dog test with, *329*
Allison, P., 50
alpha amylase, 140
altruism, 187, 189, 197
American College Health Association, 166; survey, 40–41
American Evaluation Association, 293
American Heart Association (AHA), 141
American Humane Association, 12
American Kennel Club, 36, 204, 322, 328
American Psychiatric Association, 143
American Psychological Association, 285
American Society for the Prevention of Cruelty to Animals, 193
Americans with Disabilities Act (ADA): ESAs and, 135–36; FHA and, 21; pet, ESA or trained service animal under, 116; service dogs and, 69, 73, 102–3, 104, 109, 113, 116, 119–20
American Veterinary Medical Association (AVMA), 12–13, 34, 68, 163
America's Hero Dog, 12
America's VetDogs, 109
animal, abuse, 10, 17, 186, 199

animal-assisted activities (AAA): BARK and, 263–64; therapy dogs and, 12–13; value of, 41
animal-assisted education (AAE), therapy dogs and, 13
animal-assisted interactions (AAIs): best practices for, *86–87*; education and training, 78–79; Five Freedoms and, 68; "Guidelines for Wellness of Animals Involved in AAI," 84; leashes and, 71; personnel, 79–80; planning and protocols, 80–81, *81*. See also human-canine interactions, behaviorally healthy
Animal Assisted Intervention International (AAII), 83
animal-assisted therapy (AAT), 177, 231; with emotions, positive, 42; therapy dogs and, 13; value of, 41, 249
Animal-Assisted Therapy in Counseling Competencies, 177
animal guardians, 10, 125, 323
Animal Legal and Historical Center website, 120
animals: abuse, 73; American Society for the Prevention of Cruelty to Animals, 193; "Assistance Animals Notice," 145; bonding with, 286; CARAT, 82; Central California Society for the Prevention of Cruelty to Animals, 200–201; cruelty toward, 65–66, 241; dominion over, 323; with good life, 60; "Guidelines for Wellness of Animals Involved in AAI," 84; HAB, 260; human-animal bond, 34–37, *35*; Institutional Animal Care and Use Committee, 291; medical student education and, 65; rights, 66; RSPCA, 22; Table of State Assistance Animal Laws, 120. See also companion animals; dogs; emotional support animals; homeless dogs in the care of animal welfare groups; human-animal interaction

animal visitation programs (AVPs), 167
animal welfare: canine, 69–72, 206; canines on campus and, 73–74; ESAs, 72–73; research on, 67–74
anxiety: Beck Anxiety Inventory, 286; Burns Anxiety Inventory, 286, 291; depression and, 308; diagnosis rates, 309; HAI studies and, 286; Hospital Anxiety and Depression Scale, 286; STAI, 229, 286
APHE. *See* Association for Humane Professional Educators
applied behavior analysis (ABA), 256
Articulate Learning (AL), *211*
ASD. *See* autism spectrum disorder
Assessing the Human-Animal Bond, 286
"Assistance Animals Notice," 145
Assistance Dogs International (ADI), 103, 106, 111, 113; accreditation by, 315; behavior, 115; public appropriateness and, 115; service dogs and, 327; training, 115–16
Association for Humane Professional Educators (APHE), 174
assumptions, rethinking, 329–30
ATD. *See* Alliance of Therapy Dogs
attachment, loss and, 31–33, 38–40, 51
Auburn University Montgomery, 204
Australian shepherds, as therapy dogs, *279, 310*
autism spectrum disorder (ASD), 17, 109–10, 133, 137, 260, 279
AVMA. *See* American Veterinary Medical Association
AVPs. *See* animal visitation programs

Bain, K., 244
Baker, Tricia, *260*
BARK. *See* Building Academic Retention through K9s
"Bark Against Violence," 277
Barker, R. T., 291–92
Barker, S. B., 291–92

BarkPost.com, 171
Baylor University, 40, 65
Bazelon Center for Mental Health Law, 144
bears, 65
Beatrice Humane Society, 320
Beck Anxiety Inventory, 286
Beck Depression Inventory, 286
Beetz, A., 139, 140
behavior: ABA, 256; ADI and, 115; service dogs, standards of training and, 115–16; around service dogs, dos and don'ts, 122–23. *See also* human-canine interactions, behaviorally healthy
Beidas, R. S., 285
Bekoff, Marc, 323
Bell, A., 284, 290
Bell, S. M., 38
Bergin, Bonita, 109
Berman, D., 117
Bernese mountain dog, *48*
Berns, Gregory, 6–7
Besterfield-Sacre, M., 252
bichon frise: as hypoallergenic, 322; as therapy dog, *158, 279*
Binfet, John-Tyler, 43, 48, 83, 262–63, *264*, 265, 283, 284
biophiilia: defined, 58, 64; nine approaches to, 63; students and, 64–67; theory of, 62–67
blind people: guide dogs for, 5, 101, 102, 105, 108, 125; robotic dogs and, 44
body language: of dogs, 81, 206; dogs with human, 3, 63
bomb proof, 162, 163
bonding: with animals, 286; Assessing the Human-Animal Bond, 286; Characteristics of a True Bond, 60; Human-Animal Bond Research Institute, 11; mothers and children, 38; pets and benefits of, 10–11; reciprocal, *134*. *See also* human-animal bond
border collies, with word recognition, 3

Bowlby, J., 38
Boyle, S. F., 322
Boys and Girls Club, 259, 264
Bradshaw, K., 67
brains: of dogs, 3–4, 7, 104; endorphins and, 229
Breece, Lori, 111
breeding: food and, 60; puppy mills and, 10; purpose of, 36; service dogs, 104
Brief Mood Introspection Scale, 286
Bright, T. M., 199
Brooks, H. L., 139–40
Brown University, 147
Buechner-Maxwell, V., 322
Building Academic Retention through K9s (BARK), 262–65, *264*
bull mastiffs, 212
Burns Anxiety Inventory, 286, 291
Buros Center for Testing, 285
Buros Mental Measurement Yearbook, 285

campus: canine-campus events, 258–59; canines on, 73–74; community, education of, 328–29; dogs and QoL on, 20–24; Dogs on Campus, 41; housing, 40, 142–54; Pets on Campus policy, 40; resources, 293–94; violence on, 231–32
Campus Contact, 189
campus culture, dog-friendly: assumptions, rethinking of, 329–30; with campus community education, 328–29; in context, 305–7, 333; with dog council and pet policies, 324–27; emotional lives of dogs, 323–24; with handler, stress reduction of, 330–32; infection, reduce risks of, 321–22; PERMA model and, *311*; QoL, 307–12; recommendations for practice, 321–32; research and institutional initiatives, 315–20; terminology revised, 322–23; with training level raised, 327–28; value-added, 307, 312–14

cancer detection, 4
canine-assisted interventions, 41, 43, 47, 163, *164*, 179, 296
Canine-Assisted Interventions (Binfet and Kjellstrand Hartwig), 48
canine-campus events, 258–59
Canine Companions for Independence, 75, 109, 122
Canine Good Citizen (CGC), 328; certification, 174, 204; test, 318
Canine Good Citizen Advanced (CGCA) test, 328
canines: BARK, 262–65, *264*; on campus, 73–74; learning maximized with, 227–32; welfare, 69–72, 206. *See also* human-canine interactions, behaviorally healthy; research evidence on human-canine interactions
cannabis, Iceland and use of, 318
CARAT. *See* Clothier Animal Response Assessment Tool
cardiovascular disease, 139, 141
careers, dogs and preparation for, 24
Carlson, T. C., 289
Carr, S., 39
case studies, role of, 230
Castellano, J., 41
CDC. *See* Centers for Disease Control
Cebry, A., 47, 48
Centers for Disease Control (CDC), 84, 322
Central California Society for the Prevention of Cruelty to Animals, 200–201
certifications, ATDs, 177
CGC. *See* Canine Good Citizen
CGCA test. *See* Canine Good Citizen Advanced test
The Champions (documentary), 17
Chang, C., 42
Characteristics of a True Bond, 60
Charles, N., 283, 292
Chihuahuas, *58*

children: AAE and, 13; with allergies, decrease in, 37; Boys and Girls Club and, 259, 264; with dogs, treatment of, 61; millennials, dog ownership and, 2, 35; mothers bonding with, 38; service dogs and, 110; therapy dogs and, 32–33, 74, 314
Chin, Lili, 206
Chronicle of Higher Education, 64
cigarette smoking, in Iceland, 318
Cimini, M. E., 256–57
civic engagement, students and, *211*
civic responsibility, service-learning projects and, 188
Clarion University of Pennsylvania, 326
classrooms. *See* dogs, in classrooms
Clothier Animal Response Assessment Tool (CARAT), 82
collaboration, service-learning projects and, 188
college courses, roles for dogs: classroom preparation with, 232–38; classroom visits and concerns addressed, 235–36; learner engagement strategies and, *239–40*; learning defined, 224, 225–26; with learning maximized, 227–32; recommendations for practice, 241–44; research and institutional initiatives, 238–40; student engagement, theory of, 226–27; student engagement and, 223–25, 244–45; therapy dogs, session evaluation, *237*; with therapy dogs and school counseling, 231–32
college courses, roles for dogs and, therapy dogs, *224*
collies: as mascots, 316; as therapy dogs, *329*
comfort dogs. *See* therapy dogs
commitment: service-learning and, 194–96; to volunteerism, 208–9
communication, professional development and, 256
companion animals, dogs as inside, 1–2, 3
complexity, of students, 196

concentration, engagement and, 226
Connor, D. J., 117
consent test, with dogs, 79
cooperative education, 255
Coppola, C. L., 199
Coren, S., 179
Corrigan, V. K., 322
costs: evaluations with time, staffing and funding, 295; robotic dogs, 44; service dogs, 126; therapy dogs, 157, 158
counseling services, therapy dogs, visits and, 171
COVID-19, 45, 84, 321–22, 341–44, *342*, *343*
crating, 73
credit card, service dog retrieves, *103*
crosscutting skills, 252
Crossman, M. K., 42, 62, 167, 292–93
cruelty: abuse and, 73; American Society for the Prevention of Cruelty to Animals, 193; toward animals, 65–66, 241; Central California Society for the Prevention of Cruelty to Animals, 200–201; RSPCA, 22
Csikszentmihalyi, Mihaly, 165
cultures, dogs in different, 10. *See also* campus culture, dog-friendly
Cunnien, T., 42
curiosity, capitalizing on, 228
Cushing's disease, 72
Cushing/Whitney Medical Library, 330

Daltry, R. M., 42, 47, 289
Das, B. M., 202, 279
deaf people, guide dogs for, 5
DEAL, for student reflection, *211*
Deci, E. L., 244
Delgado, C., 44
Dell, C. A., 229–30, 290
Department of Housing and Urban Development (HUD), US, 137, 145, 146
Department of Justice, US, 116, 146–47

Department of Transportation, US, 14, 136
depression: anxiety and, 308; HAI studies and, 286; homesickness and, 320; Hospital Anxiety and Depression Scale, 286; rates, 308
de-stress: with dogs event, 9, 42–43, 76, 275, 276, 277, 292; with students, 275
de Waal, Franz, 323
diabetes, 6, 101, 137
Diagnostic and Statistical Manual of Mental Disorders (DSM-5), 143
disabilities: criteria for, 137; students with, 117
Disability Services Office: with accommodation request evaluation, 146–48; ESA and approval from, 149
Disaster Stress Relief (TDI DSR), 328
disease: cardiovascular, 139, 141; CDC, 84, 322; Cushing's, 72; NCEZID, 322; zoonotic, 321, 322
Dispenza, F., 42
dispositions, dogs developing professional knowledge, skills and, 22
dispositions, with hard and soft skills, 252–54
Doberman pinschers, 36
dog council, establishing, 324–27
dogs: abilities of, 3–5; ADI, 103; Assistance Dogs International, 106; body language of, 81, 206; brains of, 3–4, 7, 104; campus life and, 20–24; children with treatment of, 61; with consent test, 79; COVID-19 and, 341–44, *342*, *343*; cultural differences and, 10; different ways of being with, 7–11; emotions and, 323–24; evaluations of events, projects, and student programs with, 280–82; experimental research and, 65; facility, 13, 17, 172; as family members, 2–3, 323; fights, 326; guilt in, 324; hearing of, 4; humanization trend toward, 2–3; humans influenced by, 40–45, *43*; hypoallergenic,

dogs (*continued*)
322; influence of, 64; as inside companion animals, 1–2, 3; medical alert, 6, 110–11; men, women and percentages with, 2; millennials, children and, 2, 35; MWDs, 17, 35; negative interactions with, 9–10; Newfoundland, 316; with physical limitations, 315; posters for welfare, 78; post-tragedy visits, 319–20; research on student wellness and, *168–69*; resident, 13, 17; robotic, 44–45, 224; roles for, 11–18, *48*; with safety improved, 21; search and rescue, 12; sense of smell and, 4–5, 110; on social media, 33, 329, 341; stray, 9, 121, 195, *195*; stress for, 69–74; students and, *2*, 14–18, *15*, *20*, 20–24, *32*, *51*, 61–62, *201*, 228–29, *306*, *312*, 332–33, *341*, *342*, *343*; training and skills acquisition, 318; training levels raised for, 327–28; vision of, 4. *See also* campus culture, dog-friendly; college courses, roles for dogs; emotional support animals; family dogs; homeless dogs in the care of animal welfare groups; research evidence on human-canine interactions; service dogs; shelter dogs; therapy dogs; working dogs; *specific organizations*; *specific types*

dogs, in classrooms: with concerns addressed, *233–34*; handler/dog team and visits, preparing for, 224, 235–36; preparing for, 232–38

Dogs for Life, 109

Dogs on Campus, 41

dog walkers, volunteerism and, *200*, 201–2, 205, 208, 210, *210*

dominionistic, as biophilic approach, 63

dropping out, of volunteerism, 205

drugs, alcohol and, 318

DSM–5. *See Diagnostic and Statistical Manual of Mental Disorders*

dualism, service-learning and, 193

Durry, D. L., 10

Eagan, Patricia, 79–80, 81

East Central Illinois, 317

Eating Disorder Awareness Week, 77

Eckerd College, 326; open-pet policy at, 61

E. coli, 321

education: AAIs, 78–79; of campus community, 328–29; cooperative, 255; IHE, 88; Ministry of Higher Education, Malaysia, 253; Research and Service in Humane Education, 203

egoistic/self-actualization, volunteerism and, 197

Egypt, ancient, 36

Ein, N., 280

Einstein, Albert, 225

elite institutions, rich families and, 312–13

Emotional and Supportive Attachment to Companion Animals Scale (ESACA), 286

emotional support animals (ESAs): ADA and, 135–36; ADA with trained service animal, pet or, 116; agreement, 150, *151*; animal welfare and, 72–73; benefits, 139; in campus housing, processes and practices, 142–54; FHA and, 136, 137, 146; residence hall and process of bringing, 149–50; residence life office and, 148–54; RHA and, 136, 146; rights of, 241; role of, 14, 17, 133–34, *138*, *141*, *153*, 155; service dogs and, 49, 135; stress mediation, theory of, 138–42; terminology and concepts, 135–38; with therapy and service dogs, *160–61*; written verification of need for, 142–45

emotional wellness, 166

emotions: AAT and positive, 42; dogs and, 323–24; dogs and human, 3, 63;

dogs counteracting negative, 21–22, 39; learning and role of, 229; mental health and, 61; positive psychology and, 165
endorphins, brains and, 229
engagement, elements of, 226. *See also* student engagement
English as a Second Language (ESL) students, 249–50
enjoyment, engagement and, 226
Enns, R. M., 199
Environmental Health and Safety Office, 325
equipment, requirements for ATDs, 81
Erichsen, K., 198
ESACA. *See* Emotional and Supportive Attachment to Companion Animals Scale
ESAs. *See* emotional support animals
ESL students. *See* English as a Second Language students
ethics, professional development and, 256
etiquette, service dog, 329
Eustis, Dorothy, 108
evaluations: with assessment methods matched to research questions, 294–95; campus resources and, 293–94; in context, 275–78; defined, 278–79; of dog-assisted events, projects, and programs with students, 280–82; focus groups and, 283–84; frequency counts, 282–83; HAI studies with psychological traits and measures, 286; informal feedback and, 283; literature review and, 294; logic models and, 278–79; naturalistic observations and, 283; program improvement and outcomes assessment, 288–89; psychometric tools and, 285–87; randomized controlled trials, 292–93; recommendations for practice, 293–95; research and institutional initiatives, 287–93; service-learning projects and, 188; standardized psychological or physiological measures, 290–92; strategies and tools, 282–87; student participation and program types, 288; student stress and well-being, 289–90; surveys, 284–85; with time, staffing and funding, 295
exam week, therapy dogs, tests and, 171
experience, respect for, 208
expertise, respect for, 208
explosives, smells and detecting, 5
external influences, volunteerism and, 197
Eyler, J. R., 227–28

facility dogs: research and institutional initiatives, 172; resident and, 13, 17; role of, 17
Fair Housing Act (FHA), 21, 136, 137, 144, 146
families: dogs as members of, 2–3, 323; elite institutions and rich, 312–13; nontraditional adults and, 309; with pets, percentages, 2, 36
family dogs: role of, 11, 15, 31, 63–64; students and role of, 15
Farm Animal Welfare Council, 59–60
fecal flotation test, 321
Fede, J. H., 256–57, 266
Fédération Cynologique Internationale, 36
feedback, evaluations and informal, 283
FHA. *See* Fair Housing Act
fights: dog, 326; rings, 10
filters, allergy, 152
Fine, A. H., 63, 139, 145, 163, 293
Fiocco, A. J., 44, 46
firearms, smells and detecting, 5
Five Freedoms, 59–60, 68
flea/tick medication, 321
Florida State University, 62
Florida State University Counseling Center, 319

flow, characteristics of, 165–66
fMRI. *See* functional magnetic resonance imaging
focus groups, evaluations and, 283–84
Fogle, Jared, 5
food: allergies, 5; breeding and, 60; shelter dog without, *208*; working dogs and, 122
Foreman, A., 50
Foreman, A. M., 74, *234*
4 Paws for Ability, 22
The Four Mood Introspection Scale, 286
Fox, R., 59
Frank, Morris, 108
Freeman, L. M., 322
frequency counts, evaluations and, 282–83
Funari, Jessica, *141*
functional magnetic resonance imaging (fMRI), 3, 6, 104, 323

Garcia, R. M., 198
gas leaks, 21
Gee, N. R., 59
Generation Z, 308
German shepherds, as working dogs, 108
Gibbs, D. M., 322
Glenk, L. M., 71
Glenn, M. K., *234*
glycemia alert dogs, 6
goldendoodles, as service dogs, *16, 121*
golden retrievers: fMRI and, 6–7; as search and rescue dogs, 12; students and, *15*; as therapy dogs, *20*, 32, 279, *290, 312*, 317
Gorman, K. S., 256–57
graduate degrees, millennials and, 35
Graham, Ashton, *138*
Grajfoner, D., 47
Grandin, T., 199
greyhounds, as therapy dogs, 35
Grief Awareness Day, 1
Groth-Marnat, G., 285
The Guardian (newspaper), 45

guide (leader, seeing eye) dogs: for blind people, 5, 101, 102, 105, 108, 125; for deaf people, 5; waitlist for, 108
Guide Dogs for the Blind, 125
"Guidelines for Wellness of Animals Involved in AAI," 84
guilt, in dogs, 324

HAB. *See* human-animal bond
Hadden, L., 199
Haggerty, J. M., 62, 284, 288
HAI. *See* human-animal interaction
Hammer, D. P., 251, 256
Handbook of Psychological Assessment (Groth-Marnat and Wright), 285
The Handbook of Animal-Assisted Therapy (Fine, A. H.), 293
handlers: in classrooms with dogs, preparing for, 224, 235–36; with negative connotations, 323; with stress reduced, 330–32; therapy dogs and, 174–75, *230*
Hanson, L. M., 291
hard skills, 252–54, 261
Harrison, P., 283
Harte, E., 47
Harvard University, 66
health, 37; American College Health Association, 40–41, 166; Environmental Health and Safety Office, 325; NIH, 72; One Health, 84; SHC, 75, 76, 77–81; Veterans Health Administration, 103. *See also* mental health
health checks: ATDs and, 158, 321; vaccinations and, 73
Healthy Pets, Healthy People website, 322
hearing, of dogs, 4
hearing assistance dogs, 109
heartworm medication, 321
Helmsley, Leona, 241
Hettler, B., 166
Hingson, Michael, 12

homeless dogs in the care of animal welfare groups: adoptions of, *51*; reasons for, 341–42; role of, 14, 17–18
homesickness: depression and, 320; therapy dogs and, 319
Hospital Anxiety and Depression Scale, 286
House, L. A., 289
housing, campus: dog-friendly, 317; with ESAs, processes and practices, 142–54; pets and, 40
Howie, A., 82
Hoy-Gerlach, J., 136
HUD. *See* Department of Housing and Urban Development, US
human-animal bond (HAB), 260; biophilia and, 64; Characteristics of a True Bond and, 60; defined, 34–37, *35*; improving outcomes of, 6–7
Human-Animal Bond Research Institute, 11
human-animal interaction (HAI): advancements in, 6; animal welfare research and, 68; benefits, 140–41, 256; defined, 34–37, *35*; evaluations with psychological traits and measures used in, 286; influence of, 139; research, 296
human-canine interactions, behaviorally healthy: AAIs, best practices for, *86–87*; animal welfare research, 67–74; biophilia, theory of, 62–67; definitions, 59–62; education and training, 78–79; Five Freedoms, 59–60; institutional initiatives, 74–81; issues of concern, 57–59; One Welfare, 84–88; personnel, 79–80; planning and protocols, 80–81; quality program example, 75–78; recommendations for practice, 81–84; students and dogs, 61–62; wellness model and, *167*
humanistic, as biophilic approach, 63
humanization trend, 2–3

humans: allergies and, 23, 322; dogs influencing, 40–45, *43*; dogs reacting to emotions and body language of, 3, 63. *See also* research evidence on human-canine interactions
Human Society, 204
Hunse, A. M., 44, 46
Huss, R. J., 67
hypoallergenic dogs, 322

IAHAIO. *See* International Association of Human-Animal Interaction Organizations
Iannuzzi, D. A., 60
Iceland, 318
identity: formation, 309; mascots and, 65; pets and, 64; shelter dogs with service-learning, student development and, 192–96
IHE. *See* Institute for Humane Education
inclusion, theory of, service dogs and, 114–18
Indiana University of Pennsylvania, *279*
Indian Institute of Management, 253
Indivisible Self Model of Wellness, 167
infection, reducing, 321–22
Institute for Humane Education (IHE), 88
Institutional Animal Care and Use Committee, 291
Institutional Review Board, 170, 285, 291, 293
insurance coverage: ATDs and, 17, 158, 175, 237, 316; for therapy dogs, 315
integrated learning, service-learning projects and, 188
intellectual wellness, 166
interest, engagement and, 226
International Association of Human-Animal Interaction Organizations (IAHAIO), 83–84, 238

International Guide Dog Federation, 108, 326
International Hearing Dog, Inc., 109
International Reading Association, 314
invisible wounds, 103, 110
Iowa State University, 317

Japan, 120
Jarolmen, J., 44
Johnson, Rebecca, 242–43
Jordan, T., 84
Julius, H., 139
Just PAWS, *290*

Kamioka, H., 292, 293
Kazdin, A., 42
Kazdin, A. E., 62
Kellert, Stephen R., 62
Kennel Club, 36
Kent State University: anniversary of tragedy at, 22; Dogs on Campus at, 41; therapy dog program at, 171; US Department of Justice and, 146–47
Kids Interacting with Dogs Safely (KIDS) package, 203
Kirnan, Jean, *257*
Kjellstrand Hartwig, E., 48
Klein, Kristen, *262*
knowledge: dogs developing professional skills, dispositions and, 22; professionalism and discipline-specific, 256; respect for expertise, experience and, 208; service-learning, 192–96
Knudson, K., 42
Kobak, R., 38, 39
Kotrschal, K., 139
Kruglikova, Y. A., 291
Kurdek, L., 38

Labrador retrievers, 307, 329; as service dogs, 12, *114*; with smells, 4–5; as therapy dogs, *276*
Lannon, A., 283

Lasikiewicz, N., 44
leader dogs. *See* guide dogs
leads. *See* leashes
learned helplessness, 68
learning: AL, *211*; canines used to maximize, 227–32; college classes with engagement and, *239–40*; defined, 224, 225–26; emotions and role in, 229; evidence of deep, integrated, 226. *See also* professional development
leashes (leads): AAIs and, 71; Love on a Leash, 177
Lee, Y., 199
Lem, M., 84
letter template, written by mental health professional, *144*
Lewis and Clark College, 316
Li, L., 280
liability insurance, for therapy dogs, 8
life: animals with good, 60; dogs with emotional, 323–24; ESAs and residence life office, 148–54; Office of Residence Life, 148, 149, 150, 152; processes of, 62; QoL, 20–24, 307–12. *See also* biophilia
Likert scale, 236, 284
Linder, D. E., 322
literature review, evaluations and, 294
logic models, 278–79
loneliness: HAI studies and, 286; University of the Philippines Loneliness Assessment Scale, 291; women and, 309
Lory Hector, B., 136
loss, attachment and, 31–33, 38–40, 51
Louisiana Purchase (1804), 316
Louisiana State University, 65
Love on a Leash, 177
loyalty, 24, 324, 344

MacLin, O. H., 291
Malaysia, 253
Maltese, 241

Manchester terriers, 36
Marks, L. I., 284, 288
Maryland Institute College of Art (MICA), 325
mascots: identity and, 65; rethinking, 316–17
material/expected gain, volunteerism and, 197
McCain, N. L., 291–92
McConnell, B. L., 203
McConnell, P., 163
McCullough, A., 82
McDonald, E., 46–47, 285, 287
McDonald, S., 46–47, 285, 287
McGourty, J., 252
McGuigan, N., 47
McKay, C., 47, 48
McLaughlin, R. H., 284, 288
Meade, B. J., 50, *234*
medical alert dogs, 6, 110–11
medical student education, animals and, 65
Mehr, K. E., 42, 47, 289
Mellor, D., 60
men, percentage with dogs, 2
mental health: Bazelon Center for Mental Health Law, 144; emotions and, 61; ESAs and, 17, *153*; issues, 162, 308; mobility issues and, 103; professional, letter template written by, *144*; services, destigmatizing of, 23; in UK, 45–46; The Warwick-Edinburgh Mental Well-Being Scale, 286
Mental Health Week, 77
mental illness: DSM-5, 143; rates of, 72
Metropolitan State University, 318
MI. *See* myocardial infarction
Miami University, Ohio, 22
MICA. *See* Maryland Institute College of Art
Michigan State University, 64, 120
military, US, service dogs and, 103, 114

military working dogs (MWDs), 17, 35, 108
Milkman, Harvey, 318
millennials, dog ownership, children and, 2, 35
Miller, M. D., 280
Millersville University Student Center, 289
Ministry of Higher Education, Malaysia, 253
mobility assistance dogs, 105, 109, *124*
mobility issues, mental health and, 103
models: aggression, 70; Indivisible Self Model of Wellness, 167; logic, 278–79; PERMA, 309, *311*; of wellness, 166–67, *167*
MOGO (most good), 88
mold, 21
mood, HAI studies and, 286
Moore, R. W., 198
moralistic, as biophilic approach, 63
most good. *See* MOGO
mothers, children bonding with, 38
Motley, P., *211*
motto, ATDs and, *310*
Muckle, J., 44
Mueller, M. K., 62, 284, 288, 322
Mueller, S. L., 198, 199
multiplicity, service-learning and, 194
Muslims, 9
MWDs. *See* military working dogs
Myers, J. E., 166–67
myocardial infarction (MI), 37

National and Community Service Trust Act (1993), 187
National Center for Emerging and Zoonotic Infectious Diseases (NCEZID), 322
National Center for Learning Disabilities, 117
National Institutes of Health (NIH), 72
Native Americans, 316
naturalistic, as biophilic approach, 63

naturalistic observations, evaluations and, 283
NCEZID. *See* National Center for Emerging and Zoonotic Infectious Diseases
NEADS World Class Assistance Dogs, 109
negativistic, as biophilic approach, 63
New Directions for Evaluation (American Evaluation Association), 293
Newfoundland dog, 316
New York Times (newspaper), 166
Ng, Z., 68, 69, 82, 83, 84, *87*, 162
NIH. *See* National Institutes of Health
9/11, 11, 12, 13, 308
911, 5
nontraditional adults, 309
Northern Illinois University, 319
nursing homes, 307, 310, 327, 342; with robotic or live dogs, 45, 224; therapy dogs and, 8, 158, 224, 328
nutrition, 3, 166, 178, 256

Office of Residence Life, 148, 149, 150, 152
"official national registry," as bogus, 145, 158
Ohio National Guard, 22
The Ohio State University, 147
One Health, 84
One Welfare, 84–88
open-pet policy, 61
organizations, therapy dogs, 8
orientations, therapy dogs and scheduled events, 171–72
outcomes: assessment with program improvement, 288–89; professional development and program, 266
oxytocin, 82, *141*; gaze positive loop, 140

Parker, L., 42
participants, professional development and program, 266
partnerships, with service dog providers, 124–25
Passmore, H. A., 43, 47, 284
Patel, G., 44
PawstoDeStress program, 76, 76–77, 77, 80
Penn State Animal Volunteers, 206
Penn State Worry Questionnaire, 286
Pennsylvania Department of Corrections, 99
Pennsylvania State University, 206
Perceived Stress Scale, 286
PERMA model, 309, *311*
Perrine, R., 64
Perry, William, 193
personal growth, students and, *211*
personnel, AAIs, 79–80
Petfinder, 33
Pet Fostering Application, 317
pet industry, in US, 37
Pet Partners, 163, 174, 177, 322
pet products, in UK, 2
Pet Program Agreement, 317
Pet Project, 74
pets: ADA with trained service animal, ESA or, 116; with attachment, 38; benefits of bonding with, 10–11; campus housing and, 40; families and percentage with, 2, 36; identity and, 64; MICA policy, 325; open-pet policy at, 61; policies established, 324–27; service dogs and, 102; zones free of, 325
Pets on Campus policy, 40
Philippines Loneliness Assessment Scale, 286
physical activity, dogs encouraging, 21
physical interaction, students and dogs, 228–29
physical limitations, dogs with, 315
physical wellness, 166
physiological measures, randomized, 290–92

PicMonkey, 33
Pierce, B. J., 322
planning, AAIs with protocols and, 80–81, *81*
Poland, M., 50
Pomeranian/Australian cattle mix, *243*
Pomeranians, 9, *243*
Poole, N., 229–30
populations: of service dogs, 111; shelter dogs, 199
Portuguese water dogs, 322
positive psychology, 165
posters: for dog welfare, 78; for therapy dog event, *76*
post-tragedy dog visits, 319–20
post-traumatic stress disorder (PTSD), 5, 101, 104, 109, 114, 118, 279
Potter, L., 47
Powers, K. R., 72
prison dog training program: service dogs in, *16*; therapy dogs in, 176
professional development: canine-campus events and, 258–59; in college learner, 254–57; description and theory of, 252–57; ethics and communication with, 256; events/activities, types of, 259–61, *260*; with hard and soft skills and dispositions, 252–54; influences on, *254*; outcomes, 261–62, *263*; with professionalism defined, 251; program outcomes and, 266; program participants and, 266; program structure and, 265–66; recommendations for practice, 265–67; research and institutional initiatives, 257–65; student assessment and, 267; therapy dogs and, *257*; with UBC as exemplary program, 262–65; understanding, 249–51
"Professional Guidelines for Humane Educators," 81
professionals, working dogs of, 16
protocols, AAIs with planning and, 80–81, *81*

providers, partnerships with service dog, 124–25
psychiatric service dogs (PSDs), 118
psychological conditions, service dogs for diagnosed, 109–10
psychological measures, randomized, 290–92
psychometric tools, evaluations and, 285–87
PsychTESTS database, 285
PTSD. *See* post-traumatic stress disorder
Public Access Certification Test, 103, 121
public access rights: for service dogs, 8; service dogs and, 104, 119–20
public appropriateness, ADI and, 115
"Puppies on the Quad" event, 67
puppy mills, 10, 328
purposive, volunteerism and, 197

Quality of Life (QoL): defined, 307–12; dog on campus and, 20–24; evolution of, 308; students and, 309

randomized controlled trials, evaluations and, 292–93
RCMP. *See* Royal Canadian Mounted Police
Reading Buddies, 202
reality, 3 Rs of service-learning and, 214
reciprocity, 3 Rs of service-learning and, 214
Reddit, 41
reflection, 3 Rs of service-learning and, 214
reflection, service-learning projects and, 188
"Regarding Animals," 305
Rehabilitation Act (RHA), 136, 146
relativism, service-learning and, 193–94
research: animal welfare, 67–74; on dogs and student wellness, *168–69*; dogs used in experimental, 65; HAI, 296; Human-Animal Bond Research Institute, 11; questions matched to assessment methods, 294–95

research and institutional initiatives: college courses, roles for dogs, 238–40; dog-friendly student housing, 317; dog training skills acquisition, 318; evaluations, 287–93; facility dogs, 172; with mascots, rethinking, 316–17; post-tragedy dog visits, 319–20, *320*; professional development, 257–65; service dogs, 118–20; shelter dogs, 197–200; spring breaks, alternative, 320; therapy dogs, 167–73; therapy dogs to address homesickness, 319; university service or therapy dogs, 315–16

Research and Service in Humane Education, 203

research evidence on human-canine interactions: with attachment and loss, 31–33, 51; with attachment and loss, theories of, 38–40; dogs influencing humans, 40–45, *43*; human-animal bond and interaction with, 34–37, *35*; recommendations for practice, 45–50, *48*

Reserve Officer Training Corps (ROTC), 17

residence hall, ESA and process of bringing into, 149–50

residence life office, ESA and coordination with, 148–54

resident dogs, 13, 17. *See also* facility dogs

rest in peace. *See* RIP

returned to shelter dogs. *See* RTS

Reveille (Texas A&M mascot), 316

RHA. *See* Rehabilitation Act

rights: animals, 66; of ESAs, 241; public access, 8, 104, 119–20

Riley, T. A., 289

RIP (rest in peace), 306

Roberts, A., 46–47, 285, 287

Robertson, R. L., 291

Robinson, G., 198

robotic dogs, 44–45, 224

Rockett, B., 39

Rooney, N., 67

Rose, C., 289

ROTC. *See* Reserve Officer Training Corps

Rottweilers, 36

Rowan, A. N., 60

Rowan University, 317

Royal Canadian Mounted Police (RCMP), 328

Royal Society for the Prevention of Cruelty to Animals (RSPCA), 22

RTS (returned to shelter) dogs, 306, 307

Ruffman, T., 63

rules, volunteerism and, 207

Rutgers University, 317

Ryan, R. M., 244

safety, dogs with improved, 21

Safewalk, 199

Saint Bernards, 49

St. Charles Community College, 21

St. Thomas University (STU), 75, 77

salivary cortisol, 69, 71, 82, 287

salukis, 35

Sanders, C. R., 117–18

Sartore-Baldwin, M. L., 202, 279

Saturday Evening Post (newspaper), 108

scheduled events, therapy dogs, orientations and, 171–72

Schoen, A. M., 330–31

school counseling, therapy dogs and, 231–32

Schubert, C. M., 291–92

scientific, as biophilic approach, 63

Scott, Taylor, *262*

Seaman, 316

search and rescue dogs, 12

seeing eye dogs. *See* guide dogs

Self-Determination Theory, 244

Seligman, Martin, 309

September 11, 2001. *See* 9/11

Serpell, J. A., 10

service dogs: ADA and, 69, 73, 102–3, 104, 109, 113, 116, 119–20; ADI and, 327; alternative assignments for, 121–24; benefits, 111; for blind people, 108; breeding, 104; children and, 110; costs, 126; credit card picked up by, *103*; defined, 7, 101–11; dos and don'ts for behavior around, 122–23; downsides, 126; ESAs, therapy and, *160–61*; ESAs and, 49, 135; etiquette, 329; for hearing assistance, 109; inclusion theory and, 114–18; issues with, 111–14; medical alert, 110–11; for mobility assistance, 109, *124*; obstacles to acquiring, *112*; pets and, 102; population of, 111; providers and partnerships, 124–25; PSDs, 118; for psychological conditions diagnosed, 109–10; public access rights and, 8, 104, 119–20; raising, 22; recommendations for practice, 120–25; research and institutional initiatives, 118–20; role of, 5, 12, 16, 21, 23, 44–45, 73, 99–100, *106–7*, *114*, *121*; therapy and, 120–21; training, *16*, *100*, 104–5, 115–16; in UK, 118, 120; university, 315–16; US military and, 103, 114

Service Dogs Program, United Disabilities Services Foundation, 111

service-learning: benefits, 189, *190–91*; colleges and benefits of, 187–92; commitment and, 194–96; contributions of, *190–91*; defined, 186–87; dualism and, 193; multiplicity and, 194; projects, checklist question to guide, 188; qualifications for, 187; relativism and, 193–94; shelter dogs and, *187*, 200–204; shelter dogs with identity formation, student development and, 192–96; 3 Rs of, 214

Sethi, D., 253

Shakir, R., 253

SHC. *See* Student Health Centre

shelter dogs: adoption of, 304, 306; emaciated, *208*; identity formation, student development and service-learning, 192–96; owner-surrendered, *200*; population, 199; recommendations for practice, 204–11; research and institutional initiatives, 197–200; returned to, 306, 307; as service dogs, 104; with service-learning, benefits of, 187–92; service-learning with, 200–204; students and, 185, *320*; volunteerism, service-learning and, 186–87, *187*; volunteerism and, *187*, 305

shelter personnel, stay-at-home environment and, 341, 342

Shernoff, D. J., 226

Shields, P. O., 197, 198

Shuman, L. J., 252

Siebens, H. C., 322

sight hounds, 35–36

Simkovic, M., 312–13

Six Dimensions of Wellness, 166

skills: crosscutting, 252; dogs developing professional knowledge, dispositions and, 22; dog training, 318; hard and soft, 252–54, 261; for workplace, 313–14

smells, dogs and sense of, 4–5, 110

social awkwardness, 17, 309, 310

social belonging, creating sense of, 228

social function of leisure, volunteerism and, 197

social media: dogs on, 33, 329, 341; influence of, 45; role of, 62

social wellness, 166

soft skills, 252–54, 261

Somervill, J. W., 291

Souter, M. A., 280

Southeastern Louisiana University, 74

Speech-Language-Hearing Clinic, 74

spiritual wellness, 166

spring breaks, alternative, 320

Staats, S., 39
staffing, evaluations with time, funding and, 295
STAI. *See* State-Trait Anxiety Inventory
"Standards of Practice" (AAII), 83
State-Trait Anxiety Inventory (STAI), 229, 286
stay-at-home orders, 341, 342
Stephens College, 317
STEP@UCF, 75
Stetson University, 326
Stewart, L. A., 42, 291
stray dogs, 9, 121, 195, *195*
stress: de-stress with dogs event, 9, 42–43, 76, 275, 276, 277, 292; de-stress with students, 275; dog handlers and reduced, 330–32; dogs dealing with, 69–74; mediation, theory of, 138–42; PawstoDeStress program, 76, 76–77, 77, 80; PTSD, 5, 101, 104, 109, 114, 118, 279; recommendations for practice, 46–49; "Stress Buster Day," 62; TDI DSR, 328; well-being and student, 289–90
stress, HAI studies and, 286
"Stress Buster Day," 62
stress-mediation framework, 134
Strigas, A., 197
structure, professional development and program, 265–66
Struik, K., 47, 48
STU. *See* St. Thomas University
Stuart, K., 37
student engagement: with college courses and roles for dogs, 223–25, 244–45; theory of, 226–27. *See also* college courses, roles for dogs
Student Health Centre (SHC), 75, 76, 77–81
students: assessment, professional development, 267; biophilia and, 64–67; complexity of, 196; in crisis with dogs, 22; DEAL and reflections of, *211*; de-stress with, 275; development with service-learning and identity formation, 192–96; with disabilities, 117; dogs and, 2, 14–18, *15*, *20*, *32*, *51*, 61–62, *201*, 228–29, *306*, *312*, 332–33, *341*, *342*, *343*; dogs and increased participation of, 23; with dogs and quality of campus life, 20–24; dogs and retention of, 22–23; dogs expanding horizons for, 23; education of campus community and, 328–29; ESL, 249–50; evaluations of dog-assisted events, projects, and programs with, 280–82; with horizons expanded, 23; as nontraditional adults, 309; participation, 288; QoL, 309; recruitment and dogs, 21; service dogs and role supporting, *106–7*; shelter dogs and, 185, *320*; wellness and dogs, *168–69*
Sturgill, A., *211*
suicide, 45, 61, 162, 308
Supplemental Nutrition Assistance Program Outreach, 256
surveys: American College Health Association, 40–41; evaluations, 284–85; Penn State Worry Questionnaire, 286; therapy dogs at the library questionnaire, 301–3
Sweeney, T. J., 166–67
symbolic, as biophilic approach, 63

Table of State Assistance Animal Laws, 120
Tannenbaum, J., 60
TDI DSR. *See* Disaster Stress Relief
The 10 Health Benefits of Dogs (and One Health Risk (Stuart, K.), 37
terminology, revising, 322–23
tester/observer, for ATDs, 244
tests: Buros Center for Testing, 285; CGC, 318; CGCA, 328; dogs and consent, 79; fecal flotation, 321;

PsychTESTS database, 285; Public Access Certification Test, 103, 121; therapy dogs, exam week and, 171
Texas A&M University, 316
therapy (comfort) dogs: AAA and, 12–13; AAE and, 13; AAT and, 13; BARK, 262–65, *264*; benefits, 268; children and, 32–33, 74, 314; college courses and roles for, *224*; costs, 157, 158; counseling services and visits, 171; defined, 7, 159–65; de-stress event with, 9, 42–43, *76*, 275, 276, 277, 292; ESAs, service and, *160–61*; handlers and, *230*; homesickness and, 319; insurance coverage for, 315; interacting with, 8–9; intervention types for, 12–13; learned helplessness and, 68; liability insurance for, 8; as mascots, 316–17; nursing homes and, 8, 158, 224, 328; organizations, 8; orientations, new experiences and scheduled events, 171–72; poster, *76*; professional development and, *257*; program at Kent State University, 171; questions and answers, 157–59; recommendations for practice, 46–47, 173–78; research and institutional initiatives, 167–73; role of, 8, 12–13, 16–17, *20*, 22, *35*, *43*, 45–47, 66, *158*, 162, *170*, *173*, *224*, *238*, *243*, *260*, *276*, *279*, *281*, *287*, *290*, *310*, *312*, 317, *329*; school counseling and, 231–32; service and, 120–21; session evaluation, *237*; situations surfacing for handlers of, 174–75; stress for, 71; tests and exam week, 171; test with ATDs, 329; traits of, 163; university, 315–16; wellness theory and, 165–67. *See also* Alliance of Therapy Dogs
therapy dogs at the library questionnaire, 301–3
Therapy Dogs International, 177, 224, 321, 328
tigers, 65

time, evaluations with staffing, funding and, 295
time-to-graduation rates, in US, 308
Toukonen, M., 44
trained service animal, ADA with pet, ESA or, 116
training: AAIs, 78–79; ADI and, 115–16; levels raised for dogs, 327–28; service dogs in, *16*, *100*, 104–5, 115–16; skills acquisition with dog, 318
trauma: post-tragedy dog visits, 319–20, *320*; psychological, 103 (*See also* post-traumatic stress disorder); service dogs to help with, 110

UBC. *See* University of British Columbia
UK. *See* United Kingdom
UNB. *See* University of New Brunswick
United Disabilities Services Foundation, 111
United Kingdom (UK): Farm Animal Welfare Council, 59–60; mental health in, 45–46; pet products in, 2; RSPCA in, 22; service dogs in, 118, 120
United States (US): Department of HUD, 137, 145, 146; Department of Justice, 116, 146–47; Department of Transportation, 14, 136; humanization trend in, 2–3; military, 103, 114; pet industry in, 37; time-to-graduation rates in, 308
universities, service-learning benefits at, 187–92
University of British Columbia (UBC), 47–48; BARK, 262–65, *264*; canine-campus events, 258; as exemplary program, 262–65; professional development outcomes from staff, faculty and students, *263*
University of California, Davis School of Veterinary Medicine, 313–14
University of Central Florida, 75, 320

University of Illinois at Champaign-Urbana, 317
University of Nebraska at Kearney, 146
University of Nebraska-Lincoln, 318
University of New Brunswick (UNB), 75, 77, 79
University of Northern Colorado, 326
University of Redlands, 317
University of Sheffield, 124–25
University of Southern California, 172
University of South Carolina, 172
University of the Philippines Loneliness Assessment Scale, 291
University of Toledo, *138, 141*, 147
University of Wisconsin Extension, 278–79
Urbanik, J., 68
US. *See* United States
utilitarian, as biophilic approach, 63
Uvnäs-Moberg, K., 139

vaccinations: health checks and, 73; proof of, 321
value-added: defined, 307; documenting, 313; dog-friendly campus culture, 312–14
Veterans Health Administration, 103
veterinary checks, annual, 321
Vick, Michael, 17
Vickers, K., 280
Vincent, A., 136
violence: "Bark Against Violence," 277; on campus, 231–32
vision, of dogs, 4
visits: post-tragedy dog, 319–20; therapy dogs, counseling services and, 171
Vitztum, C., 68
volunteerism: benefits of, *250*, 255; commitment to, 208–9; defined, 186–87; dog walkers, *200*, 201–2, 205, 208, 210, *210*; dropping out of, 205; Penn State Animal Volunteers, 206; recommendations for practice, 206–11; with

rules, adherence to, 207; shelter dogs and, *187*, 305

waitlists, for guide dogs, 108
Ward-Griffin, E., 46, 83
Warta, S., 198
The Warwick-Edinburgh Mental Well-Being Scale, 286
Washington State University, 147
Weatherly, J. J., 118
Weimaraners, 36
Weimer, M., 159
welfare: canine, 69–72, 206; Farm Animal Welfare Council, 59–60; One Welfare, 84–88; posters for dog, 78. *See also* animal welfare; homeless dogs in the care of animal welfare groups
well-being, HAI studies and, 286
wellness: categories, 166; "Guidelines for Wellness of Animals Involved in AAI," 84; human-canine interaction and model of, *167*; Indivisible Self Model of Wellness, 167; models of, 166–67, *167*; research on role of dogs in student, *168–69*; Six Dimensions of Wellness, 166; student stress, well-being and, 289–90; theory of, 165–67; Wheel of Wellness, 167
Wells, M., 64
Westgarth, Carri, 243
Wheeler, C., 44
Wheel of Wellness, 167
whippets, as therapy dogs, *175*
Williams, J., 47
Wilson, A., 253, 267
Wilson, E. O., 58, 62
Wirth, O., 50, *234*
Witmer, J. M., 166–67
Wolkowitz, C., 283, 292
women: with dogs, percentage, 2; loneliness and, 309; mothers, 38
Won, D., 199
word recognition, 3

working dogs: food and, 122; MWDs, 17, 35, 108; of professionals, 16; role of, 12, 16
workplace, skills for, 313–14
World Trade Center, 11, 12, 13
worry, HAI studies and, 286
Wright, A. J., 285
Wright State University, 317
written verification of need, for ESA as accommodation, 142–45

Yale Law School, 66
Yale University, 330
Yin, Sophia, 206
Yong, M. H., 63
Younggren, J. N., 72
Youth Service California, 187

Zamir, T., 67–68
zoonotic diseases, 321, 322

ABOUT THE EDITOR

MARY RENCK JALONGO, PhD, is the author, coauthor, or editor of more than forty books and has earned eight national awards for excellence in writing, including four EDPRESS awards. Many of her books and articles have focused on the human-canine bond, particularly on the topics of bringing therapy dogs on campus to mitigate college students' stress (*Public Services Quarterly*); motivating children to practice reading aloud in the company of therapy dogs (*Society & Animals; Childhood Education; Early Childhood Education Journal*); preparing service dogs to assist people with disabilities (*Children, Dogs and Education: Caring for, Learning Alongside, and Gaining Support from Canine Companions, 2018*); and promoting mutually beneficial child-animal interactions (*The World's Children and Their Companion Animals, 2004; Teaching Compassion: Humane Education in Early Childhood, 2014*). Working with Springer Nature, she spent twenty-five years as editor-in-chief of a professional journal and is the senior editor of a book series, a position she has held since 2008. Now a professor emerita from Indiana University of Pennsylvania (IUP), she served as director of the Doctoral Program in Curriculum and Instruction and was named the university's distinguished professor in 1991–1992. In 2019, the Pennsylvania Department of Corrections recognized her as a Volunteer of the Year for five years of teaching in and the design of a certification program that gives carefully selected inmates an opportunity to train service dogs for children and adults (*Prison Dog Programs: Rehabilitation and Renewal in Correctional Facilities, 2019*). Beginning in 2014, she volunteered with college students at a no-kill animal shelter to photograph and promote adoption of homeless dogs and cats via social media. Over the past fourteen years, she has made hundreds of visits to education and health care facilities with her four registered and insured therapy dogs—two greyhounds and two collies. She currently serves as a tester/observer of therapy dog teams for Alliance of Therapy Dogs.